Praise for *The Women's House of Detention*

"In this essential, abolitionist work, historian and author of *When Brooklyn Was Queer* Hugh Ryan uncovers the stories of this bewildering place and of the people who populated it."
—*Electric Literature*

"By using queer history as a framework, Ryan makes the case for prison abolition stronger than ever. Part history text, part call to activism, this book is compelling from start to finish."
—*Buzzfeed*

"While this book is ostensibly about the New York City Women's House of Detention, Greenwich Village's forgotten queer landmark, it is also about so much more. Ryan contextualizes the notorious prison in the realms of criminology, queer theory, women's history, geography, and many other disciplines. . . . This blend of queer history and social history is highly recommended."
—*Library Journal*

"Expertly mining prison records and other source materials, Ryan brings these marginalized women to vivid life. This informative, empathetic narrative is a vital contribution to LGBTQ history."
—*Publishers Weekly*

"A truly radical, moral, and exciting history that will blow your mind. Ryan argues that it was the creation of a women's prison in the West Village that helped center lesbian life in that area. Since lesbians are poorer (no men's incomes), de-facto marginalized, and more often deprived of family support, lesbians and queer women and trans men have also been overrepresented in prisons. Using records documenting poor, white, Black, and Latina women incarcerated for criminalized lives, Ryan shows us the profound injustices of prisons themselves, and how lesbians have been demeaned and yet tried to survive. A game changer from a community-based historian."
—Sarah Schulman, author of *Let the Record Show: A Political History of ACT UP New York, 1987–1993*

"In the 1950s and 1960s, I lived my femme lesbian life in the shadow of the Women's House of D. In the bar that was home to me, parties were held to greet released lovers or to mourn new incarcerations. The Women's House of Detention was the horizon of my early lesbian queer life; I have carried the voices of the separated lovers I heard in those hot summer streets all my years. In 1971, the building was erased from its

Village corner, but Hugh Ryan refuses that erasure. These pages are thick with women and transmasculine people stepping back into our communal history, our national history. In this portrait of one prison's life we can see the nation we have become and why, where mass incarcerations of Black, Brown, and poor people have taken genocidal proportions. Ryan uses new archival sources to emphasize the prison's role in punishing nonconforming expressions of gender and love. Read this and you too will hear the lost voices reminding us both of their vitality, and of the work that still must be done. A needed, needed history."

—JOAN NESTLE, author and founder of the Lesbian Herstory Archives

"A rigorously researched and compellingly told piece of queer history that features a memorable cast of heroic characters. Ryan squarely places his subject in the context of our contemporary society to illustrate the ugly and longstanding enactment of homo/transphobic terrorism by the carceral state."

—MELISSA FEBOS, author of *Girlhood* and *Body Work:*
The Radical Power of Personal Narrative

"A fascinating, lively, and devastating story reverberates in the pages of *The Women's House of Detention*. Hugh Ryan reveals the vital realities of people confined to the margins, whether behind the walls of the notorious House of D in the heart of the Village in Manhattan, or at the edges of complex communities in the tumult of twentieth-century New York City. Ryan's engrossing and rigorous history of one jail documents an intersection of gender politics, evolving queer identity, and brutal racial repression, and is essential reading in a nation that now incarcerates 30 percent of the world's women prisoners."

—PIPER KERMAN, author of *Orange Is the New Black:*
My Year in a Women's Prison

"Hugh Ryan has gifted us with a magnificent queer history of the notorious Women's House of Detention in New York's Greenwich Village that spans almost fifty years. With an astonishing gift for digging into archives, using their own letters and voices as much as he can, Ryan illuminates those whose lives were deemed 'irredeemable.' Stories that resonate with the humanity, resourcefulness, and loving of imprisoned Black, Puerto Rican, and working-class women are combined with those of political prisoners like Claudia Jones, Elizabeth Gurley Flynn, Angela Davis, Andrea Dworkin, Afeni Shakur, and Joan Bird. This meticulous work shines like a lighthouse beacon on a fog-shrouded shore. A brilliant achievement."

—BETTINA APTHEKER, distinguished professor emerita
of feminist studies, University of California, Santa Cruz

THE WOMEN'S HOUSE OF DETENTION

A Queer History of a Forgotten Prison

HUGH RYAN

BOLD TYPE BOOKS

NEW YORK

Bold Type Books
116 East 16th Street, 8th Floor, New York, NY 10003
www.boldtypebooks.org
@BoldTypeBooks

Printed in the United States of America
First Edition: May 2022

Published by Bold Type Books, an imprint of Perseus Books, LLC, a subsidiary of Hachette Book Group, Inc. Bold Type Books is a co-publishing venture of the Type Media Center and Perseus Books.

The Hachette Speakers Bureau provides a wide range of authors for speaking events. To find out more, go to www.hachettespeakersbureau.com or call (866) 376-6591.

The publisher is not responsible for websites (or their content) that are not owned by the publisher.

Names of some individuals have been changed.

Print book interior design by Linda Mark

Library of Congress Cataloging-in-Publication Data
Names: Ryan, Hugh, 1978– author.
Title: The women's house of detention : a queer history of a forgotten prison / Hugh Ryan.
Description: New York : Bold Type Books, [2022] | Includes bibliographical references.
Identifiers: LCCN 2021040521 | ISBN 9781645036661 (hardcover) | ISBN 9781645036647 (ebook)
Subjects: LCSH: Women's House of Detention. | Reformatories for women—New York (State)—New York—History—20th century. | Women prisoners—New York (State)—New York—Social conditions—20th century. | Transgender prisoners—New York (State)—New York—Social conditions—20th century. | Poor women—New York (State)—New York—Social conditions—20th century. | Prison abolition movement—New York (State)—New York—History—20th century. | Greenwich Village (New York, N.Y.)
Classification: LCC HV9481.N62 W6679 2022 | DDC 365/.430974741—dc23
LC record available at https://lccn.loc.gov/2021040521

ISBNs: 9781645036661 (hardcover), 9781645036647 (ebook)

LSC-C

Printing 1, 2022

This book is dedicated to the memory of the forgotten.

A Few Notes on Language

THROUGHOUT THIS BOOK I USE THE WORD *QUEER* IN A MATERIALIST, rather than identity-based, way to refer to the broad collection of people whose sexual and gender expressions were not normative in their time. Use of the word *queer* to refer to sexually nonnormative people goes back to the early nineteenth century, but most of the people I discuss in this book would not have used that word, in that way, for themselves. In that sense, it is an ahistoric term that is useful in this context.

Often, I use the phrase "women and transmasculine people." Many of the folks in this book were presumed to be women and lived lives that were masculine of center, but I have no access to how they identified. I do not want to make them invisible, presume facts I do not know about them, or project my assumptions onto them. Some clearly identified as men, and I follow their lead. Overwhelmingly, however, the people I am writing about understood themselves as women, and I do not want to obscure that fact either.

For people whose stories I've drawn primarily or exclusively from private social work files, I use only their first name and last initial, as they never chose to make their stories public. For people who told their own stories, or whose stories I found largely through published documents, I introduce them using their full name, then default to just their last name. In both cases, this is a choice made out of respect.

I capitalize Black in the same way that I would capitalize an ethnicity such as Irish or Puerto Rican (although these categories can overlap), because part of the legacy of slavery in America has been an erasure and flattening of the vast ethnic diversity of the people we today call Black—a flattening that continues to this day. Black connotes a specific experience and history, and even those Black people who do not share that experience—for instance, recent Black migrants from other countries—have the presumptions of those experiences placed on them by virtue of living Black in America, and must deal with the material realities that accompany those presumptions. As this is not true in the same way for white or brown people, I do not capitalize those terms.

Finally, I primarily refer to the Women's House of Detention as a prison, which is technically only a place where people are caged *after* they have been found guilty in our criminal legal system. Pretrial detention takes place in a jail. The House of D held both kinds of detained people.

Contents

Jay Toole Marks the Land

> The success or failure of a revolution can almost always be
> gauged by the degree to which the status of women is
> altered in a radical, progressive direction.
>
> —ANGELA DAVIS, *If They Come in the Morning*...

THE JEFFERSON MARKET GARDEN IN GREENWICH VILLAGE IS ONE OF the loveliest places I can't stand. Flowering season seems to last longer there than the rest of the city. The low-rise nature of the surrounding buildings allows precious sun to warm the ground for Lenten roses in the first weeks of March, and keeps the garden inviting until the last camellias drop their petals in November. The only potential reminder of the spot's one-hundred-fifty-year history as a prison is the high steel fence, which these days keeps the unwanted riffraff *out* rather than *in*.

I used to love this garden. I'd sit by the koi pond, do interviews on my cell phone, and think what a beautiful oasis it was—what a gift the Village had given the city. Now, I can't look at it without hearing Jay Toole's voice describing the brutal physicals that doctors had inflicted upon her there, when the garden was a prison called the Women's House of Detention.

When I go into the garden, I'm always brought back to the one time—happened many, many times but this one stands out. He's telling me to get on the table, and put my feet in the stirrups and this and that, and it felt like his whole arm went in there, you know, and they checked everywhere, every hole you have that's where they went. Then he was like "All right, get off the table. Hurry up, we got to bring the next one in."

"Hurry up?" And I couldn't move, the pain was so bad and I don't know what he did up in there but it was so, so bad. When I looked down I was covered in blood.

And they didn't do nothing.[1]

Today, it's hard to imagine that a prison once graced the rarified streets of Greenwich Village, one of New York City's most picturesque (and unaffordable) neighborhoods. But for almost as long as there has been a Greenwich Village—which is to say, almost as long as there has been a United States—detention centers have been an integral part of Village life. The last of them, the Women's House of Detention, stood from 1929 to 1974. It was one of the Village's most famous landmarks: a meeting place for locals and a must-see site for adventurous tourists. And for tens of thousands of arrested women and transmasculine people from every corner of the city, the House of D was a nexus, drawing the threads of their lives together in its dark and fearsome cells.

Some were imprisoned there once, for as little as a day; others returned often and were held for years at a time. For decades, upon their release these women navigated the streets of Greenwich Village: ate in its automats and diners; caroused in the bars that would let them in; lived in nearby tenements; slept rough in the parks; visited friends and loved ones who were on trial or in detention; worked what jobs would hire them; attended court-mandated health screenings and probation meetings; and in a million and one other ways, made the Village their own. Now, aside from a small plaque on the garden's fence, they have been almost entirely forgotten.

Almost.

The slim few who have fought to preserve the memory of the House of D are mostly working-class lesbian/bisexual women and transmasculine folks—the people most likely to fall into its clutches, and least likely to have other landmarks to call their own.

Jay Toole first ended up in the orbit of the House of D when she was thirteen, in 1960. Some friends had given her the haircut every cool boy wanted: a tight-fade flattop, just like Steve McQueen and Mickey Mantle. That was the final straw for her father—a violent, sexually abusive man who ruled their Bronx home with his fists. That night, he threw her out, and Jay lived among the queer kids on the streets of the Village for the next twenty-five years. At the age when most of her peers started high school, Jay started heroin. In 1964, she stole a taxi to drive her girlfriend to California, but they only made it as far as Texas before they were caught, and Jay was sentenced to her first bid in the House of D.

"A lot of us called it the playground. A lot of us called it a prison. I called it both," Jay told historians in 2016, "depend[ing] on what I was arrested for and how much I got."[2]

For Jay, the prison was complicated: dangerous, vile, violent, dirty, cruel—but also a place where she met other queer people, and one of the centers of her queer community. She and other butches would hang out in the shadow of the prison, at Whalen's drugstore on Sixth Avenue, where they could watch the tide of arrested women flow in and out of the prison's high stone walls. Most of the people she met in prison are gone now, dead or disappeared. But Jay keeps their memories alive. Since the early 2000s, she's organized tours of the West Village, to share the queer history of the House of D, because "young people don't know about it."[3] The landmark is gone, but she marks the land, exposing the grim roots beneath the garden's manicured paths.

And make no mistake: the House of D was a queer landmark. In truth, all prisons are, especially ones intended for women.

Today, approximately 40 percent of people incarcerated in women's detention facilities are part of the broad LBTQ spectrum[4] (compared to about 3.5 percent of the general population).[5] That percentage is based on in-person interviews with over a hundred thousand currently detained people, and researchers only identified someone as a "sexual minority" if they themselves identified that way or if they had sexual relationships with people of the same sex *before* being incarcerated. We can only speculate how high the percentage would have been had the study counted those who could not talk openly about their sexual identities, or if it had included those who had same-sex sexual relationships *while* incarcerated.

We live in the age of mass incarceration. If we extrapolate these findings to the nearly 250,000 women currently incarcerated in America, at least 100,000 are queer.[6] And that's after decades of LGBTQ, feminist, anti-racist, and anti-prison activism, which have supposedly made our criminal legal system more fair. During the years the House of D was active, which spanned the single most homophobic period in American history, the percentage of queer people it encaged was almost certainly higher. How much higher, we'll never know for sure. But records show that queer women and transmasculine people were sentenced to the House of D for such crimes as smoking, forgery, petit larceny, being homeless, attempting suicide, murder, wearing pants, sending the definition of the word *lesbian* through the mail, "associating with idle or vicious persons," staying out late, accepting a ride from a man, vagrancy, alcoholism, prostitution, possession of narcotics, "waywardism," disobedience, stealing rare books, being alone on the street, rape, drug addiction, and lesbianism itself. Yet the impacts of queer people on prison history, and the impacts of prisons on queer history, are rarely examined. Even when they are, the focus is mostly on men.

However, thanks to its age, size, and unique history as an early adopter of penal innovations, New York City "offers a unique perspective on how the rehabilitation of female criminal behavior developed as a distinct reform enterprise," according to Cheryl Hicks, author of *Talk with You Like a Woman: African American Women, Justice, and Reform in New York, 1890–1935.*[7] Furthermore, over the course of the twentieth century, New York City went from having a 98 percent white population to a 44 percent white population. Major demographic shifts like the Great Migration, the immigration of Black people from the Caribbean, post–World War II anti-urban white flight, and the influx of Puerto Rican people due to the economic devastation of American colonial capitalism have had formative effects on our city—and our prisons, and the way we treat the people incarcerated in them. Thus, New York's penal institutions for women offer unique insights into how racism, classism, xenophobia, and homophobia intertwined with misogyny to create public policy, and ruin human lives.

And the House of D, more than perhaps any other prison, had an outsized role in queer life. It sat at the end of Christopher Street, the block whose very name is a global byword for queerness. You could see the Stonewall Inn from the prison's high, small windows, and during the Stonewall Uprising, those on the inside held a riot all their own, setting fire to their belongings and tossing them out the windows while screaming "gay rights, gay rights, gay rights!"[8] Yet still in 2016, the *New York Times* would refer to the protest as being all gay men, and only grudgingly issue a correction stating there was "at least one lesbian involved."[9] Jay Toole, a Stonewall veteran herself, could have told them that—if only they had bothered to ask.

The House of D helped make Greenwich Village queer, and the Village, in return, helped define queerness for America. No other prison has played such a significant role in our history, particularly for working-class women and transmasculine people. For them, as pioneering historian Joan Nestle (founder of the Lesbian Herstory Archives) once wrote, the House of D was a constant "presence in our lives—a warning, a beacon, a reminder and a moment of community."[10]

Many—perhaps most—formerly incarcerated people talk rarely about their experiences, and many—perhaps most—non-incarcerated people refuse to listen when they do. At most, we get *data* about people in prison: aggregated statistics that reduce them down to fungible numbers, not human beings with specific thoughts and experiences. As Nicole Hahn Rafter wrote in the preface to *Partial Justice: Women, Prisons, and Social Control,* "Like others who have attempted to study prisoners of the past, I was constantly frustrated by lack of information on individual inmates."[11]

In the thirty years since Rafter wrote her book, little has changed. In the introduction to a 2015 study of prisons in early America, Jen Manion wrote that "without diaries or letters written by the women themselves, I accepted that I would never really know what they thought, felt, or strived for," and bemoaned "how incomplete our understanding of state authority has been without attention to the actions, thoughts, and experiences of those subjected to its reach."[12]

The bulk of the work of this book has been to undo this silence, to find and follow the lives of imprisoned women and transmasculine people, and to allow revelations about the Women's House of Detention, Greenwich Village, queer history, and prisons generally to arise from *their* lives, *their* ideas, *their* stories. This is the biography of a unique building, but the building only matters because of the people who passed through it. By reconstructing the experiences of hundreds of incarcerated New Yorkers, I've identified a representative few whose lives were particularly well-documented. They have acted as the Beatrices for my descent into what one prison social worker called the "hellhole" that was the House of D.[13]

When I began sketching out the idea for this book five years ago, I had a naive understanding that prisons were bad, and should be made better. I might even have described them as "broken." But to look at prisons historically is to see a monstrously efficient system, doing exactly what it was designed to do: hide every social problem we refuse to deal with.

Prisons have very little to do with "justice" or "rehabilitation." If they did, we would care about the 83 percent recidivism rate for people currently incarcerated in state prisons.[14] Or we would be up in arms about the fact that two hundred thousand people are sexually assaulted while incarcerated *every single year*—and that's not even counting those who are violated by the routine procedures of "health care" in prisons and jails, or those who never report being assaulted, out of fear or shame or simple recognition that the system does not care.[15]

If one in twelve people sentenced to prison were also sentenced to be raped for their "crimes," we would call that barbaric. But when one in twelve people is sexually violated as collateral damage to their imprisonment, we call that justice.

As noted abolitionist, author, and community organizer Mariame Kaba writes in her brilliant book, *We Do This 'Til We Free Us*, calls for prison reform "ignore the reality that an institution grounded in the commodification of human beings, through torture and the deprivation of their liberty, cannot be made good....Cages confine people, not the conditions that facilitated their harms or the mentalities that perpetuate violence."[16]

Justice deals with root causes; punishment and confinement do not. For that reason, following the example of Kaba and other abolitionists, I use the phrase "criminal legal system" instead of "criminal justice system."

Most people in detention are there because they are poor, Black, female, queer, gender nonconforming, brown, mentally ill, chemically addicted, indigenous, abandoned by their families and the state, or some combination of the above. Discussions of "crime" are a distraction from this reality. Many abolitionists thus differentiate "crime"—the violation of specific statutes, many of which are inherently unjust— from "harm," a violation inflicted on a person by another person or by the state, which must be redressed for true justice to exist but which is often considered perfectly legal.

Criminal detention almost always leads to increased harm—for the person incarcerated, for those who depend on them, and for the communities they come from. The only twisted sense in which detention creates *less* harm is if we disregard the humanity of those incarcerated (and their communities) and focus solely on the incarcerated person's potential to harm someone the system cares about: usually a white person of some means or a business.

Researching the House of D has shown me the consistency of this truth, over decades, through liberal moments and conservative ones: the prison system is irredeemable. These detention warehouses are stopgaps and pressure valves for every other system that actually *is* broken, from education to mental health care, and without fundamental change, any minor reform to the prison system is simply overwhelmed, over time, by that reality.

But through this research, I also began to see the connections between abolition and my hopes for the queer movement writ large. Abolition moves us away from a paradigm of "legal" versus "illegal," and toward one of "harm" versus—what?

To me, the opposite of harm is care—the thing we owe one another, the thing we cannot live without, the thing the government should take a vested (and financial) interest in promoting. Yet we starve our systems of care while we feed the beast of incarceration. Our social safety net, from health care to the shelter system to welfare, is badly frayed, and our government has confused promoting a specific family type (heterosexual and nuclear) with promoting interpersonal care generally.

I had many criticisms of the movement for gay marriage, but at the most fundamental, my frustration was this: it accepted, unquestioningly, the idea that certain kinds of sexual relationships deserve to be rewarded. Yet the government has no fundamental interest in our sex lives. It does, however, have a vested interest in seeing that we are cared for. The uncared-for person ends up on the street, in the emergency room, in foster care, in asylums, in nursing homes, and, all too often, in prison. The uncared-for person costs the state time and money, one way or another.

Marriage law is a clumsy, limited solution to this problem: an attempt to promote relationships of care in hopes that this work will not end up on the state. Why unnecessarily limit it to pairs of people who like each other's genitals? Why not extended families, why not friends, why not sexual relationships beyond monogamy?

A need for care connects so many parts of the broad queer agenda. What do children abandoned by their families need? Care. What do elders without descendants need? Care. What does the support to form a chosen family ensure? Care. What is access to medically safe, socially supported gender transition services? Care. What does the AIDS crisis show our government's lack of? Care. What do LGBTQ immigrants, refugees, and asylum seekers need? Care. Care. Care.

Because queerness is not a vertical identity, so long as our society sees personal care as something that should mainly come from the nuclear family, there will always be queer people in need of care.

In 1998, Jay Toole got sick—couldn't walk for a while. Some friends on the street took Jay to a shelter, where she got sober and connected with a woman who brought her to the LGBT Center. At first she thought, "'Fuck no. I'm not going to that place.' I used to sleep outside of it in the front when it first opened and they chased me [off]."[17]

But she went, and at the meeting, they were talking about welfare, about substance use, about homelessness, and she kept thinking—that's me, that's me, that's me. For once, they were talking about her. So she talked too:

> I don't know how but the microphone ended up in my hand? I got up and I started telling them what I thought they needed to do, coming from the shelter system, and that there's so many of us in there and no one knows about it.
>
> I haven't fucking shut up yet.[18]

In 2002, recognizing the limitations in the liberal LGBTQ movement, that group became Queers for Economic Justice, an anti-poverty advocacy group with a queer lens. For the next twelve years, Toole was the director of their Shelter Project, which advocated for queer homeless people. Thanks to her work with QEJ, New York City allows shelter residents to self-determine whether they want to be placed in men's or women's facilities, and they recognize domestic partners on an equal plane with married couples.

Despite all that she has done on behalf of so many others, however, Toole's own future is still insecure. "I would say I feel discouraged by what our community is not doing," she told an interviewer in 2011. "I wonder what's going to happen to me when I won't be able to work or do anything....Who will take care of us?"[19]

These are the questions abolition asks: Who is harmed, who is cared for, and where is the state putting its thumb on the scale?

The vast changes that our systems need cannot happen all at once, but every step we take must be in the direction of our ultimate goal of true liberation. As Huey P. Newton, cofounder of the Black Panther Party, once said,

> I believe that reform must be integrated with revolution. Reforms are alright. Reforms are good! So long as they don't put up an obstacle to your final revolutionary goal....We must make very sure that our reforms are well thought out, and [that] we explain to the people on the way the significance, and also the dangers, of accepting certain compromises.[20]

I am not an organizer. I do not have the answers. But by looking closely at the history of the Women's House of Detention, I can clearly see the development of our modern system of mass incarceration, how it has affected queer people and our communities, and just how little justice there is in it.

In writing this book, I have lost a garden—and gained a new vision for the world.

— CHAPTER 1

The Prehistory of the Women's House of Detention (1796–1928)

THE SETUP OF MABEL HAMPTON

On the night Mabel Hampton was arrested the weather was, in a word, "unsettled": cloudy and warm, with winds that spent the whole day twisting back on themselves, flying up the long avenues of Manhattan from the southwest before doing a 180 to catch you from the north side too.[1] It was July 5, 1924, on 123rd Street: the heat of summer, in the heart of Harlem, as the twenties roared—a moment of unimaginable potential for a young Black lesbian like Mabel Hampton, who could find friends, lovers, a job, or an all-Black party around any corner.

But it was a moment of great danger as well. Before the night was over, the state would steal the next three years of her life.

From the police file of Mabel Hampton: "A small rather bright and good looking colored girl. 21 years old but appears to be younger. Has bushy black hair, is slim but not lacking in nourishment. Dark brown eyes. Friendly. Alert. Composed. Pleasant voice and manner of speaking."[2]

In actuality, Hampton had just turned twenty-two a few months before her arrest. How do we know this? Because Hampton had the (rare) opportunity to record her side of the story.

In many ways, Hampton's life was typical for working-class women of her day. Like most of her contemporaries, she entered the historical record the moment she was arrested, throwing her into a diffuse network of police, jails, courts, prisons, hospitals, reformatories, and social service organizations, all of which kept copious files. Unfortunately, many of our oldest and most extensive records of queer history come from our carceral system, and they are some of our most homophobic and ignorant ones as well. While they provide *data*—names, addresses, ages, etc.—they lack real descriptions of the experiences, feelings, and thoughts of the people they chronicle, and depending on the diligence of the individual who created them, carceral files contain many errors, small and large.

But in another way, Mabel Hampton was a true trailblazer—an out, Black, working-class lesbian dedicated to developing queer community. Through the connections she forged, her story has been preserved in greater and more personal detail than any of her contemporaries', and her work helped pave the way for the Lesbian Herstory Archives, where her story lives on today in a series of oral histories done in the 1970s and '80s.

The dynamic tension between her two sets of records—one produced about her and one produced by her; one contemporaneous and one retrospective; one for straights and one for queers—creates an incredibly robust picture of Hampton's life, while simultaneously highlighting the limits of each record when examined independently.

A few months before her arrest, Hampton had been cast as one of the "bronze beauties" in the chorus of *Come Along Mandy*, a popular musical farce at the Lafayette Theater, a pillar of the Harlem Renaissance.[3] *Mandy* was known for casting chorus girls who weren't light-skinned, women who were "dark clouds" or "smokey joes" rather than "high yellow" or "red bone," according to the argot of the Black theater at the time.[4] Backstage, Hampton met some of the most famous Black queer women in showbiz, from Gladys Bentley, to Ethel Waters, to

Jackie "Moms" Mabley. But the theater was a come-and-go job, and generally, Hampton remembered, she would go as soon as the men came on to her. Every show she worked, she said, "some man would feel my pussy and I'd have to leave."[5]

Like many working-class women, Hampton often held multiple jobs simultaneously. When she wasn't dancing in the chorus, she did domestic work, living with white families, taking care of their apartments and children—which is why she was on 123rd Street that night, in an apartment belonging to Mrs. V. K. Howard. Howard and her children were in Europe that summer, and Hampton managed their apartment in their absence. The night before, to celebrate July 4th, she and her girlfriend Viola had gone to a cabaret, where they met a white man who asked to call on them the next evening. He'd bring a friend, he said. Meet them at Howard's apartment. Take them out for a Coke.

In the end, Abraham Schlucker brought two friends: Patrolmen Dorfmen and Holmes of the NYPD, who burst through the doors of the apartment and arrested Hampton and Viola. The charge? Violation of Section 877, subdivision 4 of the New York Code of Criminal Procedure: vagrancy prostitution. Of the 17,000 women arrested in New York that year, one in eight was arraigned for vagrancy prostitution, and hundreds (perhaps thousands) of others were arrested on sex-work-related charges. Queer working women like Hampton were in particular danger because one telltale sign of prostitution, according to police informants, was being a woman out at night without a man.

Like the vast majority of other women arrested in New York City at the time, Hampton was quickly whisked down to Greenwich Village, which was, throughout the twentieth century, the epicenter of women's incarceration in New York, *and* the epicenter of queer life in America. These two histories twine round each other like grape vines—twisting, interconnecting, and reinforcing one another, until it's impossible to tell where one ends and the other begins.

Yet for too long, only half the story has been told. The whiter half, the richer half, the half concerned with famous artists—and, mostly, the half about men.

To understand what happened to Mabel Hampton on the night of July 5, 1924, and how women like her created the Greenwich Village we know today, requires drawing together thousands of threads, stretching to the furthest bounds of America's global empire and going back almost to the founding of this country. The history of women's incarceration is not simply a small mirror held up to the incarceration of men; rather, it is about the development of a distinctly unjust system of justice, violently dedicated to the maintenance and propagation of "proper" femininity.

Mabel Hampton was arrested five years before the Women's House of Detention was built. But it was built for women *like* her, and because women like her were increasingly a part of civil society, whom the government wanted to control. In fact, Hampton was brought to Greenwich Village by the same forces and laws that were already working to build "the House of D." Their shared prehistory, however, goes back all the way to 1796—a bare twenty years after the birth of America.

THE FIRST 114 YEARS OF PRISONS IN GREENWICH VILLAGE

Greenwich Village today is known for its beautiful, twisted streets; its history of artistic creation and gay liberation; and its hyper-gentrified real estate market and blighted luxury storefronts. It's the kind of place cops take you *away from*, not *down to*. But from the dawn of the country all the way up to the close of the twentieth century—from 1796 to 1974—prisons, in one form or another, dominated life in Greenwich Village. The first was Newgate (nicknamed for the famed London gaol), which opened just a few years after the US Constitution was ratified. Newgate was a high-walled stone complex spread over four acres where Christopher Street met the Hudson River. Prisoners from "the city" (what is today downtown NYC) were transported there by boat—the origin of the phrase "sent up the river."[6]

Newgate was a penitentiary, so called because it operated under the idea that the role of prison was to bring the convict to salvation, to make them *penitent*. Compared to most prisons of the day, it was a paragon of progressive penology, which embraced prisoner reform through hard labor and vocational education. Before Newgate, convicted people were permanently marked via barbaric punishments like having their "ears cropped" or "being branded," or else they were put in the stocks to be publicly humiliated.[7] The idea that arrested people should be detained *as* punishment was relatively new in the late eighteenth century, as was the idea that incarcerated people could be reformed.

Newgate was conveniently located not far from the potter's field where paupers were buried and convicts were hanged, which today is Washington Square Park. And it was far from any real estate that was considered valuable. In fact, what few neighbors there were greeted the construction of the prison as a fortuitous event, "look[ing] on the scheme as one promising a future rise in value of their holdings." Also, "it gave a stately air to the rural scenery."[8]

Women at Newgate were held together in a communal room in an isolated wing, where they did the prison laundry and sewing.[9] In early America, women who committed crimes were considered vastly more troublesome than men. As women were "naturally" more virtuous, the reasoning went, only the most vile could be induced to criminal behavior. Their life in detention combined the malign neglect that all imprisoned people received with toxic misogyny that made life behind bars almost unlivable. Their facilities were fewer, smaller, less funded, and less staffed; they received little to no vocational training or health care; and they were constantly in danger of sexual violence. A prison chaplain in New York observed in 1833 that "to be a *male* convict...would be quite tolerable; but to be a *female* convict, for any protracted period, would be worse than death."[10]

However, few women ever served time in Newgate, as most were denied the kind of public lives that gave them the opportunity to commit crimes. They were daughters, wives, mothers, and slaves, and in each case, some man in their life replaced judge, jury, and jailor. The discipline and punishment of "unruly" free women, of all colors, were mainly handled in the home, by their families, fathers, husbands, and brothers (part and parcel of our never-ending cycle of gendered intrafamily violence).

Those women who were imprisoned in Newgate were generally accused of crimes against property (such as theft) or crimes against persons (such as assault). Prostitution, intoxication, and other "crimes against the public order"—the kind of "crimes" that would one day fill the cells of the Women's House of Detention—rarely resulted in prison sentences in early America.

But over the course of the nineteenth century this system—which was designed to punish the antisocial (usually violent) acts of white men—was repurposed as a method of social control over women of all colors and Black people of all genders. As slavery was abolished and New York's Black population grew, prisons took on the punishment and persecution that had once been the provenance of the owners of enslaved people—"locking people of color into a permanent second-class citizenship," as Michelle Alexander wrote in *The New Jim Crow*.[11] At the same time, as white women moved further into the public sphere, the legal system took on the patriarchal duties of their families: the violent enforcement of virtue, chastity, femininity, submissiveness, motherhood, etc.

By the 1820s, Newgate was dangerously overcrowded, causing numerous escapes and a return to the public whippings and violent humiliations the prison had earlier eschewed. Additionally, the prison itself was crowded by the expanding neighborhood of Greenwich Village, which had experienced a strange and unexpected growth spurt in the summer of 1822. As the rest of the city succumbed to a particularly virulent outbreak of yellow fever, Greenwich's distant and underdeveloped streets were seen as a refuge; in a single week, the custom house, post office, and numerous banks and newspapers all decamped to the Village.[12] The city had come to the prison.

Around the same time, the last public hanging—of Rose Butler, a nineteen-year-old Black girl accused of arson—was held in the nearby potter's field.[13] A few years later, in 1826, a celebration was held to re-designate the field as Washington Square Park, a military parade ground. The earth was so rotted with corpses that some of the cannons crashed through the ground and into mass graves. Even so, the new houses surrounding the square quickly became prized real estate (for many years, NYU held its graduation ceremony there).[14] From this point on, the Village was firmly incorporated into the social fabric of New York City.

In 1829 Newgate closed for good, but soon after, in 1838, the Jefferson Market Watch House opened on the other end of Christopher Street, at 10 Greenwich Avenue. The Watch was like a police force that worked only at night, and the Watch House had a few jail cells that held people for short periods. For the next 140 years, until the closing of the Women's House of Detention, there would be some kind of jail located at this spot.

In 1844, as New York City expanded exponentially thanks to new trade from the Erie Canal, the Watch was replaced with a professional police force (the first in the country). Three police districts were established; the Second District was headquartered at 10 Greenwich.[15] This was a one-stop shop for nineteenth-century justice: aside from the police HQ, there was also a police court, a jail (which held men who had been arrested but not sentenced), and a detention pen, where men and women were held together on the day of their trial. The pen, in particular, was a cold and dangerous place. According to the *New York Times*, it was a "perfect icebox, where prisoners of both sexes, young and old, innocent and guilty, are huddled together."[16] And like Newgate before it, the Jefferson Market tank would sink to new lows as time passed.

This is the stark truth of prison history: most reforms are quickly overwhelmed or abandoned as soon as civic interest shifts away. Public outcry sweeps in like the ocean, upends everything, and rushes out, leaving the correctional system jumbled, but no less dysfunctional. In fact, reform almost always comes with increased funding or more square footage for human cages, meaning that when the system relapses to cruelty, it's usually bigger than it was before.

But the next tick of the wheel, the next cycle of reformation and retrenchment, would set Greenwich Village on track to become the queer, bohemian neighborhood it would one day be known as, and indelibly thread together the history of Greenwich Village with that of incarcerated women.

In the second half of the nineteenth century, prison reform became a hot button issue in America. The country's exploding population and increased urbanization had created an overcrowding crisis in detention facilities from New York to California. The Civil War had only recently ended, and the all-too-brief period of Reconstruction, when progressive and anti-racist politics were ascendant, was in full swing. The entire purpose of the correctional field was coming into question globally. Were prisons *custodial*—places where defective criminals were segregated and punished? Or were prisons *reformative*—places where the immoral, the spiritually fallen, and the mentally defective were transformed into useful members of society?

In 1870 the first meeting of the National Prison Congress, a gathering of prison activists, was held in Cincinnati, Ohio, to tackle these questions. Overwhelmingly, the participants embraced a reform model built around separating different kinds of prisoners. "Classification was touted as the crucial preliminary step in…encourag[ing] prisoners to reform," according to Nicole Hahn Rafter, historian of women's prisons. "This preoccupation with classification logically led to a call for entirely separate institutions for women."[17]

With the best of intentions, these concerned reformers created an entire world of separate and unequal jurisprudence, where women were arrested and confined on a whole host of charges for which men received fines, citations, or no punishment at all. Hand in hand with the coming expansion of anti-Black Jim Crow laws, these reformers helped oversee a massive expansion of the American prison system, which would in particular target generations of people who were young, Black, working-class, and/or queer, who were mostly guilty of the "crime" of being the wrong kind of woman.

This new concept of incarceration-as-punishment went hand in hand with the emerging medical-scientific field of eugenics, which was primarily concerned with saving the white race from external threats (people of color) and internal threats (queer people) via proper breeding. While these reformers thought of themselves as helping incarcerated people, they built a system that saw those people as cancers, to be removed as thoroughly as possible from the American body politic.

When a series of scandals turned a harsh light on the conditions at Jefferson Market Prison, and on the exploitation of arrested women throughout New York City, the resulting outcry opened the door for reformers to bring this new world of uneven justice to New York City. And it all began with the arrest, in Greenwich Village, of a man named Azel P. Newkirk.

THE TRAGIC DEATH OF AZEL P. NEWKIRK

Azel P. Newkirk was a handsome, square-jawed lawyer, with Abraham Lincoln muttonchops and one wildly cocked eyebrow in every photo. He was twice elected assistant secretary to the Indiana State Senate before the age of thirty, but his fortunes had fallen since, and he arrived in New York City in the winter of 1871 as the advance man for Van Amburgh's Menagerie, a once-famous animal circus.

On the evening of Sunday, December 3, 1871, Newkirk was invited to spend the night in the room of William Dunham, "out of charity," since Newkirk had squandered his paycheck.[18] The next morning, Dunham accused Newkirk of stealing his clothes, and had him arrested and packed off to Jefferson Market. The Northeast was experiencing an epic cold snap that week; the low for the day was fifteen degrees and the high wasn't even above freezing.[19] At one p.m., Newkirk was placed in the court detention pen, where "the windows [were] all broken...and the floor [was] always soaked with wet, except when covered with ice."[20] There had once been a stove, but it had been stolen and sold by the man responsible for installing it, a flunky for the corrupt city government who would soon be arrested for charging the city over $25,000 for six weeks' worth of "matts, brooms, spittoons, and water-coolers" (that's a little more than half a million in today's money).[21] Not that it would have mattered if the stove had been there; the court hadn't received a single shipment of coal that entire winter. At three p.m., the guards had to carry an unconscious

Newkirk out of the court pen and into the police jail, where at least there was heat. When he started to convulse, the guards "thought he was only shamming," and when next they checked on him—around one a.m.—Azel P. Newkirk was dead.[22]

Public outrage erupted immediately—primarily, according to one newspaper, because Newkirk was "a man of note."[23] Had he been "common," they acknowledged, "his death would not have created the excitement it has."[24] A grand jury was quickly called to investigate. In their report, they acknowledged that "little attention has been paid to the repairs of Courts and prisons generally" in New York City. They found that the Jefferson Market detention pen in particular was "neglected," and that "persons there were confined sometimes for hours" in conditions that were "undoubtedly grave."[25] Yet still, the jury determined that Newkirk's death was an unfortunate accident, perhaps related to his rumored alcoholism, and that the guards had done all that "circumstances permitted."[26] (Historically and today, any history of drug or alcohol use is used to blame arrested people for their own suffering, imprisonment, and death.)

The grand jury did, however, condemn one aspect of the Jefferson Market police complex: the mixing of all kinds of prisoners—particularly men with women, and those already found guilty with those awaiting trial—in the same pen. "A needful remedy in this respect will probably be had without much delay," the *New York Times* opined.[27]

Newkirk's death was, indeed, the final straw for the police and court complex at Jefferson Market. The whole rotten shebang was demolished in 1874 and replaced by a beautiful redbrick, neo-Gothic jail and courthouse, replete with a central spiral staircase, stained glass windows, and a clock tower that can still be seen for blocks around. Many prison reformers in this generation believed that their charges needed to be properly inspired in order to live better lives, and it showed in their architecture, if only occasionally in the detention facilities they ran. The jail held about a hundred people, approximately one-third of whom were women. The first person imprisoned was, in the words of the *Brooklyn Daily Eagle*, "a little boy 14 years of age."[28] Before the year was out, the prison had its first suicide attempt, and in the coming decades, it would be plagued by all of the same problems as its precursors: overcrowding, underfunding, corruption, neglect, violence, and despair.[29]

However, the new Jefferson Market Prison *did* provide the necessary space to begin segregating different kinds of imprisoned people—male from female, young from old, recidivists from first-timers, etc. And Greenwich Village was now considered centrally located, making it an ideal location for new experiments in penology meant to serve New York as a whole. In the first years of the twentieth century, these two factors made it the natural home for the next step in the development of women's jurisprudence in New York—the Night Court—which inevitably led to the building of the Women's House of Detention.

THE NIGHT COURT, WHERE TRAGEDY BECAME FARCE

Prior to 1907, a person arrested after the courts had closed for the evening was held at the nearest police station, where she was arraigned, meaning she was officially given notice of the charges against her. Most women were arrested for minor violations called summary offenses—vagrancy, intoxication, loitering for prostitution, etc.—and given a "station house bond," which was a kind of bail, determined solely by the police. If a woman could pay her bond, she was released on her own recognizance and got the money back when she appeared in court. Otherwise, she spent the night in the station house pen.

The vast majority of these arrested women were destitute and could not pay. Instead, they relied on bail bondsmen, who would furnish the money for their bail in exchange for a nonrefundable fee of anywhere from 5 to 50 percent of the original amount. "Bonding out" not only prevented the ten or twelve hours of discomfort and abuse an arrested woman would have endured overnight in a police cell, it also made her vastly more likely to be released at trial. Overwhelmingly, court records show that "the woman who did not secure bail was more likely to be convicted than one who did," a fact that is still true today.[30] After all, who seems more innocent—the woman who arrives at court under her own power, in an outfit she's chosen, or the one who is dragged there in handcuffs by the police, wearing what she had on the night before? Although the concept of bail was theoretically designed to minimize the time an arrested person spent in a cage before trial, it has from the very beginning been a way to privilege wealthier defendants. It is just one of the highly visible, publicly acknowledged ways in which our legal system is far from being a justice system, particularly for the poor.

Station house bonds, in particular, proved remarkably easy to exploit. Since they were already detained, arrested women only had access to bondsmen approved by the police, creating a pay-to-play system wherein bondsmen bribed officers for access to incarcerated people. The more people the police arrested, the more they were paid, and if the charges were subsequently dropped, the bondsman received his money back without ever having to ensure the arrested individual showed up in court. The women were released back onto the streets, minus the bondsman's fee, where they were easy targets for future arrests. It was a revolving door for extortion.

In an effort to stem this tide of police corruption, in 1907, New York created the Night Court, to take after-hours arraignments out of the hands of the police and cut down on the business of bail bondsmen. Once the court opened, "all persons charged with misdemeanors" and "women arrested for whatever crime in any part of the city" were routed through the new Night Court at Jefferson Market, where there were (at least theoretically) enough cells to separate different kinds of offenders.[31]

The New York City police were firmly opposed to this new court, claiming that requiring them to bring arrested women to Greenwich Village, instead of to their local precinct, would leave the city undefended at night. No crime wave manifested after the court opened, however. In fact, both journalists and magistrates were quick to point out the astonishing fact that as soon as it opened, arrests for prostitution fell by more than 50 percent, as police adapted to the new, less lucrative system.

But very quickly thereafter, the number of arrested women ticked right back up to where it had been. In the year the Night Court was instituted, nearly 7,400 people were arrested on prostitution charges; by 1909, that number had only decreased about 5 percent.[32] And while sex work arrests were down, incarceration time was up—suggesting that there weren't fewer sex workers in the city, they were just being held on longer sentences after each arrest. And nearly all of those arrested were women.

According to a report written by Judge Anna Kross, a magistrate in the Night Court who was later named commissioner of correction for all New York City, "The business of running a disorderly house is comparatively safe for men...it is the women who pay the penalty of publicity and shame. Of the 7,054 people arrested [for prostitution-related crimes] in 1909, 98.4 per cent were women."[33]

Kross went on to point out that this gendered imbalance remained true even when looking at prostitution-related offenses that were often committed by men, such as running brothels. In 1909, 148 brothel keepers were arrested—120 of whom were women.[34]

When it came to its original purpose, the Night Court was a spectacular failure. The bail bondsmen simply moved their trade from the station house to the Jefferson Market courthouse. Since the courts were open to the public, the bondsmen no longer needed to bribe the police or judges for access to prisoners (although they still did). Moreover, the police never really fully cooperated with the Night Court; one organization that worked closely with the court estimated that about a quarter of the women arrested for prostitution-related crimes were still being brought to the station house, where they were subjected to the same costly rigmarole as before.[35]

In the words of Magistrate Kross, "by 1909...the Night Court had fallen heir to the evils of the Station House Court and had added to them."[36]

Recognizing the failure of the court administration to deal with these issues properly at the city level, the state government empaneled the Page Commission, which wrote the Inferior Criminal Courts Act of 1910. The act mandated sweeping changes to the administration of justice in New York State—many of them aimed at women arrested for prostitution. The creation of a Women's Court, as mandated by the act, happened immediately. The Night Court was split in twain, and the women's part remained in the Village at Jefferson Market.

However, the act also required that there be a detention center exclusively for women, located conveniently near the Women's Court. It would take another two decades for the city to break ground on the Women's House of Detention, but from here on out, the clock was ticking. All that was left was to wrangle (and wrangle, and wrangle) about when, and where, and how much to pay for it.

Despite its name, the Women's Court was not a court for all arrested women, or even for all women arrested at night. Instead, it was dedicated to two kinds of offenses: prostitution and intoxication (and eventually shoplifting). But in the eyes of the courts, the police, and most respectable citizens, almost any disreputable woman was considered an opportunity for prostitution to occur, regardless of whether she actually exchanged sexual acts for money. In 1916, this would be codified in New York State legal precedent, thanks to a case known as *People ex rel. Miller v. Brockman et al.* In his decision, the presiding magistrate wrote that "prostitution has been defined as…the common lewdness of a woman."[37] In discussing this decision, another magistrate later clarified that "the element of hire or money does not appear to be essential."[38] In 1921, it was ruled that men who hire sex workers cannot be charged under prostitution laws because the crime lay in the *offer* of sex, not the act.[39] Finally, in 1936, a court found that "a male person cannot be convicted" of being a vagrant prostitute, thereby completing the illogical syllogism: in the eyes of New York City, all prostitutes were women, and all lewd women were prostitutes.[40] (Eventually, some men would be targeted under these solicitation and prostitution laws—almost always queer ones.)

In truth, the Women's Court was a court for women who were improperly feminine, women accused of "crimes" that would rarely, if ever, have put them in front of a judge in an earlier age—or if they were men. Overwhelmingly, regardless of the specifics of their cases, they were charged as prostitutes.

In the first full year the court existed, over four thousand women were arrested for prostitution and sent through its doors at 10 Greenwich. Over the first twenty-five years of its existence, it would see about twenty-five hundred prostitution cases a year, with a 75 percent conviction rate, well over the average in other city courts.[41] Black women, in particular, came in for harsh sanctions, so much so that even one of the moral reform organizations that pushed for the creation of the Women's Court noted it in their internal reports. In 1922, two years before Mabel Hampton was arrested, they found that Black women made up just 5 percent of the city's population but accounted for 20 percent of the prostitution arrests.[42] Once arrested, these women faced an 80 percent conviction rate, as compared to a 69 percent rate for white women arrested as prostitutes.[43]

Examining these figures, Magistrate Anna Kross wrote that "*arrests for prostitution bear no relationship whatever to the growth of the total population of the city, nor do they carry out the oft-repeated statement that economic depressions increase the number of women forced into a life of shame*" (emphasis in the original).[44] This makes sense: if the charge of prostitution was no longer related to a specific act, arrests for it would bear no relation to things that might increase the number of people committing those acts, such as a rise in overall population or a decline in economic security.

Magistrate Kross's final verdict on the Women's Court? "No judicial institution has done more to destroy the public confidence in the integrity of the judiciary, of the police, [and] of our laws."[45]

From this point on, thousands of women who were unable or unwilling to obey the dictates of proper femininity were brought to Greenwich Village every year. *At the exact same time*, the Village suddenly developed a reputation as a bohemian destination, rife with sexual freedom and illicit entertainments. This was no coincidence. The area already had pockets of artists and bohemians, stretching as far back as the 1850s, when Walt Whitman caroused in a bar called Pfaff's. But it wasn't until after the Women's Court opened that the neighborhood as a whole gained a reputation as a bohemian nightlife destination. According to *Steppin' Out: New York Nightlife and the*

Transformation of American Culture, by the 1920s, the Village had "become a tourist area...a playground where uptowners could indulge in wilder forms of sensuality...[where] conventional whites could see lesbians and homosexuals on the streets."[46]

Steppin' Out pegs the start of this increase to 1917, when café culture took off. It fails to mention, however, that the Women's Court had already been a slumming destination for those same thrill-seekers for a decade at that point. By 1912, one woman lawyer wrote that the court was frequented by a "shifting but almost always present group of fashionable men and women, who drop in after theater or dinner as they would perhaps to some vaudeville show."[47]

This was a feature of the system, not a bug. Although the officials involved in the Women's Court may not have intended their audiences to get quite so much entertainment out of their work, they intentionally set up a system that would publicly humiliate arrested women. As the court's first probation officer later wrote, "more important than granting immediate trial to offenders and freeing them from the evil of professional bondsmen...has been the service of the Night Court in showing the public a long procession of the girls bound to a life of prostitution."[48] This was but a small step away from the stockades and public beatings of the eighteenth century.

Eve Rosahn, an activist in the early radical lesbian movement, grew up in the Village in the 1950s. Her mother told her stories of frequenting the Night Court in the twenties, and compared it to "going to dance in Harlem."[49] She was "not a Lady Bountiful" type, just a young, working-class teen looking for some excitement—exactly the audience the Night Court was looking to scare straight.[50]

The court went so far as to produce publicity materials encouraging the public to attend; they noted there was "considerable space for spectators" and that the floors were sloped, "so that all have a clear view of the proceedings."[51] Newspapers hailed court watching as a "metropolitan institution."[52] As for the guests? "Women in furs and silks...seemed to enjoy the sight of shuddering at the raw, open running sores of the city," one columnist reported.[53]

(This practice sounds antiquated. Barbaric even. Yet it continues to this day; in 2014, the Associated Press recommended New York City's Night Court to tourists as "gritty entertainment" and "a chance to experience real-life law and order on a New York scale."[54])

To the public, the Women's Court was an amusement that charged no cover, was open every night, kept late hours, always had new stars, and could not be raided by the police. In 1918, as the more conventional entertainment scene in the Village was taking off, the *New-York Tribune* documented the already well-established tradition of attending the Women's Court for fun.

> "Chinatown or the Night Court, which shall it be?" has been a usual after-dinner question on the part of aristocratic slummers or diners in uptown restaurants or Greenwich Village. Motors have stood for hours outside of Jefferson Market courthouse while the occupants in evening dress have watched the tragic procession of women, in turn defiant, sullen, whimpering, pass before the magistrate for sentence.... Gray-haired women with shifty eyes and bold-faced little girls of sixteen...stand before the judge while their offence is discussed in the presence of unsympathetic and sensation-seeking spectators.[55]

Most histories of Greenwich Village don't connect these arrested women with the changing reputation of the area, even though the Women's Court was located in the Village until 1943. Even in books about the women of Greenwich Village, arrested and incarcerated people are virtually nonexistent. According to *All-Night Party: The Women of Bohemian Greenwich Village and Harlem, 1913–1930*, the "revolutionary years" for women in the Village did indeed start in the teens, but instead of mentioning the Women's Court, the book focuses only on "bohemian" artists and women of means.[56]

But what made *those* women bohemians? According to Caroline Ware, a pioneering sociologist from Columbia University who conducted a decade-long study of Greenwich Village in the 1920s, bohemians were characterized by free love, unconventional dress, erratic work—if any—indifference to physical surroundings, all night parties, crowding, sleeping where one happened to be, walking the streets in pajamas, girls on the street smoking, plenty of drink, living from moment to moment, with sometimes a pass at creative work but often not even that.[57]

In other words, they did the same things for which working-class queer women were being arrested. The vast majority of people who bucked the conventions of gender were punished for it, while a select (white) few were christened the harbingers of modernity.

So just who were these *other* Greenwich Village women? Unlike with bohemians, stories involving "criminals" usually end when the police arrive and "justice" is served. What happens to them inside the legal system, and after they get out, is mostly hidden from view—and what isn't hidden we turn away from, unwilling to face the cruelty that undergirds our so-called justice system. We know little about these women because records of queer, formerly incarcerated people (particularly pre-1930) are rare, which makes Mabel Hampton's story all the more important.

Women like Hampton, arrested in the years immediately preceding the construction of the Women's House of Detention, were the ones for whom the House of D was created. Simultaneously, they were the ones who had the least say in its creation. But without them, the House of D would not exist: not as a building, nor as a landmark. The state built the House of D to hold these women and transmasculine people, but they are the ones who invested it with meaning. Like Jay Toole in the 1960s, Hampton found ways to turn the state's carceral infrastructure to her advantage. The prison would never be anything more than a prison, but the people inside it were always so much more than "prisoners."

THE SETUP OF MABEL HAMPTON, REPRISED

After her arrest on July 5, 1924, Mabel Hampton spent four nights in the Jefferson Market Prison. Fifty years earlier, after the death of

Azel P. Newkirk, the "new" Jefferson Market had been hailed as the apotheosis of proper detention facilities. But like all reformed prisons, it was quickly forgotten, leading once again to severe deterioration and overcrowding. According to the Department of Correction, by the 1920s the prison was "indescribably gloomy, with narrow cells which would only permit a cot two feet wide. At times, due to the terrible overcrowding, it was necessary to have two women sleeping on one of these narrow cots, and this too, in a penal institution where homo-sexuality is always to be expected."[58]

At the time Hampton was arrested, Jefferson Market was a mixed-sex institution, but it was women-only on and off throughout the 1920s. In 1921, due to overcrowding, the city started juggling arrested women from one site to another, keeping them at Jefferson Market during the day, then bringing them over to Welfare Island (now Roosevelt Island) at night. This was an unrealistic solution that pleased no one, but the city continued this practice until the State Prison Commission declared it not only impractical but in fact illegal. The procedure violated the Inferior Criminal Courts Act of 1910, which mandated that women be detained near the court where they would be arraigned. By 1922, women were once again being kept at Jefferson Market full-time, and the city returned to exploring options for creating the now twelve-year-delayed Women's House of Detention.

On her first night at Jefferson Market, Hampton was fingerprinted— a recent advance in police procedure. In 1910, the same Inferior Courts Act that created the Women's Court and commanded the eventual creation of the House of D, also "mandated the taking of prostitutes' fingerprints in New York City magistrates' courts."[59]

Fingerprinting was pioneered on women arrested for prostitution for a few reasons. First, there were many of them, so the police had a large pool upon which to experiment. Additionally, previous anthropometric techniques of tracking criminals (what were known as Bertillon measurements) had been developed on men, and they didn't work well on women. Most importantly, however, women who were repeatedly arrested for prostitution were considered naturally criminal—like "perverts," or drunks, or vagrants, or "born tireds."[60] As their deviant bodies supposedly led them to commit crimes, it made sense to track those bodies themselves.

Thus a stunning perversion of justice was accomplished: recidivism became a stand-in for being born bad. Judges began to base sentencing not on the crimes in front of them but on a biologically based assumption of inherent criminality—the "proof" of which was a previous history of arrests. That recidivism might indicate a failure in the system, or that the arrested individual might be experiencing persistent poverty, societal persecution, racism, misogyny, etc. did not seem to occur to the rich, white, straight men who made the system.

This leads to the final reason fingerprinting was pioneered on arrested prostitutes: they were considered fundamentally disposable, and if it turned out that fingerprinting did not work for identification, "the consequences of an error in a prostitution case was not all that dire."[61] Unless, of course, you were the arrested person. Soon, fingerprinting would be expanded to other disposable classes of feminine people, particularly abortionists and men arrested for homosexuality. Only after it had been thoroughly tested on these groups would fingerprinting be expanded to common procedure.

Fingerprinting put women like Mabel Hampton at a unique disadvantage: unlike men, they couldn't give a fake name to avoid outstanding warrants or hide previous arrests. Unsurprisingly, the Fingerprint Bureau found that during the 1920s "the problem of the female offender [grew] increasingly difficult." In the Department of Correction annual report for 1929, they speculated this was caused by "the comparative emancipation of woman, her greater participation in commercial and political affairs and the tendency toward greater sexual freedom."[62] Or, they acknowledged later in the report, "the figures may merely represent an increased activity on the part of the police."[63] Nowhere did the Fingerprint Bureau acknowledge that their own practices might have influenced these statistics.

Most women's organizations and white "social feminists" of the day supported this radical expansion of policing and incarceration of other women. Social feminists were generally upper-middle-class white women raised in Victorian morality, who believed they had an obligation to work as caretakers for their less fortunate sisters. In other words, they took up roles as doctors, social workers, and lawyers, not because men and women were equal, but because men and women were so different that women needed their own professionals in order to fathom them.

While social feminists understood themselves as *helping* other women—and on an individual level, they often did—they promoted a system that was, at its core, deeply unequal. Moreover, they looked down on the women they were helping and saw them as analogous to children who needed a firm hand. This led them to support not only the fingerprinting of arrested women but also the enactment of more and longer sentences, particularly what were called "indeterminate sentences," which allowed a woman to be incarcerated *until those holding her decided to let her go*. In general, these feminists were among the fiercest supporters of the Women's Court and the Women's House of Detention...until it opened.

Gabrielle S. Mulliner, a New York City poet and lawyer, was one of these social feminists. Writing in the *Brooklyn Daily Eagle*, she argued strongly *against* using fines or citations on arrested women— the kinds of punishments men often received for violations of the public order. Instead, she wrote, "every woman who is arrested for a crime, no matter how petty," should be incarcerated until "she can show herself capable of earning her own living, or has some one who will take care of her."[64] It went without saying that this would mean training these women to be "properly" feminine, as who would marry a wife—or hire a maid—who didn't show the virtues of true womanhood?

Along with increasing the length of sentences, Mulliner also proposed sweeping changes to the *character* of women's incarceration, such as treating all arrested people with dignity regardless of the length of their criminalized history, and creating women's detention centers with an eye to "sanitation, physical comfort, [and] moral decency."[65]

Unlike Mulliner's call for increased sentencing, however, these more forward-thinking ideas were never enacted. For all their cooperation with the state, social feminists generally received half measures in return—mostly, the punitive half. But their attitudes and ideas (good and bad) would animate an entire generation of women working with incarcerated people and thus in turn have outsized effects on those, like Mabel Hampton, who came under state control.

After she was fingerprinted, and spent a few nights at the Jefferson Market jail, Mabel Hampton had her day in court on July 9th. There, she faced Magistrate Jean Norris: a renowned legal mind, a social feminist icon, the first woman appointed to a judgeship in New York State, and a profoundly racist jurisprudent who would soon be disbarred.

Even fifty years later, Hampton's righteous anger at Magistrate Norris still ran hot when she described her trial in her oral history. "No lawyer, nothing—she railroaded me," Hampton remembered.[66] Hampton described Norris as a lot like "that hussie" Anita Bryant, the former beauty queen who was the pinched and disapproving face of late-1970s homophobia.[67]

Hampton had no lawyer because in cases dealing with low-level summary offenses like prostitution, the magistrate replaced judge, jury, and counsel. And by redefining prostitution as the common lewdness of women, which did not require the *actual* payment of *actual* money for *actual* sexual deeds, the city had circumspectly abrogated even the need for evidence in these trials. Thus, women arrested as sex workers were denied their rights to an adequate defense, a jury of their peers, and a presumption of innocence. Or as a scathing article in the *New Republic* put it, "in the New York Women's Court...the assumption seems to be that all defendants are guilty."[68]

The only witness at Mabel Hampton's trial was Abraham Schlucker, who was clearly working with the police to set her up—and who failed to disclose that he was *also* a New York City police officer.[69] This kind of corruption was rampant in 1924. The same day that Hampton was arrested, the *New York Age* (one of the most influential

Black newspapers in the country) published a stinging exposé on the NYPD's use of crooked informants and evidence-less trials in prostitution cases. They documented one informant's confession of how he

> succeeded in luring girls and women into situations where he could counterfeit the appearance of wrongdoing on their part, and that policemen, acting in cahoots with him, have followed behind and made arrests of the females on charges of moral delinquency....In most cases, the woman, frightened through inexperience and mostly without friends who were able to advise, have had to pay the law's penalty, thus allowing unscrupulous police officers to add to their record of supposed efficiency.[70]

But the NYPD did not have an exclusive market on corruption in New York City, or on abusive practices toward women arrested for prostitution. In 1930, Magistrate Jean Norris was at the center of a corruption scandal called the Seabury Investigation, and the next year, she was disbarred for faking evidence in prostitution cases, convicting women she knew were innocent, and using her position for personal gain (because she appeared in an ad for Fleischmann's Yeast while wearing her judicial robes).[71] This wasn't just one or two injudicious acts; according to scholar Cheryl Hicks, "In over 5,000 cases 'overwhelmingly related to prostitution and disproportionately involving African-American defendants,' Norris handed down 40 percent more convictions than her peers."[72]

For the "crime" of allowing a man to take her out for a Coke, Magistrate Norris gave Mabel Hampton a three-year sentence to the Bedford Hills Correctional Facility for Women, which had opened in 1901 as a reformatory. Reformatories were the social feminists' answer to women's prisons: large, rural campuses where young women (mostly first-time offenders, and mostly white, initially) could be taught the value of true womanhood. More than thirty reformatories opened around the country in the first part of the twentieth century, and they pioneered a wide variety of programs for (and on) imprisoned women.[73]

However, reformatories were expensive to run, and they often re-fused to take older women, repeat offenders, those convicted of more serious crimes, Black women, women considered mentally ill, etc. Although they were sometimes successful at helping those women they deigned to allow in, by the time Mabel Hampton was sent to Bedford, reformatories were widely seen as inefficient. They were also frequently overwhelmed with many more cases than they had been designed to handle. Much like Newgate Penitentiary and the Jefferson Market police complex before it, Bedford Hills sunk deeper into depravity over the years.

In 1919, the governor of New York started an investigation into allegations of staff cruelty at Bedford Hills. The director admitted "that girls had been handcuffed, their faces dipped in water, and their diet cut to bread and water," but argued that this was therapeutic, and that in fact some women "liked the handcuffs and would not take them off because [they] enjoyed the soothing effect."[74]

"Big Cliff" Trondle, a gender nonconforming person who was sent to Bedford Hills in 1913 on a charge of "masquerading in boys' clothes," told a very different story, detailing punishments that included

handcuffing the hands over one's head and hanging that way with the big toe just touching the floor for hours at a time until one fainted. Other things were the straight jacket, and strapping the girls to springs of beds without any mattresses for hours and hours without even being able to properly take care of their bodily needs.[75]

In detention, Trondle learned two things: how to turn tricks, and how to shoot heroin. For the rest of Trondle's life, he would be in and out of prison—often at the House of D.

Bedford Hills, as a reformatory, was one of the *progressive* prisons, the *kinder* alternatives. And, in truth, Mabel Hampton's experiences at Bedford Hills were 180 degrees away from Big Cliff's. In all likelihood, this was because of the publicity over the tortures that people like Big Cliff faced, and because Hampton was more feminine, and willing to work in domestic service.

Over the course of her three-year sentence, Hampton met a number of other queer women at Bedford Hills. The administration considered her a smart student, a good worker, and at all times well-behaved. She was granted probation to work as a maid, and when that job turned abusive, she voluntarily returned to Bedford Hills, where the administration advocated on her behalf and helped her secure a new position. Reformatories like Bedford Hills trained women to take up two kinds of post-prison lives—wives or maids—and if a woman was willing to go along, they would help her.

After her time at Bedford Hills ended, Mabel Hampton rarely worked in the theater again, and at this far distance, it is impossible to parse out how much of that choice was due to the coercive effects of reformatory life, and how much from frustration with life on the stage. She would continue to work as a domestic, and in the 1930s, she met the love of her life, Lillian Foster. The two became fixtures in the lesbian community, and in 1985, Mabel Hampton was named the grand marshal of the New York City Pride Parade to celebrate her decades of activism.

THE WOMEN'S HOUSE OF DETENTION FINALLY MATERIALIZES

In Mabel Hampton's last year at Bedford Hills, 1926, a state-level Department of Correction was created in New York, which tried to reorganize the entire correctional system to be more efficient and less expensive. This was the death knell for reformatories, which were both inefficient and costly. For the next few years, the state would do-si-do incarcerated women through a variety of different institutions, trying to find a workable alternative, while slowly stripping away the most progressive features of the reformatories that remained. In 1932, the Bedford Hills Reformatory was officially rechristened the Westfield State Farm, a prison for women, and the reformatory movement, in New York, was dead—a sign of the waning power of social feminists and the Progressive movement of which they had been part.[76] Today, the former reformatory is known as Bedford Hills, a maximum-security prison and the largest women's prison in New York State.

Increasingly, a Women's House of Detention in New York City seemed to be the answer—a place that could hold a large number of women in a denser, more vertical, less costly arrangement, while still (in theory) providing the same redemptive value as a reformatory. In 1914, the city had actually begun work on a site on West 30th Street, but with the encroachment of World War I, the idea was abandoned. By the mid-1920s, that site no longer seemed viable for the prison. Instead, the city focused on 10 Greenwich Avenue.

Primarily, this was because the neighborhood was still disreputable. Thanks in part to the Night Court, and the institutions that had appeared to serve those arrested by it, the Village was "noted as the home of 'pansies' and 'Lesbians,' and dives of all sorts featured this type," according to pioneering sociologist Caroline Ware, who spent the entirety of the 1920s studying the neighborhood.[77] Most of these were not what we today think of as "gay bars"; rather, they were bars that catered to the hip and happening, for whom homosexuality was suddenly, briefly, hot.

As Ware described the scene in one basement bar, "Jo's,"

By 1930, promiscuity was tame and homosexuality had become the expected thing. One girl who came nightly was the joke of the place because she was trying so hard to be a Lesbian, but when she got drunk she forgot and let the men dance with her....To lend a touch of intellectuality and to give people a sense of activity, the proprietor set aside two nights each week for discussion or performance by regular patrons. These evenings, however, did not interrupt the group's major preoccupations, for the subjects chosen for discussion were such things as "the social position of a gigolo" and "what is sex appeal?" On the latter subject, the views of the Lesbians present were especially called for.[78]

Throughout her study, Ware continually noted the distinct and unique lesbian presence in the Village. Of the many bars she examined, only four catered primarily to locals, one of which "had a Lesbian reputation and used some local girls as hostesses and attracted a few others as patrons."[79] Even the other areas of the city that had businesses that served queer men—Coney Island and Sands Street in Brooklyn, Times Square and Harlem in Manhattan—did not yet have public institutions for queer women. For these women, the Village was unique.

Moreover, many Village residents had their own direct experiences with the criminal legal system, making the presence of a prison not as onerous in their minds. In fact, for some, the idea that their arrested loved ones would be nearby was a positive, not a negative. Incarcerated and formerly incarcerated people were understood as part of the neighborhood—as stakeholders in a world they were all co-creating—not as interlopers who had been inflicted upon the "proper" owners of the area. One of the great tricks of mass incarceration (perhaps, in fact, a necessary step for it to exist at all) was the removal of incarcerated people from the bounds of civic life, physically and spiritually. Over the course of the twentieth century, they would go from people to be helped, to problems to be solved.

This othering had already begun in the Village in the 1920s. In her study, Caroline Ware distinguished between "local people"—Irish and Italian immigrants, "mostly tenement dwellers"—and "the Villagers," who had been drawn to the area for its beautiful buildings and bohemian reputation.[80] One of the major distinctions Ware noticed between the two groups was that "although most of the local people lived relatively law-abiding lives, the wall which separated them from the underworld was a thin one which might at any moment be broken."[81] For the Villagers, on the other hand, incarceration was something you read about in the papers.

In the late twenties, the Villagers went through successive waves of home remodeling and "became a direct danger to those [local people] who desired to remain in the neighborhood."[82] The Villagers fought against the nearby placement of the House of D, but they were few and not well organized (for now). In 1928, excavations for a new subway line (today's A/C/E trains) created "serious cracks" in the foundation of the Jefferson Market Prison, forcing the city to make "preparations for an immediate evacuation."[83] This seems to have been the deciding factor: as Jefferson Market would now have to undergo major structural renovations no matter what, Mayor Jimmy Walker finally pulled the trigger and proclaimed it the site for the now eighteen-year-delayed Women's House of Detention.

For the first new penal institution built in New York in thirty-five years, the city planned to go all out. According to the 1929 Annual Report of the Department of Correction, the Women's House of Detention would feature a massive hospital, covering several floors, with state-of-the-art medical equipment and extensive psychological services. Most importantly, in the eyes of the city, there would be enough space to ensure complete segregation of the imprisoned population at all times. The hospital would function independently from the prison, and incarcerated people would be separated by age, type of case, health status, drug use, arrest history, etc. All told, the initial concept for the Women's House of Detention was a triumph for progressive reformers of the day.

Those, however, were summer plans, made while the twenties were roaring. All prison reforms naturally sink back to a baseline close to—or worse than—what came before. Imagine what would happen to a prison opened amid the worst depression the country had ever seen, followed immediately by a world war.

Is it any wonder that the House of D would come to be known as "Skyscraper Alcatraz," "the shame of the city," or simply, the "Hell-Hole"?

Psychiatrists, Psychologists, and Social Workers—the Prison's Eyes, Ears, and Record Keepers

A DARK DAY DAWNS

On the morning of October 30, 1929, New York awoke a vastly different city than the day before. In the preceding twenty-four hours, the stock market had lost some $14 billion in value—about $206 billion in today's money—starting an economic slide that wouldn't bottom out for another three years.[1] The Roaring Twenties had ended with a bang; the Great Depression had begun.

We can thus forgive the newspapers for failing to cover another momentous event that occurred that afternoon: the laying of the cornerstone for the Women's House of Detention, the eleven-story prison that would loom over Greenwich Village for the next fifty years. Only the *Brooklyn Standard Union* covered the groundbreaking that day, according it one-half of one sentence in an article about Mayor Jimmy Walker's reelection.[2] Walker was New York City's good-time mayor. The Night Mayor, he was called, or Beau James, for his beauty.

A college dropout from Greenwich Village, he was the mayor of the speakeasy and the chorus girl. But like a good machine politician, he always turned up for events in his home district. Despite the rainy fall weather, some two thousand other New Yorkers joined him on the 30th, all eager to memorialize the first step toward the new, long-promised prison at 10 Greenwich Avenue.

Just two years later, the prison was complete. Despite the deepening Depression—which, by now, the country realized was no temporary downturn—1931 was actually the single busiest year for skyscraper construction in New York City history *to this day*, with thirty-two buildings going up from Midtown Manhattan to downtown Brooklyn.[3] This was the last gasp of the era of prosperity. Buildings were built so fast because the money had been secured before the Depression, and with workers now desperate it was easy to employ big, round-the-clock crews for very little pay. But while they could build them, they couldn't force anyone to use them. The Empire State Building, also completed in 1931, was called the "Empty State Building" for years because the owners couldn't secure paying tenants.

An oft-overheard joke in the Village that year was that every day several women dropped in at the House of D to ask how to get an apartment. The answer was always the same: "shoot your husband."[4]

It was easy to mistake the House of D for an apartment building. The architects were Sloan and Robertson, who were responsible for a number of other well-known New York City buildings, including the Chanin, which can still be seen at the corner of Forty-Second and Lexington. They brought the simple, elegant, rhythmic geometry of art deco to all of their projects, including the prison. All told, it cost about $2 million to build, and was widely called the only art deco prison in the world. The cells ran along the exterior of the building, so they had windows—small, mostly opaque, and crisscrossed with saw-proof wire, but not barred—and the two-tone stone used for the exterior facing gave the impression that the windows were much larger than they actually were. Right above ground level, some of the windows were placed inside delicate ogee arches, whose sinuous curves had a Moorish cast. Interspersed with these were copper facings of stylized leaves, thrusting out and up, like the carvings at the top of a Corinthian column.

In the estimation of one journalist, "It would be far sweeter to live in this modern 'jail' than to work and pine away in a boarding house."[5] He went on to suggest that this "new style penology" was really just "criminal coddling."[6]

Already there was a souring of opinion, a growing negativity that cropped up in almost every article about the House of D, before a single woman had been incarcerated. The Progressive Era that kicked off the twentieth century—when reform-minded activists were ascendant—had shattered at the beginning of the twenties. Partially, this was due to internal disagreements among progressives over World War I, about whether pacifism trumped fighting "the Great War." Partly it was due to the movement's twin successes in 1920: the constitutional amendments that gave women the vote and enacted Prohibition. But regardless of the reasons, with the Great Depression now in full swing, the Progressive Era's etiolated beliefs about prison reform and human rehabilitation were being weighed against their costs, and found wanting.

Even before the prison was completed, the state began making plans to shut down other facilities that held incarcerated women, from a correction hospital located on Welfare Island, to a women's workhouse located outside the city. The officials knew this would cause severe overcrowding, but "New York City was close to bankruptcy...[and] it was not very concerned about the needs of an incarcerated population which, at least, was given food, shelter and clothing."[7] The House of D began its death from a thousand cuts before a single person ever entered its doors.

Initially, the House of D was to be a jail, which meant it would only house women awaiting trial or sentencing, or those otherwise detained *without* being sentenced (such as material witnesses)—not women who had been convicted. Since these women were supposedly held for a short time, from a few days to a few weeks, little room was made for recreation or social services in the initial design. A large hospital was included in the plans instead, intended primarily to treat narcotics addiction and sexually transmissible infections.

However, male wardens from the other prisons pushed back against these designs, urging the creation of a more "practical" institution, by which they meant one that would hold more people, in a smaller space, with fewer costs.[8] Their voices carried the day, and the House of D was made to hold both women awaiting trial and those serving sentences—populations with very different needs. According to Clarice Feinman, author of *Imprisoned Women*, this was the original sin of the House of D, "leading to consistent problems of overcrowding, lack of facilities, and riots."[9] In the future, both state and city governments would claim that this mixing of inmate populations was necessitated because another New York prison was closed in 1934, but the paper trail makes it clear that this was the city's intention stretching back as far as 1927.

To make room for the dual population, plans for the hospital were scaled down. All told, the prison was designed to hold four hundred people at a time, in individual cells spread out over the fourth through tenth floors. Each residential floor was vaguely H-shaped, with a set of cells on each of the legs of the H, allowing for four units per floor. At the intersection of one leg was a communal dining room, and at the other, a multiuse space (starting in 1935, however, some of these rooms were cannibalized to make dormitory-style cells).[10] In between the two, at the center of the H, was a guard station, set up to see down every part of the floor at the same time. Individual cells were all on the outside of the building, and each had a toilet, sink, cot, and window. The eleventh floor was the hospital. In the end, it had only twenty-nine beds. The roof, sometimes called the twelfth floor, was caged over and used as recreation space in the summer. The first floor was for receiving new inmates and visitors, the second for staff housing and a chapel, and the third for the kitchen and laundry.

People brought to the House of D were made to run a gauntlet on arrival. Although some of the details changed over the years, their experiences followed along these lines: They were brought via police van through the exterior wall to a small courtyard, out of sight from the street. They waited together in a large room on the first floor until the intake process began. They were made to shower and given a forced enema, an invasive medical exam, and a probing genital search, after which their belongings were taken and they were given a set of sheets (which were changed, on average, once every two weeks—quite a bit more frequently than the blankets, which were only cleaned "every few months," no matter how many people used them in that time).[11] Detained people were allowed to keep their outside clothes; those serving sentences were given uniforms. (The true unfortunates were those detained for so long they crossed a season, and were stuck wearing summer dresses in a stone jail in the encroaching cold of winter, or wool underwear in the heat of summer.) Finally, after hours of processing, arrested women were assigned to their cells.

Day-to-day life in the prison was a mixture of tedium and despair. Cell doors opened at 6:30 a.m. and were locked again at 8:30 p.m., with lights out by nine. It was noisy at all times, and filled with vermin. Once every two weeks, imprisoned men from other institutions were supposed to act as exterminators, hosing the cells down with insecticide, with "special attention being given to the beds" (most likely because bedbugs were still a serious urban problem when the prison opened). Often, those scheduled exterminations never happened.[12] Complaints about the food were constant. A small percentage of women were given psychological exams and services; most were not. As the first superintendent reported in 1934, "Only a comparatively small group can be assigned to any educational or vocational work."[13] Women incarcerated for under three months were generally given no activities to do whatsoever. Some twenty to thirty were employed in the laundry (where they did unpaid work cleaning the linens from penal institutions around the city, in what was deemed a vocational training program), and a similar number were employed in the kitchens. Sometimes there were classes (in literacy, beauty arts, and the "rudiments of culture"), or discussion groups, or visits from volunteers.[14] In the spring and summer, if the weather was good, each woman could spend one hour a day on the roof. The art deco chapel had a tripartite altar for weekly Jewish, Protestant, and Catholic services. Sentenced prisoners were allowed one visitor every two weeks; those on trial were allowed one visitor a day. At first, inmates could write one letter a week; later, they were allowed to write as many as they could afford postage for. All outgoing and incoming communications were censored. There were no phone calls—instead, women wrote down the messages they wanted to send and guards made calls for them (illiterate people had to find someone to help them).

The prison's lack of social, educational, and psychological services virtually guaranteed that it would function mostly as a revolving door. A report by the New York State Commission of Correction, issued a year after the House of D opened, mentioned that there were only seven social workers servicing the entire prison system in New York City.[15] Moreover, these positions were not included in the city budget, which would have at least offered a thin guarantee they would be continued year to year. Instead, social workers were paid out of money made from purchases in prison commissaries—a $300,000 per year business, which journalists described as "the pet private project of the Commissioners of Correction," who also used the funds to expense lunches and pay for travel.[16] If an incarcerated person wanted sugar, milk, a comb, or cigarettes, the commissary was her only option. Since at least the time of the Tammany Hall scandals in the late nineteenth century, there were many complaints about the corrupt nature of the commissary racket in NYC prisons. Then, just one year after the House of D opened, all city commissary funds were poorly invested in a bank that went under. As a result, it was "necessary to curtail [social service] activities" throughout New York City's detention facilities.[17]

The House of D's psychological services didn't even receive that minimal guarantee of funding—despite the fact that the State Commission of Correction deemed them "a very valuable aid in the administration of the institution and in the follow-up of cases after discharge."[18] Instead, the House of D relied on private funding to pay the salaries of a part-time psychologist and a visiting psychiatrist, who concentrated their services on "women who are shown by the tests to be of higher intelligence than the average but who have not had the advantages of higher education."[19]

These tests (intelligence, aptitude, and Rorschach) were pseudoscientific and deeply defective. They were a major part of prison reformers' vaunted system of classification, despite their wide-scale flaws, which included inbuilt racial and class biases and the basic irreproducibility of their results. Their use in women's prisons was largely developed at Bedford Hills during the years when Big Cliff Trondle reported being tortured by the staff there.

These tests were used to apportion out critical prison services from education to psychiatry, but more fundamentally, they were used to divide arrested women into the good and salvageable versus the defective and incorrigible. Those who were deemed least intelligent or most damaged risked being sent to an institution for the "feebleminded" or "psychopathic," which would transform their criminal sentence into a civil one—meaning they could be detained for any amount of time, even life, regardless of the severity of their original offense. The goal was not only to prevent future crimes, but to remove these women as thoroughly as possible from the social fabric of America so they couldn't have children and pass down their quote-unquote biological inferiority.

Much like social feminists, these early psychologists helped to greatly expand the reach and power of the criminal detention system, putatively in order to help incarcerated women. But when their charges failed to reform adequately, their medical model was "used to place the blame for institutional failures on the inmates."[20] It wasn't the system that was fundamentally broken, it was the women themselves.

The organization that provided the funding for psych services at the House of D was called the Women's Prison Association (WPA). In 1845, the WPA split off from the mixed-sex Prison Association of New York, becoming the first organization in the country to focus solely on women involved in the criminal legal system. Like most women's reform groups, the WPA was predominantly run by middle- and upper-class white social feminists, but they often took a more progressive—and aggressive—approach to their work than did other organizations of the time, particularly before World War II. Aside from the staff they funded at the House of D, they also ran a short-term home for formerly incarcerated women, called the Hopper Home (which still exists today), and provided extensive social services to an even larger network. Their case notes were rigorous, detailing every conversation, point of contact, and service given. The resulting files could run over eight hundred pages, and included everything from photographs, to high school transcripts, to love letters, to medical reports. Although they generally began seeing women during or immediately after their incarceration, WPA services (including psychiatric and medical care) often continued for years—sometimes decades—after release, and frequently included the psychiatric staff they funded at the House of D. In this way, the House of D remained a dominant force in the lives of many women long after their incarceration ended.

These social work files are an unparalleled resource for researchers interested in the lives of incarcerated women, particularly in the 1930s and '40s, when there are few other sources to draw from. In 1931, the New York City government was so underwater that neither the court system nor the Department of Correction published an annual report of their work—and they wouldn't publish one again until the 1940s. Although a number of women in the WPA files attempted to share their own stories in memoirs, articles, and speeches, they were almost uniformly denied the opportunity to do so until well after World War II. When their cases did get publicity, they were treated with disdain, disgust, and morbid curiosity. The 1920s and '30s saw a "boom in autobiographical and fiction writing by prisoners," according to *Criminal Intimacy: Prison and the Uneven History of Modern American Sexuality*. But almost all of those authors were cisgender white men.

Although the information in the WPA files was mediated by the social workers who recorded them, they are still the closest thing we have to these women's stories, told in their own words. To be clear: This is an imperfect archive (as are all archives). The people who received aftercare services were a small, selectively chosen group, which tended to be younger, straighter, and whiter than the prison population as a whole. But the histories these files recorded were captured nowhere else, and in the aggregate, they offer a unique view into the lives of formerly incarcerated queer people. All historians must account for, and work around, the inbuilt biases of the archives they use; thankfully, the WPA proclaimed those biases openly. As far as I am aware, no other researcher writing about New York City, women's prisons, or queer history has ever looked at these files—all 148 boxes of them.

From the moment the prison opened, the WPA was tightly imbricated with its staff and residents, seeing its successes and failures play out in the lives of hundreds of women every year. Through their files, we can see how the lives of these women were changed by the prison, and how these women in turn changed life in Greenwich Village.

Two of the earliest House of D referrals that the WPA worked with were a study in oppositions: a butch Brooklyn runaway named Charlotte, arrested for waywardism, and a Maine farm girl turned femme fatale named Virginia, arrested on a charge of murder—two teenagers whose lives would be forever altered by their chance meeting in the House of D. For many young people in this decade, like Charlotte and Virginia, the criminal legal system was *the* vehicle through which they learned modern, upper-class ideas about sexuality and gender—but more importantly to them, it was where they met their lovers.

THE LOVE SONG OF CHARLOTTE AND VIRGINIA

Charlotte B.'s troubles began in 1930, the summer she turned fifteen, when her mother died of a sudden illness. Charlotte and her three brothers were taken in by their aunt, who lived next door to them in Crown Heights, Brooklyn. Despite their physical proximity, however, there was no love lost between Charlotte's mother and her aunt, and that animosity transferred quickly to Charlotte.

Charlotte's aunt blamed Charlotte for her mother's death, and informed her that "if she did not mend her ways she would grow up to be nothing more than a maid."[21] Up to this point, Charlotte had been a decent student with college aspirations, but she soon began skipping school, disappearing for longer and longer jaunts as time passed. In the 1920s, mass production had flooded the streets of America with affordable cars, and Charlotte was fascinated by them. Hitchhiking became her escape of choice, and she spent much of the next three years on the road. In fact, when she met her first social worker at the WPA, Charlotte informed her that she was "the famous Charlotte B. who had hitch hiked across the continent and back again."[22]

Increasingly, her aunt found Charlotte ungovernable, and started bringing in professional help—the Missing Persons Bureau; the Board of Health; the Crime Prevention Bureau; and, eventually, the Girls'

Service League (GSL). The GSL's mission was similar to that of the Women's Prison Association: they provided services to troubled young women through a privately run shelter. But the GSL was much more conservative than the WPA, and in 1933 they worked with Charlotte's aunt to have Charlotte arrested "as a Wayward Minor and a chronic runaway"—despite the fact that she was now eighteen and legally an adult.[23] Charlotte was summoned to the Women's Court in Greenwich Village, but instead she hitchhiked to Maryland, where she remained for four months, working in restaurants. When she returned to Brooklyn in April 1934, the police picked her up and took her to the House of D.

This pattern of youthful indiscretions that turn into criminal proceedings is overwhelmingly common in the lives of incarcerated queer women, historically and today. The Williams Institute found that nearly half of the incarcerated queer women they examined were under the age of twenty-nine, more than double the percentage for straight-identified women. In a separate study from 2016, the Center for American Progress found that 20 percent of all youth in detention—and 40 percent of girls—identified as LGBTQ.[24] Today, youth of color are particularly in danger, thanks in part to the increased role of police officers in schools with primarily Black students, creating what is often referred to as the school-to-prison pipeline. In an interview, the author of the Williams study noted that "there is an over-representation of sexual minority youth" in detention centers, and there is a direct "pathway between being a young person held in custody...to being incarcerated later."[25]

This pathway was built by many of the same Progressive Era reformers who pushed for separate women's prisons in the late nineteenth and early twentieth centuries, who believed that bringing wayward young women under the arm of the state would put them on the right road to adulthood. Instead, for the majority of these youths, their early involvement with the criminal legal system would follow them for life, precluding them from many kinds of employment, removing them from their communities, and introducing them to new and sometimes dangerous associates.

The first Wayward Minor law in New York State was passed in 1882. It applied only to girls and women aged fourteen to twenty-one who had been arrested for prostitution and expressed a desire to reform.[26] Within a few years, the law was greatly expanded—to include women who were not prostitutes but who might be someday. In 1886, "incorrigible girls" were added to the Wayward Minor law, and parents were given the ability to have a girl committed without having her arrested. The law wasn't applied to boys until 1925.[27] At the same time that the Women's Court was being developed (during the Progressive Era at the start of the twentieth century), New York State instituted Children's Courts, which were intended to keep youth accused of crimes out of the adult legal system. But in 1927, the New York Court of Appeals ruled that defendants in the Children's Court had "neither right to nor necessity for the procedural safeguards described by constitution and statute in criminal cases"—meaning that in an effort to protect youth like Charlotte from the carceral system, the city made it easier to find them guilty and have them detained.[28] Once these youth were in the system, it made it far more likely they would be arrested again later. Today, approximately 55 percent of all juvenile detainees are rearrested within one year of being released.[29]

The Williams Institute study noted one trait, in particular, that seemed to put youth in increased danger of criminal legal involvement: being gender nonconforming. Certainly, that was an issue for Charlotte (as it had been for Big Cliff Trondle and, at times, for Mabel Hampton—who preferred slacks to skirts—as well). As "the only girl among a great many cousins," Charlotte said that she was "brought up almost as a boy."[30] Even as a child she was tall, broad shouldered, and athletic, and her behavior around other girls was considered suspect. Although today we tend to assume there existed a uniform ignorance and silence around queer identities pre-Stonewall, by the 1920s and '30s, our modern ideas of sexual identity were being developed and discussed openly, in some places—including the criminal legal system.

As historian Gillian Rodger points out in her work on drag kings in vaudeville, before the concept of homosexuality was widespread, "there was a place within working-class culture for strong assertive women" like Charlotte—women who defied gender norms both consciously and instinctively.[31] In the Victorian era, some people (particularly upper-class, educated individuals with connections to the growing sexology movement in Europe) might have called Charlotte an "invert," which was an idea that combined our concepts of being homosexual, being transgender, and being intersex. Inverts were thought to have bodies that were different from men and women, and their abnormal desires and behaviors came directly from those deviant bodies. For this reason, it was almost impossible to think about "curing" or changing an invert—they were, literally, born this way (although inverts would still be pitied, shunned, abused, and held up as examples of how *not* to live).

But in the late nineteenth and early twentieth century, social workers, medical professionals, psychiatrists, newspapers, and the criminal legal system spread the idea of "the homosexual"—a person attracted to people of the same gender, emotionally stunted, morbidly obsessed with sex, predatory, and unidentifiable (perhaps even to themselves). Jen Manion, author of *Liberty's Prisoners* (one of the few other books to look at women's prisons historically), points out that at this moment, gender nonconformity ceased to be seen as a discrete phenomenon in and of itself; rather, it was considered "a sign of something innately different and pathologising" inside a person—homosexuality.[32] In this new schema of identity, your sexuality was rooted in your mind, so your body was only, at best, a clue to who you were.

This had three profound consequences for queer people. First, it made thinkable the idea that there were gender conforming people who were attracted to members of the same sex. In the Victorian era, when men were expected to spend all of their time with other men, and women with other women, these people would have been unremarkable, and probably didn't even understand themselves as being that different from those around them. But as the separate spheres of men and women collapsed, largely thanks to urbanization, these people became more obvious. Their desires were suddenly strange, and that strangeness could not be blamed on their bodies. This is why homosexuals seem to emerge from the woodwork at the turn of the twentieth century: because straight people started acting differently.

Secondly, if all queer people weren't inverts, who had (or at least desired to have) bodies that were different, then those who did needed a specific name—eventually this would give rise to our modern categories of "intersex" and "transgender."

Finally, moving sexuality into the mind made it secret and dangerously mutable. You *knew* if you or your best friend or your mother was an invert just by looking at them, but a homosexual? They could be anywhere—any *one*—and it required constant vigilance to avoid them, or avoid becoming one. This would eventually lead to both conversion therapy and the aggressive performances of heterosexuality that we call homophobia.

These ideas were brewing in Europe, and eventually America, by the late nineteenth century. But it would take the popularization of Freudian psychology in the early twentieth century to give them mass appeal. For working-class people, with little access to higher education or books about sexuality (which were usually banned or heavily regulated), a primary vector spreading these new ideas was the criminal legal system. Because homosexuality was seen as preventable and/or curable (unlike inversion), the work of preventing and curing it became the job of those concerned with the welfare of young women.

This was exactly what happened to Charlotte. While her aunt and the Girls' Service League technically took her to court over her hitchhiking, the WPA noted in their files that she was only labeled a "serious problem" when she began "influencing girls" to hitchhike with her.[33] It was because of this that she was taken to the Women's Court and "attempts were made to have her committed to an institution," her file notes.[34] It was in court that her education—and humiliation—began. Her aunt, the GSL staff, and the judge "had a rather extensive conversation before Charlotte regarding the possibility of her being homo-sexual," and accused her of seducing girls at the GSL shelter.[35] Charlotte, who at this point seems to have never had a relationship with anyone, found the experience "extremely painful."[36] She said it wasn't her fault the girls admired her as they would "a good-looking football hero."[37] This was the first time she heard the word *homosexual*, and while she understood the implications, it was a full year before she summoned the courage to ask someone the definition.

Later, Charlotte's WPA social worker confronted the GSL staff, who admitted her case "had been very badly handled by all concerned," before casually mentioning "how many other similar situations have resulted in commitment to an institution and a long career of delinquency for the person involved."[38]

Charlotte's rescue from this fate came from an unexpected source: Dr. Marion Stranahan, the WPA-funded part-time psychiatrist at the House of Detention, who not only arranged for Charlotte to receive probation, but also convinced the court to assign *her* as Charlotte's probation officer. During the three weeks Charlotte spent at the House of D waiting for her arraignment, Dr. Stranahan had begun seeing her and was convinced that "if she can continue her contact with her over a long period, she may be able to help the girl quite materially."[39] Their therapeutic relationship would continue on and off for the next six years, during which Charlotte sometimes saw Dr. Stranahan two or three times a week, in appointments that could last up to four hours.

For Charlotte, who coped with stress by taking flight, even a short time in detention was highly traumatic. Afterward, she couldn't sleep with the door closed, and would get up in the night to make sure she wasn't locked in. She made her social worker promise not to involve the police in her welfare, for fear of being rearrested. She was so traumatized by the medical exam she received in the House of D that she avoided even routine care afterward.

Charlotte came to refer to her time in the House of D as "the turning point" of her life—not because of the trauma inflicted upon her, nor because of her long-term relationship with Dr. Stranahan, but because, as she said, "I met Virginia there."[40]

Virginia M. was one of the first celebrity criminals held at the House of D, though she was far from the last. In photos, she had a zaftig appeal, with sensuous lips, a mischievous expression, and eyebrows that she kept plucked pencil thin. Her early beauty was the road she took to escape small-town life in Bangor, Maine, but it was a road full of dangers she couldn't yet see. "I was still only 14," she would later write in a newspaper exposé about her life, "but I was physically mature. I wore grown-up clothes. I'd been around and I knew the answers, even if I didn't know what they meant."[41] By fifteen, she was living on her own in the Bronx, working in cafeterias and dance palaces. "You understand I wasn't a bad girl at this point, not really bad," Virginia wrote, sounding like the femme fatale in every film noir, "just out for a gay, irresponsible time."[42] Almost certainly, Virginia was working with a ghostwriter or editor who was influencing her diction, but aside from that, her story in the newspaper seems to have hewed close to the truth.

She soon caught the eye of mob boss Lucky Luciano, who installed her as a taxi dancer (so called because they were paid per dance) at a club on Mulberry Street. One night, one of his lieutenants invited Virginia to a party. "I knew if a man like that took a fancy to me I should go places," she recalled. But when she arrived, the lieutenant was missing, and six mafiosos attempted to rape her instead. "It's a favorite amusement of certain types of thugs, these gang attacks," she wrote. Only invoking the specter of Luciano's wrath saved her that night. She quit the dance halls the next day, opting for the safer life of a call girl working for a madam. Her regulars were the dukes of the underworld: men like Owney "The Killer" Madden, who ran the infamous Cotton Club, and "Tough Joey" Rao, who controlled smuggling and narcotics inside city penitentiaries.

But the life of a good-time girl was beginning to wear on Virginia, physically and mentally, and a doctor warned her that if she didn't slow down, she was headed to an early grave. Around this time, she had a full hysterectomy, though why was never recorded. Even though she was only eighteen, she'd learned how to use a gun and had been a fly on the wall for all kinds of criminal activity. She developed an idea for a way out. She'd briefly worked as a hostess at a gambling joint in Harlem called the Benizen Club, a private, integrated spot, serving Black and white men and women, which was run out of someone's home. "I knew the owner had no license and wouldn't dare call the cops in case of trouble," she said. She also knew "he had plenty of dough in the till."[43]

Together with three men—Albert, K.O., and Slats—Virginia decided to rob the place. Instead of a gun, she carried a small metal cigarette case shaped like a pistol. At first, everything went like gangbusters. The fourteen or so customers forked over their money and jewelry, and Virginia ran down to start the car. As she got in the driver's seat, she heard a shot; then two men came racing out the front door of the building and leapt into a taxi. Virginia waited alone in the getaway car, with no idea where to get away to, so she crawled into the back seat and hid beneath some old clothes and blankets.

It turned out that Albert had shot a man in the stomach, convinced he was reaching for a gun. In the ensuing melee, K.O. and Slats escaped. Albert hid in the apartment building next door, but someone had heard the gunshot and called the police. When he saw that they were searching building by building, apartment by apartment, Albert had the brilliant idea to hang out a window until they were gone…only he chose a window at the front of the building, not the back, and he was spotted instantly. When they managed to get Albert down, they discovered the car registration in his pocket, put out an all-points bulletin, and found Virginia. She tried to pretend she wasn't one of the robbers—just some woman hiding in the car under some blankets, officer—"but one of the club's customers had remembered [her] funny-looking 'gun,'" and she was nabbed.[44]

When the man Albert shot died the next day, Virginia was charged with robbery and murder in the first degree, and she spent the next eight months in the House of Detention.

Her beauty won her just as many suitors in prison as it did outside. There was Minnie L., who was "white haired, very masculine," and "a rather notorious homo-sexual."[45] And there was Ruth K., who was so into Virginia that she showed up on Virginia's mother's doorstep four years later and threatened to kill Minnie to get Virginia back.

Then there was Charlotte.

Their relationship in prison was brief—no more than three weeks, at most—but intense. With Virginia potentially facing the electric chair, Charlotte formulated a plan straight out of the comics: the two would use their bed sheets to make a rope, knock the matron unconscious, tie her up, and escape. But their plan was discovered, Charlotte was labeled a troublemaker, and the two were separated. A few days later, Charlotte's case came up in court, and she was released (largely at the urging of Dr. Stranahan). Virginia pled down to manslaughter and was sent to Bedford Hills on a sentence of three to twenty years.

Virginia seemed to have perfected a veneer that allowed everything to slide off her. Her mother called her a "yes girl," and said that all her life "she had been pleasant and agreeable verbally but that she usually did exactly as she pleased."[46] No one—not Charlotte, nor Virginia's mother, nor the staff at the WPA—ever felt they had a good handle on what was happening in her head. She was "cagey," "evasive," and "hardened," and aside from Charlotte, she formed few lasting relationships of any kind.[47] Even Charlotte worried that Virginia would one day "stab her in the back," though it appears that Virginia was as devoted to Charlotte as she would be to anyone in her life.[48]

Certainly Charlotte was devoted to Virginia. After she was released from the House of D, one of the first questions Charlotte asked her social worker was if she knew Virginia. She also asked about the newspapers that prisoners at Bedford Hills received, so she could communicate with Virginia via code through the personal ads.

While she waited for Virginia to be released, Charlotte worked, saved money, and spent much of her free time in the Village. Her social workers spotted her at the drugstore across the street from the House of D (where Jay Toole and other butches would still be hanging out in the 1960s, waiting to see who was released and who was taken into custody that day). Charlotte was still seeing Dr. Stranahan, and she killed time leaning against the prison gates before and after her appointments. In the evenings, when she didn't have plans, she would drift down to the Village to see if she would be "stopped by some one of the Lesbians there."[49] For a while, she had regular dinners in the Village with Ruth—the same Ruth who had competed for Virginia's affections and threatened Virginia's other suitors—although whether they were fighting or secretly seeing each other the files can't reveal. But to the social workers at the WPA, "Greenwich Village" was clearly a byword for temptation, and they noted it when women spent too much time there. Women like Charlotte were both drawn to the Village for its queer reputation and, simultaneously, creating that reputation by being queer women, unable to afford private space, living their queer lives on the street—a queer, working-class feedback loop that is still operative to this day in every gayborhood in America. Regardless of who owns the real estate, it is largely working-class and young queer people who create the street culture that gives these neighborhoods their reputations.

Finally, two and a half years after they first met in the House of D, Virginia was released in the fall of 1936 and returned to New York City on probation, precipitating a major crisis for Charlotte.

There had been other women in Charlotte's life while Virginia was in jail—Ruth, Virginia's ex; Mamie, a coworker; Vivian, another client at the WPA—but publicly, she always talked about them breezily, and never as more than friends. Her social workers worried about these relationships, but decided that none of them had reached what they called the "overt homosexual" stage.[50] Whether this was the truth, or willful ignorance, or true ignorance, or a polite fiction that they maintained so as not to out Charlotte in their paperwork, it's impossible to say. But once Virginia returned, any fig leaf of deniability was torn away.

From the very first day Virginia appeared at the WPA, workers were inclined to separate her and Charlotte. Once again, Dr. Stranahan stepped in. "Even though this friendship might not have a constructive value," she told the staff, "it would be inadvisable...to try in any way to keep these two girls apart."[51]

Virginia began working as a live-in maid, and in mid-October, her employer found a "very passionate love letter, which revealed, unmistakably...that the two girls were having an overt homosexual relationship."[52] Charlotte had gone down on Virginia—perhaps, it seemed, for the first time—and wrote that she hoped "that it gave you as big a thrill as it did me."[53]

Virginia's employer was levelheaded about the whole matter. "She has no objection whatsoever to what Charlotte and V. do outside of the house but she does object to them making love there," the social worker noted. More than anything, however, her employer was "especially anxious that V. not know she read the letter....She does not want to lose V."[54]

On Thanksgiving, Charlotte joined Virginia and her mother for dinner—a serious step for any relationship, let alone an only somewhat acknowledged lesbian relationship taking place during the Great Depression. A few days later, Charlotte had a breakdown. As a young teen, she had seen her interactions with other women as natural, and their feelings for her as comparable to the way they felt about men. Now, she had learned that those feelings were a sign of that dreaded thing that was so awful that her aunt, the Girls' Service League, and a judge who had almost sent her to an institution over it—homosexuality. To embrace her feelings for Virginia would now mean that "all she has worked for during the past two years…she would have to give this all up."[55] Overwrought, she repeatedly asked her social worker at the WPA the same question: "What would you do if you were faced with this problem in your own daughter?"[56]

After trying to avoid answering, her social worker Barbara Manley Philips gave Charlotte a surprisingly compassionate response: "Worker told C. that if this were the case she would talk the problem over with the daughter very frankly and that if she felt that her daughter was really happy…worker felt she would accept the situation—under no circumstances would she condemn the daughter."[57]

Over the next two decades, Philips would be an important advocate for many queer young people caught in the net of the House of D. Critically, she was empathetic to them (rather than sympathetic or pitying), and she recognized—and fought against—the deficiencies of the system she was embedded in.

A QUAKER REFORMER IN NEW YORK CITY

Like many women prison reformers before her, Barbara Manley Philips came from a New England Quaker family that believed in education for women. She was born in 1901, graduated with highest honors from Swarthmore College in 1922, and briefly worked as a laboratory assistant in astronomy at Wellesley College in 1923. Around that time, she married Tom Philips, with whom she would stay for the rest of her long life.

Almost certainly Philips met queer women during her education. At her graduation, an honorary degree was given to M. Carey Thomas, the president of Bryn Mawr College, who had long-standing, openly acknowledged relationships with several women during her tenure.[58] As a progressive Quaker, Philips was likely inspired by Swarthmore alumna Alice Stokes Paul, a queer Quaker feminist who spent nearly a hundred years fighting for justice, from women's suffrage in 1920, to the Civil Rights Amendment in 1964. Stokes's legacy was well-known on campus, in part because Stokes's grandfather had founded the school.

In the mid-1920s, Philips began working at the Women's Prison Association. But in the thirties, during the years she worked with Charlotte B., she moved to a new position, managing all aftercare services for the Women's House of Detention. Like most of the psych services at the House of D, this position was funded by the WPA, keeping the two organizations tightly entangled. In this role, she worked closely with Dr. Marion Stranahan, as two forward-thinking voices in the field of services for incarcerated women in New York City.

In 1971, many years after she retired, Philips was profiled by a newspaper in Cocoa, Florida, where she explained that she was no "do-gooder."[59] "I really loved those girls," she told the reporter. "They weren't bad. They just tried to cope with their circumstances and environment as best they could."[60]

Philips swept in to the House of D as a reformer, with ambitious goals: she would do a thorough intake on the first two hundred women to enter the institution under her watch, instead of waiting for other staff to refer the clients they felt were most likely to respond positively to social work. The first hundred women she saw would be given the "maximum of case work and after care service," while the second would be given "a rather different type of service—less personal and consisting mainly in routine referrals."[61]

The latter method was the one already used for discharging formerly incarcerated women, and it was an utter failure. "Referral at the time of release is to be avoided if possible," Philips explained, because it required the woman to establish a new, confidential relationship with a new worker, at a new organization, right at the same moment when everything else in her life was being upended.[62] It was a recipe for failure and recidivism, made worse by the fact that the prison gave women only a dime at the time of their release. As the

State Commissioners of Correction wrote in 1936, the same year that Charlotte and Virginia got together,

> If she has no home to return to nor friends who will assist her, of what avail is the ten cents? Not even sufficient to purchase a lunch! There can be but one result; she must eat and in order to do so probably will be forced to beg or steal or become the prey of the procurer…the present arrangement is socially and economically unsound and should be changed.[63]

It wasn't.

For as long as the House of D was open, reformers (and the Department of Correction itself) would continually draw attention to the way formerly incarcerated people were abandoned as soon as they left the prison gates. Ten cents, a quarter, five bucks —the amount given to those leaving the prison changed with the decades, but it was never more than a pittance. That's remained the case for other prisons in the decades since the House of D was torn down: in 1999 New York City would be sued over a similar practice of releasing mentally ill inmates in the middle of the night, with only $1.50 and two subway tokens. To this day, the city is required to be monitored by an outside nonprofit to ensure compliance with the ensuing court decree, known as Brad H.[64] As of 2021, New York State mandates that indigent formerly incarcerated people be given $40 upon release.[65] Ask yourself: How long could you live on $40?

Six months into her test project, Philips wrote a report for the WPA. She had only been able to see 113 cases, not the 200 she hoped, largely because of the overcrowded and understaffed nature of the House of D. Her idea to examine every woman had been abandoned almost instantly, and unfortunately, "after-care work was reduced to a minimum" and only given to those with "sentences of thirty days or less who had asked for immediate after-care service."[66] She could maintain a maximum of thirty clients at a time, she wrote. That year, the daily average census for the House of D was 608, and a total of nearly 9,000 women and transmasculine people flowed through its doors.[67] In fact, the House of D was officially overcrowded for thirty of the thirty-nine years it existed, and even when it wasn't, it didn't have enough staff, space, or funds to provide adequate programming for the people it held. The vast majority of incarcerated people poured through the House of D like water through a sieve, untouched by its services. Even the best-intentioned reformers like Philips could do little to change the system, although they were incredibly important in the lives of the individual people they did help.

Historically and today, the kinds of aftercare services that Philips provided are recognized as being critical for formerly incarcerated people who are trying to get back on their feet and deal with their trauma. Yet they are routinely underfunded, understaffed, and the first to be cut when the winds of conservative reform or financial recession blow. According to the author of a 2014 American Psychological Association report on incarceration and mental health care, "Prisoners essentially fall out of the system because there's not an effective pass-off to the service providers in the community."[68] Barbara Manley Philips, and a few others, fought valiantly against this reality, but to no avail.

It's impossible to tell if Philips sought out or was purposefully assigned clients who presented as queer, but she ended up with a lot of them. In these relationships, she showed herself to be open-minded and knowledgeable about modern ideas of sexuality and psychology. She did not automatically shut down conversations about same-sex desire or steer her clients toward heterosexuality, nor did she hide their desires in her case notes, as other workers seemed to do.

This kind of openness around sexual identity and variation was not unheard of in the early part of the twentieth century, particularly among women in social work and adjacent fields. After all, many of them were also considered improperly feminine because of their desire to be educated and employed. Others were themselves queer or had met queer people in their pursuit of higher education. Their more progressive ideas existed side by side with the growing conservatism that would dominate public opinion after World War II. The history of this progressive strain of thinking has been largely erased by postwar homophobia, which was a triumph of Orwellian thought, defining homosexuality for the public and, in the same breath, declaring that we have always been at war with it.

The very first time Charlotte openly talked about homosexuality, Philips assured her that her sexuality was not a deficit. When Charlotte learned that she had been labeled a homosexual in court, it was Philips who told her that "there were a great many professional people who were looked up to and respected who were at the same time so-called homosexuals."[69] When Charlotte finally admitted her own homosexuality, Philips told her that if she were happy, that was great. But she also said that if Charlotte were unhappy, "no matter how much she was in love," Philips would recommend she see a psychiatrist and "solve the problem there."[70] Here again we can see the influence of emerging upper-class ideas about sexuality: unmoored from the body, it was a changeable thing, to be dealt with by psychologists.

Charlotte, who was overwhelmed by the implications of her growing relationship with Virginia, leapt at this idea, stating, "This is exactly my case."[71] Convinced now that she could be fixed, she would fault herself when she couldn't turn straight.

YOU CAN'T OUTRUN YOURSELF

After that Thanksgiving dinner with Virginia and her mother, and her conversation with Barbara Manley Philips, Charlotte began to avoid Virginia. In her case notes, Philips characterized the next six weeks as "a period of extreme emotional stress for Charlotte," as she tried to deny the fact that she was in love with Virginia and all that now implied about who she was as a person.[72]

In December of 1937, she told Philips that "the problem regarding her homosexuality was more than she could face or solve."[73] In just a few short years, the criminal legal system had transformed Charlotte's understanding of other women's attractions to her. She no longer saw herself as a dazzling football hero but as a sexually broken person.

In crisis, she turned to her oldest coping mechanism: flight.

Right before Christmas Charlotte ran away to Florida, where she worked as a chauffeur and childcare attendant for a rich white family.

Except for missing Virginia, it was one of the happiest times of her life. She wrote to Barbara Manley Philips to ask if Philips remembered her desire "to get out in the country, because it gave [me] sort of a comforting feeling?"[74] Well, Florida was "the fulfillment of my dream...too bad Virginia isn't here then it would be perfect. IF she was down here I don't think I would ever leave."[75]

Still, she lied to Virginia about it, saying that she was on the run over a gambling debt. When asked about Charlotte's absence, Virginia professed indifference, telling her social worker, "I like Charlotte but I don't miss her."[76]

Secretly, however, Virginia and Charlotte were in close communication the entire time Charlotte was in Florida, and once Virginia made it clear she wanted Charlotte to return, Charlotte immediately hitchhiked back. In a passionate letter to Philips, Charlotte declared,

> I guess I tried to push something aside that can't be pushed aside. I thought that by going to Florida I could start anew and get a different kind of friends but I now see I am putting up a useless fight. I guess I am just meant to be something that I thought I wasn't but I am. I have decided there is nothing else in the world that I want more than Virginia. So I am returning soon to her and if there ever comes a time that it would mean a definite split between the family and me because of her it will make no difference because I will still stay with her. God help the person or persons that try to take her away from me.[77]

But the people who separated Virginia and Charlotte, in the end, were Virginia and Charlotte themselves. In Charlotte's absence, Virginia had fallen back in "with the old crowd with whom she was associating before she got into prison," and shortly after they reunited, the two separated for good.[78]

As soon as Charlotte was out of the picture, Virginia stopped reporting for parole, visiting the WPA, or going to her job. When asked in mid-1938, Charlotte told a social worker that she hadn't seen Virginia in months. When Virginia began to serialize her experiences as a "New York City Gun-Girl" in a weekly column for the *Sunday Mirror* magazine that same year, Charlotte told the WPA that she would sue Virginia if she mentioned her by name. But it was worse than that: Virginia didn't mention her at all.

From this point on, their paths diverged sharply. Virginia never re connected with the WPA. She was picked up for a parole violation in November 1938, and they had no word of her again until 1948, when she died by suicide after OD'ing on sleeping pills in her apartment on Second Avenue.[79]

For Charlotte, the relationship with Virginia had brought her "face to face with an aspect of her emotional life that had sent her into a very real panic," but she emerged from it sure about—and comfortable with—who she was.[80] She told Philips that "for the first time ever she felt that she would be able to really talk with Dr. Stranahan," the psychiatrist at the House of Detention, who had guided Charlotte through her relationship with Virginia every step of the way.[81] Their appointments became less and less frequent, as Charlotte got her high school equivalency diploma and developed a network of friends who seemed aware of her sexuality.

Charlotte was working as a grill cook at Stouffer's Restaurant on Forty-Second Street when World War II really kicked into gear, and she was profiled in the *New York World-Telegram* as a leader in New York City's "big farmerette movement."[82] She joined a program known as the Women's Land Army, through which women worked as volunteers on farms across America. Here again, women flocked to her. Or as the paper put it, "Despite the supposed dislike of city girls for the farm, all the waitresses at the restaurant are interested in Miss B.'s new occupation. 'They're all asking me for my address and they want me to write them when I get up there and tell them all about it.'"[83]

The last the WPA ever heard from Charlotte, she was in Des Moines, Iowa, where she had been promoted to captain in the Women's Army Auxiliary Corps, and was driving an ambulance. By the mid-fifties, she was a prize-winning dog trainer, specializing in boxers, living in upstate New York. For decades, she owned and operated her own kennel in Hopewell Junction, which sounded exactly like the kind of outdoor paradise she had dreamed of all the years she lived in New York City. "Located in middle of 40 acres," she wrote in a newspaper ad for the kennel. "Each dog has large heated inside kennel with swinging door...large outside run. Well balanced diet. Tender loving care."[84] After a brief illness, Charlotte died at the age of sixty-nine in 1984—a year before Mabel Hampton served as grand marshal in the New York City Pride March.[85]

For Charlotte and Virginia, the Women's House of Detention seems to have provided their first opportunity to understand and explore their sexuality, both in theory and in practice. But other women sent to the House of D were already well aware of their desires, long before they were arrested. Many of these women never received services from places like the WPA after their time at the House of D; their queerness was already a strike against them, and if it had caused them to be previously incarcerated, or if in addition to being too queer they were also too old, too masculine, too angry, too Black, etc., they were considered unredeemable. After 1945, as America embraced suburban conservatism, there would be fewer and fewer of these vocally queer women and transmasculine people in the WPA files. But before the war, there was a small but steady stream of women like Elaine B., a California teenager who mostly dated trans women; Alison C., a grifter who scammed her way from woman to woman; and Louise B., a Brooklyn teen whose theatrical aspirations had a particularly queer bent.

The three came from wildly different backgrounds. Two were young, one was older. One had graduated high school, one had dropped out, and one claimed to have a master's degree in English lit. Two were white, one was Black. One was a runaway, one lived with her mother in Brooklyn, and one had traveled the world (maybe). One was arrested for prostitution, one for shoplifting, and one for forgery.

In fact, the only traits that united all three were an acute verbal intelligence (which won them allies at every step of their incarceration and post-prison lives), their connection with Barbara Manley Philips, and a penchant for spending time in Greenwich Village. Thus, their files are a tantalizing record of what some women in the queer community in New York City knew, where they went, and what they did in the mid- to late 1930s.

---CHAPTER 3

Where the Girls Are: Greenwich Village and Lesbian Life

THE QUEER ROMANCE OF THE ROAD

In the spring of 1931, a sixteen-year-old Elaine B. published a short lyric essay in her Sacramento High School yearbook. "Oh, what is Life?" she cried at the beginning, before enumerating the joys and fears that made up hers:

> Tiny happinesses that help to make life for me are many—and various....The wind that stirs strange unmanageable longings within me...the road that leads ahead—when a friend walks by my side. "For a road is romance, and roads can whisper"—of things unexplored and waiting for us. The poet's dream of death—wherein life is renewed in a violet blossom, that one's beloved might wear....
>
> And tiny fears are as many and as important....The fear of cowardice where I must not falter. The fear of convention that binds like cold steel fetters. The fear of intolerance—of the pain that lodges deep in the heart of the stranger and the lonely person.[1]

Although she was often described as a "dreamy" or "imaginative" girl, this wasn't just the poetic waxing of a well-read teen.[2] Elaine knew what she wrote from deep personal experience. Her father had run off when she was four, leaving her mother to fend for Elaine and her younger twin sisters. Although once prosperous, they lived a threadbare existence; Elaine told the WPA that "we get corn meal mush for breakfast and potatoes for supper."[3] Her mother worked constantly, while Elaine professed that she herself was "simply vile" at housework.[4] At the start of her senior year of high school, she told her mother she was leaving, and not to call the cops—the road, it seemed, was whispering.

First, Elaine stopped in San Francisco to visit her father—a man "as unintelligent as the usual salesman," in her estimation.[5] From there, she hitchhiked to Los Angeles, where she fell in with an older woman who seemed a bit like the master thief Fagin in Charles Dickens's *Oliver Twist*. This woman made a living as a fortune-teller and shoplifter, and she trained Elaine in the latter—which is how Elaine ended up getting arrested for the first time. A court psychiatrist asked Elaine whether she loved this woman (she did), and if she'd kissed her (she had). The state of California returned Elaine to Sacramento, put her on probation for four years, and told her mother "that she had been living with a homosexual woman and involved in a homosexual relationship."[6] Like Charlotte B., Elaine didn't know the word, but she was determined to find out what it meant, and "it was not long before she had learned a great deal."[7]

In telling the WPA about her experiences with this woman, Elaine breezily explained that she "had read all of Kraft-Ebbing [*sic*] as well as other books on psychology," which is how she came to understand the word *homosexual*.[8] Richard Freiherr von Krafft-Ebing was the author of one of the foundational texts of modern sexology, 1886's *Psychopathia Sexualis*. When the book was translated into English, it introduced America to the terms "homosexual," "sadist," "masochist," and "necrophilia," among others. Krafft-Ebing's writings on homosexuality represent a transitional point between older theories of bodily inversion and newer theories of psychological damage; he viewed homosexuality as a mental illness caused by inherited degeneracy of the body. It was the rare nineteen-year-old who was familiar with his writing, and it may well have influenced Elaine's travels, as Krafft-Ebing called cities (and prisons) "breeding places" for perversion.[9]

Los Angeles was not the first time Elaine had gotten close to an older woman, causing trouble with her family. When an English teacher offered to help Elaine afford college, Elaine's mother told her she would be a "parasite" if she took the money, and would wake Elaine in the night and beg her not to go. But after Elaine's arrest, things changed—"her mother want[ed] to keep her as far as possible" from her sisters.[10] Once Elaine left, her mother told her "never to write home again."[11]

Perhaps this rejection is why, even years later, when Elaine was embedded in the queer community, her desires for cis women would be difficult for her to accept. The "idea is repulsive to her," she informed her social workers at first, before telling them about her "homosexual affairs with women in NY as well as other parts of the country."[12]

She seemed to tease the WPA with the idea of lesbianism, constantly testing their reactions, like when she gave them a copy of her poem "Liebestraum"—the title of a popular waltz, which Elaine said "reminds me of the only girl I ever loved."[13] On the page, she was less restrained, writing,

> *Violins soaring and dreaming—*
> *Blue noon outside and twilight within the curtained room—*
> *And my young blood pulsing like maddened flame—*
> *And my lips curving themselves in meaningless jests*
> *Lest the gypsy wanton of me*
> *Let down her dark hair and call you*
> *Too urgently.*[14]

To escape the opprobrium and drudgery of her home life, once Elaine graduated high school, she hit the road again (much like Charlotte B.). By the time she landed in New York City in 1935, she liked to say that she had been everywhere "except Bar Harbor and South Dakota."[15]

"I hitchhike with homosexual men," she informed her social workers. They were safer, she explained. Also, "she was attracted by their
beauty."[16]

Before New York, she'd spent months in Chicago, enjoying "the
Century of Progress," as the 1933–1934 World's Fair was called. There,
she fell in love with "the Countess." Also known as the "blond Venus,"
or "the painted Virgin," the Countess worked as a female impersonator at the fair.[17]

"Elaine usually referred to the Countess as 'she,'" Barbara Manley
Philips noted in her WPA file. "The first time she remarked on this
apologetically, but did not appear to notice it after that."[18]

Here, Elaine seemed to be bumping up against the limits of the
English language (and the American mind) when it came to discussing
gender and sexuality. She knew many "homosexuals," but her attractions and relationships were with people who worked as female impersonators, for whom she used female pronouns, like the Countess or
La Violette (a night club entertainer in Manhattan). Elaine clearly saw
these individuals as different from homosexual men; she explained
that they "were at least a step and an attempt to break away from her
more serious affairs with women."[19] The word *transgender* did not yet
exist, but trans people (of some stripe) clearly did.

Elaine lived with the Countess on West Erie Street in Chicago for
months, but eventually took to the road again, because the Countess's
family—whom she'd met—"were all morons."[20] Moreover, the Countess was cheating on Elaine, and she discovered she was just one of a
number of women who "chiseled" for the Countess.

To chisel, Elaine explained, was to "stop a man in the daytime, say
she was hungry and get 50 cents or a dollar."[21] Sometimes, she'd pretend to be soliciting and disappear once she'd gotten the money from
the would-be john. This was how she supported herself in New York
City—and how she ended up in the House of D. On a cold January
day in 1935, she bummed a ride from a driver in Manhattan, heading
to her apartment on Sixty-Fifth Street, and offered to have "abnormal
sex relations" with him (probably a blowjob) for $5—but he was a
cop, and she landed in the House of Detention.[22] Over the next ten

years, she would be in and out of the prison, always on the same charge: Section 877, vagrancy prostitution—the same statute under which Mabel Hampton was arrested.

Vagrancy prostitution was a particularly abuseable law, if your goal was to remove the arrested individual from society as thoroughly as possible, thanks to a wrinkle written into the New York State parole laws. In 1915, New York State created a parole commission, which interviewed people who had been convicted of certain crimes, in an effort to separate those who had accidentally fallen on hard times from those "failures of society" who were inveterate criminals.[23] Those who were found to be redeemable were eligible for release after serving only a portion of their sentence, although they would have to check in regularly with their assigned parole officer.

When the law was written, it was necessary to change the sentencing guidelines around those specified crimes, to give the parole commission the legal wiggle room to release people early. Any crime that carried a sentence to the workhouse now could not exceed six months—*except* for a small class of crimes, all of which were used to arrest sex workers (including vagrancy prostitution).[24]

In these cases, if the parole commission discovered that a woman had been convicted two or more times in the past two years, or three times in her life, she would be given an indeterminate sentence of up to two years in the workhouse (later this would be expanded to three years). Because fingerprinting had been pioneered on sex workers, it was now easy to track their past convictions, and treat those with records more harshly. They were not sentenced based on the crime they were accused of, but based on their history, which almost ensured that poor women—who worked as sex workers out of necessity—would eventually end up with longer sentences.

For such a low-level crime—one that wasn't even thought to require a lawyer in the court—this punishment was incredibly high. Why? Because sex workers were seen as a danger to men, particularly soldiers, at the start of World War I, when the law was enacted. Repeat sex workers were considered disease vectors, so the law was designed to put them away for as long as possible. Parallel to this, johns weren't usually prosecuted, because they *weren't* a danger to other men. (Similar forms of "preventative detention" weren't widely used on men until the War on Drugs of the 1970s and the War on Terror post 9/11.[25])

One of the main proponents of the parole commission law was the woman who had been in charge of Bedford Hills when Big Cliff Trondle was detained there. She understood herself as a reformer, and in one sense, parole is certainly a better alternative to prison time. In her eyes, this law allowed reformatories like Bedford Hills more discretion to help incarcerated people, and more time in which to do it. But the reformatory system was already an overcrowded failure, and this law simply made it worse. And for the people who came under the law's hand, it was a punitive measure that turned a five-dollar blowjob into a two-year prison stay. Any reform that gives more power to the penal system, or longer sentences to those under its thumb, is ultimately a regressive action, no matter its intentions.

At the House of Detention, Elaine underwent the same degrading entrance inspection that Jay Toole spoke of in the 1960s, which included forced enemas and invasive vaginal and rectal exams. These were performed even on people under the age of eighteen, *and* on those who were only being held as witnesses, not accused of any crime. In part, these exams were searches for hidden contraband, but they were primarily concerned about sexually transmissible infections (STIs), particularly gonorrhea and syphilis.

In New York, the origin of these inspections goes back to the same 1910 law that created the Women's Court, which mandated that those convicted in the court receive an immediate examination. And they meant "immediate." As historian Scott W. Stern described,

> In full view of an ogling audience, court officials would immediately drag convicted women into a small side room with an eight-foot-high board dividing it in half. On one side, a patrolman took the women's fingerprints; on the other side, a female physician poked and prodded the women's vaginas.[26]

This was part of the "theater" that slumming uptowners found so entertaining.

This section of the law was struck down in 1911, but the government was not so easily defeated. Seven years later, at the close of World War I, proponents saw their chance to bring back these mandatory invasive examinations, now fully supported by the power of the federal government, as part of something called the American Plan.

According to Scott W. Stern, "Initially conceived at the start of World War I to protect soldiers from sexually transmitted infections... the American Plan became one of the largest and longest-lasting mass quarantines in American history."[27] All told, it's likely that hundreds of thousands of women and girls around the country were detained without due process, thanks to the American Plan. Through crafty coordination with local authorities, the legacy of the plan lasted in some places (including New York City) up through the 1970s.

Here's how it worked: In 1918, the attorney general wrote a letter to every US attorney in the country, urging them to join the fight against venereal disease in their hometowns. "As prostitution is a prolific source of these diseases," he specified, "this campaign includes both the suppression of prostitution, and the medical examination, quarantine and cure of prostitutes afflicted."[28]

New York was one of the first states in the country to comply, and in 1919, they passed a law that mandated that any vagrant suspected of having "any infectious venereal disease" be detained, tested, and if found to be infected, held until they were cured—at which point, they could be tried or begin their sentence if they had already been found guilty.[29] Although the wording did not specify women, in practice, only women fell under the law's grabbing hands. And because all incarcerated women were seen as invitations to prostitution, in the eyes of the state, they were all potential Typhoid Marys who needed to be inspected.

In 1935, the year Elaine was arrested for vagrancy prostitution, the federal government tucked approximately $1 million for fighting STIs into an earmark on the act that created Social Security. In

1938—again amid wartime fears that sex workers would spread disease to the military—the government set aside some $15 million for this work (which would be more than $270 million today). Almost all of the money would go toward harassing, surveilling, arresting, and detaining women assumed to be prostitutes.

In 1936, the House of D saw 692 cases of gonorrhea and 713 of syphilis.[30] By 1938, those numbers had almost doubled, with the prison hospital recording 1,348 cases of gonorrhea and 975 cases of syphilis.[31] Each case took anywhere from four months to a year to treat, and the women would not be released—even if their sentences were up—until they received a clean bill of health (though they could be transferred to other detention facilities). In 1938, state inspectors wrote that "there were a large number of convicted women who had been given a prison sentence so that they might have the benefit of venereal disease treatment…this practice is partly responsible for the overcrowding" in the House of D.[32]

For poor women, imprisonment replaced medical care, mental health care, housing, vocational training, and education.

Nearly every woman and transmasculine person who passed through the House of D was traumatized by their examinations. The same doctors who performed the inspections provided all other prison health care as well, meaning that for any routine care, imprisoned people were forced to interact with someone who had violated and humiliated them. When Charlotte B. was released, she repeatedly refused to ever see a doctor again, unless she was assured it "would not be like the House of D."[33]

Some of the earliest public protests against the prison were over these examinations. In 1936, the League of Women Shoppers (an organization of mostly middle-class white women fighting against racial discrimination and for the rights of working women) convinced the mayor to publicly call for an end to this practice, although the *Daily News* sarcastically noted that he had already done so two years prior, to no apparent effect.[34] Throughout the thirties, women would protest these dehumanizing exams, which were tantamount to state-sponsored sexual violence. And they would continue to protest them in the forties, the fifties, the sixties, and right up until the day the prison closed, to no effect. If anything, things got worse—by the time Jay Toole was incarcerated, they let male doctors do the examinations. Toole called the physical the single worst part of being at the House of D, saying, "The pain was so bad…when I looked down I was covered in blood, and they didn't do nothing."[35] Some women she met at the House of D were so brutally scarred by these inspections, they were effectively sterilized.

Adding insult to injury, at the time Elaine was arrested, there were no good cures for gonorrhea or syphilis. As a result, many women picked up under the early years of the American Plan were held in limbo for months, while receiving highly toxic injections of compounds like neosalvarsan, an arsenic derivative. In 1936 alone, the House of D administered more than five thousand doses of neosalvarsan. Moreover, the tests for these diseases weren't much better, as they were often riddled with user error—which is exactly what happened to Elaine, with tragic consequences.

Upon arrest, Elaine tested positive for gonorrhea and was sent to a detention hospital (on the day that state inspectors visited the House of D that year, about 38 percent of the women were considered "active venereal cases" like Elaine).[36] But the course of treatment wasn't finished before she was transferred to Bellevue for mental examination, where she was told she was now negative for gonorrhea.

The psychiatrist at Bellevue was a conservative Freudian whose interpretations of Elaine's behavior were miles away from the forward-thinking attitude of Dr. Stranahan in the House of D. He saw Elaine's chiseling as an expression of her "very infantile nature" and "desire to punish and hurt [men]."[37] He dismissed her queer relationships out of hand, telling Elaine that "she may have had one or two affairs with women but many people do this and it does not imply that she is definitely attached to women."[38] Her affairs with trans women, he explained, were really about protecting herself from true intimacy with real men. He told her she needed to get a job and get married. Unsurprisingly, Elaine didn't keep up her appointments with him after she was given probation and released, in the spring of 1935.

Believing herself to be free and clear of the penal system, Elaine settled into life on probation in queer New York. In fact, when Elaine wasn't in Greenwich Village *behind* bars, Elaine was in the Village *in* bars.

She told the staff at the WPA that she loved "to go to all the 'drags'"—which Barbara Manley Philips clarified meant "masquerade balls."[39] Elaine "always dressed as a man for these parties," but made sure to paint her nails—no real butch would have been caught dead with nail polish on, so the femmes would understand that she was just playing pretend.[40] The only notable friend she made during her time at the WPA was Alice, a six-foot-tall powerhouse of a woman who had recently had a traumatic breakup with her lover, an opera diva. Alice had also been arrested for prostitution (although in her case, it was almost certainly a setup, as she'd been arrested while wandering the streets in the midst of a psychiatric break). The two seemed to recognize a queer kinship in one another right away, quite possibly because of their shared arrest and their affinity for masculine garb.

Elaine also "dressed as a man" when she hung out at Stewart's Café, one of the most notable queer spots in Greenwich Village in the 1930s.[41] Stewart's was located just one block from the House of D, at the corner of Seventh Avenue and Christopher Street, and had opened around the same time as the prison. The café's "large plate glass windows put gay life on full display to the late-night crowds who frequented this busy intersection," according to the New York City LGBT Historic Sites Project.[42] A contemporary source was more blunt about it, writing that Stewart's was a home for "that nocturnal clan, the third sexers. Dykes, fags, pansies, lesbians, and others of that unfortunate ilk convene there nightly, parading their petty jealousies and affairs of the heart."[43]

Elaine hung out at Stewart's in order to "pick up tourists whom she piloted through the Village showing the sights"—always, again, dressed as a man.[44] Being visibly queer, it seems, marked her as an expert on the Village to newcomers looking for excitement. Unlike most of the formerly incarcerated people in this book, Elaine was able to blend in with the bohemians...at least for a while, largely because she was white, had read all the right books, and was trying hard to hide her poverty.

But Elaine soon found that she didn't like New York City. "It is like a sexy, voluptuous gin-y woman," she told Philips at the WPA, "and she hates that sort of person."[45] So, when the spring of 1935 came, Elaine packed her bags and followed "the winter inhabitants of Greenwich Village" to Woodstock, New York, which they treated as an artist colony. In order to get permission from her probation officer, Barbara Manley Philips warned Elaine against acknowledging "her usual interest with homosexual people" as her reason for going.[46]

For a few weeks, Elaine lived a joyful life in Woodstock, juggling a series of jobs—assistant to a French painter named Euginie McEvoy, waitress at a hip restaurant called the Nook, etc.—until her incarcerated past came back to haunt her. Elaine's record would be an albatross around her neck, as it is for all formerly incarcerated people to this day: preventing them from getting jobs, joining professional associations, receiving certain kinds of loans and government assistance, and in a million other ways ensuring they remain second-class citizens for life.

When Elaine was hired at the Nook, they learned about her arrest and demanded she produce a clean bill of health. Not only did Elaine not have a health certificate to show, worse, her symptoms had returned. Desperate, she wrote to the WPA and explained that she was "doctoring it with potassium permanganate 'internal baths,' drinking no coffee, tea or alcoholic liquors; leaving salt, pepper, and spices alone; [and] drinking quarts of milk and water." Pitifully, she ended the letter, "I don't know what else to do."[47] Of course, she had no access to or money for a doctor.

Douching with potassium permanganate was a common treatment for venereal disease, despite the fact that it was toxic when taken intravaginally, causing "acute gastroenteritis" and in extreme cases "circulatory collapse."[48] But it was no worse than the drugs that doctors generally prescribed, which ran the toxic gamut from arsenic to mercury. The first real treatment for gonorrhea would arrive with the sulfa class of drugs, which were tested (nonconsensually) on incarcerated prostitutes at the House of D, starting in 1938—too late to help Elaine.[49]

The WPA recommended Elaine return to New York and get tested, which she did. On May 13, 1935, she tested positive for gonorrhea again. That was the end of her summer dreams—her waitress gig at the Nook had come with a small room, and without that, Elaine could no longer afford to play country bohemian with the richer denizens of Greenwich Village. Instead, the WPA arranged for Elaine to be sent to Inwood House, which was like a homeless shelter where women with sexually transmissible infections were kept until cured. Elaine disliked the place from the very beginning, particularly the curfew, and disappeared her first night there. She spent one night on the floor of La Violette's room, and the next she tried to sleep in the New York Times building in Midtown (where her friend Alice had once given her a tour). When that didn't work, she joined the other street girls who slept rough in Bryant Park, and for a few weeks, she disappeared.

If Elaine had only lasted one night at Inwood House, she would have discovered the next day that there had been a mistake: her test was clean; she *never* had gonorrhea, and she was free to return to Woodstock to pursue her dreams of being an artist's assistant (and eventually, she hoped, an artist herself). Instead, she ended up on the doorstep of a man she had briefly dated, whom she described as "bi-sexual" and "look[ing] like a rugged sailor edition of Rudy Vallee."[50] When she discovered he had inherited some $4,000, she made the spur of the moment decision to accept his marriage proposal.[51] By July, they had left New York, and it was only via Elaine's friend Alice that the WPA learned the pair ended up in Los Angeles.

Their marriage did not last long. By 1942, Elaine was single and back in New York—now going by Dorothy O.—when she was arrested for prostitution again. In 1947, she was back in the House of D, going by Elaine again. In her last interaction with the Women's Prison Association, they sent the poems she wrote in the 1930s to the staff at the House of D, "so that we might show Elaine what good work she did 10 years ago."[52]

In between those last two arrests, Elaine's sister Zelpha died tragically young in 1944, and her obituary listed Elaine as a surviving relative.[53] But when Elaine's mother died in 1953, her obituary mentioned Elaine's sister Nadeen but not Elaine herself.[54] And when Nadeen died in 2011, there was no mention of Elaine either.[55] Perhaps Elaine passed away sometime between her arrest in 1947 and her mother's death in 1953, or perhaps, under a new name, she continued to crisscross the country.

Only the road knows for certain.

But right as Elaine was preparing to leave the Village with her new husband, another queer woman was moving in with her much younger girlfriend. Like Elaine, Alison C. was drawn to the Village for its queer vibe—but with much darker intentions.

THE MANY LI(V)ES OF ALISON C.

Alison C. might just be the most mysterious woman in all of the WPA files. Her life story was epic. Orphaned in the 1906 San Francisco earthquake, her comatose body was rushed to a hospital in Vancouver, where her grandparents rescued her and brought her back to their ancestral manse in Lochie Valley, Scotland. She attended convent school in Paris, before getting her bachelor's and master's degrees in English literature at the University of Edinburgh. At twenty-one, she joined the Howard Carter expedition that explored the interior chamber of King Tut's tomb, and then did fieldwork in Sumatra. Somewhere along the line, she learned to speak Italian, Danish, Icelandic, and Norwegian. Somewhere along the line, she married a twisted sadist of a husband, from whom she was on the run. Somewhere along the line, Paramount Studios hired her to create animated cartoons. Somewhere along the line, Alfred Harcourt—cofounder of the publishing house Harcourt and Brace—called her up and said she simply *had* to write her memoirs…

It is—and was—impossible to separate truth from fiction when it comes to Alison. From the very beginning of their time working with her, the staff at the WPA noticed holes in her story. For instance, when they tried to get copies of her school transcript to help her look for work, the University of Edinburgh said they knew of no such student. Alison breezily explained to Barbara Manley Philips that "while she had a perfectly legal right to the name of C. this was not her own name nor the name under which she had attended the U. of Edinburgh so that it was quite obvious [why] they had not been able to verify her record there."[56] Yet this didn't prompt much suspicion on the part of the WPA, nor did they terminate services for Alison, as they often did with women they felt were lying. Instead, Philips simply noted that Alison "did not volunteer any more information about herself and worker felt that it was not wise to press her."[57] In many ways, Alison was similar to the WPA staff—white, (seemingly) college educated, middle-aged, and with a middle-class affect—and this kinship meant they gave her far more trust and latitude than most of their clients.

At the time of her arrest in 1935, Alison was living with her girl-friend, Ginny, in the Hotel Malton, just down the block from the House of D. Ginny was a senior at NYU, and the two had been living together for some six weeks when the Salvation Army had Alison arrested on a charge of forgery. Alison had been working for the Museum of Natural History and was accused of passing fake checks in the name of a coworker. The truth of the matter, Alison insisted, was that a Salvation Army major and Ginny's mother had cooked up the whole business to separate her from Ginny. At first, the WPA had their doubts, but as they investigated, they came to believe Alison's story. Certainly, the court records indicated an unusual focus on homosexuality during the proceedings. The court report on Alison stated, "Altho there is no evidence to indicate any overt homo-sexualities she probably belongs to a group of persons who have submerged homo-sexual tendencies. There is a certain looseness in the moral code which can be seen in her attitude toward basic things in life."[58]

The court let her plead down to petty larceny and sent Alison to the House of D for ten months. Alison "felt keenly the unjustice of her sentence"—but also admitted that she had, indeed, forged the checks.[59]

Rumors about Alison's sexuality followed her into prison, and every day she was "pointed out to someone either by an inmate or a matron as an abnormality of nature."[60] Many men's prisons, including Rikers Island in New York City, had separate "fairy wings" for effeminate men. Yet the same was rarely true in women's prisons, where "the practice of segregating homosexuals was virtually unheard of."[61] In the House of D, there were sporadic periods in the 1960s when gender nonconforming women were made to wear the letter D on their uniforms—for "degenerate"—and many queer women and transmasculine people were placed in solitary holds because they were considered sexually aggressive or mentally ill. But routine and consistent segregation was never practiced.

By the time Alison was incarcerated in 1935, the Women's House of Detention had already begun to sink beneath the waters of oblivion, leading once again to the overcrowding and neglect that had plagued every previous detention institution in Greenwich Village. That year, the House of D recorded a one-day population high of 568 people in a building meant to hold 400.[62] To accommodate this overflow, they simply lashed a second cot onto the existing ones in each cell, creating an uncomfortable double bed. The crusading new mayor, lawyer Fiorello LaGuardia, was another Greenwich Village native, and he took as personal an interest in the prison as his predecessor, Mayor Jimmy Walker—although with a very different point of view. The luxury prison that Mayor Walker inaugurated in 1932 was now "antiquated and cruel" in 1935, according to LaGuardia.[63]

From this point on, a bare three years after the prison opened, single-inmate cells—one of the most vaunted aspects of the House of D—would largely be a thing of the past. Most inmates would be forced to double up, while some true unfortunates were housed in nonresidential spaces that were hastily converted into dormitories. Sexual activity (consensual and not) and other kinds of physical intimacy would be a routine part of life at the House of D from now on. But only some prisoners—like Alison—were singled out for their queerness. Overwhelmingly, it was butch and gender nonconforming individuals who bore the brunt of institutional homo- and transphobia. Most carceral institutions, because they are segregated by sex, have no framework within their rules for consensual intimacy between imprisoned people. Sex is understood only through a lens of assault, which has "disproportionate and serious consequences for sexual minority populations" still to this day, according to the Williams Institute.[64] Masculine women like Alison, in particular, are often viewed as inherently aggressive.

Outside of prison, Alison lived as public a queer life as seemed possible in the 1930s. To be "out" in this era meant to be out to other queer people and oneself—not necessarily to the straight world—and Alison was adept at living this double life. Before she met Ginny, she'd lived in a cheap rooming house on Thirteenth Street, "but was asked to leave because she brought a young girl to her room and they both slept on a very narrow bed."[65] The WPA described her best friend, who helped Alison get back on her feet after her arrest, as "a very mannish person…[who] might, because of this, not be entirely helpful" to Alison.[66] Other WPA clients repeatedly warned the staff that Alison was both untrustworthy and queer, with one going so far as to point-blank state that Alison "made a habit of getting hold of young girls and…threatening to tell their parents of their homosexual relations if they did not give her money."[67] The response from Barbara Manley Philips showed both an open mind around sexuality and an implicitly assumed connection between lesbianism and Greenwich Village: "Worker promised she…was well aware of the fact that Alison had been involved in a great deal before her arrest but that worker had not seen anything to indicate that she was even going to Greenwich Village at this time."[68] To those in the know, the Village was code for lesbians.

When Alison got an apartment of her own again in 1936, she told the WPA that her roommates were graduates of the Sargent School of Physical Education in Boston, two women named Bobbie and Betty. But Betty, it turned out, was actually Alison's old girlfriend Ginny, who *had* briefly attended Sargent but had more recently graduated from NYU while waiting for Alison's release. Soon Bobbie moved out, leaving Alison and Ginny to feather a cozy nest together. Alison's caseworker at the WPA made a number of social visits "in order to observe her in her own home setting and with Ginny."[69] She found their apartment pleasant and pretty, and described Alison as "whim-sical" and "childlike" when in private.[70] In describing their home for the WPA files, Philips scrupulously avoided mentioning the number of bedrooms, writing that the apartment "consists of three rooms on the top floor of an old apartment house which was in the process of being remodeled. One room A. uses as a workroom. Their living room is large, attractively furnished and home-like in general atmosphere, and they have a bath and small kitchen."[71] Their relationship walked a careful line, managing to be public but still unspoken when necessary.

Other institutions also seemed to treat Alison and Ginny as a couple. For instance, the WPA worked closely with the Home Relief Bureau, a Depression-era program that supported adults without dependents. When they refused to provide Alison with full benefits, the worker at the bureau told the WPA that she had heard "many hints as to [Alison's] homosexuality and her activities in Greenwich Village."[72] Her decision around benefits was based on the fact that Ginny "was working and earning money," so because Alison "was part of her family setup in a sense she would not be entitled to full relief."[73]

For two years, Alison and Ginny seemed to be the definition of domestic bliss. Alison's relationship with Ginny's family underwent a dramatic thaw in the summer of 1937, when Ginny's father gave Alison a job for $25 a week. But at the end of July 1938, Alison's probation finally ended, and within two months she was gone. She stuck around just long enough to lift some expensive knickknacks from Ginny's parents and pawn them on her way out of the city. Alison's job with Ginny's dad? Most likely just a cover for blackmail payments to prevent Alison from exposing Ginny's sexuality.

Finally, the WPA admitted that they had been thoroughly had by a talented gay grifter. In the summer of 1939, after not seeing her for a year, Barbara Manley Philips closed Alison's official file with a final note saying she was "a very difficult case," with a "personality disorder that could respond only to intensive psychiatric treatment."[74] Two years later, Alison stopped by the WPA office one afternoon, looking "much less masculine than usual," and made an appointment to talk with the executive director. But when the day came, Alison never showed.[75]

Alison's case makes obvious the fact that there was one powerful thing that could sometimes trump the deleterious effects of having a criminal record: white, middle-class privilege.

In the early years of the twentieth century, most women incarcerated in New York were white. But this changed dramatically over the course of the Great Depression. Unfortunately, these years are a blank spot in the statistical history of the House of D, as neither the Department of Correction nor the municipal courts wrote annual reports during them. However, in their first post-Depression report, covering 1940–1941, the Department of Correction devoted an entire section to "The Problem of the Negro." They wrote that in 1930, Black women constituted 32 percent of incarcerated women in the workhouse, and 41 percent of incarcerated women in the penitentiary. Ten years later, in 1940, Black women were 58 percent of people in the workhouse, and 54 percent of the penitentiary (although these stats were tracked separately, both "the workhouse" and "the penitentiary" were now the House of Detention).[76]

In 1940, the census found that only 6.15 percent of New York City's population was Black. This was likely something of an undercount; overall, the census left out some 1.2 million Black Americans that year.[77] Still, the percentage of Black women being incarcerated in New York City was severely disproportionate. And not just in comparison to white women; the city's men's institutions were, at this time, between 60–70 percent white.[78] There *were* slightly more Black women living in New York than Black men, but not enough to even come close to accounting for this discrepancy. Many Black people were moving to New York City at this time, primarily from the rural South, but also from Puerto Rico and the Caribbean, looking for better opportunities. Unfortunately, for many Black women, they found prison cells instead—much more often, proportionately, than did Black men. Given that a woman's incarceration was largely based on her perceived failure to conform to proper—white—femininity, it seems almost certain that this was due to the consistent, racist view of Black women as more masculine, more sexual, more violent, and in general, less feminine and deserving of care than their white counterparts. As Andrea Ritchie writes in *Invisible No More*, as soon as a Black woman deviates from a subservient role, she is presumed by police and the carceral system "to be unacceptably aggressive," and "the physical threat she poses [is] drastically overblown, her sexuality is automatically deviant, her body devoid of feeling, [and] her personhood undeserving of protection."[79]

Economic forces were almost certainly involved in the over-incarceration of Black women as well, as they were (and are) much more likely than white women to have to work outside the home, which made them infinitely more vulnerable to (already racialized) policing.

Although they did absolutely nothing to fix the situation, the Department of Correction was surprisingly broad-minded in diagnosing it. There was no "problem of the Negro," they wrote—rather, Black New Yorkers faced the problem of consistent and overwhelming racism. From the 1940–1941 annual report:

> Amongst this group we find that poverty is more prevalent and more intense than among other groups; many avenues of gainful employment are closed to them; they are more discriminated against in every avenue of gainful employment; housing and living conditions average the worst in the city....
>
> [And] where under similar circumstances, a considerable percentage of white offenders are released on bail or placed on probation, the very poverty of the Negro and of the resources available, preclude any alternative other than remaining in jail while awaiting trial or being sent to an institution, after conviction.
>
> At the time of release following sentence, again, lack of employment opportunities and of decent housing conditions, complicate the Negroes' chances of being absorbed into a normal existence. Obviously the net result of this is to have a greater percentage of "failures on parole," and a greater number of "returns" to our institutions, either as "parole violators" or on new charges....It is our challenge to see the fault and to remedy it rather than condemn.[80]

But they didn't.

Just as the Department of Correction would continually note that poor women should be helped rather than arrested as vagrant prostitutes, they acknowledged the racism Black New Yorkers experienced but did not work against it.

The WPA was more progressive than many other similar institutions, but they were a majority white organization, and they were unprepared to fully help Black women. And when the Black women they did help pushed back against their racism, they reacted poorly.

Such was the case for Louise B., a precocious, talented Black teen. Louise was one of those first 113 cases seen by Barbara Manley Philips when she left the WPA and went to work at the House of D. Louise closely fit the pattern of Charlotte, Elaine, and Alison. Yet in large part because she was Black, her experiences with the WPA were very different from those other women's.

HOW LOUISE B. GOT TO PARIS

Louise B. lived with her mother in the shadow of Brooklyn's majestic Prospect Park, in a middle-class neighborhood that was (like Louise's family) beginning to fray around the edges. Her father, Frederick, had been a pianist and composer of some renown. When she was young, Frederick promised to someday take Louise to Paris, where he had studied music, starting Louise's lifelong fascination with Europe. When he died in 1929, the *New York Age* called him a "prominent figure in musical circles in New York," as well as a "prolific composer" who had won several national awards for his work.[81] The family owned their home and took in boarders to make their mortgage payments, but as the Depression wore on, Louise's mother had to work harder and harder simply to hold the family together. Her mother was everything that white America wanted a Black woman to be in the 1930s: young, attractive, light-skinned, meticulous, "clean," intelligent, well-mannered, and unwilling to date another man after her husband died (at least at first).[82] The WPA contrasted Louise as being dark, slovenly, heavyset, "high hat" in her attitude, and lazy—but also prodigiously intelligent.[83]

Louise excelled at languages and eagerly practiced French, Italian, and German with any native speakers she met. From an early age, her parents pushed her to be a musician, like her father, but while she had aptitude, she had no real interest, except as a listener. She also excelled in visual art—so much so that the WPA brought her drawings to Dr. Florence Cane, a pioneer in art therapy who was at the time the director of art at NYU's Counseling Center for Gifted Children. Dr. Cane felt that Louise "undoubtedly has talent and should be trained but that she needs about three years of art school before much could be expected of her."[84] Far from going to art school, however, Louise barely made it to high school.

Louise ran away for the first time in 1935, when she was twelve, after she was mistakenly accused of stealing a dollar. She made it to Canada (hoping to find a place where people spoke French, as her father had) but was refused entry and found work in a small town along the border, before eventually turning herself in to the police. She asked to be sent to a reform school but was returned to her mother instead. For months, she was "depressed and talked about killing herself," her mother told the WPA.[85] She ran away again that September, a week after her thirteenth birthday, and this time spent three months working as a live-in domestic in Chicago. When she returned home, she suffered from severe depression and night terrors. Shortly thereafter, Louise's mother began having her committed. She spent two months at Kings County Hospital in 1935, and three at Brooklyn State Hospital in 1937. She was labeled "despondent, uncooperative, resistive, [and] difficult to control."[86] At first, she was diagnosed with dementia praecox (an outdated classification similar to schizophrenia), before that was scrapped for a very different diagnosis: psychopathic personality disorder.

Louise did not display the traits that we today associate with psychopathy (except perhaps for a degree of narcissism, according to her case file). She was not violent, did not lack empathy, was not a pathological liar, etc. But the concept of psychopathy was incredibly important to the criminal control of women in the early twentieth century.

In the nineteenth century, imprisoned people who failed to cooperate or adequately reform were often labeled feeble minded, which greatly curtailed their freedom and in effect made them wards of the state. Their criminality was linked directly to their defective bodies (in this case, their brains), and this justified keeping them permanently imprisoned, or even sterilizing them, to prevent them from spreading their taint to the greater world.

However, thanks in large part to research performed on imprisoned people at Bedford Hills Reformatory, by the twenties, prison administrators were well aware that most of their charges were of average intelligence (even by the measure of their flawed tests). Thus, resistant inmates—like Big Cliff Trondle—could no longer easily be labeled feeble minded and packed off to asylums. This was a real problem for the reformatory, and specifically for its biggest private backer, who funded almost all of their research and wanted results: John D. Rockefeller Jr.

The reformatory staff needed a diagnosis, something to blame when their work did not, in fact, reform someone. Moreover, it needed to be something that would allow them to remove resistant women from their facilities, and recidivists from their statistics. As the field of psychology became the dominant way of understanding human personality, the theory of psychopathy "would, they hoped, account for resistance that was articulate, organized, and evidently fearless."[87]

Rockefeller agreed to continue funding Bedford Hills *only* if New York created "a state-wide system for the care of mentally defective women," so they could be pushed out of the reformatory.[88] So, in 1920, New York State passed its first ever defective-delinquent law, which decreed that any imprisoned woman over the age of sixteen who was found to be "mentally defective to an extent to require supervision, control, and care" would be transferred to the new Division for Mentally Defective Women, which, although on the same campus as Bedford Hills, was *technically* not part of the reformatory.[89] Their new sentences would be indefinite, and their eligibility for release would be determined solely by the administrators of the reformatory, not by the courts. By 1931, there were so many of these imprisoned people at Bedford that the state moved them to Albion, a larger, more remote, and higher security women's prison on the outskirts of Niagara Falls.

Tellingly, the 1920 law did not apply to men or create a "custodial institution…for male defective delinquents."[90] Over and over again, women were punished in harsh and unique ways not because of what they had done but out of fear that they would pass criminality down to their children. In the eyes of the law, men were people and women were vehicles for the creation of people and the temptation of men. (There are strong parallels between this preventative incarceration of women and the way in which the "deliberate arrest and incarceration of young African American men became a strategy to prevent future crime" in the 1970s, right at the start of our modern crisis of mass incarceration.[91] Our criminal legal system punishes white men for what they have done, and everyone else for what they *might* do *to* white men.) Much like fingerprinting, though, the idea of the psychopath would soon be used against queer men, as Anna Lvovsky documented in her book *Vice Patrol*. Lvovsky writes that in the late thirties, "sexual psychopath" was a "new legal category disguised as a medical one," which was epitomized by "violent or predatory offences" but was written into laws broad enough to cover "consensual same-sex acts."[92] The first of these laws was passed in Illinois in 1938, and by the mid-fifties, they had spread to more than twenty states. By that point, queer women had been struggling against the psychopath label for decades.

By the time Louise was hospitalized in 1937, psychopathic personality disorder had become a catchall for girls and women who did not cooperate with authorities, and a dangerous diagnosis to have on your file. Only Louise's education (and her quick tongue) saved her from a lifetime of institutionalization.

In 1938, when Louise was about to turn sixteen—the magic age that made you vulnerable under the defective-delinquent law—her mother brought her to the Children's Court and asked to have her committed. For a few weeks, she was seen by the court psychiatrist, with whom she got along surprisingly well "because they discussed

Wagner."[93] He refused her committal, and once again, Louise returned home to her mother in Brooklyn. Her seeming depression continued unabated and untreated, and on two back-to-back days in October 1939, she was picked up by the police for shoplifting at Macy's. She was back in school, now older than her classmates (because she missed so many days due to her hospitalizations), and had been embarrassed by her clothes, so she had tried to steal a hat. For this, she spent ten days in the House of D.

Louise, by this point, was an expert when it came to institutions. She handled the House of D with the equanimity that sometimes comes with great depression or great fortitude, "looking upon it mainly as an opportunity to make observations of other people."[94] The other incarcerated women did not seem to feel the same way. They "resented her superior attitude," and "there was real trouble on the floor because of the violence they attempted to do to her."[95] The only person she connected with, she said, was Barbara Manley Philips, who guided her to the WPA—but without Philips there, the WPA was not as progressive as it once was, as Louise soon discovered.

Louise persevered because she believed it was all training for her true calling: the stage. Louise wanted to be a serious dramatic actor—something that was almost unheard of for Black women in the early twentieth century. "She did not want to do musical comedy or tap dancing or singing or all of those other things colored people do," her WPA social worker wrote in her file. "She wanted to be a greater actress than Ethel Waters was in 'Mamba's Daughters.'"

Mamba's Daughters opened on Broadway in January 1939 and became an overnight sensation. In the lead role as Hagar, Ethel Waters became "the first black actress ever to star in a serious Broadway drama."[96] Behind the scenes, her involvement in the show went much further. A few years before at a party, Waters had casually struck up a conversation about the opera *Porgy and Bess* with Dorothy and DuBose Heyward. She confessed that she thought the story hadn't seemed "quite true to life" and enthused instead about the novel *Mamba's Daughters*.[97] The Heywards, it turned out, had been the ones who dramatized *Porgy and Bess*—and DuBose was the author of *Mamba's*

Daughters. Waters told them how deeply she connected with the character Hagar, who reminded her of her mother. "All my life I'd burned to tell the story of my mother's despair and long defeat," she told the Heywards, sparking *Mamba's Daughters'* long journey to the stage.[98]

There was another story that Ethel Waters had never had a chance to tell, not publicly, one that Louise shared: her attraction to women. In the 1920s, she'd lived in Harlem with her girlfriend, the dancer Ethel Williams. Although some historians still debate Waters's sexuality, their relationship was known in their day. Mabel Hampton mentions "the two Ethels" several times in her oral history, including in a discussion of women who were "in the life."[99]

It's possible that Louise didn't know about Waters's sexuality—certainly, her caseworkers (plural, as Louise bounced through several) did not seem to. But the more time Louise spent with the WPA, the more queer hints she dropped. Again and again, Louise found ways to steer the conversation back to folks who lived queer lives, even if it was not yet possible for them to be publicly out in the way we can be now. On the same day that Louise enthused about Waters, she told her social worker that she was reading two biographies, of Eva Le Gallienne and Kit Cornell.

Le Gallienne was not only a successful stage actress, she was also a director, translator, and the manager of the Civic Reparatory Theater, which produced dozens of works throughout the Great Depression. Her affairs with women were numerous and well documented, including with the great Russian actress Alla Nazimova, the writer Mercedes de Acosta (whose infamous "sewing circles" connected queer women across the arts), the gold heiress Alice DeLamar, and the married actress Josephine Hutchinson. It was her 1930 affair with Hutchinson that turned Le Gallienne's sexuality into semipublic knowledge; the newspapers had a field day with it, referring variously to La Gallienne as Hutchinson's shadow, and to Hutchinson as "the shadow actress"—shadow, at the time, being a euphemistic way to suggest lesbianism.[100]

Kit Cornell was considered one of the greatest, if not *the* greatest, American stage actors of her time. She was the first person to ever receive the Drama League Award, for *Romeo and Juliet* in 1935.

Although she was married, it was widely understood that both she and her husband, Guthrie McClintic, were gay. Cornell's life crossed paths with Le Gallienne not infrequently; they both dated Mercedes de Acosta, for instance. Kit Cornell and Ethel Waters were also friendly, and correspondence between the two can be found in Cornell's archive. The only male actor Louise enthused about was Maurice Evans, a British stage actor whose queer sexuality was also commonly known in gay circles.[101] Evans played Romeo in the production for which Kit Cornell won the Drama League Award, and he shared the stage with Ethel Waters on at least one occasion. The New Yorker who was knowledgeable about one of their personal lives might well have known about all of them.

Louise's clues about her sexuality were not confined to discussions of famous actors. Her file noted how "she would go on all night subway rides, sit on hard benches or wander about Coney Island and Greenwich Village"—two of the city's queerest neighborhoods.[102] She also told the WPA that she considered getting an apartment in the Village with another woman she'd met through their shelter, though that didn't work out. This engendered the one moment when Louise's social worker might have tangentially been acknowledging Louise's sexuality, writing that

> in none of this was there any indication of sexual activities, her relationship with the Village intelligentsia being confined to long and heated discussions on art, music and the theatre, and joining them in unconventional intrusions on their friends for rest and meals at odd hours.[103]

By 1939 (the year of Louise's first arrest), the relationship between Greenwich Village, working-class lesbians, and the House of Detention had become public knowledge. In April of that year, Walter Winchell had mentioned it in his nationally syndicated gossip column, "On Broadway," which ran in papers from Tampa to Texas. "Ask the owner of the Jefferson Diner (across from the Women's House of Detention) why he charges a 25c cover charge between 1 and 5 ayem," Winchell wrote. "Sort of a Greenwich (Howdy Club) Village atmosphere, they say."[104]

The Howdy Club was one of the most famous lesbian joints in the Village, a place where the butch waitstaff wore football sweaters or tuxes, and male and female impersonators performed on the stage. Not only was Winchell suggesting that the lesbian vibe of the Howdy Club was the same as the vibe of Greenwich Village as a whole, he was also pointing to a fundamental shift in the acknowledged geography of New York City. Neighborhood boundaries are always in flux, but before the opening of the House of D, it was generally agreed that Greenwich Village was west of Sixth Avenue (where the House of D was located). But as the prison brought more queer women into its orbit, year in and year out, the border of the Village began to shift eastward, encapsulating more of the area immediately around the House of D. Winchell's column was a rare public acknowledgment that the queer women and transmasculine people in the House of Detention were already changing the city in profound ways. By the time the prison closed in the 1970s, the intersection where the House of D was located would be considered central to the Village.

Louise must have been deeply embedded in the New York theater community, because in 1941, she talked her way into the rehearsals for Orson Welles's Broadway adaptation of Richard Wright's novel *Native Son*—and then, in "the most valuable experience she had ever had in her life," she was allowed to audition.[105] Welles "complimented [Louise] upon her ability but advised that her physical size prevented her from being considered for the cast."[106] Despite not getting a role, the play seemed to have a profound effect on Louise, and her thoughts about race in America. Its central tragedy—a poor, young Black man caught up in a system that doesn't value his life, who accidentally kills a white woman—was one that Louise could relate to. It was also a story her white social workers at the WPA could, at best, only try to understand from the outside.

The ignorance of Louise's workers at the WPA was not constrained to queer life; they were also ignorant about Black life in New York, and the parallel world of Black organizations that could have assisted Louise. The WPA had no Black staff at this time, and while they mentioned organizations like the Urban League or the Harlem branch of the YWCA to Louise, they lacked the connections to facilitate any introductions. Instead, they relied on the tried and true method of foisting the work off on random Black people they knew. "Several of the people in the colored population could be approached and might be of some help to Louise in looking for work," her social worker conjectured limply in her notes.[107] When Louise wanted help finding a more welcoming educational environment, her worker did an "extensive survey of boarding schools"—all in the South.[108] The WPA also lacked the cultural competence necessary to talk to Louise about internalized racism, which she struggled with her whole life. As a result, she looked down on other Black teens and refused to socialize with them. "She is unhappy and miserable with members of her own race," her social worker wrote, because Louise felt they did not share the same interests, education, or cultural touchstones.[109]

After Louise auditioned for *Native Son*, however, the tone of her file shifted. She discussed her childhood experiences with white racists in Mississippi and began reading the *New York Age*, one of New York's most prominent Black evening papers (although she found it often "amateurish").[110] When Pearl Harbor was bombed in December 1941, Louise was listening to the philharmonic on the radio in the WPA's Hopper Home. The broadcast was cut short to cover the news, and Louise "critically denounced the United States and disclaimed any patriotic feeling because of the unfair treatment and inequality shown colored people."[111]

Her social workers, who had previously been ignorant but relatively supportive of Louise as she embraced her Blackness, now began to push back against her vocal anti-racist attitudes. "The culture of negroes and whites was compared to the development of a person in youth and maturity," her worker noted in her file, in a conversation about the Pearl Harbor bombing.[112] Unsurprisingly, Louise would soon sever connections with the WPA, after an incident that exposed both her sexuality and the racism of our carceral system.

In truth, Louise's social workers didn't need her theatrical hints to know about her desire for women. All they needed to do was look at her file. When Louise had first been hospitalized, at the age of twelve, she met another girl named Ann C. Both were young, stubborn, and queer; treated by the same doctor; and diagnosed as psychopathic personalities.

After they first met in a hospital in 1935, Louise and Ann were suspected of a "homosexual relationship and prolonged teamwork," but as they were shuffled back and forth between different institutions, they lost touch. Six years later, however, in 1941, they were reunited at the Hopper Home, where a staff person caught them in the kitchen, giggling and smelling of marijuana. Together, they planned a clever heist.

A few days before Christmas, the two girls put on their heavy winter coats and separately went in to Scribner's, a fabled multilevel book emporium located on Fifth Avenue in Manhattan. Each made their way to the rare book department, and together they hid a three-volume set of *The Naval Chronology of Great Britain*, valued at $500, under their coats.[113] When asked about it later, Louise would say she chose them in part "for their beautiful leather bindings."[114]

The two were in and out without a problem, and Louise used the phone book to find a rare book dealer who would meet them on Monday morning. When the time came, Ann overslept; Louise went on her own, even though she knew it was a bad idea—a "large Negro girl, having such valuable books" was never going to be trusted by the salespeople in such an establishment.[115] But it was worse than she thought: there was a hidden mark in the book, Scribner's had already alerted other booksellers to the theft, the dealer they were visiting had called the police, and a plant was waiting in the store when Louise arrived. The police grabbed her as soon as she tried to sell the books, but Louise broke free and managed to make it out of the store, across Fifth Avenue, and all the way to the steps of St. Patrick's Cathedral, where they collared her. At the station house, she "did nothing but quote Shakespeare at them and talk about Nostradamus."[116] She was booked for grand larceny and sent back to the Women's House of Detention.

Ann, meanwhile, had no idea what happened until she opened the newspaper on Christmas Eve and read about Louise's arrest. Immediately, she headed to see Louise but "was refused permission because she was white and Louise was colored."[117]

The House of D had an uneven record on segregation. Before it opened, the city's commissioner of correction announced that the prison *would* be segregated, but he quickly backtracked in the face of public outcry, alleging that NYC prisons *only* allowed for racial segregation when requested by Black prisoners themselves, to protect them from racist whites. These "Jim Crow blocks" were strenuously opposed by civil rights organizations, who rightly saw them as punishing imprisoned Black people rather than dealing with the root issue of white supremacy. As the NAACP put it,

> It would seem that instead of granting the request of any Negro prisoners who would seek to avoid contact with prejudiced whites, anti-Negro manifestations by white prisoners should be promptly dealt with. We respectively but vigorously urge that no segregation on the basis of race or color be considered even though some Negro prisoners may of their own volition otherwise appear to favor such segregation.[118]

In 1936, an inspection report stated that Black prisoners were assigned to "separate corridors as a general rule."[119] But this was an inconsistent situation. Absent any official policy, individual staff seem to have acted on their own impulses and biases when it came to allowing interactions between imprisoned people of different races, which is why Ann was never able to speak to Louise.

Stymied, Ann left Louise some cash for the commissary and headed to the Women's Prison Association for advice. She thought perhaps she'd go to Scribner's and offer them some money, in return for dropping the charges. They had the books. No harm, no foul. But the WPA called their lawyer, and the lawyer recommended Ann turn herself in or the WPA would be an accessory to a felony.

The district attorney "could scarcely believe the girl had done what she said...and of her own free will unnecessarily confessed to it."[120] Ann also admitted that this was not the first time the pair had worked together to steal and sell rare books. The WPA pleaded on Ann's behalf, but it did no good. The detectives said Louise's bail had already been set at $1,500. Ann couldn't afford that. They asked if she could raise a $200 bail for herself. Ann, shamefaced, said no. $50? Nothing. Soon, Ann joined Louise in the House of D—a place she was already well familiar with.

First, however, Ann contacted her lawyer, the infamous Gertrude Gottlieb, aka "Dirty Gertie."[121] Short, stout, and a master at playing the press, Gottlieb was the lawyer women called when they'd been arrested for particularly disreputable crimes—pimping, baby-killing, lesbianism, etc. In her fur coats and fascinator hats, she looked like a high femme Ethel Rosenberg. It's unclear how she and Ann first connected, but Gottlieb repeatedly provided Ann with free legal services in the late 1930s and early 1940s. It seems possible that this connection came through the queer community, as by the 1960s, Gottlieb had a near monopoly on representing men arrested for soliciting other men for sex. "As the mythology of the day had it, even before family or friends had heard the news, Gottlieb...would appear at the police station, apparently tipped off by the cops," according to historian Martin Duberman.[122] Neither Louise nor Ann could pay for Gottlieb's services, but still, she argued the charge down to petty larceny from grand larceny, and the two girls received a month in the House of D and a year on probation each. The two must have been quite an item behind bars, as Ann "was deluged with notes from girls in the Hse. of Detention suggesting that she 'give up Louise and be their "daddy."'"[123] According to her social worker, Ann pretended "to be bored and disgusted, but was obviously somewhat intrigued" by the notes, though she continued to deny that she had a physical relationship with Louise.[124]

This, for the most part, marked the end of Louise's time with the Women's Prison Association. In the House of D, she "found some Nazi spies who were willing to talk German to her...requested Shakespeare's Tragedies and Esquire for reading material, and...complained of the lack of milk in the diet."[125] She continued to see Dr. Marion

Stranahan from the House of D on and off for a few years, but never truly connected with a worker at the WPA. In late 1942 she was arrested for assault. After this, she left the city. "Off the record," Dr. Stranahan told the WPA that she had moved to Connecticut in 1943 to work in a defense plant for the war effort.[126]

For the Black community in New York, 1943 was a terrifying year, scarred by police violence. James Baldwin, who turned nineteen that year, wrote about it in his famous essay "Notes of a Native Son" (the title was a play on the same Richard Wright novel that had so affected Louise):

> Racial tensions throughout this country were exacerbated during the early years of the war, partly because the labor market brought together hundreds of thousands of ill-prepared people and partly because Negro soldiers, regardless of where they were born, received their military training in the south. What happened in defense plants and army camps had repercussions, naturally, in every Negro ghetto. The situation in Harlem had grown bad enough for clergymen, policemen, educators, politicians, and social workers to assert in one breath that there was no "crime wave" and to offer, in the very next breath, suggestions as to how to combat it....The Harlem police force had been augmented in March, and the unrest grew—perhaps, in fact, partly as a result of the ghetto's instinctive hatred of policemen....I had never been so aware of policemen, on foot, on horseback, on corners, everywhere.[127]

In August, a white police officer shot a Black soldier, starting the bloodiest riot New York had seen in decades. Before the night was over, five people were dead, five hundred were injured, and there was an estimated $5 million in property damage in Harlem. The city's response was to pour more cops into the situation. "For days after the rioting, 6,000 city policemen, military policemen and air raid wardens patrolled the streets of Harlem," according to the *New York Times*.[128]

Louise had been smart to get away when she did.

Thirteen years later, a woman who worked with Dr. Stranahan told the WPA that Louise now lived in Paris, and she occasionally sent postcards to the doctor. Years before, Louise had informed the WPA that France was the one place where "colored people would be accepted by whites."[129] Her father was never able to take her to Paris, so it seems Louise took herself: A manifest for the SS *Liberté* showed Louise headed to Le Havre, France, on September 14, 1954. In the column for her intended length of stay, the form simply said "indefinite." In the very last sentence of her file, the WPA wrote, "We asked what Louise was doing." The only answer they received was, "Probably what she did here."[130]

This was a good time to escape New York, if you were a formerly incarcerated woman. The war created jobs—decent jobs—that working-class women could have, but they were only temporary. Afterward, wartime patriotism would lead directly into the reactionary and conservative politics of the 1950s; women would be asked to leave the factory and return to the kitchen; and the GI Bill would underwrite the boom in racist suburban construction that would leech cities of tax revenue and vital infrastructure. Progressive organizations floundered during and after the war, with their membership again riven between pacifists and those eager to fight fascism. The upshot? Fewer and fewer had the time or money to focus on incarcerated women.

Ann C. stayed behind when Louise left New York. For a few years, she treaded water—a small butch boat in a rising wartime tide. But by the end of the 1940s, Ann had spiraled out of control. Like many formerly incarcerated women, three interrelated forces would dominate, and ultimately ruin, Ann's life: the stigma of her incarceration, the lack of treatment for her mental health, and her inability to find and keep a good job. For Black women like Serena C. (another WPA client), these forces were compounded by the corrosive toll of white supremacy and anti-Blackness. Ann and Serena were about as different as two WPA clients could be, and they would meet only once, in Bellevue's psych ward in 1952. But the tragic paths that brought them to the hospital were eerily similar, and indicative of what life was like for formerly incarcerated queer women in New York City during the tumultuous 1940s.

World War II fundamentally changed New York and the experience of queer life in America, but paradoxically, the fight for freedom abroad ushered in the most conservative decade of the twentieth century.

CHAPTER 4

Rosie the Riveter Gets Fired

THE ONSET OF WORLD WAR II

In the aftermath of the attack on Pearl Harbor, the United States officially entered World War II in December 1941. Thanks to government intervention, the country was already emerging from the Great Depression, but the war turbocharged the recovery. By 1945, "the United States was the wealthiest society in history."[1]

Oftentimes, the story we are told about women in World War II is a triumphant one of Rosie the Riveters, doing their part to fight fascism abroad while simultaneously making America a freer and more feminist place. Indeed, some working-class women, like Louise and Charlotte, used this moment of opportunity to set themselves on a new path, one that allowed them to escape the city and the revolving door of the House of D. Between 1940 and 1944, nearly eight million private, nonagricultural jobs were added to the economy, while simultaneously, ten million working-age men were called up for military service.[2] As a result, in just four years, the percentage of women working outside the home leapt from 27 percent to 37 percent, until nearly twenty million American women were employed. Many of these new jobs were in arenas that women had traditionally been kept out of, such as factory work. In 1940, there were only 340,000 women working in "durables manufacturing"; in 1943, there were 2.1 million.[3]

These new industrial jobs paid much more than being a maid, waitress, or washerwoman. Thus, the number of women employed in domestic work fell by 20 percent during the war, and "regions with a high concentration of factories"—like New York—"found it difficult to induce women to take low-paying, unpleasant jobs in laundries and restaurants."[4]

Also on the list of bad, low-paying jobs that women with options didn't want anymore? Working in prisons.

In the spring of 1943, there were fourteen staff vacancies at the House of D (about 20 percent of the full-time employees), many of which were "comparatively long standing," according to state inspectors, because the city's policy was "not to fill vacancies because of reasons of economy."[5]

In private correspondence, the superintendent of the prison also admitted that "the failure to fill them is due, in large measure, to [the] non-existence…of available candidates."[6] As a result, when older workers (like Barbara Manley Philips) left, they were replaced by ones less qualified and more conservative—when they were replaced at all. In 1942, funding for the teachers in the part-time education program at the House of D was cut, and the librarian was fired—just one year after the superintendent praised the "unquestionable value of a library for prisoners" in her annual report.[7] Although guards would take over these programs for short periods, there would be no real education staffing for the rest of the decade.[8] In 1946, a report on the entire NYC Department of Corrections would scathingly find that

> the personnel, particularly the custodial force, had been depleted in number far below the danger point, the morale of the employees was at a very low ebb, many vacancies remained unfilled, promotional examinations in many categories were not held for a long period of time and, generally speaking, the department might be regarded as having been neglected.[9]

If the *staff* were neglected, imagine what was happening to the people incarcerated.

Across the board, resources for imprisoned women were dwindling, even as the economy boomed. In 1941 the Department of Corrections put out their first annual report since the start of the Depression. In a spew of doublespeak, they admitted that the House of D was in trouble. Largely thanks to disappearing federal anti-poverty funding, "some of the services—particularly Educational and Social Welfare—are not at the peak level attained during this administration, and it is hoped that their proved value will not be permanently impaired. However, it is not to be implied that real advances have not been permanently achieved."[10]

Their contorted diction would be humorous were it not for the magnitude of the failures it hid. But it is indicative of the defensive position from which all public-facing correctional documents are written. These are never neutral records—they are arguments for more money, excuses for past failures, and professional attempts to spin shit into gold.

So, what did this gobbledygook mean in reality?

First off, a decade of extreme overcrowding and underfunding had taken a hard toll on the physical condition of the prison. Right before the war started, the city had set aside $1.25 million to build a much needed extension on the House of D, but the project was put on hold for the duration of the war and then abandoned.[11] In 1944, inspectors found the halls "were littered with cigarette ends and matches."[12] They reported "dirt behind cell doors and under radiators," "papers and magazines…stuffed under mattresses," and mirrors that were "so worn as to be useless."[13] They found what they euphemistically called "mouse dirt" in the kitchen and the food, and open containers of insecticide and other chemicals stored cheek by jowl with bulk food items.[14] They boasted that some 1,400 women had taken part in recreation programs during their incarceration—which sounds great, but in reality meant that about 80 percent of the women in the House of D that year took part in no activities whatsoever. The inspectors hedged on what these programs even were, saying things like, "There is said to be a class in music appreciation."[15] They noted that women were still occasionally being doubled up in cells, even on days when the population was low enough that each individual could have a cell of their own (for several years during the war, the average population of the prison dipped below the overcrowding threshold, largely because of the wartime development of effective treatments for syphilis and gonorrhea—the sulfa drugs that were tested on imprisoned women at the House of D).

Private interest (and investment) in the prison also stalled during the war. The Women's Prison Association disbanded their Psychiatric Aftercare Clinic in 1941, and stopped paying for a prison psychiatrist in early 1947.[16] Other private sources of funding also dried up, or concentrated their efforts elsewhere, such as the Women's Federal Jurors Association, which began splitting their annual fundraiser between the House of D and the Red Cross, although "until this nation entered the war, the association only contributed to the House of Detention."[17] Although New York City would not officially admit this until a 1960 annual report, "at the end of World War II all post-war budgeting had been aimed at the needs of housing, sewage, schools and hospitals. Correction was allowed to struggle along without replacements and additions."[18]

For formerly incarcerated people like Yolanda E., a young Black woman who spent nearly three years at the House of D on a charge of "impairing the morals of a minor," the collapse of post-prison support infrastructure had terrible consequences. Yolanda was just eighteen when she was incarcerated, after a sexual encounter with her common-law husband and a twelve-year-old girl. Originally, she was charged with rape and sodomy, but the case seemed to fall apart and the charge was reduced. The incomplete records left behind make it difficult to sort out what happened. Regardless, in 1949, as she prepared to leave the House of D, Yolanda began a desperate attempt to get ready for life on the outside. She had hoped to receive employment help from the WPA, but they were stretched too thin. In March, she wrote a letter to their executive director, asking her to "please help if you possibly can because I've been in here since October 20, 1945 and I'd like a chance when I meet the [parole] board to prove to them I can be good." Four months later, when she still hadn't gotten a reply, Yolanda wrote plaintively, "I've been waiting to hear from you but it seems you have forgotten me."[19]

Yolanda's mother lived in Maryland, and she wrote to the parole board saying Yolanda could live with her—and that she had a job lined up for Yolanda—but this was deemed "inadequate."[20] Instead, the parole board felt it was best to simply release her, with no plan, onto the streets of New York City. She arrived on the doorstep of the WPA's Hopper Home in October 1949 "without any announcement to us...[from] the parole department."[21] The WPA gave her shelter, but they were unwilling or unable to do much more. "[Yolanda] came in for her things," her social worker noted a few weeks later, "but she was not asked where she was going as she has not been very welcome in the house."[22] Yolanda turned to the City Mission, where she had received help before being imprisoned, but they said "they could do no more for the girl."[23] Similarly, the Salvation Army told Yolanda's WPA social worker that they had "no further interest in this case."[24] Without resources, support, a steady job, or a home, Yolanda turned to sex work and was rearrested several times before her case was closed for good in 1955. There's no way to know how things might have turned out for Yolanda otherwise, but certainly, her experience was made infinitely worse by the prison's lack of aftercare planning and the financial constraints of the few nonprofits that still provided the services she needed.

Even as the war distracted the country from the plight of formerly imprisoned women like Yolanda, it shone a harsh light on modern ideas about sexuality, with profound ramifications for the queer community that was now firmly established in Greenwich Village. In the words of historian Allan Bérubé, author of *Coming Out Under Fire: The History of Gay Men and Women in World War II*, "The military's mobilization for war made soldiers confront homosexuality in their personal lives and changed the ways that homosexuality fit into American institutions."[25]

Many people discovered or learned to name their own queer desires in the intense, sex-stratified life of the military. Margaret B.— "a large, blonde, blue eyed white girl who looks rather hard"—was one such individual.[26] Her wealthy family had lost their oil money during the Depression, and when her inheritance ran out at twenty-two, she joined the Women's Auxiliary Volunteer Enlisted Service, or WAVES—the navy reserve force for women. She served from 1944 to 1946, before returning to New York City, where she quickly developed a severe alcohol problem, which (indirectly) led to her arrest. Her boyfriend, a policeman named Reilly, had been passing bad checks, and the cops had nabbed her along with him. There was no evidence that she was involved, but Margaret suspected she received her three-month sentence to the House of D because she had "been drunk when she came to Court."[27]

She drank, she told the WPA, "to forget her troubles"—her sadness, her feeling out of place, her struggles with men and keeping a job. One afternoon, while waiting to see a doctor at the VA hospital, Margaret told the WPA that "she had made quite a number of friends in the WAVES with whom she was still maintaining a friendship.... Margaret also told the worker that these friends were Lesbians."[28] Isabelle, the woman who had accompanied her on many appointments, was one of those friends. A lightbulb went off for Margaret's caseworker upon learning this, and she wrote in her notes,

> It is the worker's impression about M. that she presents the true academic picture of the alcoholic: M's choice of a vocation, the fact that she was an only child, the choice of her friends, her promiscuity, her unhappy sex relationship—all indicate that there might be a basis of Lesbianism in this particular alcoholic pattern.[29]

Margaret was comparatively lucky during the war: she hadn't been injured or killed; her sexuality hadn't been discovered (except, apparently, by other queer women); and she was given an honorable discharge, which enabled her to get health care from the VA and educational benefits from the GI Bill.

Many others endured far harsher conditions during the war, which provided endless opportunities for the government to broadcast propaganda about LGBTQ people around the country. For the first time in American history, homosexuality was explicitly ruled to be incompatible with armed service, which meant that everyone who signed up had some version of homosexuality explained to them as a danger, a flaw, a weakness, or a psychological defect. They were given induction lectures about sexual dangers, including homosexuality, and watched other service members get investigated and drummed out for their sexuality or gender identity (often referred to as "being given a blue ticket"). They learned what behaviors to suspect in friends and to hide in themselves, and they brought that knowledge home with them after the war. What the court system had done teaching women like Charlotte and Elaine about homosexuality on a small scale, the military did on a national level. Many of these women, even those who had good experiences in the service, found no place to be themselves when they returned home.

The spreading fear of the "hidden homosexual" made straight people less willing to be seen in queer spaces. The tourist trade that had funded large parts of the queer world in Greenwich Village was no longer very interested in the fairies, butches, and drag balls that Elaine had once shown them. By the end of the war, the fancy queer bars with floor shows began to disappear, and they were replaced by the smaller, dirtier, more secretive gay bars we associate with mid-century America. The Howdy Club, which Walter Winchell had used as a byword for both lesbianism *and* Greenwich Village in 1939, was forced to suspend its drag shows in 1944. When their lawyer pointed out that they "had been doing the same act for about 10 years without complaint," the city government simply didn't care.[30] In the same raid, the police went after Tony Pastor's Downtown, a cabaret just four blocks from the House of D, for "permitting Lesbians to loiter on the premises."[31] The Howdy Club folded in 1945; Tony Pastor's survived by getting in bed with the mafia, who provided enough protection for the bar to remain open until 1967, when it was closed for serving homosexuals.[32]

Around the same time, the last gasps of the Progressive Era feminist movement collapsed, further marginalizing queer people in public life. According to *The Woman Citizen*, a history of feminism in the early twentieth century, after winning the vote in 1920 many feminist organizations de-radicalized. They went from advocating for broad social change to working on issues "of more particular concern to business and professional women," which meant that they rarely, if ever, thought about imprisoned women.[33]

Early radical feminist organizations like the Heterodoxy Club, a political and social group that formed in Greenwich Village in 1912, had openly queer members and leaders. But the passage of time—and the conflict around the two world wars—made many of them abandon their radical views, and Heterodoxy became smaller and less important as the years went on. They shuttered for good sometime around the start of World War II, and no large, queer-friendly feminist organization would take their place for decades. When one member—Communist activist Elizabeth Gurley Flynn—ended up in the House of D in the fifties, she was a progressive political voice on every issue *except* homosexuality, which she coldly condemned.

But if Heterodoxy folded in part over politics, one member said it was also largely because "prices of food and meeting places" in the Village had become exorbitant.[34] The Village's unique winding streets, its charming architectural details, and its now-storied history were becoming selling points for real estate interests and landlords. In the forties, the Village would emerge as a battleground between government urban renewal projects, local landowners, and the diverse communities (many of them immigrant, working class, or queer) that lived and socialized on its blocks—a battle that continues to this day.

Visible displays of queer sexuality or gender disidentification were no longer exciting signs of bohemianism, but dirty signifiers of disordered minds (and dropping property values). In the late forties, construction on Washington Square "altered the physical character of the neighborhood by demolishing many 19th century structures."[35] As a result, homeowners and businesses organized around the idea of creating some kind of historic, landmarked district that would prevent both growth and change in the physical structure of the neighborhood while accelerating the change in the population from working class to middle and upper class. Although it was a slow and uneven process, the modern gentrification of Greenwich Village had begun.

The world was changing. The Village was changing. But through it all, the Women's House of Detention remained much the same—uniquely so, for queer people. Unlike with any other commercial, public, or private space in the city, the government couldn't drive homosexuals away from the House of D, because they were the ones actively concentrating queer women and transmasculine people there. Bars could be closed, private residences could be raided, and the streets were fair game for brutal police sweeps. But the prison was untouchable. Those arrested on sex-work-related charges continued to make up approximately 50 percent of the prison's population, but there would be more and more women arrested for drugs and political organizing as the forties bled into the fifties. These women would be some of the first former inmates of the House of D to publish their memoirs—although they wouldn't see print until many years later.

Ann C. and Serena C. couldn't have foreseen these changes when they were both sent to the House of D for the first time in the late 1930s, but by following in their footsteps, a seeming paradox becomes evident: as the economy boomed, incarcerated women did worse.

THE UNEMPLOYABLES

The first note in Ann C.'s WPA file is one of the most telling—a retrospective reconstruction of the first two years she received services, written in 1940, shortly before Ann and Louise B. were arrested for shoplifting rare books. Why was this reconstruction necessary? Well,

> Ann was accepted for case work and during the following two years established an excellent relationship with her worker. She was very disturbed by a necessary change in personnel in July of 1940 and manifested it by several episodes of delinquent behavior, one of which was

to steal her record from the file, carefully read it, taunt her mother with appropriate excerpts, and then tear it to bits and burn it.[36]

Ann's childhood had been one of violence and deprivation. Her maternal grandparents were well-off alcohol importers, but her father was a dandy who alienated his wife's family and drank away their money. When he became semi-incapacitated due to tuberculosis, he got violent, repeatedly beating Caroline (his wife), until she miscarried. Eventually, he was taken to court for raping one of his grandchildren. Ann was a witness, and it was suspected that she herself had survived the same abuse.

Caroline, Ann's mother, testified on behalf of her husband, and seemed to live in a world of paranoid delusions. She "resented any outside interest which Ann developed, called her vile names, always suspected her of immoral relations, [and] taunted and ridiculed the girl unmercifully."[37] She institutionalized Ann for the first time at age five and used mental hospitals as a "punishment measure" when Ann acted out.[38] Ann bounced from Catholic charity to state hospital and back, accumulating a file full of "violent temper tantrums" and suicidal ideation.[39] Shortly before she destroyed her first WPA file, Ann got into a fight with her mother, beat her with a teakettle, and blinded her. As a result, she spent months in the House of D on a felony assault charge. Like many queer women before her, Ann was offered psychological services while in jail. However, Ann didn't see progressive Dr. Stranahan but instead was assigned to Dr. Henriette Klein, a new hire who toed the line of working only with clients who were deemed redeemable. Dr. Klein's opinion of Ann? "Her dull normal mental ability, unattractive physical appearance, very limited understanding of her own motivation, and her thirst for excitement would make it difficult for her to compete in any field."[40] It was true that employment would be a constant problem for Ann, but not because of her abilities—because of her arrest record.

Serena C. was a few years older, and although she also came from a poor Brooklyn family, her life in the late 1930s was very different. Her mother was illiterate, and her father likely was as well. Both pushed

Serena to leave school early—it was the Depression, and the family needed her income desperately. But Serena persisted. By 1938, when she was twenty-two, Serena had completed regular high school and enrolled in a night school to prepare her for college. She hoped to work full-time as a clerk or telephone operator during the day to save money for tuition—the kind of jobs she'd held previously. But when she applied at the Home Relief Bureau (a Depression-era government program) the administrator told her the "quota was closed" for clerks, and that Serena "must go to a housekeeping school to learn that kind of work, under penalty of being cut off relief."[41] When challenged, the Home Relief administrator informed Serena that "Negro families lived happily and Negro women should be glad to work for $25 a month"—the usual wage for a domestic position in Brooklyn at the time.[42] This was less than Serena's rent, and certainly not enough for food or bills or tuition.

Furious, Serena turned to the Worker's Alliance, a Socialist Party initiative that sought to unionize unemployed people around the country. The Alliance ensured that her case made headlines in Black and socialist newspapers. "This is an outrageous case of discrimination," fulminated one organizer to the press, "and is typical of the treatment accorded Negroes."[43] With their help, Serena received rent assistance and a new apartment. But to get a good job, or money for school, Serena had to be creative. While she had the attention of the press, she announced that she was going to travel to Detroit to ask the manager of John Lewis (the famous boxer) to help her afford tuition to Howard University. Serena had met him previously through the Urban League (a Black civil rights organization), and he had encouraged her to ask for assistance.

And this, she told the staff on her first day at the WPA, "was how she got into trouble."[44]

To get to Detroit, Serena bought herself a pair of new shoes and a bus ticket, using the only money she had: her Home Relief rent payment. But Lewis's manager said he couldn't help her. "Her feeling was that he never intended her to follow his suggestion," her worker noted sadly in her file. Dejected, broke, and back in New York, Serena shoplifted fifty cents' worth of stationery, so she could write to Howard University—but she ended up with an eighteen-day sentence in the House of Detention instead.

Serena "had hysterics practically all the time" she was in prison, feeling that she had "worked hard for an education and…had ruined the whole thing by this experience."[45] After she was out, however, she occasionally showed up at the House of D to talk over her problems with the new psychiatrist, Dr. Klein, who took notes on her "hypomanic tendencies and…great concern over her sexual adjustment."[46] In the more than twenty years that Serena was in contact with the WPA, she explicitly mentioned having sex with only one woman, once, telling a worker that "she was not confused over her sex but she had had homosexual relations with a girl at the House of Detention…[who] continues to haunt her."[47] Her file contained hints of what might have been other queer relationships, but they were ignored. At one point, Serena mentioned one woman repeatedly over the course of a year, saying, "they see a good deal of each other," referring to her as her "girlfriend," and requesting tickets to take her to the theater. The WPA workers never inquired about her, or even wrote down her name. Those few workers who understood the implications of Serena's conversations continually tried to guide her back to heterosexuality. For instance, when Serena mentioned that she was occasionally going on dates with a neighbor but was feeling "considerable conflict about her relationship to him and to all men," her worker simply told her she "needed the definite continued help of a psychiatric case worker" and repeatedly enthused about the importance of marriage.[48]

Serena's stint in the House of D slowed, but didn't stop, her fight to go to Howard. She took her battle with the Home Relief Bureau all the way to the mayor, and finally secured a full-time clerk position. The WPA helped arrange money from private sources, and Barbara Manley Philips at the House of D took up a collection among concerned Brooklyn women who volunteered at the prison. But the hustle and insecurity came with a high price, and Serena started to express "considerable worry about her physical and mental condition," because "she regards herself as lacking in self-control."[49] After a fight with her landlady, Serena checked herself into City Hospital for temporary supervision, but they called her a difficult patient, and after some disturbance with a nurse, she was transferred to the psych ward at Bellevue. There, she was held for a month but ultimately released. Bellevue informed the WPA that Serena was "very near a manic depressive break," but they only told Serena that she had gonorrhea.[50] Over and over again, because she was poor, Black, formerly incarcerated, and involuntarily committed, doctors and social workers treated Serena without any regard for her autonomy, deciding what was best for her and telling her only slivers of the truth.

The WPA was already aware of Serena's manic tendencies. Her tremendous drive radiated off her in spiky waves, and while she impressed the WPA staff greatly, they were concerned from her very first visit:

> S. talked very rapidly. She sat on the edge of her chair and occasionally became so tense in her talking that she clipped her words. She would talk very rapidly about one subject and just before finishing that would switch off onto another one. It was at no time hard to follow her and there did not seem to be any particular confusion in her doing this. It was as if she was thinking too rapidly for her words.[51]

This was an early preview of the mania that would, over the next twenty years, occasionally take hold of Serena, particularly when she was under severe stress, and would eventually leave her incapacitated and institutionalized. It was a dangerous energy, but one that she could at times harness to her advantage. It took years, but Serena's hard work paid off, and she cobbled together the necessary money to go to a one-year dental hygienist program at Howard.

Serena excelled at university. In a supportive Black environment, and without the constant fear of ending up on the streets, her mental health concerns seemed to evaporate. In 1941, she won a National Youth Administration Award and a prize for her essay writing.[52] The WPA staff wrote in her file that "the Dean had written a very favorable report on S. She is doing very good work and is the second highest in her class....He believed that she would make a real success of her studies as well as of her future life."[53] But leaving Howard put Serena back at the mercy of a white supremacist power structure that continually devalued her, with devastating long-term effects.

In June 1941, Serena returned to New York filled with hope. But after a month of being unemployed and living with her mother, she asked to move back into the WPA's Hopper Home. "She is not discouraged over her prospects," the WPA wrote in their notes. "She realized that it may take some time for her because she is colored and because of the limited facilities available to colored people."[54]

Despite her high marks and good references, every door closed on Serena. The Dental Hygienist Employment Agency told her "they seldom had a call for a colored worker."[55] The Gordon Employment Agency found her a position, but instead of the work she was trained for, her duties would have been "the cleaning of the dentist's apartment and the ironing of his coat."[56] The WPA took out an ad for Serena in the *New York Times*, but the first dentist to respond said "she was too dark."[57] The next offered Serena $10 per month—*half* of what she had been offered years earlier to work as a maid. In August, Serena went back on Home Relief, and also took an emergency loan from the WPA. In September she finally got placed at a school-based dental clinic in Brooklyn, but that was soon changed to two separate placements, at two different schools, and then on October 3rd she was moved again, this time to a Boys Club Dental Clinic in Manhattan. Her new supervisor, a white woman dentist, was known to be "difficult, officious and eccentric," and their relationship was never good.[58] In an effort to find decent work—and, just as importantly, the kind of Black social circle she had cultivated at Howard—Serena took on a second job in the private office of a Black dentist.

The stress of the two positions, and of being a working-class Black woman in World War II America, quickly began to wear on Serena. At the Boys Club Clinic, her white supervisor was high-handed and disrespectful, and accused the few Black workers of being "leagued against her."[59] But even if they had gotten along, it wouldn't have mattered. The Depression was over, and the government programs that funded the clinic (the same ones that had supported the educational and social services in the House of D) were closing. What appeared like a good government job in actuality came with very little security, the thing Serena needed most.

At her second workplace, the private dentist's office, Serena was put off by the doctor's behavior toward her and his general attitude toward women, though the WPA told her it was just "kid[ding]," and she needed to learn how to take it.[60] Instead of becoming the center of her social life, as she hoped, the dentist and his family became a preoccupation for Serena's mania—was he making a pass at her? What would she do if he did make a pass at her? Did the dentist's wife hate her? Serena was certain she did.

Looking for other social outlets, Serena got involved with the war effort. Despite her experiences with racism in government programs, Serena was strongly patriotic, because she "knew no other country or no other Government would have permitted her the opportunities for advancement which she has enjoyed in the United States."[61] Yet despite her education, position, and new, expensive clothing, she found herself sidelined in volunteer groups, largely because she was Black—or as the WPA put it, "she has succeeded in making it more difficult for herself by raising a loud and minority voice....And in general showing very aggressive behavior."[62]

By midsummer 1942, the WPA noted that "with all this combination of irritants, plus real physical fatigue, Serena began to develop manic symptoms...internal pressure, excessive laughing, [and] incoherence being present in her speech."[63] A few months later, the government stopped funding the Boys Club Clinic where she worked. While "all the white hygienists on the project were 'snatched right up' by other employers," Serena found herself commuting to Coney Island to learn industrial machine operating instead. At the end of the year, she took the Civil Service Exam and passed with good marks. The dean at Howard recommended her for a government job in Washington, DC, but there was a seven-part section on the application about arrests. Serena answered honestly, and the WPA wrote her a glowing recommendation explaining her arrest and subsequent triumphs, but Serena never heard back.

Increasingly, having an arrest record was an inescapable censure that permanently destabilized the lives of working-class people. Arrested for being poor, the criminal legal system did its best to ensure they stayed poor forever. Regardless of whether they were convicted, for the rest of their lives they would face questions about their arrests in job interviews, on applications for government assistance, and while trying to get career licenses or join professional organizations. This was a truth universally acknowledged among formerly imprisoned people and those who worked with them. But it wouldn't be until the second half of the twentieth century that academics began to seriously study the stigmatization of arrested individuals—and what they found was deeply disturbing.

One of the earliest criminal stigma studies was done in 1959 by researchers Richard D. Schwartz and Jerome H. Skolnick. The pair employed a law student to pose as an employment agent connecting working-class men with manual labor jobs in the Catskill region of New York. The hypothetical employees were identical except for their arrest records, which were divided into four groups: those who had never been arrested; those who had been arrested and acquitted; those who had been arrested, acquitted, and given a special recommendation from the judge emphasizing their innocence; and those who had been arrested and convicted.

The results were stark. Only 4 percent of those who had been convicted were offered positions (as compared to 36 percent of those with no record), proving that "conviction constitutes a powerful form of 'status degradation' which continues to operate after the time when, according to the generalized theory of justice underlying punishment in our society, the individual's 'debt' has been paid."[64] When it comes to the failure of prisons to "rehabilitate" those they incarcerate, this is the other half of the equation: not only do detention institutions offer few to no services or vocational training, but once formerly incarcerated people are back on the outside, no one gives them a chance.

Even more damning, according to Schwartz and Skolnick, was the treatment of those who had been acquitted. Despite being just as innocent as those without any record, only 12 percent of those resumes received positive responses. Having a letter from the judge made some difference, but only some, as those resumes were called back just 24 percent of the time. Any brush with the criminal legal system seemed to taint these individuals for life, making a lie of our supposedly fundamental belief that an arrested person is innocent until proven guilty, or is redeemed after doing their time.

On the flip side, while there is no "causal link between incarceration rates and crime," in 1974, federal researchers discovered there is a "direct correlation between unemployment rates and incarceration."[65] In other words, our criminal legal system makes it harder for people to be employed, while knowing full well that unemployment is directly correlated to crime.

In the decades since these studies were done, remarkably little has changed. In 2001, Harvard sociologist Devah Pager created a more robust version of the resume experiment. This time, pairs of testers were sent to act as actual applicants at 350 entry-level positions in Milwaukee. In each pair, one person had no arrests while the other had a single nonviolent drug conviction. The size of Pager's study allowed her to look at the effects of racism as well as incarceration. White applicants with no criminal records faired the best, with 34 percent being called back (almost identical to the results Schwartz and Skolnick found forty years earlier). White applicants with a criminal record were called back only 17 percent of the time—which was still more often than Black applicants with *no* criminal record (who were called back only 14 percent of the time). Black applicants with a criminal history fared the worst, receiving callbacks a paltry 5 percent of the time. Much as it was for Alison C. in the 1930s, whiteness is still a powerful force when it comes to overcoming the stigma of incarceration.

Prison administrators at the House of D were well aware of the difficulties that formerly incarcerated people faced, and while they noted the importance of employment and vocational training, they were never able to provide them adequately. A few years after the Schwartz and Skolnick study, the Vocational Rehabilitation Administration—part of the US Department of Health—came to the House of D to create "a definitive plan for the restoration of [incarcerated women] to the community...which would substantially reduce the incidence of recidivism. This plan was to incorporate vocational training, or re-training, as a central theme."[66] Unfortunately, at the end of the initial planning period, the authors abandoned the idea, concluding that "the program of vocational education...was very much needed but the facilities in the Women's House of Detention were not appropriate."[67] The prison was overcrowded, underfunded, and serving multiple pop-ulations with conflicting needs; nothing functional could be built on those shifting sands.

The only vocational opportunities that ever existed in the prison "trained" women for the same work they had always been given, as maids or wives: working in the laundry (which employed a few dozen women at a time) or in the kitchen (which took a smaller number). A beauty parlor was added to the House of D in the early 1950s, but al-though the training was useful, formerly incarcerated individuals were banned from obtaining beauty licenses in New York State until 1957, and in 1958, the program graduated a single licensed beautician.

For Black women like Serena, this stigmatization was com-pounded by racism and assumptions of Black criminality (as Devah Pager's study showed), but formerly incarcerated working-class white women—like Ann—were also routinely denied employment because of their records.

While Serena was being ignored by the Civil Service, Ann was bouncing from nursing job to nursing job. Despite the low expecta-tions of her family, according to Dr. Henriette Klein at the House of D, and nearly every person she encountered at the WPA, Ann was a hard worker who was determined to support herself. Nursing had some excitement and variability to it, which suited her personality, and there were always jobs to go around—especially during the war (if you were willing to lie about your record). Indeed, unlike Serena, Ann had few problems *getting* work, but invariably either her arrest record or her sexuality was discovered and she was let go. As much as anything else, she was a victim of the US administrative state and its surveillance, both of which expanded exponentially in the forties.

After a year of glowing reviews, Ann was fired from her first hospital placement because "her fingerprints were checked and it was discovered that she had a record."[68] Ann left her next job under strange circumstances, with her file noting only that her work was praised but she was fired after she "got into an argument with the superintendent" because he had caught Ann and her female "roommate" going to a tavern.[69] She lost her next job because she was in the House of D on another shoplifting charge and missed work. While in prison, her mother died, and Ann was forbidden to go to the funeral (though she was allowed, while handcuffed and under guard, to see her mother's body in the funeral home). When she was finally released, the WPA acted as her reference for yet another nursing gig, but when her supervisor discovered how Ann knew the organization, she was dismissed.

Out of work again, and now living with her brother, Ann took a bottle of sleeping pills. She quickly changed her mind and raced out to a candy store, where she used the phone to call the WPA. But no one answered, and Ann passed out and was rushed to the hospital in a coma. When asked why she had done it, Ann gave two reasons: "difficulty about jobs" and "her constant worry over the heavy growth of hair on her face and body."[70]

Three months later she was back working at a new hospital—a job she walked out of to go hitchhiking with another girl. Her next job lasted a month before they discovered her arrest record and fired her. She was at her next job for over a year, but her coworkers taunted her about her facial hair. One told Ann that "probably the reason she had such a growth of hair on her face and neck was that she was homosexual," a word Ann had trouble pronouncing.[71] Ann disagreed, saying she would believe that if she were "'flat in front,' but she has 'a large bust.'"[72] Still, she followed her coworker's advice and went to see the woman's mother for electrolysis—but her mother, it turned out, had volunteered as a doctor in the House of Detention. Terrified, Ann broke off the appointment and soon quit that job.

This pattern would continue for the rest of Ann's life.

Distrusting someone because of a previous arrest was not a new phenomenon. But the world was growing ever more interconnected and well recorded, making it harder and harder to escape your past. According to queer historian Christopher Mitchell, in the mid-twentieth century, life was "increasingly regulated, and the regulations were increasingly uniform" around the country.[73] "Police and vice squads start[ed] to be more purposefully organized...and [were] obviously coordinating with each other."[74] In his research, Mitchell found that police around the country started to warn each other about specific individuals, shared techniques for conducting raids and sweeps, developed mutually agreed upon definitions for what qualified as things like "disorderly conduct," and distributed information about the psychological and sociological makeups of criminal types, including "the homosexual."

Fingerprinting—pioneered on women arrested for sex work in New York—was now routine in police departments around the country, creating long paper trails with every arrest—and during the mobilization for World War II, it spread far beyond police usage. In 1939, the military pushed to create "an accurate and complete record of the fingerprints" of every service member, held not at the War Department (where they had been previously) but in the Department of Justice, where they could be examined for nonmilitary purposes more easily.

By 1940, the army had around 5 million fingerprints on file, and the navy 1.5 million.[75] But these were far outstripped by the Federal Bureau of Investigation, which had collected "about 18 million sets" of fingerprints.[76] New York City police had 1.7 million additional "criminal fingerprints," as well as the fingerprints of "all civil service employees of the city government, including policemen, firemen, clerks, and hospital employees" (like Ann and Serena), "some 27,000 subway employees," and 150,000 civilians who voluntarily requested fingerprinting.[77] Members of juries were routinely fingerprinted, as were audience members who came to hear the police speak about their activities, members of the Boy Scouts, schoolchildren, bank tellers, and airline employees. In August 1940, the New York City police decreed that anyone who worked in entertainment—"financial backers, operators, maîtres d'hotel, waiters, busboys, everyone down to the lowest scullion"—was to be fingerprinted, as part of a massive attempt to contain and control the city's nightlife.[78] For this, they set up a special fingerprint drive, located (of course) in Greenwich Village.

Other nonpolice, government administrative initiatives were also making it more difficult for formerly arrested people to make new lives. The 1940s saw the entrenchment of the modern American administrative state, which emerged initially as a response to the Great Depression but was expanded and legitimated by the war, which required massive government coordination around the country. According to law and political science professor Mariano-Florentino Cuéllar, "By the end of the war…the public was far more exposed to powerful, adaptive federal agencies of nationwide scope.…The resulting framework led to a surge in the power and size of the federal administrative state."[79]

As just one example, the 1936 creation of the Social Security Index (SSI)—intended to facilitate the government provision of care to incapacitated individuals and families—was also the development of a countrywide database of permanent identification information. As organizations like the WPA helped their clients sign up for SSI (something they did with almost every woman they saw in the forties, including both Serena and Ann), they bound them more tightly to the web of the government, which made them trackable, traceable, and virtually unemployable.

For Ann and Serena, this meant a lifetime of surveillance and punishment.

During the war, the need for workers was so great and the intervention of the government into the labor market was so widespread that even with all of these issues, Serena and Ann largely managed to get by. Serena was eventually hired by the Civil Service of New York City, and Ann by Bellevue Hospital, so the WPA closed Serena's case in the summer of 1944 and Ann's in the fall of 1945.

Within a few years, both would be unemployed, back getting assistance from the WPA, and on their way to being involuntarily committed for most of the 1950s.

But at the same time that Ann and Serena were moving on, a new crop of women was filling up the House of Detention—narcotics users. Post World War II, drug use would join sex work as *the* major cause of incarceration at the House of D.

Using, abusing, manufacturing, transporting, selling, and policing drugs has a long and complicated history in America, but in the postwar period, the same expanding administrative state that bedeviled Ann and Serena would fundamentally alter our relationship to narcotics, flooding the House of D with users.

One of those users was Big Cliff, the gender nonconforming person who had been held at Bedford Hills Reformatory in the 1910s. Cliff was joined by a huge number of younger, newly arrested people—women like Tonie B., a young orphan who learned to shoot heroin while in the House of D, and Florrie Fisher, who became the most infamous antidrug campaigner of the 1970s (and the inspiration for Amy Sedaris's character Jerri Blank on the cult classic television show *Strangers with Candy*).[80] Together, their stories illustrate the hidden evolution of our modern war on drugs, which has redefined American incarceration ever since.

CHAPTER 5

The Long Tail of the Drug War

AFTER WORLD WAR II, NARCOTIC USERS RAPIDLY BECAME THE LARGEST population in the Women's House of Detention. In 1932, the year the prison opened, there were just 175 women arraigned on any drug-related (nonalcohol) charges in New York City, and not all served time.[1] In just twenty years, there was a more than 700 percent increase, as the number of people incarcerated on drug charges in the House of D rocketed to 1,317 in 1952.[2]

However, even these escalating incarceration numbers don't capture the full picture, because many people arrested for other reasons were found to be addicted once they were in detention. By 1965, the Department of Correction estimated that 60 percent of people sentenced to the House of D had substance use issues,[3] while the Women's Prison Association estimated it was more like 85 percent.[4] (For comparison, in 2020, the US government estimated that about 65 percent of all incarcerated people nationwide have substance use issues.)[5]

Where was this apparent boom in narcotics addiction coming from?

The drugs these incarcerated people were using—mostly heroin and cocaine—were not new. Instead, the government's approach to

drug use had shifted rapidly over the first few decades of the twentieth century, literally creating hundreds of thousands of new "criminals." Although World War II turbocharged the drug war, to fully
understand the increased criminalization of women and transmasculine drug users, we have to go back to the early twentieth century,
when Big Cliff Trondle was just a kid.

BIG CLIFF LEARNS TO SHOOT HEROIN

One afternoon in August 1913, Big Cliff Trondle was hanging out in
the back of a café on Flatbush Avenue in Brooklyn, having a smoke,
wearing one of his nattiest outfits: a blue serge suit, silk hose, tan ox-
ford shoes, and a newsboy cap. For some unspecified reason, he came
to the attention of a passing police detective, who realized he was
transgender and arrested him for "masquerading in men's clothes."[6]

Prison records are full of "mannish" or "masculine" women, who
may have considered themselves "normal," butch, lesbian, trans, invert, intersex, or something else entirely, but Cliff was the rare early
twentieth-century transmasculine person who had the chance to articulate his gender more specifically to the world.

Cliff caused a spectacle in court when he repeatedly refused to
give his birth name or change into a dress. On the steps of the courthouse, Cliff told the press, "I've always been more boy than girl," and
he sent a letter to President Woodrow Wilson asking for permission
to dress that way, though the president doesn't seem to have ever responded.[7] The first judge to hear Cliff's case threw out the arrest, ac-
curately noting that it was legal for Cliff to dress however he wanted.
Although many people would be arrested for cross-dressing over the
course of the twentieth century, the actual 1845 New York State law
criminalized "masquerading" *only* if it was done as a disguise while
committing another offense.

Unfortunately, the legality of Cliff's clothes made no difference.
While he was in pretrial detention, a court-appointed probation officer discovered Cliff's birth name. With that, she found that Cliff was
seventeen (not twenty-four as he claimed). He had been thrown out

by his well-off family and had passed through a number of institutions for "wayward girls." The probation officer took it upon herself to ensure that Cliff would be incarcerated and thus, in her eyes, fixed. When the judge threw out his original case, she immediately had Cliff rearrested, this time under a charge of "associating with idle and vicious persons"—aka smoking with men in a café.[8]

This charge was brought in front of a new magistrate, who made it clear that Cliff's gender identity was the reason he was given a three-year sentence (the maximum possible). "I sent her to the Bedford Reformatory," the magistrate told the papers, "because I believe she is a moral pervert. No girl would dress in men's clothing unless she is twisted in her moral viewpoint."[9]

(Given Cliff's chosen name, public statements, and usual manner of dress, I use male pronouns for him, but his gender journey is a long one that can only be partially reconstructed from the existing record. But however he understood his internal gender identity, he was masculine of center, and persecuted for it.)

At the reformatory, Cliff heard some incarcerated women talk about the good money they made as prostitutes, and listened closely. When he was released in 1916, he started turning tricks, and he was arrested in 1918 on a charge of vagrancy prostitution. It was then that he first started using heroin, which was easily smuggled in and out of detention institutions by both incarcerated people and guards. He "was the non-drug inmate in a whole cell block of drug addicts" and "found it almost impossible to sleep," so he asked a cellmate to give him a shot.[10] For the next twenty-five years, he would be on and off opiates and in and out of jail. Sometimes he would kick it—usually after a cold-turkey stint in the "junkie tank" in prison—but he always went back.

In 1918, it was legal, under some circumstances, to shoot heroin in New York (although not in jail). By the time the House of Detention opened in 1932, not only was it illegal, it was considered such an irredeemable vice that most social service organizations, like the WPA, would not work with drug users like Big Cliff.

What had changed in the interim?

Up through the earliest part of the twentieth century, the most common opiate users in America were middle-class white women, who got drugs legally from local pharmacies, the Sears and Roebuck catalog, and their family physicians. The most common use for opiates was menstrual pain, but they were also taken for everything from asthma to surgery. Starting in 1909, however, the US government slowly began to criminalize these drugs. In the beginning, these laws weren't really even about drug use, they were exercises in state power—compromises, distractions, and bargaining chips in the game of empire. As drug war historian Kathleen Frydl put it, "The modern drug war is, almost entirely and most importantly, a way for the state to accomplish something else."[11] But once the door was opened, temperance true believers—the same ones who would enact Prohibition in 1920—smashed right through, turning America year by year into the moralizing, backward, alarmist, antidrug, and anti-science country we have been ever since.

America's first national attempts at drug criminalization were aimed at opium. At the turn of the twentieth century, the government was looking for a way to thaw relations with China, as it had spent much of the late nineteenth century agitating against—and ultimately banning—Chinese immigration. The Chinese government had long been frustrated by the British empire's "compulsion to allow the opium trade," so banning the drug in the United States seemed like an easy peace offering.[12]

In order to avoid interrupting the booming American opium business, offending rich white opium users, or pissing off state governments (who had the power to directly control medical regulations), the federal government carefully crafted the Opium Exclusion Act in 1909 to ban *only* the importation of smoking opium. By focusing on imports, not use, they avoided interfering with the powers of the states, and by focusing on *smoking* opium, which was almost exclusively used by people of Chinese descent, they avoided criminalizing rich white people. Even the name of the act was carefully chosen, based on the law that had banned Chinese immigration, the Chinese Exclusion Act.

This was our first national drug prohibition law, and its racist distinction between acceptable and unacceptable kinds of opium would be echoed in later drug policies (such as the incredible disparities in the treatment of powder cocaine and crack in the 1980s).

Arrests of people of Chinese descent on drug-related charges immediately skyrocketed, public acknowledgment of legal white women opium users decreased, and the racially coded image of the criminal, poor, urban "dope fiend" was born. By 1910, newspapers would go so far as to claim that the word *dope* itself was "coined by Chinamen" and "can be traced back to Frisco's dingy opium dens"—when in fact it came from the Dutch word *doop*, for a thick liquid dipping sauce.[13] Although the cities, races, and drugs would change, this racist boogeyman would endure.

The American public had been fed stories of drug-addled, dangerous "Chinamen" for decades (to fuel the campaign to outlaw Chinese immigration), so the Opium Exclusion Act met little organized resistance. But for true believers, it didn't go far enough.

Out on the edges of the American empire, the United States was still happily making money on opium. Since 1898, when the United States colonized the Philippines during the Spanish-American War, the government had been collecting taxes on the large opium business that occurred on the islands. This angered temperance activists at home, particularly those who also believed in American exceptionalism, an ideology that sees the United States as a moral beacon to the world. Christian missionaries urged the US government to crack down on opium in the Philippines, and in 1912, twelve countries (including the United States) signed the International Opium Convention, in which they pledged to ban opium. As this new international treaty made no distinctions between *kinds* of opium, prohibitionists saw an opening to further criminalize drug use in the United States, and used the existence of the treaty to help pass a new federal law: the Harrison Narcotics Tax Act of 1914.

Even as this was being done, comparatively little was said about drug use or drug users like Big Cliff. According to drug war historians, the act was sold in Congress as being about "international obligations rather than domestic morality."[14]

Why?

Largely because most American citizens didn't care much about drug use, and trying to outright ban drugs would probably have failed. Grandmas used opium. Coca-Cola had cocaine in it. Edibles were sold for menstrual cramps. Drugs were as American as apple pie.

So the teetotalers had to get creative.

The Harrison Act actually didn't *ban* opium. What it did was require anyone who imported, manufactured, or sold opioids or cocaine to register with the government and pay regulatory taxes. These kinds of taxes aren't really intended to raise money, but instead, to punish those involved in the taxed goods, in an effort to regulate their use. It's the way we treat cigarettes today, and once upon a time, all drug enforcement in the United States operated on this kind of regulatory model.

The act was mostly aimed at large-scale drug production and importation. Technically, it didn't penalize the use of the drugs themselves, because again, that was seen as infringing on states' rights. However, it contained an important clause, which made it illegal for a medical professional to dispense a narcotic to a patient *solely* to prevent withdrawal symptoms. Not only did this clause prevent individual doctors from helping individual users, it also made it impossible to do most treatment research on drug addiction (because you couldn't give drugs to people with opioid addiction *just* for being addicted).

Prior to this point, all someone like Big Cliff had to do was get a doctor to write him a prescription for heroin, and he was set. Now, unless that person had a specific medical condition, that was illegal. Big Cliff could legally possess heroin, and he could legally take heroin—but he couldn't legally *buy* heroin without proof of an approved medical condition.

Thus, the government created a large, unregulated, and underground demand for drugs. Unsurprisingly, illicit supply chains arose to meet the needs of nonprescription users like Big Cliff—the beginnings of the international drug trade. In fact, the more we criminalized drugs, the more we created criminals, both by outlawing previously legal behaviors *and* by creating whole new classes of criminal activity.

Step by step, the government was forging an understanding of addiction not as a medical issue but as a moral and legal one. As one textbook for hospital administrators put it, "The six years following the passage of the Harrison Narcotic Act is unparalleled in medical history....At least a million citizens were turned, by a wave of the legislative wand, from sick people into criminals."[15]

Why "six years"? Because while the Harrison Act punished importers and doctors, it didn't criminalize users themselves. That needed to happen at the state level, which meant that prohibitionists needed a PR campaign to push states to pass their own laws modeled off the Harrison Act, but aimed at drug *users*. Since it had worked so well with smoking opium, prohibitionists returned to their racist, hyperbolic playbook—now with government support. They pushed a new party line, which said that all drugs were inevitably habit forming, all drug users were violent criminals, and there was an inherent connection between people of color and drug use. They spread their new antidrug gospel in every way they could, from organizing public lecture tours to feeding stories to friendly journalists.

For instance, here's how the *Buffalo Sunday Morning News* described "the character of the Mexican" the year the Harrison Act was passed:

> To Europeans (of course I include Americans in that term) the Mexican mind is a mystery; just as much a mystery as the Chinese mind....
> But clearly the Mexicans are Asiatic....A Tehuantepec woman smoking a cigar could pass easily for "the Burmese girl a-sitting" on the road to Mandalay....They [both] madden themselves also with a drug called marihuana. This has strange and terrible effects.[16]

From this point on, as the *Virginia Law Review* pointed out in 1970, "with ever-increasing frequency and venom, [the drug user] was portrayed in the public media as the criminal 'dope fiend.'"[17]

Locales around the country raced to pass new laws based off the Harrison Act and its propaganda. That same year, New York State passed the Boylan Act, which was basically the same as the Harrison

Act, except that it placed criminal punishments onto the *users* of "habit-forming drugs" rather than their doctors.[18] Anyone possessing heroin or cocaine without a doctor's prescription could be fined up to $500 and sent to jail for up to a year.[19] Simultaneously, New York City amended its health code to place similar punishments on users of marijuana. There was remarkably little understanding of what these drugs actually were or did; in praising these new laws, the *New York Times* reported that "[marijuana] has practically the same effect as morphine and cocaine."[20]

The Boylan Act was the law that sent Big Cliff to the House of D repeatedly, and it would provide the template for the next evolution in the drug war, twenty years later.

In the meantime, however, negative press poisoned the public against drug users, and new laws packed them into our overcrowded, underfunded, and ultimately unprepared prisons. New York City knew this would happen, but no one cared. The year the Boylan Act was passed, the commissioner of correction admitted there would be "a great increase in the number of prisoners committed to city institutions after the new law gets to work," and that "these institutions are now [already] full."[21] The reason the House of Detention had originally been designed to have a large hospital was in part to treat these newly criminalized drug users. But the increasing racist stigmatization of users meant that when the time came to build the prison, no one wanted to spend money on them. Instead, the hospital was reduced to just twenty-nine beds to handle *all* medical needs in the House of D (including the American Plan's ongoing imprisonment of women suspected of having STIs).

As for users like Big Cliff?

By all accounts, addicts in the House of D were abandoned to their withdrawal. In official documents, administrators euphemistically referred to giving people like Big Cliff "the cure," but that usually meant two weeks cold turkey, with perhaps an occasional aspirin. Even the prison staff wrote the word "cure" in scare quotes. For many drug users, withdrawal symptoms commenced almost immediately upon arriving at the House of D. As one wrote about her experiences there years later,

At 2 A.M., about six hours after I was busted, it really broke loose. I vomited, my bowels and bladder couldn't be controlled, I was wetting and dirtying myself and screaming for help. Right away, I was busted to the junkie tank....The next morning I was in the shower with the dry heaves, sweating, then freezing with chills, my insides ripping apart.[22]

Though the "junkie tank" was usually physically segregated from the rest of the inmates, sometimes by as many as four floors, the excruciating sounds of users going through withdrawal reverberated throughout the House of D at all times.

Big Cliff didn't talk much about his experiences in the House of D (though he was in and out many times over the course of the 1930s and early '40s), but he made an impression on Polly Adler, an infamous madam who later wrote about her time in the House of D.

This was how Polly was introduced to Cliff:

I was awakened out of a deep sleep by frightened cries from the floor above me. A woman was screaming, "Please, God, let me die." Then she called for help again and again. Then, suddenly, the screams were shut off. In the silence I wondered what time it was. I tossed from side to side. The last hour of rest was interrupted by screams from the floor below. A woman kept shouting hysterically, "You dirty sons of bitches, let me out of here. I'll kill you for this, you sons of bitches...." Suddenly it was six thirty. The main switch that opened the cell doors creaked into action. I rushed off to the shower room. "Jeez, I didn't get a wink last night," said one inmate. "Me neither," chimed in another. "I felt sorry for the poor dame. I think it was Big Cliff; she musta wanted to die; it's her fourth day in the tank and that's the worst."[23]

Drug users were stuck in a negative feedback loop from hell: They had to get drugs illegally, so they were sent to prison, where they were tortured and then released. With a record, they could no longer be employed, and because of the Harrison Act, they couldn't get treatment either. So why not go back on drugs? To the rest of the country, opioid users now looked like pathetic, criminal failures, rather than society ladies with jeweled lockets full of laudanum. The prohibition PR campaign that taught Americans to hate drug users had become a self-fulfilling prophecy.

By the time Big Cliff first showed up at the WPA in 1935, the staff there "felt justified in closing its doors" on users, but they made an exception for Big Cliff.[24] Why? Because the staff at the House of D said that Big Cliff "seems completely changed."[25] Partially, this was because he said he wanted to get off drugs—but that had been true many times before. In the main, it appears that Big Cliff was accepted for services because he also wanted to stop being Big Cliff.

According to his WPA file, Cliff was struggling with "great guilt concerning homosexuality," and it seems that he may have been trying to socially de-transition or go stealth, turning away from the life—and gender—he had lived for so many years.[26] He began telling people to call him by his birth name instead of Cliff. He asked the WPA to help him afford a dress (they noted the rest of his clothing was uniforms), and he aggressively pursued psychiatric therapy.[27]

Cliff also tried to reconnect with his sisters, but when the WPA contacted them, they "spoke with disgust of the life" Cliff had lived, and refused to introduce him to his nieces and nephews (though he was allowed to meet them once, under a fake identity).[28]

From the records, it seems as though this may not have been Cliff's first attempt at conforming to a gender role to please his family—in 1925, he was listed in the New York State census as being married to a man named Billie, and living with his mother. But that relationship was long over by the time he was at the WPA. Perhaps after a lifetime of fighting to live as he wanted, he simply didn't have it in him to fight anymore.

For the first eighteen months he received services from the WPA, Cliff stayed sober and straight and worked as a hospital attendant, but it didn't last. He hooked up with a woman who gave him a shot, then he used on his own, lost his job, started looking sick, and eventually, with the assistance of a doctor at the House of Detention, voluntarily checked himself in to detox at Metropolitan Hospital. But "the nurse on duty told [him] that they planned to make it as difficult for [him] as possible as they did not want drug addicts there any way."[29] He checked out after only one day and was rearrested shortly thereafter.

Unfortunately for Big Cliff, things had changed since his early drug arrests. In 1922, the federal government passed the Jones-Miller Act, which banned the importation of heroin. Anyone found possessing the drug was *presumed* to have imported it illegally—a clever work-around to keep the law within the bounds of the powers of the federal government. The penalty for a first arrest was incredibly harsh: a minimum of five years.[30] However, Cliff continued to be arrested and charged only under New York State's Boylan law, *until* the passage of the next major step in federal narcotics regulation, the Uniform State Narcotic Drug Act (USNDA) of 1932.

In essence, the USNDA provided model legislation to the states, which took the reach of New York's Boylan Act—covering many more drugs than just opiates—and combined it with the harsh penalties of the federal Jones-Miller Act. The government's model legislation included a mandatory minimum two-year sentence for a first violation; five years for a second (or a first violation of this law plus a violation of any other drug law); and a minimum of *ten years* for a third. Anyone with multiple convictions was not eligible for parole, probation, or a suspended sentence. (In 1951, these mandatory minimums would be made even harsher by the federal Boggs Act, which also added marijuana to the law.)

Much as the Harrison Act had sundered drug users from doctors, cutting them off from one of the few legitimate sources of support they had, the USNDA cut away at the ability of judges to mete out sentences that were proportionate to the cases in front of them— further isolating drug users from those with the most institutional power to help them and greatly expanding our prison populations.

The real problem for Big Cliff, however, was that the USNDA *also* melded federal and local law enforcement, giving the federal government infinitely more soldiers for their budding drug war.

Immediately after the passage of the USNDA, the federal government started to flex its new muscle. In December 1934, federal narcotics agents conducted simultaneous raids across the country, arresting over five hundred people. Not coincidentally, the raids were conducted "on the eve of a national crime conference called to weld all Federal and local agencies in a combination to put still greater pressure on the underworld."[31] Larger raids soon followed, such as one in March 1935, when the Treasury Department coordinated their "greatest [raid] ever undertaken," using twelve thousand local law enforcement agents in a hundred cities.[32]

When Big Cliff started using again, it was only a matter of time before he ran afoul of the increased federal power of the USNDA. When he was arrested in June 1937, he was tried in federal court and given five to ten years—one of "the severest [drug] sentences given here," according to a newspaper report.[33]

Cliff had been incarcerated fifteen times in the last twenty years, yet somehow, he remained hopeful. He knew that what he really needed was a job, and to be separated from the acquaintances he had made in his years in New York's underworld, so he begged to be sent to Alderson Federal Prison Camp in West Virginia, where he could "take advantage of the excellent training resources"—resources that were nonexistent in the House of D.[34] He hoped that if he did so, he wouldn't be returned to New York when his time was up.

But nothing worked out the way Cliff wanted, and in 1941 he was sent back to New York City. In prison, he'd trained for factory work, but "the machine cutting which [Cliff] learned at Alderson is of no use to [him] now as that is generally considered a man's work and [Cliff] could only do it because of [his] unusual masculine strength. Only men are employed at it in NY."[35]

Cliff tried to return to nursing, but much like Ann and Serena, he quickly discovered that "hospital work...is out of the question with the new rules about fingerprinting and employing no one with a record."[36]

In 1941, the Home Relief Bureau contacted the WPA for assistance on Cliff's behalf. The WPA curtly responded that they "had spent a great deal of time and money on [Cliff]" and they "did not believe there was more" they could offer.[37]

One year later, Cliff's "bruised and battered body" was found in the Elmwood Hotel, presumably murdered by a john (who was never arrested).[38] Cliff was identified by the pawn tickets in his pocket, and neither his family nor the WPA would claim his body. According to his parole officer, "The 'street girls' took up a collection...and kept [Cliff] out of potters field." The WPA recorded his final resting place as Mount Cedar Cemetery, Staten Island, but no such cemetery exists. Instead, Cliff is buried in an unmarked grave in Mount Olivet Cemetery in Queens: Lot 49A, Section E, Grave 14Tem. He seems never to have known his birthday—it isn't even listed on any official documents, like his Social Security application—but the census says he was born in March, should you care to visit him.

Despite the increasingly punitive approach to drugs that developed over Big Cliff's lifetime, it wasn't until after World War II that arrests really took off. Initially, this was about supply. "The near total cessation of commercial trade" during the war induced a "remarkable, albeit temporary, drought in illicit narcotics," according to historian Kathleen Frydl.[39] America's antidrug warriors incorrectly interpreted this as a sign that their moralistic approach to narcotics was working. So, when trade and tourism rebounded after the war, bringing drugs along with them, they doubled down on their criminal approach. As true believers in their own propaganda, they refused to see drug use and addiction as common features in all human life, and instead spun complicated conspiracy theories that demonized nonwhite drug users almost exclusively, at home and abroad.

Additionally, World War II had—quite by accident—put the final nail in the coffin of the regulatory tax approach that had ruled drug policy in the nineteenth and early twentieth centuries. Wars were expensive, and to pay for this one, the US government turned to an underutilized, highly contentious source: the federal income tax. Before the war, most Americans didn't pay income taxes, and they viewed them with the jaundiced eye of a people whose founding mythology was tightly tied up in refusing to pay the government for things. Patriotic fervor changed all of that, and "in 1943, the government mandated extension of the income tax to everyone with an income of

$600 or more."[40] About twenty-six million people paid income taxes in 1942; in 1943, the year before Big Cliff was murdered, it was nearly forty million.[41] All other functions of the Treasury Department were swamped by the need to collect, manage, and disperse this phenomenal volume of revenue. Piddly little regulatory taxes—which raised no money and required much oversight—were now seen as distractions, at best. In the end, the regulatory approach lost, not because it didn't work, but because the federal government wanted to use taxes for other things. The administrative state was left holding the bag on drug control, and they were eager to let it go.

Antidrug prohibitionists rushed to fill this enforcement void, using their two favorite tools: over-criminalization and racist hysteria. Black communities around the country would bear the brunt of our expanding racist drug war from now on. Not only did these tactics do nothing to stop drug use, many of the Black women who were arrested post World War II would, like Big Cliff, first be exposed to drugs in prison.

So it was for Tonie B., a young Black orphan from the Bronx who was initially arrested after a robbery in 1946. After the end of World War II, it was increasingly rare for drug users, particularly if they were Black and/or queer, to receive any kind of post-prison services—making their experiences some of the hardest to document from existing records. An exception was made for Tonie…for a time.

THE LONELINESS OF TONIE B.

Tonie B.'s young life was marked by uncertainty. Starting at the age of two, her mother handed her off to institutions and relatives; she ran away for the first time at just four years old. She had a son at fifteen and put him up for adoption; she hoped to be able to get him back when he turned ten. She was short, stocky, and very light-skinned; people variously responded to Tonie as white, Black, or Latina, depending on the context in which they met her. In all her official records, however, she was simply listed as "Negro" or "mulatto."[42]

No one knew quite how to handle Tonie. In fact, no one seemed to know Tonie very well at all, except perhaps for her boyfriend, an Italian man who was forty years older than she was. Police, prison officials, parole officers, and nearly everyone else involved in the carceral system labeled Tonie angry, closed off, depressed, uncooperative, and—eventually—a "psychopathic personality," just like Louise and Ann in the 1930s.[43] Yet even the court psychiatrist who labeled her psychopathic admitted that she was "without psychosis," showing that this diagnosis was still being used, not to arrange for appropriate care for incarcerated women, but simply to blame them for the system's failures.[44]

Thankfully, a psychiatrist at the House of Detention pushed back against the diagnosis, telling the staff at the WPA that "there is nothing psychopathic about [her] attitude…the girl's withdrawn and remote appearance is simply a conscious effort to keep people from finding out more about her."[45] In juvenile detention, Tonie was found to have a low-average IQ of 85; tested again, on the outside, by a psychiatrist who knew little of her history, she scored 123, or "superior intelligence."[46]

Tonie began receiving services from the WPA in early 1947, after an arrest for robbery in the first degree, the circumstances of which seem as odd and unreliable as the rest of her official history. On a hot night in June 1946, she was hanging out in the cool green shade of Mt. Morris Park in Harlem (which is today Marcus Garvey Park), drinking whiskey with some friends. In the park at the same time, a man named Robert Scott was mugged and beaten by several people. His assailants made off with his wallet, $45 in cash, and an expensive watch. The police were called and a crowd formed around them. Seeing Tonie in the throng, Scott told police she was the one who had beaten him over the head with a bottle, and she was arrested. Inexplicably, in Scott's version of the events, Tonie had stayed to wait for the police while her co-conspirators fled.

Tonie had neither the watch, wallet, nor cash on her. There were no other witnesses. Tonie proclaimed she was innocent; the cops added charges of resisting arrest and assaulting an officer, which were dropped with no explanation before the case came to trial. When asked later, Tonie continued to deny the mugging but was resigned to being punished regardless, saying there "is just nothing one could do about it" and besides, "there might have been other crimes for which she was not apprehended."[47] Tonie was found guilty and sentenced to six months in the House of Detention.

In all likelihood, Tonie was arrested simply for being a Black woman in the wrong place at the wrong time (that place and time being as much post–World War II New York as Mt. Morris Park after a mugging). In the aftermath of the Second World War, several major trends—the growing surveillance of Black communities by the police (which was both part of and fueled by the drug war); a growing Black population; and a violently segregated housing market—intersected to disastrous effect for women like Tonie.

At this time, America's top dog in its war on drugs was a man named Harry Anslinger, a racist, Prohibition true believer, who led the Bureau of Narcotics for thirty-two years, from 1930 to 1962.

According to meticulous research done by drug war historian Kathleen Frydl, Anslinger "believed himself to be squaring off against a largely black population of addicts."[48] He claimed—with zero corroboration—that "85 percent" of drug users were Black.[49] He then used those claims as a basis for directing punitive policing at Black neighborhoods, using the federal and state coordinating abilities created by the USNDA.

Unsurprisingly, arrests of Black people on drug charges went up as a result, justifying more over-policing, harsher punishments, and more vitriolic abuse of Black Americans in the press, ad nauseum.

Even the richest, most famous Black women in America weren't safe. The same year that Tonie first tangled with the law, blues singer Billie Holiday was arrested on drug charges in her own New York City apartment. Holiday's lawyer asked that she be sent to a hospital, for rehab; instead, the judge sentenced her to a year and a day in a reformatory, where "the government was going to give her 'benevolent' treatment."[50] If so, she would have been the first to receive it.

At the same time that these arrests were rising, New York (like many northern cities) had a growing Black population that was demanding the full rights of citizenship. Having fought for freedom abroad in World War II, they saw no reason to settle for less at home. Between 1930 and 1950, the Black population in New York City doubled, to nearly eight hundred thousand people. For the rest of the twentieth century, the Black population in NYC would increase steadily.

Simultaneously, the postwar period was "characterized by large waves of Puerto Rican migration...throughout the Bronx, Manhattan, and Brooklyn."[51] By the end of the 1940s, there were some 190,000 people of Puerto Rican descent living in the city, as well as increasing numbers of people from the Dominican Republic, Haiti, and all around the Caribbean. In official records they were haphazardly coded "Negro" or "white" depending on their skin tone, name, self-presentation, and the biases of the person recording their race.[52]

New York was finally becoming the global, multiracial city we know it as today. However, thanks to racist zoning laws, bank mortgage agreements, property deeds, real estate agents, and housing developers, most Black and Puerto Rican people were forced to live in a select few neighborhoods—Manhattan's Harlem district, Bed-Stuy and Brownsville in Brooklyn, Jamaica in Queens, the South Bronx, etc. This unnatural density created incredible competition for housing in these areas, allowing landlords to jack up prices and refuse to do repairs, degrading the available housing stock, further limiting housing options for Black people, and forcing much of Black community life to happen in public—where it was easily targeted by racist police enforcement. According to Kathleen Frydl,

> Law enforcement in the United States...previously had neglected inner city minority neighborhoods; during the postwar era, they provided service in these areas for the first time, but only with the benefit of the discretionary power afforded to them under illicit drug enforcement, a policing agenda that, unlike other discretionary tools, remained impervious to civil rights reform.[53]

In New York City in the late 1940s and early '50s, "there was an explosion of police violence against Black people...and police officers moved to the front lines of defending white supremacy," according to a history of the city's civil rights movement.[54] The NYPD treated Black neighborhoods almost like occupied territories, and viewed Black residents not as a constituency to be served but as a problem to be controlled.

The occasional federal drug raids of earlier years turned into more generalized police occupation efforts centered in majority Black areas, like Operation 25, which "flooded the precincts" of Harlem with beat cops, or Operation Hazard, which did the same with Brownsville.[55] In 1954, "the entire graduating class of the Police Academy, 413 rookies," were assigned to just two (majority Black) neighborhoods: Brownsville and Jamaica.[56] Who could possibly have believed that filling primarily Black neighborhoods with inexperienced, primarily white, armed cops was a good idea? As Michelle Alexander, scholar of the modern racist drug war, wrote in The New Jim Crow, "Tactics that would be political suicide in an upscale white suburb are not even newsworthy in black and brown communities."[57]

As a result of all these forces, "from 1949 to 1957, the average sentence for narcotic offenses more than tripled, from 19 months to 61.4 months…[and] the percentage of African Americans among those convicted of federal narcotics violations [rose] from 13% in 1946 to 53% in 1957."[58] Harry Anslinger had decided that Black people were criminal drug addicts, and then he created the conditions to make it true.

These police raids didn't target queer people in particular; according to the files of a doctor involved in treating men arrested for homosexuality at this time, "The cops don't bother about the homos in Harlem, they are too poor, not enough graft in it."[59] But Black queer people, like Tonie, were caught up in the raids all the same.

As a medical report so delicately put it, in the House of D, Tonie was "approached by a homo."[60] This contemptuous familiarity was a marked change from the more confused, conflicted, and coded condemnations of earlier years—an indicator of the cultural sea change brought about by World War II. The staff at the WPA were very concerned, feeling that "this was a great danger for [Tonie], because she has never had anyone pay any attention to her on any basis and would probably respond with undue eagerness even to an abnormal approach."[61]

This was something of an odd statement, considering that just a few sentences later, they wrote about Tonie's boyfriend, whom she was hoping to marry when she got out of the House of D. He was a garbage man with the city who had recently retired with a full pension. But right as Tonie was released, disaster struck, and after a short hospitalization, Tonie's boyfriend died, leaving her adrift.

Now free and very much alone, Tonie was desperate to get in touch with her mother, whom she hadn't seen in years. She contacted the Missing Persons Bureau, who started to help her, but when they discovered that Tonie lived in a halfway house, they closed her case.

Depressed and isolated, Tonie told another woman at the WPA that "life wasn't worth living."[62]

Recognizing that Tonie was desperate for connection, the WPA tried to help find her mother, but as they dug into her family history, things became even more confused. Her father had never been in the picture, but Tonie knew his name was Eugene La Fantue and that he was originally from Panama. However, when the WPA dug into *his* history, they found a family court deposition in which he said he was not Tonie's father, but that instead, her father was a Spanish sailor, and her mother was an entirely different woman whom Tonie had never met, who'd left her, as a baby, with Eugene La Fantue and his girlfriend. That girlfriend was the woman Tonie believed to be her mother, and because she was Black, Tonie would be listed as Black in official documents as well—which she may well have been. Certainly, she was raised in Black neighborhoods and institutions. But when she needed to, she easily passed as white, as the WPA discovered by accident while trying to figure out if she was a lesbian.

From the very beginning of their time with her, thanks to her refusal to wear dresses and that "homo" in the House of D, social workers worried about Tonie's sexuality and tried to keep her away from other women. She never connected well with the WPA staff, whose help came with a strong side of surveillance and pity. They didn't even spell her name right, constantly putting it down as "Toni," even on official correspondence. She was eager to move out of their halfway home and into an apartment of her own, so when she found a rooming house nearby, the WPA subsidized her weekly rent. But one evening, when she wasn't at the rooming house, her worker mentioned to another client that she couldn't find Tonie. The other client told her that Tonie had "gone out to meet the girl who is supporting her....She spends most of her time with this girl."[63]

Her social worker rushed to confront Tonie about whether she was still living in the rooming house, and Tonie quickly admitted she wasn't. She didn't mention any woman but said it was because the other residents "found out she was colored."[64] But she still wanted to live in lower Manhattan—a neighborhood that was largely closed off to Black people. She had heard rumors of a building on East Third Street in Manhattan, "where there is a colored superintendent," and she hoped to move there soon.[65]

Her worker, uninterested in the racism or housing issues Tonie was facing, cut her off and "asked if she were involved with some other girl."[66] Tonie was surprised but admitted that yes, she was. Her worker was eager to let her know that this was something they could fix and "point[ed] out that this is not an unusual problem."[67] Tonie's response—"Oh, but I am abnormal"—threw her worker for a loop.[68]

Her worker noted Tonie's "smile of satisfaction" when she said she was abnormal and wrote, "It was hard to discern whether she had a guilty feeling about this or felt that it in some way distinguished her."[69] The worker flailed, suggesting Tonie talk to a psychiatrist or Barbara Manley Philips, and fled the conversation.

This precipitated a downward spiral for Tonie, who ended up back in the House of Detention a month later, where she told them that for the last three weeks, she'd been on heroin. Like Big Cliff, Tonie said she heard about heroin from another woman in the House of D and wanted to try it (most likely, it was that "homo"). Seemingly for this reason alone, the staff at the WPA decided that Tonie was responsible for a recent break-in at their halfway home, in which someone had stolen a radio and silverware. Suddenly, their attitude toward Tonie chilled immensely. Who knows what Tonie's life might have been like if someone had supported her relationship with this other woman, but no one at the WPA even bothered to ask her name.

While detained in the House of D, Tonie kicked heroin cold turkey in the tank, but at trial, her probation officer still recommended the judge lock her away.[70] Thanks to the USNDA, Tonie was looking at a minimum two-year sentence for this, her first drug charge. The judge took pity on her because he felt the mandatory sentencing was unfair, and he dismissed her case entirely. The probation office assumed she would start using again and "refused to work with her," meaning that suddenly, surprisingly, Tonie was completely free.[71]

One would assume that this would be the moment social workers would swoop in: Tonie was out of jail and off probation, and had gone through a brutal three-week detox. Instead, the WPA wrote "D.A." ("drug addict") in red pencil on the front of her file, typed out "DRUG ADDICT" in red ink on the first page of her file, and closed her case.[72]

The closure notes hint at some internal disagreement at the WPA, with the first note saying simply, "It is this organization's policy not to work with drug addicts," and "this girl should be referred elsewhere."[73] The second note, however, suggests this policy chafed at least some workers, in some cases:

> In the opinion of some of us, this was the most interesting and challenging young woman referred to us in some time. It was with a real sense of failure that we had to admit losing her and we would welcome the opportunity of working with her again even within the limits of our policy on drug addicts.[74]

Six years later, in 1954, Tonie popped back up at the House of Detention (vagrancy prostitution this time), looking "exactly the same… except she has a great many tattoos on her arms."[75] Her former worker stopped by briefly to see her, but "did not speak to [Tonie] about her addiction," and the WPA never contacted Tonie B. again.[76]

The queer Black women like Tonie, arrested as a result of our intensifying, nonsensical drug war, are some of the hardest to locate in the historical record. Tonie's story was preserved because she started using drugs only *after* her first interactions with the WPA—and she was likely taken up for those services in part because she was so light-skinned.

Rarely were women like Tonie allowed to publish their own stories. Most social work organizations (like the WPA) refused to work with them. There was no LGBTQ press, social services, or organized infrastructure at this time, and issues of addiction in the queer community were not on anyone's radar (although some people were bemoaning the lack of social outlets aside from bars). People with substance use issues were often considered pariahs in their own communities, and so, while the Black press consistently pushed back against racist over-policing, they still presented Black drug users as villains, or at best, failures. The white press eagerly wrote about Black users and dealers as well, but mostly as stereotypical racist caricatures, and mostly men. When Black women did appear, they were proto welfare mothers or slutty Jezebels—roles that were almost inseparably connected to heterosexuality. Even among other queer drug users, women of color were judged to be particularly licentious. For instance, Florrie Fisher, a white heroin addict who was incarcerated many times in the forties and fifties, opened her memoir with a scene of her forty-third birth-day party, held in the House of D, during which several incarcerated women took turns stripping. Fisher's memoir was filled with lurid de-tails about her sexual exploits, but these were always connected to her drug use. The women of color in the House of D, on the other hand, were "natural strippers" whose bodies gyrated "effortlessly."[77] Their dancing was almost magical, driving men and "lezzies" mad.[78] Fisher was sexually depraved because of drugs; incarcerated women of color were simply sexually depraved, full stop.

This racist exoticization notwithstanding, more women like Tonie were starting to appear at the House of D and the WPA—not just more drug users (though they were brought there too), but more women who saw their sexuality—rather than their gender—as something that distinguished them from other people, in a way that wasn't negative. Unlike the generation before them, these women had grown up with the concept of homosexuality. They didn't need it explained the way Ann, Elaine, and Charlotte once did. They weren't yet organizing politically as queer women (the first group for lesbians in America, the Daughters of Bilitis, didn't start until 1955), but these young women—butches, studs, ky-kys, femmes, lesbians, and bisexuals—were the backbone of early dyke culture that made that organizing imaginable. And many of them were Black women, or women—like Tonie—who slipped uneasily between our limited, binary understanding of race.

Two such women, Renée S. and Bernice D., met through the Women's Prison Association in 1949. Renée was a tall, dark, seventeen-year-old from Georgia; Bernice, a short, twenty-five-year-old, racially ambiguous (but white-identified) orphan from Vermont. Though their lives were incredibly different, they were united by one core belief: that their love for each other was not a problem, pathology, crime, or moral failing.

Throughout the 1950s, women like Renée and Bernice would be joined in prison by another demonized group, who were also unwilling to hide their true selves to avoid being incarcerated: Communists. As America became more conservative, activists like Elizabeth Gurley Flynn, Rosa Collazo, and Claudia Jones faced lengthy prison sentences, police violence, and extradition for their political beliefs.

Unsurprisingly, Communists and homosexuals would become melded together in the American mind—even if the two groups rarely found common cause.

CHAPTER 6

Flickers of Pride

"I LIKE MY OWN KIND"

Renée S. was a tall, dark-skinned girl from Georgia, with an archipelago of white vitiligo spots spread across her neck and face. Like many Black teens, she was assumed to be older by the white social workers and police officers she interacted with, who were surprised to learn she was just seventeen. She was shy and spoke slowly, but she was steely underneath. Unlike most of the girls who passed through the WPA, she hadn't been arrested for anything. Instead, she was on the run from her father, who had beaten her severely for being a lesbian.

From her very first day at the WPA in February 1949, Renée told staff that she had been "that way" since she was just ten or twelve years old.[1] At first, her social worker guessed she meant pregnant. When asked to clarify, Renée said, "I like my own kind."[2] This had caused a rift with her mother back in Thomasville, Georgia, so she'd been sent to live with her father in Harlem—although no one told him why. Her father's new wife, realizing "the hard role that a step-mother plays in a second marriage," put out every effort to get to know Renée, and soon, the two were like sisters.[3]

Nearly a year after she moved to New York, Renée developed a crush on a girl in her neighborhood and wrote her a love letter; disturbed, the girl brought the letter to Renée's stepmother. The stepmother had "a long talk" with Renée, during which she explained "what this type of behavior might lead to."[4] She didn't tell her husband—rightly fearing what would happen if she did. Although it doesn't seem like he'd ever hit Renée before, he'd been "rather brutal" to her stepmother.[5] Her stepmother didn't feel "moralistic" about Renée dating other women, but she did suggest Renée might want to see a psychologist.[6]

Soon, however, rumors started circulating that Renée was dating a new girl, and this time, the stepmother told her husband—likely to preempt his hearing about it from someone else.

Renée's father "seemed understanding" at first, but behind his wife's back, he paid a woman in the neighborhood to have sex with Renée "so that he could get the full details."[7] This backfired and Renée started dating the woman, enraging her father. One day shortly thereafter, he went out all night, got drunk, came home, and demanded his wife have sex with him. She was angry at his behavior and put off by the "liquor on his breath," so she said no.[8] At this, he attacked her savagely, knocked her to the ground, kneeled on her chest, and started to choke her. "You are so cold," he told her, "you must be having an affair with Renée."[9] Then, he turned on Renée and beat her too.

In the morning, the stepmother gathered her stuff, got Renée, and headed to a shelter. When the two were then hooked up with the WPA, she told them "she will never live with the husband again, and wants very much to protect Renée."[10]

A week later, Renée and her stepmother went to Girls' Term (the children's court for girls). Renée's father was there as well, and he insisted on reading the love letters he'd found among her things out loud to the court. He seemed shocked when Renée was removed from his custody.

As for Renée, this hurt her terribly. The first ten months she'd been in New York had been some of the best of her life. Until this happened, her "father was nice to her and did a lot of things which won Renée's respect," and her stepmother was "the only one who has ever understood her" and her sexuality.[11] She thought they'd been able to discuss it openly and that things were fine, never knowing that her new girlfriend had been her father's spy.

Normally in a situation like this, Renée would have been put on probation—not because the court felt she had done anything wrong, but because there were few systems set up to provide care for poor young people, particularly Black people, aside from our carceral one. There was no structure in place to support a family consisting of a teen and her homeless stepmother. Because of the court proceedings, her love letters to other girls were entered into Renée's official file, which would follow her any time she was involved with courts or government agencies. Her only access to psychotherapy would be a doctor at the House of Detention. Through no fault of her own, Renée was now bound up in the carceral state.

However, the WPA intervened in Renée's case, and the court probation officer agreed to let Renée stay off probation, so long as she remained in the WPA halfway house, which was a congenial place with shared bedrooms, living and dining space, and a wealth of programming and services for young women. Renée was one of the first completely out lesbians to live there, it seemed, and this sometimes caused fights with the other girls. After about a month, Renée got into a physical altercation with an Italian American woman named Anna, who mocked her lesbianism. When the WPA staff talked to Anna, she claimed that Renée and another client had attacked her in the bathroom and tried to fondle her. Renée said that wasn't true, but that Anna had bitten her and she had hit Anna, and now she was scared the WPA would throw her out on the street. Her worker assured her that wouldn't happen, but the next day the director of the WPA decided that it would be better for everyone if Renée moved into a Salvation Army shelter—where she would have to pay her own way. Unless she wanted to go on probation, Renée had no choice but to agree. Surprisingly, her father agreed to pick up the tab, though he didn't want her to come home.

This move was "much to the regret of several girls" in the Hopper Home with whom Renée had become good friends. But Renée still spent a lot of time there, hanging out with the girls, taking art class, and having conversations with her social worker. This was how she ended up meeting—and eventually dating—Bernice D.

Bernice had arrived in New York City around the same time that Renée was attacked by her father. She was almost immediately arrested for prostitution and packed off to the House of D, where she tested positive for gonorrhea and was held for treatment. When her case came to the Women's Court, a probation officer was so impressed with her self-presentation, she recommended that Bernice receive a suspended sentence, so she could be hooked up with the WPA for help. In a beautiful colorized photo clipped to the front of her file, Bernice had thick brown hair and prominent front teeth, and wore a small double loop of pearls and stud earrings. She was just over five feet tall. Twice in their very first description of her, the WPA noted her racial ambiguity, saying she "looks very Oriental," and then specifying that she seemed Chinese.[12]

Although the WPA found her "timid," "tense," and "withdrawn" on the surface, they also noted that she had "a great deal of pride," and was determined to make her own way.[13] Soon, however, that pride would manifest in ways the WPA did not expect or encourage.

Like Tonie B.'s, Bernice's childhood was something of a mystery, and as a result, so was her racial identity. She told the WPA that she moved in with her maternal grandmother in Vermont in 1930 and stayed with her for the next decade, until she was sixteen. However, the 1930 census lists her as living at the Providence Orphan Asylum, and she doesn't appear again in public records until 1940, when a newspaper article mentions that she had just moved to South Dorset, Vermont (where her grandmother lived), from Burlington (where the orphanage was located).[14] The 1940 census *does* list her as living with the woman she said was her grandmother—not as her granddaughter, but as the wife of that woman's son. Moreover, Bernice spelled her last name differently from her grandmother, father, and half brother (although the same as her sister, who was also in the Providence

Orphan Asylum), and when asked about her birthday, she said it was in February 1924—one month after the death of the woman she said was her mother.[15] In fact, she told the WPA that all of her relatives were dead.

Official records of the lives of poor people are never very well taken, and as time passes that neglect compounds, degrading what little there is. It's impossible to draw too many conclusions from a tiny pile of hundred-year-old documents.

However, Bernice herself also expressed anxiety about her race, or at least how it was perceived. A few months into her time at the WPA, she suddenly asked her social worker "in a most serious way if worker thought she looked Chinese."[16] She added that "millions of people had mistaken her for Chinese."[17] Despite what she had already written in Bernice's file regarding her race, the worker assured Bernice that Asian people did not have brown feathery hair, and said she should take any such comments as compliments. In a curious note at the end of the transcript of that conversation, the worker added, "She said nothing about being part Indian," though whether this is a reference to something Bernice had mentioned previously or simply a supposition on the worker's part is unclear.[18]

Shortly after she started staying with the WPA, Bernice mentioned to the staff that "she was planning to go in the afternoon to visit" Renée's stepmother, with whom Renée had remained close.[19] Whatever relationship had developed between Bernice and Renée up to this point, it hadn't been considered worth noting, but this was cause for alarm.

Immediately, her worker, Nannie Spraggins (who was now also Renée's social worker), tried to dissuade Bernice from going. She suggested a family visit was too intimate for new friends; Bernice said Renée's stepmother had welcomed her over. Spraggins suggested that instead Bernice take a class at the YWCA, maybe shorthand? But Bernice wasn't interested, and instead they "talked about professional sports" and Bernice's desire to see a real baseball game.[20]

In part, Spraggins seemed unwilling to directly express her fear that the two girls were dating because Bernice was so proper and feminine. "She is always very neat and always pleasant," she wrote. Everyone, staff and clients alike, loved Bernice. Within a week of moving into the Hopper Home, she had a good job at a hospital, and she soon saved up enough to open a bank account. With the money she had left over, she bought fabric and sewing supplies, and began making herself several dresses.

Even though Renée was eight years younger than Bernice, Spraggins had no compunction directly addressing "the problem" with her, likely because she was out, and judged by most people to be masculine (over and over again, Black women, especially those who are dark complected, are judged to be more masculine, aggressive, and less deserving of care than other women). When Bernice didn't catch her hints, Spraggins cornered Renée, "who went so far as to admit this relationship."[21]

Renée was terrified of what might befall the two of them since they'd kicked *her* out of the Hopper Home over just an accusation of lesbianism. She begged Spraggins to bring any consequences down on her and "not accuse Bernice."[22] For the moment, Spraggins decided to ignore their budding romance, hoping it would collapse on its own, as "Bernice seems a very hopeful girl and is bright, etc. and [Spraggins] would hate to see her become involved in something which hinges on the perverted."[23]

Spraggins's hesitance to take action seemed to stem from her having an older, upper-middle-class, body-based understanding of sexuality—similar, perhaps, to what Elaine B. might have learned from reading classic sexology books. At the beginning of the twentieth century, as sexologists could no longer ignore the existence of gender conforming homosexuals who did not fit their theory that deviant sexuality was based on inverted bodies, they began to elaborate between different kinds of inverts. A classic, or congenital invert, was masculine when they should have been feminine (or vice versa), and had a body that was inherently contra-sexed as well. In some cases, congenital inverts may have been people we would today call intersex, but often they were simply presumed to be bodily different because inversion theory proclaimed them so. To this classification, sexologists added the idea of the acquired invert, who was normal in body and properly gendered but had same-sex desires because they were either insane, uncontrollably oversexed, drug-addled, or seduced by a congenital invert.

Upon first meeting Renée, Spraggins told her and her stepmother that "in some cases the condition [homosexuality] was biological and in others acquired."[24] In her case notes, she followed this up by saying that Renée was "physiologically a female, has all the feminine characteristics and…was menstruating."[25] Spraggins clearly hoped that she was not a born invert. There was no question about Bernice, who was definitely the femme to Renée's butch. In Spraggins's mind, if neither of the girls were congenital inverts, it stood to reason that the relationship would peter out.

Over the course of the next month and a half, Spraggins watched the two girls closely. Bernice, she noted, was friendly, cooperative, quiet, and interested in dressmaking, nursing, and other appropriately feminine activities. Renée was "masculine," wanted to wear pants, and got into fights with other women.[26] To Spraggins, this made things clear: Renée was an inverted homosexual, but Bernice was "normal," and "something should be done to break up this relationship."[27]

At the end of May 1949, Spraggins confronted Bernice—who, in turn, confronted Spraggins. With "great precision," Bernice informed Spraggins that she had been waiting for Spraggins to say something: she was in love with Renée and "had no guilt feelings."[28] Bernice then articulated a perfect summation of the mindset of the early homophile rights movement that was developing around the country: "She feels that this kind of abnormal behavior is a way of life and that people should be permitted, without interference, to go on living in this way if it pleases the parties involved."[29]

A shocked Spraggins suggested a psychiatrist, but Bernice wasn't interested. She didn't have a problem; she didn't need a solution. Stymied, Spraggins turned on Renée, who informed her that "no kind of help will 'change me.'"[30] Furthermore, she told Spraggins, "people should be left alone and permitted to live their own lives, even though their way of living may be different from other people who consider themselves 'normal.'"[31] Just a few years earlier, Tonie B. had flaunted being "abnormal"; now, Renée was pushing back on the very idea of "normal" itself.

From this point on, the WPA schemed ways to break the two up. Spraggins told Renée that she'd broken a promise not to develop relationships with other women in the house; Renée, seeing the writing on the wall, stopped visiting the WPA for weeks. This, the workers realized, provided an opening, and they began to invite Bernice to events more frequently, in the hopes of connecting her with more wholesome (heterosexual) people. They sent both women to see psychiatrists who worked at the House of D. Renée, realizing what was going on, skipped her appointment. Bernice went—but only to discuss some employment issues, *not* her sexuality.

Bernice and Renée spent the spring and early summer of 1949 together, largely away from the prying eyes of the WPA. But at the end of July, Nannie Spraggins noted that Bernice was talking about another woman, not Renée anymore, and in August Renée called the WPA and asked them to tell Bernice to return the ring she'd given her (a sign of just how central the WPA was in the lives of these women, even when they were disapproving).

The end of their relationship, however, didn't trigger any kind of sexual identity crisis in either Bernice or Renée, who both continued to have relationships with women. Once she was no longer staying with the WPA, Renée returned to her father's home, and surprisingly, the two made a good go of it—for a while. According to Spraggins, "Her father's attitude had changed somewhat and…he seemed to be making a real effort to understand [Renée] better."[32] He taught her to play golf, and she kept house now that her stepmother was gone. But in October 1949, they got into a fight—apparently over Renée's smoking weed. In response, Renée smashed up her father's car with a javelin, and her father had her arrested and sent to the House of D. When asked where the weapon came from, "she would not tell on the grounds that it might involve the owner of the javelin."[33]

By the time Renée was back out on the street, in 1950, the WPA had officially washed its hands of her, but she stayed in touch with them. Over the next few years, she dropped back at the Hopper

Home a few times—after she had a son; after she joined the Catholic Church; after her father died. "She does not drink as much as she used to," the WPA wrote in 1952, but she was still engaged in "homosexual activity."[34] She worked and lived in the Bronx for the rest of her long life, before passing in 2007 at the age of seventy-five.

After their breakup, Bernice concentrated on her schooling and was determined to get a white-collar, secretarial job, like the other up-and-coming young (white) women of her era. She seemed to have learned her lesson about discussing her personal life with the WPA, and though they kept track of the other gay women with whom she was spending time, she never talked about them. On the spur of the moment one day, she moved to Boston, and when she returned to New York she "kept referring to 'we'"—a hint that the WPA took to mean she had a new girlfriend.[35] A few years later, she followed that woman, or perhaps a different "roommate," to Florida. If she didn't like it there, she told the WPA, "she would be in touch."[36] They never heard from her, and after the 1940 census Bernice D. never shows up in official government records again.

Bernice and Renée declared their pride a year before the initial meeting of the Mattachine Society (the first significant LGBTQ rights organization in the country) and twenty years before the Stonewall Riots gave gay liberation a public face. The traditional story about the birth of gay pride in America sidelines people like them. They are the backdrop to the stories of "important" early organizers, the lumpen proletariat in the bar and the "street people" outside it. In histories of twentieth-century LGBTQ life, working-class, butch-femme, role-playing, and bar-engaged people are generally depicted as self-hating, apolitical, or lacking in self-knowledge—masses awaiting a messiah. The experiences of Bernice and Renée flip that story on its head, and suggest that ideas of self-acceptance and queer liberation were percolating among the most marginalized even before they manifested in well-heeled homophile organizing. But across the board, these first flickers of pride can probably best be understood in terms of the radical Black activist tradition of "freedom dreams"—communal coming to understandings of life as it could be lived, outside of the oppressive forces of white supremacist patriarchy. As trans artist and activist Tourmaline has written, freedom dreams "are born when we face harsh conditions not with despair, but with the deep knowledge that these conditions will change."[37] Crucially, however, these dreams are *communal*—they cannot come about in isolation. For every courageous early homosexual organizer we celebrate—for every Del Martin or Phyllis Lyon, every Harry Hay or Frank Kameny—there were hundreds, perhaps thousands more like Renée and Bernice, dreaming the same freedoms into existence.

At the same time, America was about to enter its most homophobic period, the long national nightmare of idealized heterosexuality that was the 1950s and early 1960s. During the late nineteenth century, sexologists had defined the modern homosexual. In the early twentieth, that definition spread far and wide, as queer people found each other, and were in turn found by doctors, politicians, police, and psychologists, who inherently viewed them through the lens of their professions—which is to say, as problems to be solved. An understanding of what queerness *was*, and what should be done about it, developed gradually, through a process of contestation, a constant drawing and crossing of behavioral lines. These developments carried the baggage of earlier sexual ideas (about sin, about inverted bodies, about disease and insanity, etc.), but they were separate from them. As the records of the House of D show, this evolution was already well under way before World War II, but the war accelerated everything. It provided servicemembers (and their spouses at home) with space to explore these desires, but simultaneously gave the US military the final word in defining homosexuality for most Americans. Drawing from the same poisoned well of psychology as the court system, the military defined homosexuality as a "constitutional psychopathic state."[38] After the war, the image of the duplicitous, pathetic, psychologically stunted, unfit, inherently anti-American homosexual would reign. Its most well-known proponent was a Marine Corps veteran and morphine addict who was plagued by rumors about his own sexuality, who employed as his righthand man the infamous homophobic homosexual Roy Cohn, and who would eventually die of an acute, untreated case of hepatitis—but he's better known today as Senator Joseph McCarthy, the architect of the Red Scare.

THE RED SCARE, THE LAVENDER SCARE, AND THE QUEER COLLATERAL DAMAGE WE DON'T MUCH TALK ABOUT

In February 1950—the same month that Renée and Bernice saw each other for the last time—Senator Joseph McCarthy of Wisconsin threw America into a panic by announcing that he had a list of 205 Communist Party members currently working at the State Department. McCarthy's campaign for his Senate seat had been fueled by a message about being a tough military veteran who would fight the "bureaucrats...seeking to perpetuate themselves forever upon the American way of Life."[39] Communists were both a real concern for the government (this being the beginning of the Cold War) and a convenient line of attack on the growing Democratic administrative state.

Democrats in the State Department quickly responded that they employed no Communists, and had in fact for years been quietly forcing out suspected security risks—including ninety-one homosexuals. Instead of quieting the uproar, this redoubled it. Republicans in the federal government, who had long been out of power and were looking to demonize the party that gave America the popular social programs of the New Deal, seized on homophobia as the perfect weapon—layering a Lavender Scare over the Red. One Republican senator asked during a debate on the Senate floor if his colleagues could "think of a person who could be more dangerous to the United States of America than a pervert?"[40] Communists and homosexuals were linked together as un-American potential security risks, and while this connection was new, it rested on the same homophobia that had been peddled for years: that homosexuals were weak, not to be trusted, invisible, and dangerous to "normal" people. Call it the contagion theory of queerness.

Many Democrats held much the same opinion of homosexuals and were fine with offering them up as sacrificial lambs to quell McCarthy's rise to power. Additionally, a number of Southern Democrats saw the growing federal government as a potential check on states' rights and, specifically, their "right" to enforce white supremacy. Although they found McCarthy and his bombast distasteful, they were in agreement with some of his ultimate goals.

According to David Johnson's incredible book *The Lavender Scare*, although it is much less remembered today, the purge of homosexuals from the government was both widespread and well-known at the time. "While the historical literature about the McCarthy era focuses on the hunt for Communists," Johnson writes, "the typical case involved a homosexual confronted with circumstantial evidence that he had associated with 'known homosexuals' or been arrested in a known gay cruising area."[41]

Over the course of the 1950s, thousands of people would be purged from their government jobs; an unknown number would quit, transfer, or commit suicide to avoid discovery; high-profile, public condemnations of homosexuality would flood the media; and "the notion that homosexuals threatened national security...became accepted as official fact."[42] But the Lavender Scare mostly focused on men (when confronted with the idea of lesbianism during the investigations, one of the leading senators whined, "Can you please tell me, what can two women possibly do?").[43] And it wasn't just *any* men—it was mostly white men with the right background, connections, experience, and education to get good government jobs. The women and transmasculine people who were incarcerated at the House of D had already been blackballed from those positions, already had government files that proclaimed them homosexuals and criminals, and were always already condemned by the good men in the Senate. Had the Lavender Scare been constrained to the back halls of the State Department, it might have missed them entirely. But in this proxy war between pro- and anti-federal-government forces, queer people far from the State Department quickly became collateral damage, as the country gorged on a steady diet of homo-pinko fearmongering.

Rusty Brown was one of the many whose lives were permanently—but almost accidentally—altered by the Lavender Scare. She had heard rumors about antigay purges when she was in the navy during the Korean War, but there were so many queer servicemembers, she assumed it had to be all talk, or perhaps just a danger for those at the very top, the brass in Washington. But when she returned to New York City in 1953 and started working as a drag king, she "was really shocked at the phobia in the United States."[44] Communists and homosexuals were now interchangeable boogeymen. As Brown recalled, "One word against the government, and you were automatically classified as a Communist. And if you were a Communist, you had to be a homosexual."[45]

Fear flooded the country, Brown said. Gay bars (particularly the fancy show bars that catered to tourists) lost patrons and shut down, and no one stepped up to replace them. Businesses instituted loyalty oaths and background checks. In New York, the entertainment industry was particularly hard hit, to the point where even the stagehands were hounded about their sexual and political lives. "They were just seeing hobgoblins behind every tree," Brown recalled.[46] "There was tolerance in the '30s and the '40s," she said. Even while in the navy in the early 1950s, Brown recalled, there were "no snide remarks made or ... [people] trying to make a fight just because they figured I was gay."[47] But the McCarthy era was the turning point, she said, after which regular harassment and homophobic street violence ratcheted up.

For Brown, that homophobia manifested itself in the form of increased police harassment. "I had been arrested in New York more times than I have fingers and toes, for wearing pants and a shirt," she told an interviewer in the early 1980s.[48] Like Big Cliff, Brown found herself running afoul of New York City's anti-masquerade law, or perhaps a more general charge of "disorderly conduct," if she were arrested during a bar raid when she was performing. When that happened, Brown said, the club bosses (most likely mob members or affiliates) would send their lawyers to pay the $50 bail or the $150 fine, and she'd be back out by morning. But a general miasma of hatred toward sexual nonconformity was settling over the country, and in Brown's estimation, even by 1983 (when her oral history was taken), America had never recovered the more tolerant attitudes that existed before World War II.

One thing about the whole Lavender Scare confused Brown: "I never figured out how [McCarthy] equated homosexuality with Communism," she told interviewers. "The Communist Party is as much against homosexuality as anybody else."[49]

This was undoubtedly true about the party itself, but the attitudes of individual members (many of whom had been drawn to the party because of its progressive social positions) ran a wide gamut—as people in the House of D were soon to discover. Under McCarthyism, the prison began to fill with political prisoners for the first time, primarily women arrested for Communist organizing. Just five months after the Red Scare began, Julius Rosenberg was arrested on a charge of espionage, for passing atomic secrets to the USSR. A month later, his wife Ethel was arrested as well. She spent eight months in the House of Detention before being transferred to Sing Sing prison, where she was executed in 1953. The Rosenbergs were "the first U.S. citizens to be convicted and executed for espionage during peacetime" in America.[50]

The women of the House of D remembered Ethel as a bright presence in a dark time. "She had taken a sick prostitute into her cell and cared for her. She sang for the inmates....When she left the House of Detention there was not a dry eye in the place."[51] Stories about her kindness were passed on to the next infamous Communist prisoners at the House of D, who arrived just a few weeks after Rosenberg was sent to Sing Sing: Elizabeth Gurley Flynn, Claudia Jones, and Betty Gannett. All three were part of a wave of arrests designed to break the Communist Party in America. All told, "the Smith Act trials" lasted nine years, were held in more than a dozen cities, and twice had appeals go to the Supreme Court. In total, 144 people were indicted and 105 convicted—most, simply, for being members of the Communist Party.[52]

The real name of the Smith Act was the Alien Registration Act. Passed in 1940, it was a reaction to both the approach of World War II and the growing power of labor, Communist, and socialist organizers during the Depression. As with the drug laws of this period, the Smith Act was designed with an imagined group of external evildoers in mind—in this case, immigrants who wanted to overthrow the government. Thus it did two things: required all adults living in America who were not US citizens to register with Immigration and Naturalization Services, and "made it a crime to advocate the overthrow of any U.S. government."[53]

During World War II, when the United States needed the cooperation of the USSR, no Communist Party leaders were targeted under the Smith Act (though Socialist Worker Party leaders, like the ones who had once assisted Serena C., were). However, the FBI built files on Communist leaders preemptively, and starting in 1948 began arresting them in droves. They were never accused of actual violence, or even specific plans to overthrow the government; instead, the convictions rested on the fact that works like *The Communist Manifesto* predicted or advocated for violent revolution when necessary. Even though the constitution of the Communist Party of the USA specifically "rejected violent revolution and advocated a peaceful transition to communism," almost all of those tried were found guilty and given multiyear sentences in maximum-security federal prisons.[54]

Between 1951 and 1955, Flynn, Jones, and Gannett were in and out of the Women's House of Detention as their trials stumbled forward, before eventually being found guilty and sentenced to Alderson Federal Reformatory for Women in West Virginia. Jones had immigrated to America from Trinidad at the age of nine, and Gannett had come from Poland at the age of eight, so they were additionally held in detention at Ellis Island at times. However, in the end, Gannett (who was white) was allowed to stay in the country, while Jones (who was Black) was deported to England in 1955 (Trinidad's British colonial governor refused to allow her back into the country on the grounds that she was too dangerous).

Of the three, only Flynn wrote much about their time at the House of D—a damning portrait of a place virtually abandoned to its corruption. In her memoir, *My Life as a Political Prisoner*, she included an entire chapter on lesbians in women's prisons, which she opened with an anecdote she heard from Dorothy Day, a Catholic socialist organizer. When Day confronted a lesbian in the House of D, the woman told her, "'Here we are treated like animals. So why shouldn't we act like animals?'" According to Flynn, Day responded, "This is a libel on the animals, as perversion does not exist among them."[55] Lesbianism, in this view, was deviant, animalistic yet still unnatural, and a failure of personal morality.

Flynn wrote at length about her time in the House of D:

Inside the building pandemonium reigned supreme. The noise was deafening, from the shrill incessant chatter of the inmates, the hysterical laughter, the screams of suffering addicts suddenly cut off from narcotics, and the weeping and cursing of forlorn and desperate women, crowded together in small quarters. The majority were awaiting trial or were there during their trials, because they could not secure bail. Some stayed there for months and then were acquitted as innocent, but there was no redress....Some women serve sentences there up to three years. I did not ascertain on what basis they were kept in such a place, where there were no facilities for exercise or fresh air except a small wire-enclosed roof.

The cells were open, with a short curtain over the toilet as a concession to privacy. In each cell was a narrow iron cot with a thin mattress, a covered toilet which also served as a seat before a small iron table, a washbowl, and a couple of stationary wooden hangers for clothing. The blankets were old and worn beyond all possibility of real cleanliness, though they were disinfected regularly. It was a filthy place, overrun with mice and cockroaches. The food was indescribably revolting, unfit to eat. Watery spaghetti, half-cooked oatmeal, coffee that was hardly more than luke-warm water, wormy prunes, and soggy bread baked by the men on Welfare Island, very little meat and that usually an unsightly bologna—are items I recall. There was never any fruit. Sugar and milk were scarce and both had to be bought in the commissary....

The dehumanizing degradation of the House of Detention commences immediately. All your possessions are surrendered, except glasses, and one gets a receipt upon entry. But rumor had it that officers borrowed the costly mink coats of the $100-a-night call girls to wear out in the evenings....

The second step after entering was to strip and leave all one's clothes in a side room where they were searched by an officer, while the prisoner was wrapped in a sheet and taken to the showers. Next we were ordered to take an enema and climb on an examining table....All openings of the body were roughly searched for narcotics by "a doctor"—a large woman who made insulting remarks about Communists who did not appreciate this country. I told her to mind her business. Once she became so animated in her opinions while she was taking a blood specimen that she allowed the blood to run down my arm. "Watch what you are doing," I said. "Never mind my politics, watch my blood...."

No matter what lay ahead of us, it was a relief to leave the House of Detention. The vile language, the fights, the disgusting lesbian performances, were unbearable. Our only regret was to leave behind three Puerto Rican nationalists.[56]

Flynn never described the "lesbian performances" at the House of D, but soon upon arriving at Alderson Federal Penitentiary she was given a questionnaire that asked if she was a lesbian—a word some of the other imprisoned women did not know. After she explained the meaning, one responded, "Not now, but from what I've heard about this place, anything can happen!"[57] Flynn frequently referenced queer women in her memoir, usually to condemn them. She was a skilled tailor and often received requests from other incarcerated people to alter their garments—but she "made it a rule not to alter slacks or shirts so as to masculinize them."[58] She vacillated between pitying and excoriating queer women. She noted that "'masculine' inmates" were "quite often homely, as women." Many were violent and predatory, she wrote, and "such concepts as self-control, discipline, or sublimation were foreign to them."[59] She condemned "prostitutes" as living "twisted and sordid lives" that led them to trade sex in prison with other women, regardless of their orientation. To prevent these perversions, Flynn believed, "those known to be lesbians should be isolated from the young and first offenders"—one of the few beliefs she had in common with prison administrators.[60]

Why were Communists like Flynn so opposed to homosexuality, when they were—for the most part—on the progressive side of so many other civil rights issues? Bettina Aptheker, a queer feminist academic who was raised in the party (and who knew Elizabeth Gurley Flynn), cites three reasons. First, paralleling the claims of the US government, the Communist Party USA expelled homosexuals as potential security risks, because they could be blackmailed into naming other party members. When Aptheker came out as a lesbian in the late 1970s, an older comrade told her that "sex was solely for reproduction," and during the 1950s "she was instructed by the Party leadership to talk with several women comrades about their sexuality...[and] ask them to leave the Party" for security reasons.[61] Neither this comrade nor the women she helped expel ever protested the party line.

On a deeper level, Aptheker points out, the party was as misogynistic as any other institution in the 1950s, and there was "no critical analysis...of the family, or of its patriarchal character."[62] Questions of domestic violence or sexual abuse were considered "private and personal matters."[63] The party conjured up an imaginary, idealized working-class (heterosexual) family, which was the archetype we would all return to when the toxic effects of capitalism had been destroyed. Under this rubric, queerness was envisioned as (at best) a decadent by-product of the capitalist system, which would naturally go extinct when the workers' revolution came.

Finally, the party was firmly opposed to any politics that undermined the central place of the class struggle, whether they were feminist, homophile, or anti-racist. As much as these issues could be integrated into a worldview that prioritized class, the Communist Party embraced them. And much as individual members of the party were more accepting of queer sexuality than the party line acknowledged, some were also critically engaged in anti-colonial, anti-racist, and feminist organizing, despite the party's overall hesitance on these issues. But officially, this work was often seen as a distraction, or even a sign of capitalist indoctrination—a mode of thinking that would be carried over to many of the activist movements of the next two decades.

Yet the party had many queer members, particularly in the early twentieth century. Harry Hay, the founder of the Mattachine Society, America's first significant LGBTQ rights organization, was a Communist organizer, and he designed Mattachine along the same lines as the party, with anonymous, linked cells of members. Some queer people even had respected roles *in* the party, Aptheker points out in her work, like Anna Rochester and Grace Hutchins. However, in order to be accepted, they pretended to be "romantic friends," which convinced the party that "their lesbian relationship was in no way a challenge to the patriarchal family; it was not in any way connected to a feminist movement, and their work was solidly within the fold of Marxist political economy."[64]

For years, rumors have suggested that the homophobic passages in Flynn's book were put there at the demand of party leadership. Aptheker points out that Flynn lived in a close, passionate relationship with Dr. Marie Equi (an out lesbian) for over a decade. As well, Flynn was a member of the Heterodoxy Club in Greenwich Village, which included many queer women. After Flynn's death, the party claimed to have lost her papers, and it took years for biographers to gain access to them. What may have been hidden, destroyed, or lost during that time is unknown.

Certainly, though, Flynn's memoir is more vociferously homophobic than comparable other documents. For instance, one of the "three Puerto Rican nationalists" that Flynn mentioned meeting in the House of D was Rosa Collazo, a New York City–based leader in the Puerto Rican Nationalist Party.[65] The PRNP was not Communist, but it was a working-class-led, anti-imperialist group that was part of the broad, socialist/communist international. In 1954, Collazo was arrested and eventually imprisoned for six years on a charge of "seditious conspiracy" after four other members of the party attacked the US House of Representatives, shooting several officials in the process. Collazo had previously been arrested on the same charge in 1950, when her husband was part of an assassination attempt on President Truman. Both times, she spent months in the House of D.

In her autobiography, *Memorias de Rosa Collazo*, she made no reference to lesbianism. She mentioned the fights between inmates, the violations of the intake process, the corruption of the guards, and the animal shit in the food; she was even in the House of D long enough to note how, on days when state investigators were sent, the entire place changed and they were served "gallina, papa majada y ensalada [chicken, mashed potatoes and salad]" instead of the usual mush.[66] The only time Collazo made what could even be interpreted as a slant reference to queerness is when she called the House of D a "casa de perversion," or house of perversion, but she never explained her word choice.[67]

Political prisoners like Rosa Collazo and Elizabeth Gurley Flynn would never make up a large percentage of those incarcerated at the House of D, but from the 1950s on, they were a continual presence. For the last two decades of the prison's existence, the makeup of the inmate population remained largely stable. The percentages of various groups changed throughout the years—reflecting shifts in New York City and the country as a whole—but the overall picture remained the same. The post-1950 prison was made up of more Black women than white women (and increasingly of Latina women, who would be designated in a variety of official ways); more women who understood themselves to be homosexual or bisexual (and were not ashamed of that fact); and more women who were arrested for drug use or political action.

The single biggest trend in the post-1950s prison, however, was simply that it would be filled with more women, and more women, and still more women. The brief population dip brought on by the advent of antibiotic sulfa drug treatments for syphilis and gonorrhea quickly proved to be an aberration. After 1953, the House of D was permanently overcrowded, with sometimes as many as nearly eight hundred people being caged in a building designed for four hundred.

For imprisoned people—and New York City as a whole—the overcrowding could not have come at a worse time. At the end of World War II, America had invested in a massive welfare program for returning veterans called the GI Bill, which included provisions for homeownership loans with no money down, at extremely good rates. Simultaneously, the Federal Housing Authority prioritized loans to vets, and funding to suburban housing projects intended for them. Racial codes were written into this funding, making the vast majority of these homes and loans available only to white people. An explosion of cheap, segregated suburban towns flooded the market, leading vets (and their families) to flee urban centers like New York City—with devastating long-term effects on city budgets and the infrastructure that depended on tax revenues. In 1950, the *New York Times Magazine* published a Sunday feature whose headline blared "The Suburbs Are Strangling the City," and New York began its long, slow slide toward bankruptcy.[68] Since the first American census was taken in 1790, New York City's population had trended steadily upward. The city grew despite every war, every depression, every political controversy, and every new state—until the 1950s, when it lost a hundred thousand residents over the course of the decade. And that's just the cumulative number. Many more New Yorkers left and were replaced in the '50s, creating a city in rapid flux.[69] By the end of the decade, the House of D had a daily average population of 594. In 1950, a total of just 2,044 admissions were made to the prison; by 1960, the number of admissions had increased nearly 700 percent, to 14,141.

Midway through the decade, Mayor Robert F. Wagner attempted to stem some of the troubles at the House of D (and in the correctional system as a whole) by appointing Magistrate Anna M. Kross as the city's new commissioner of correction. Kross was a progressive crusader in the city's criminal legal system, and had been one of the first and most persistent critics of the Women's Court. She believed that many of the "crimes" filling the House of D—prostitution, drug use, alcoholism, etc.—should never have been dealt with through the courts in the first place. When she began her tenure as commissioner in 1954, she wrote to the mayor that

> when we took office on January 1, 1954...we found the morale of the Department low, due in great measure to understaffing and

employees working out of title. Inmates were locked in their cells for the major part of the day due not only to shortage of staff but also to the lack of any realistic rehabilitation program. The physical facilities of the Department had been permitted to deteriorate to a dangerous stage both from a sanitary point of view as well as mechanical efficiency....We believe we have made some progress in meeting the emergencies of overcrowding, personnel, [and] lack of professional, medical and rehabilitative staff.[70]

Despite her hopeful words, nine months after Kross took over, the House of D was struck by riots—the first of many, inside and out, that would characterize the prison's last decades. The Stonewall Uprising is Greenwich Village's most famous riot, but it's far from the only one. Queer people, incarcerated or not, were fed up, and they were beginning to realize that publicity (on their terms) could be as powerful a weapon *for* them as it was *against* them. From fliers to fireballs, they would fight back against the strangling conformity of the 1950s with whatever weapons they had at hand.

They were fighting for their very survival. The only other choice was death, one way or another. Many of them did not make it, particularly as they grew older and the indignities and violations added up. Young women are overrepresented in the WPA files because they were considered more redeemable. But the WPA had provided near-continuous services to two women since the 1930s—Ann C. and Serena C.—and their experiences in the 1950s show the heavy toll that years of oppression could take on a person.

CHAPTER 7

Conformity and Resistance

A PLACE WORSE THAN PRISON

Ann C., the young butch who had stolen a few rare books with her girlfriend Louise in the 1930s, was finally able to get her feet under her in 1945, when she lied on the application for a job at Bellevue Hospital's Psychiatric Division, saying she had never been arrested. As she explained in a letter to the WPA, having a criminal record "means I have to tell lies for the rest of my life in order to gain employment and I wonder if it is worth it! Must mistakes that were made in the past forever be held against a person? It seems so."[1] But if that was the case, she would make the best of it.

For six years, Ann somehow dodged every attempt to have her fingerprints checked, and she seemed happy and stable. She gave the WPA a couple of photos of her in those years; in them, she's always standing straight and tall, with an impish grin. She was quite proud of her starched white nurse's uniform and cap. She saved enough money to buy a car, donate $100 to the WPA to help other girls like her, and even put a down payment on a house. But in 1951, while trying to move a patient, she injured her back and was out on workman's comp for months. At the same time, the hospital finally succeeded in check-ing her fingerprints. Because of her workman's compensation claim, it took them awhile to fire her, but in early 1953 Ann was removed from her position because she "falsified her employment record" and "her physical condition."[2]

This couldn't have happened at a worse time. A few months later, Ann was arrested on a felony obscenity charge. She was dating a mar-ried woman named Ruth, and someone—Ruth's husband, or perhaps Ruth herself—had given their letters to the cops. It was a felony to send "obscene" material through the mail, and until a Supreme Court case in 1958, basically anything queer was considered obscene. In Ann's case, her letters were declared obscene because she defined the word "lesbian" and also "used certain scientific words" related to homosexuality.[3]

In detention, Ann plunged back into the depths of despair she had experienced in the early 1940s, when she attempted suicide. When the WPA went to see her at the House of D, they reported that

> for the first time since we have known her Ann cried. She said she had not wanted us to know that she was there—she thought that Jail was over for her. She looks very physically ill as if she were in pain. She is thin and her skin looks blue and transparent. She said that when she first got there she leaned over to pick up a tray and her back-bone slipped so that she could hardly stand up again. She was in such pain she asked for a doctor. She was told that it was Sunday and there was no doctor. She then asked to go to Bellevue and this was refused.[4]

Furious, Ann smashed a window and the guards threw her into solitary, where she got her period and asked for a sanitary napkin and a glass of water. These requests were also refused, so Ann set fire to the mattress in her cell and ranted that she would kill Ruth for getting her into this situation.[5]

The obscenity charge would eventually be dismissed, but the dam-age was done. The House of D sent Ann to Bellevue Hospital—her old workplace—after the fire, and she was soon committed to a state mental hospital. They had every legal right to hold her indefinitely as a "psychopathic personality." The year before, in 1952, homosexuality had been added to the American Psychiatric Association's *Diagnostic and Statistical Manual*, making it even easier to have women like Ann involuntarily detained. In one of her last fully coherent letters to the WPA, Ann documented how hospital staff used electroconvulsive therapy as a threat and punishment:

> I was told if I didn't behave I would get shock treatment. Their idea of behaving was weird. If a patient assaulted me I was not to hit back, I was to call for help. When one person hits another there is an automatic reflex on the part of the person assaulted to strike back. Self preservation is the law of nature.
>
> The same threat of getting shock was used when I used obscene language. Some people hit when they are angry. I can't hit because if I'm angry enough to strike a person, I'm angry enough to want to kill them and will try to do exactly that. I release my anger by cursing….Yet on the few occasions I used obscene language the charge nurse threatened to tell Dr. H., which meant I would get shock as he claims I use profanity when I'm tense and that shock would relax me. I'm wondering now if I did the right thing by repressing my anger and promising the nurse not to curse if she would promise not to tell Dr. H. A vicious circle to say the least.
>
> Maybe I should have released my hostility and taken shock treatment as "punishment" but the two ECST I had were terrifying and a constant threat of the same if one did not behave was too much. The Drs gave shock in Bellevue and we never held it as a threat or punishment to the patient. We explained to the patient it was a treatment that would enable him to get well much sooner. Such was not the case in Creedmoor. ECT is quite helpful in many cases of mental illness but never when it is used as a threat or punishment. Unfortunately, too many people working in state hospitals do not realize that or if they do they just don't care….I think many of the psychiatrists are much more psychotic than I'll ever be. At least I

don't have the delusion that I am God, as Dr. B. from Rec 7 seems to have. He should drop dead twice, once isn't enough for his inflated ego.[6]

Ann said the shock treatments did nothing but "make [her] forget...give [her] a terrific headache and make [her] feel very depressed."[7] Other equally brutal therapies, like locking her in a straitjacket, injecting her with insulin to produce a shocked state, and throwing her in solitary confinement unsurprisingly did not help Ann. Instead, they broke her. For six years, she had finally been free of the stigma of shoplifting a book during the Great Depression; now, it all came falling down on her. She lost everything: the house, the car, her friends, and even her family.

For the rest of her documented life, Ann was in and out of hospitals and prisons. In 1962, she stopped coming to the WPA for services, and in their final evaluation of her, they wrote that Ann was just "a lonely girl."[8] A lonely woman, really, who at forty-two years old had spent the majority of her life in one institution or another.

While in Bellevue in 1952, Ann was in the same ward as Serena C., with whom she got along well. For Serena, the late '40s and early '50s had been nowhere near as good a time as they were for Ann. She was never arrested again after she stole the stationery to write to Howard University, but that stigma—and the racism she was subjected to— were enough to ensure that she would never have steady employment, and her mental health deteriorated drastically in just a few short years.

Serena's experience of hospitalization was even worse than Ann's. In 1945, during a routine operation to remove a fibroid tumor, she was forcibly sterilized. Despite telling the WPA about it, no outcry was ever raised, and Serena was never told exactly what kind of procedure was performed on her.

There is a long history in America of involuntary and coerced sterilizations of Black and brown women, poor women, immigrants, and women judged to be mentally ill. Civil rights leader Fannie Lou Hamer had a nearly identical experience to Serena, when during a routine operation to remove a tumor in 1961 she was given a full hysterectomy.

In 1927, the Supreme Court ruled that states had the right to "forci-bly sterilize a person considered unfit to procreate," and an estimated seventy thousand women were forcibly sterilized in America during the twentieth century.[9] How many others were coerced into agreeing to sterilization, or never told what was done to them, is unknown. Although it is less remembered today, the early reproductive justice movement focused as much on preventing forced sterilizations as it did on access to contraception and abortion.

Serena knew that she needed mental health care. But over and over again, she was denied treatment at private institutions that would not serve Black women, even when she had the money to go. Untreated, her mental health deteriorated to the point where her family was forced to institutionalize her in state hospitals—they felt financially unable to care for her, and unsure about what she needed. Eventually, they were railroaded into signing paperwork approving electroshock therapy. Serena was also drugged with Thorazine (an antipsychotic/ sedative), which would soon be used at endemic levels in the House of Detention. Due to the effects of these two "treatments," she was left "rambling and incoherent."[10] Her penmanship deteriorated to scribbles and painstaking block letters.

When the WPA visited her in 1954, Serena told them that she received no psychotherapy, and aside from when she was getting shocked "she [was] kept in restraint almost all of the time."[11] The WPA was so surprised to hear this, they asked the attendant if Serena was telling the truth. Not only did the attendant verify this, "she ex-pressed surprise over the logical way in which Serena had spoken, say-ing they did not know it was possible for her to do this."[12] The hospital staff never saw (and had no interest in) the woman who fought racist city administrators in the 1930s, who escaped poverty and made it to Howard University and excelled. They saw only a poor, sick, crazy Black woman, whom they kept in bondage and refused any care.

In the spring of 1956, Serena was discharged from her most recent hospitalization with no warning, and ended up staying in a small room in the house of an old friend in Brooklyn. Her "personal condition... was worse" than the WPA had ever seen it.[13] Soon after, her mother died, and Serena stopped responding to all attempts at contact. After six months of silence, the WPA closed her case, and I can find no records of her life after this point.

In a decade devoted to celebrating white suburban homemakers and rooting out hidden homosexuals, queer formerly incarcerated women like Serena and Ann had few allies. But they had each other. As the forces against them mounted, these queer people fought back by any means at their disposal and, in doing so, discovered the power of organized resistance. Stonewall was on the horizon, and even if they couldn't see it yet, they were practicing for it.

THE RIOTS BEGIN

Friday, September 24, 1954, was one of those beautiful, early fall days when New York City is at its best. The sky was clear, temperatures hit the low seventies, and the streets of Greenwich Village must have bustled with apartment dwellers luxuriating in the sun before the long, cold New York winter began. But as the last golden glints of sun snuck below the low horizon of the Village's row houses, a howling began to reverberate through the streets. Somewhere, dozens—perhaps hundreds—of women were screaming. "We want to get out! The food is no good! They've killed a girl in here!"[14]

Tourists and locals alike were drawn to the source of the screams, until a wild crowd clogged the intersection of Greenwich and Sixth, staring up at the pandemonium that had taken over the House of D. The presence of spectators—the way they represented freedom, or perhaps just someone who would listen—drove the imprisoned people inside to new heights. They pounded their institutional metal cups against the cell bars, giving their screams a sharp and tinny backbeat. If the crowd looked closely, they would have seen the flickering light of a fire raging somewhere on the fourth floor. But getting too close to the prison was a dicey proposition, as those on the inside began hurling ceramic dishes and lit cigarettes at the crowd. It took hours for the guards to regain control.

As the *New York Times* wrote the next day, "Prisoners staged a noisy two-hour demonstration last night over the disciplining of a narcotics addict for an obscene remark to a guard. The outburst, which started at 8:30 o'clock, spread rapidly from the fourth to the eighth floor of the building."[15]

What exactly happened in the House of D that night is a mystery that can only be partially reconstructed from records that seem to have been intentionally destroyed. What is unarguable, however, is that the people imprisoned in the House of D discovered a powerful new weapon that night—publicity—which they wielded with a chaotic and baleful hand from then on. There would be several more riots in 1958, as well as ones in '69, '70, and '71, right before the prison closed for good. These later riots were all connected to larger movements, either held in sympathy with queer, Black, or feminist protestors gathered outside the building or inspired by the wave of prison protests that rocked the country in the early 1970s.

The riots of the 1950s arose sui generis in the House of Detention (which may be why they've been forgotten). But across the country, an escalating drug war was creating massively overcrowded prisons, where conditions were unlivable. In 1952 alone, there were seventeen major prison riots in America. As prison historians have noted, "Rioting was, and remains, one of the few ways for prisoners to ensure that they would not be ignored."[16] In part for this reason, most prisons are now built far away from people who might act as witnesses to what happens on the inside.

The riots in the House of D in the 1950s shook the prison to its core, exposed its many flaws to the public, generated several internal and external investigations, caused the entire prison administration to be upended, and started the (long, frequently delayed) process of tearing the place down. Though the inciting incidents varied, the riots had several important features in common: they occurred when the prison was desperately overcrowded; they began over minor infractions; they were initiated by drug users going through withdrawal, wayward minors, and understaffed/undertrained guards; and they seemed to be bookended by weeks of tension in the prison, which often focused around queer women and transmasculine people.

"Cherokee" was one of the girls in the prison in the summer of 1954 and into that fateful September. A wayward minor of seventeen, she'd grown up in New York City, though her father was from Georgia and her mother from Fajardo, Puerto Rico. She'd been institutionalized for two years on a charge of "delinquency" but had only the slimmest of files—she had a tendency to disappear quickly. The prison officials noted her "psychosexual confusion" and desire to wear slacks, her "destructive influence over others," how "something electric seems to happen when she walks in the room," and how "girls vie with one another to be near her."[17] The matrons considered her an invitation to trouble.

Around the time Cherokee was incarcerated, city officials labeled the entire Department of Correction "extremely understaffed and almost completely demoralized."[18] The House of D in particular was hemorrhaging personnel. At the time of the riot, they were about thirty guards short of being fully staffed, and 60 percent of the entire staff had been newly hired as of 1952.[19]

While the guards were few, the imprisoned women were many. That September, the city's correctional system hit an all-time population high.[20] There were some 452 people imprisoned at the House of D the week of the riot, which meant that at least a hundred of them were doubled up in cells that were only seven feet long by six feet wide, or stuffed into temporary dorms made from converted dining rooms. The housing floors were tense and overcrowded. Sutter's Bakery, a fancy French pastry shop, had recently opened across the street—a sign of the Village's escalating gentrification—and many women in the prison recalled the smell of baking pastries as a painful daily reminder of the world they were kept from (particularly those experiencing withdrawal, who often had intense sugar cravings). Instead of crème patisserie, they were served gray meat with animal shit, and "for many years" there were no beverages served at lunch or even a water line in the dining rooms because the facilities were in such poor condition.[21] Often, reports on the prison only noted these kinds of issues as they were being fixed, making it impossible to determine how long-standing the problems were, but they pointed to an institution that was crumbling under its own weight—and trying to hide it.

While in the House of D, Cherokee kept herself busy by writing personal notes to her girlfriends—women on the outside or at one of the other institutions she'd been at before, like the Hudson Training School for Girls or Bedford Hills. Shortly before the riot, a matron discovered her love letters and destroyed them, sending Cherokee into a fury. It was one thing for the prison to censor outgoing letters, or notes passed between imprisoned women, but these were private notes for herself, which (theoretically) Cherokee should have been allowed to write undisturbed. As punishment, she would have been sent to the fourth-floor isolation cells, where addicts and (increasingly) queer people were sent—the same floor where the riot soon began.

Conditions on the fourth floor were some of the worst in the House of D. Imprisoned women in general were treated poorly, but those who had drug addictions were treated worst of all. According to investigations done after the riot, about 35 percent of those imprisoned at the House of D that year were drug users.[22] They were forced to wear institutional blue chambray dresses so everyone would know and thrown together in their misery to kick on the fourth floor without any real assistance, just like Big Cliff and Tonic.[23] Is it any wonder they were always among the first to resist? Over and over again, the most marginalized queer people would be the ones on the front lines, literally fighting the system to survive.

After the 1954 riot, the House of D finally discontinued the fourth-floor junkie tank and began sending addicts in withdrawal to the tenth-floor hospital. This was at best a marginal improvement. A new deputy warden had been appointed—a man, as it was assumed he would be better at providing discipline—and one of his first duties was to conduct a thorough audit of what had led up to the riot. No full copies of his report (or a second report commissioned at the same time from outside medical advisors, or the state annual inspection of the prison for that year) seem to still exist. But summary excerpts saved in other documents provide a damning picture of what passed for health care in the House of D.

According to the new deputy warden, medical facilities at the House of D were "badly understaffed" and capable of doing a "token job" at best.[24] The head physician, a woman with twenty years of experience, was paid about the same as a freshly hired guard; the other doctors made less. The hospital beds and multiple operating rooms were "not used due to insufficient or incompetent staff," making the decision to place addicts there much less magnanimous than it seemed.[25] For the entirety of the 1950s, the operating rooms were abandoned.[26]

The dentist had so little time per prisoner that all he did, regardless of the complaint, was pull teeth. There was no gynecologist, or any doctor at all on premises most nights and weekends (as poor Ann C. discovered). Without the funding provided in previous decades by the Women's Prison Association, psychiatric services had shriveled—"one psychiatrist came...four hours per week and functioned primarily to determine whether inmates should be sent to Bellevue Hospital for testing or whether to commit a woman to a mental institution."[27] Overall, the hospital was a collection of "miserable facilities."[28] Only in their 1960 annual report would the city finally admit that the hospital at the House of D, during the 1950s, "had been allowed to deteriorate to an infirmary status."[29] Among the numerous problems they observed were "obsolete" and "hazardous" essential equipment; "inadequate" supplies; poorly maintained patient records "with no case history follow up"; no educational, rehabilitation, or occupational therapy programs; and nonexistent sanitary standards.[30]

The new deputy warden endorsed the same prescription for fixing the prison that had now been repeated for years: the overcrowding needed to be eased; a new building needed to be built; and most of the "crimes" for which women were arrested should never be handled in the criminal legal system.

Commissioner Anna Kross trumpeted the report throughout her administration (and even seemed to leak parts of it to the press) in an effort to bring real, substantive changes to the House of D. In 1956, following her lead, Mayor Robert Wagner officially endorsed a plan to relocate the House of D to North Brother Island—a craggy, cursed spit of land near Rikers Island (the men's prison) that had previously served as a smallpox sanitarium and the prison hospital where Mary Mallon (aka Typhoid Mary) lived the last twenty years of her life. As anyone ashamed of their cruelties will do, the city was attempting to hide the evidence. For the next decade, the government would wrangle over plans and costs, and while some improvements would be made to the House of D, the idea of the soon-to-come new building was frequently used to deny budgetary requests and other improvements at the existing prison. In the end, it was all for nothing: North Brother Island would become a drug treatment center, and the House of D would remain at 10 Greenwich until 1971.

In the wake of the 1954 riot, Commissioner Kross was able to make *some* changes. Two social service workers were added to the staff of the House of D, as were nearly thirty guards. Every prison in the city was equipped with a Diagnostic Unit, which provided (limited) psychiatric treatment and counseling—and, *finally*, these services were put in the official budget, not funded with money spent by inmates in the commissary.[31] Three vocational programs were established in the House of D, one for waitresses, one for seamstresses, and one for hairdressers, though each served fewer than thirty people a year, out of thousands. A Medical Advisory Board was launched to offer outside consultation and oversight for prison health services, and Quaker volunteers were brought in to provide entertainment and discussion groups. Heating was added to the roof, to allow for some limited outdoor recreation time during the winter, and televisions were added to the indoor recreation spaces (greatly increasing the noise in the building). Finally, in 1957, the policy of giving women a mere dime upon release was abolished. For the rest of the prison's existence, women sentenced for misdemeanors would receive a whole quarter on their way out the door! Felons could get as much as five dollars.[32]

Not all the changes made were positive, however. In 1956, the Department of Corrections finally codified in writing the process for segregating queer women and transmasculine people:

Should there be any information on the accompanying card or commitment that might indicate sex deviation by an inmate or should
the receiving room officer have knowledge through past experience
that the inmate is known to be homo-sexual, then the receiving
room officer makes the assignment to a single cell in a proper location and informs the floor officer by telephone concerning the char-
acteristic of the inmate.[33]

Technically, this policy remained in effect at least until 1964,
when a researcher reported that queer women in the prison were not
only segregated, they were forced to wear a "D" on their clothing, for
deviant.[34] However, her report also makes clear that the vast majority
of people in the prison lived queer lives (at least while in the House of
D), and that this form of public humiliation was used both arbitrarily
and as a way of punishing people who were too masculine or too
difficult. Jay Toole, the activist who today leads tours of the Village,
laughed when asked if queer people were segregated during her time
in the prison in the '60s, saying it just wasn't possible—"there were
too many of us."[35]

Other problems were noted by Commissioner Kross or her investigators but never dealt with. In the Department of Corrections annual
report for 1955, for instance, the new deputy warden noted that upon
entering or returning to the prison, all incarcerated people were given
forced enemas to find hidden narcotics—part of the degrading intake
process that women had been protesting since 1934. Parenthetically,
he noted, "none ever found," yet this ineffective, humiliating policy
was never changed.[36] Similarly, no real effort was made to separate
pretrial from sentenced prisoners, even though that was named a top
priority by all of the investigators.

Imprisoned women themselves made many complaints that were
never responded to in any way, about the mirrors (they were all
broken); the clothing (women awaiting trial were allowed a single
outfit—the one they were arrested in—which they had to continually wash. As one woman wrote, "We cannot imagine what happens

when a woman is admitted during the winter months wearing heavy woolens that can't be washed or dried"); the cold-turkey treatment of addicts ("An abrupt withdrawal is actually more detrimental to health and spirit than the drugs themselves....Not only are these methods unsatisfactory, as proven by statistics, they are not even humane"); the lack of aftercare services ("Leaving prison, in itself, is terrifying....For the indigent inmate, this is often disastrous. Not only have they ceased to function normally for a long period of time…they have no funds to see them through the ordeal of adjusting"); the lack of dental care; and more.[37]

The biggest and most consistent complaint, however, was about the lack of anything to *do* at the House of D, be it recreational, educational, or vocational. The prison had been intended to hold women for a few days before their trials, and was never designed for long-term living, even before it was dangerously overcrowded. Now, it packed sentenced people together like sardines for months, sometimes even years, in an excruciating monotony that gave them nothing to do but stew. Moreover, thanks to the slow and overcrowded legal system, sometimes the wait to go to trial could take months all by itself.

So it was for Bertha D., an "ash-blonde" butch with short hair and sticky fingers, who first ended up in the House of Detention a few months before the 1954 riot.[38] Unlike most of the imprisoned women, she was a skilled professional, with a background in medical stenography. But recently, she'd begun hitting large five and dimes all around the city with a simple trick. First, she'd find a manager and flirt with him publicly. Then, when he left the floor, Bertha would tell one of the counter girls that he needed her in the back and had sent Bertha to take her place. When the girl left, Bertha would clean out the till and take off. When she was caught, the police found a toy gun in her possession, and Bertha admitted that she had been planning to hold up the cashier at a Times Square movie palace next. She was given a $2,500 bail she couldn't pay and sent to the House of D for the rest of August. And September, October, November, December. When 1955 rolled around Bertha was still there, thanks to some holdup on her trial—a missing report? No one was clear on what exactly was happening.

Nannie Spraggins from the Women's Prison Association had met Bertha early in her incarceration, so when she visited another woman at the House of D in late February 1955, she randomly inquired about Bertha, assuming she'd probably be long gone. Spraggins was shocked when the guards ushered Bertha to her. "She wept compulsively and swore quite emphatically," Spraggins wrote of their meeting, and if Bertha had to survive another week in the House of D, "she will certainly commit suicide."[39]

She was bored, Bertha explained, desperately, painfully bored. So bored, she said, "she will blow up any day and…hurt somebody."[40] The only thing to do in the House of D was hang out with the other girls, pick fights, and learn bad habits. "She is very hostile now and trusts no one," Spraggins wrote in March, a big change from the first reports on Bertha, which called her "bright," "quite animated," and possessed of "considerable ability."[41] In part, Bertha explained, her hostility was a response to the overwhelming homophobia that pervaded the prison staff. "Because I'm a homosexual," she told Spraggins, "the officers watch me very closely."[42] As they did with Cherokee, the guards confiscated Bertha's love letters to other women and put her into segregation for them. Spraggins was surprised they weren't used as an excuse to hold Bertha even longer.

Spraggins anticipated (correctly, it would turn out) that Bertha "has fully decided what her life on the outside will be—one of crime."[43] Now, Bertha told Spraggins, "I know about these things," and then she listed the possibilities: abortion rings, liquor smuggling, shoplifting, and more. She left the prison shortly thereafter and made good on her word. She passed bad checks. She impersonated a maid and stole from some of the biggest hotels in the city. She plied other women with sob stories and asked for money, which she then turned around and spent on "the four or five women in her life" with whom she regularly "frequented the Village."[44] She wasn't ashamed to be a lesbian, she told Spraggins, and she was "accepting of the fact" that "she will play the role of the male."[45] For this, however, she needed money—more money than a stenographer's paycheck. Her only concession to straight life was to grow her hair out a little and find some women's slacks, because "she really didn't want to advertise what she is to the world."[46] Even the streets of Greenwich Village—the ones Elaine B. had once guided eager tourists through while dressed like a man—had become too dangerous for the most visibly queer people.

The last time Bertha was arrested (theft again, to support a girl-friend's drug habit) she told Nannie Spraggins she was actually hoping to "get a long sentence."[47] She would rather take more time, in a higher security facility, far from New York, than put up with another day in the House of D—just like Big Cliff in the 1940s. At least in those places there were things to do, a modicum of services, and a chance for some psychiatric care, which Bertha was interested in (though not for her sexuality).

Bertha's wish was granted in late 1955, and she was shipped off to Westfield Farm. According to a psychiatrist, Bertha found Westfield "a paradise after the close and long confinement" at the House of D.[48] She appreciated "the scenery, the private room, the food, and all the sympathetic people."[49] She told the doctor that she "likes activity" and "looked forward to 'doing' things at Westfield."[50] As a result, on the last page of her file, the psychiatrist wrote that her "intense hostility to society, seen in the H. of D. seemed gone and [Bertha] stated she would try hard to adjust."[51]

THE RIOTS RETURN

In the wake of the first riot, Commissioner of Corrections Anna Kross received much praise for trying to fix the correctional system, and the city certainly generated reams of reports, and hundreds of hours of meetings discussing its issues. But despite the changes, the House of D remained toxically overcrowded. The situation was so dire that, in 1957, the prison demolished a good portion of the hospital and re-placed it with a dormitory-style room to house fifty women at once.[52] This appeared to be a bit of realpolitik on Kross's part. Without full hospital facilities, the House of D was able to get around a public-health law that had existed for as long as the prison had, which allowed "self-committed" drug addicts to request treatment from any city-operated hospital. In reality, these requests were mostly shunted to the House of D and the prison hospital for men on Rikers Island. Commissioner Kross, in a press release, called it "a bad practice...[as] we have no proper facilities for these non-criminal addicts. Nor are they given any proper medical treatment for their illness."[53] By turning the hospitals at both Rikers and the House of D into dorms, she hoped to force the city to fund real treatment facilities in real hospitals. This did happen, to some degree, but slowly, and not for many years. Instead, the House of D simply had fewer facilities and way more addicts. In 1958, just three years after it had been discontinued, the junkie tank was quietly reinstated.

In the year of the first riot, there were 7,644 admissions to the House of D—meaning 7,644 useless enemas and forced vaginal examinations. By 1958, the year the riots returned, that number had nearly doubled, to 13,356 admissions. During the 1954 riot, there were some 452 imprisoned people at the House of D; in 1958, there were 512—meaning 200 of them were doubled up in cramped, tiny cages, or smashed into a dormitory with no privacy whatsoever.

As a result, this time around, the riot was much bigger, as was the crowd watching. Thousands of people gathered around the prison on the night of Saturday, April 26, 1958, as the people inside shouted, fought guards, and "threw burning sheets and crockery" out of the windows.[54] It took ten police officers and twelve firemen just to control the crowd, and additional male guards had to be sent from other prisons to restore order inside the House of D.[55] This time, there was no way to cover up what had happened.

According to the press, the women's main complaints were the lack of edible food and the fact that "their protests against the food had resulted only in beatings."[56] Commissioner Kross pushed back in the press; yes, she admitted, "the food budget had been cut," but she denied that they were starving or abused for complaining about it. Instead, official reports painted the following picture:

The night of the riot, the prison was once again severely under-staffed and overcrowded. On the sixth floor, there were eighty-eight imprisoned people and only a single correctional officer, who was expected to "patrol 4 corridors, serve supper, supervise recreation, send inmates to medical clinic, lock-in at 8:00 pm, and maintain over-all discipline and control."[57] About half of the people on the floor were inmates under the age of twenty-one—forty of them, doubled up in rooms built to hold twenty-five people, max—and it was there the trouble began. The wayward minor floor was known throughout the prison as a problem. The older women called the girls "diddy bops," and they had a reputation for being a bunch of hell-raisers.[58]

Nora Ann and Desiree were "cellies." Nora Ann was twenty and had been arrested for grand larceny; Desiree was sixteen, in on a prostitution charge. After they were locked in together for the night around eight p.m., they started fighting. A journalist reported that one called the other "glamorous," she then retorted that the first girl was "sexless," and within moments, "a free-for-all hair pulling session was underway."[59] The guard on the floor testified that when she arrived at their cell, Desiree was beating Nora Ann and wouldn't let the officer in, or Nora Ann out. A captain from the seventh floor heard the commotion and ran down to assist. Together, they separated the pair, sending Nora Ann to the hospital and Desiree to a punishment cell.

However, this meant the two officers had to split up. When the captain escorted Desiree to solitary on the fourth floor, Desiree kicked her in the stomach and smacked another guard in the face. On the sixth floor, meanwhile, the other women began shouting and banging on the gates in support of Desiree. A woman named Barbara started screaming that her mattress was on fire. The sole guard ran to her corridor, discovered that she was telling the truth, and opened the cell to deal with the fire—at which point Barbara slipped past her, ran to the guard post that sat at the center of the floor, and turned the control lever, unlocking all the cells at once.

Instantly, the diddy bops went crazy. Pandemonium reigned on the sixth floor, where the majority of the riot occurred (on other floors, women yelled and made noise, but did not seem to physically fight back). According to the guard, "Hysterical outbursts followed, and the cry went up to 'burn sheets and break windows.' Linens and newspapers were set afire and thrown into the corridors....Books, magazines and bedding were set afire and thrown out of windows."[60] It took over an hour to restore order, and even that only came after they'd hosed the corridors down to the point where all the halls were covered in an inch of water. All told, eighty-two windows were broken and one mattress was burned, as were ten sheets, five blankets, and eight pillowcases.[61]

Officially, the riot was blamed on overcrowding and "general restlessness."[62] Reports made by correctional officers suggested these problems were habitual: a list prepared in May 1958 showed five separate incidents that year in which staff and imprisoned people had come to blows, ranging from guards being punched in the face to guards being shoved into walls (violence *by* guards *against* imprisoned people was rarely admitted to exist).[63]

Thomasina S., an eighteen-year-old queer Black girl who had been raised by her extended family in the South, was one of the girls on that list. "Tommy," as her girlfriend Rayleen called her, was "sort of an underdog," even though she often seemed like a leader in the group of young queer women she hung out with.[64] A tiny bit of a thing, Tommy had come to New York to live with her mother after her Southern relatives had all passed, but it was a terrible situation. As Tommy once tearfully told her parole officer, "I am her oldest child and she ought to love me as much as she does the others," but instead, her mother "used her as a servant" and eventually had her committed as a wayward minor.[65] When she was released on parole in early 1958, her mother kicked her out and washed her hands of Tommy, which is how Tommy ended up at the WPA's Hopper Home, where Rayleen was also temporarily living.

The two had much in common. Rayleen was white, just a few months younger than Tommy, and also came from a troubled family. Rayleen had been regularly raped by her stepfather starting at the age of eight. Her mother found out when Rayleen was around thirteen and called her "the aggressor" in the situation.[66] Rayleen's mother began encouraging her to sleep with other boys and men in the neigh-borhood, as a distraction. Rayleen became pregnant at fifteen, which is when the government first became aware of her family situation and removed her from the home.

Shortly before the April 1958 riot, the staff at the WPA began to feel there was something unhealthy in the relationship between the two young women, and in particular, that Rayleen was out to seduce Tommy. Both girls denied it. In response, the WPA began mak-ing thinly veiled threats to send the girls back to prison, telling them that parole officers "did not approve of people associating together who were on parole."[67] Of course, many of the other clients at the WPA were also on parole and regularly associated with one another. In case she didn't get the hint, Rayleen's worker made the real issue clear: "We also straight-forwardly asked R. if she was having any kind of homosexual relationship with Thomasina and she stated that she was not."[68]

And yet someone—Thomasina suspected her mother, but it may well have been the WPA staff—told her parole officer she was dating Rayleen, and she was sent back to the House of D.

One night in late March or early April, while Tommy was on the diddy bop wing, "the whole Ward…erupted and seven of the girls [were] put into confinement including T."[69] Whatever happened that night, it was never officially documented, and Tommy was released from the House of D shortly thereafter. When the official riot hap-pened later that month, neither Rayleen nor Tommy could be found by their social workers, and both skipped appointments with the WPA during that period. They may well have been in the House of D for the riot. Certainly, Tommy was back there just a few weeks later, when a guard accused Tommy of shoving her against a wall and tearing her uniform.

According to the WPA, in the House of D, Tommy's "anger and hostility" were of "a psychotic level."[70] Why was Tommy so angry, the staff wondered? They didn't seem to notice or reflect on their own treatment of Tommy, such as when her social worker called Tommy "flagrantly mannish."[71] Nor did they protest when Tommy was kicked out of the halfway home where she had been living because "of her obvious homosexual acquaintances."[72] Nor did they say anything when her parole officer wrote that Tommy "was going from bad to worse…[and] she would have to return her to Westfield."[73]

If Tommy was angry, she had more than enough reason to be.

As threatened, at the end of May 1958 Tommy's parole officer sent her back to Westfield State Farm. While Bertha had wanted to go to Westfield, Tommy dreaded it, probably because she knew it was meant to separate her and Rayleen. Sending imprisoned people to institutions far from their families, homes, friends, and lawyers is to this day a common form of punishment. Euphemistically, it's often passed off as an attempt to rehabilitate the person by removing them from bad influences, but the complete lack of post-prison support lays bare the essentially punitive nature of these transfers. (In the 1970s, after a major riot in Attica prison led to several deaths, a number of imprisoned leaders brought cases to the Supreme Court, alleging that they were being transferred as punishment, or in an attempt to destroy their legal cases. While the justices agreed that transfers could make the lives of imprisoned people much worse, and that there should be more oversight of correctional officers, they ultimately allowed punitive transfers to continue.[74])

No doubt Tommy was furious by the time she arrived at Westfield— furious, experienced in prison life, and well versed in the value of public resistance. Coincidentally or not, on the afternoon of June 7, 1958, two weeks after Tommy arrived, Westfield was consumed by a riot of its own.

According to the press, "screaming women rag[ed] out of control for four hours"[75] and had to be subdued by male guards from Sing Sing prison, armed with "tommy guns [and] tear gas."[76] A young woman named Shirley told the Women's Prison Association there had been a troubled undercurrent in Westfield "for a long time."[77] In fact, the imprisoned people had begun to organize, and, according to newspaper reports, on the morning of the riot, "fifteen leaders sought to present a list of demands" to the superintendent.[78] Those demands have been lost to time, but according to Shirley, "The real reason for the riot was…an order that the girls would not be allowed to wear slacks."[79] Shirley's account is backed up by numerous reports, which stated that "parole violators" had caused the demonstration over "mail restrictions and the wearing of slacks."[80] In both the House of D and the WPA home, Tommy, Bertha, and Cherokee had been regularly reprimanded for wearing pants, and Cherokee and Bertha for their love letters. Whether or not Tommy was involved in the Westfield riot, other young butches like these three were surely at the heart of these protests.

After the riot was quelled, Tommy was held at Westfield for over a year, before moving back home with her mother. She never again made contact with the WPA. The social workers got what they wanted: her relationship with Rayleen fizzled out, and soon Rayleen drifted away from their services as well. The staff members who had connected closely with young queer people in the past—folks like Barbara Manley Philips or Dr. Marion Stranahan—were gone, and without them the creeping homophobia of the '50s infected the WPA, as it did every other part of American life. Queer women would still appear regularly in the WPA files, but their sexuality would be seen as a problem they needed to overcome, and many would be denied services entirely.

However, these queer people were starting to find more reliable allies than the caseworkers at the WPA: each other. As Hannah Walker wrote in a historical analysis of the Westfield riot, "Although the protest was ultimately unsuccessful…women were beginning to utilize the strength of coalition building, coupled with persistent pressure, to generate change."[81]

This wasn't just happening in the prison, it was happening in the streets, in the bars, at their jobs, and—often—in Greenwich Village.

In some of the final entries in Rayleen's WPA file, her worker suggested that she and Tommy were part of "a Group which is spending a great deal of time in the Village." A few entries later, she spelled out her fears more blatantly: the "Gay Crowds" had enticed the pair down to Greenwich.[82]

And oh, how gay those crowds were! Despite the decade's embrace of stultifying conformity; despite the endemic misogyny, racism, homophobia, and class oppression queer people endured; and despite the city's fast-crumbling infrastructure, queer people in the 1950s were building strong, sub-rosa connections, which powered the homophile and gay liberation movements. For queer women and transmasc people in particular, the House of D would be *the* New York City landmark around which their communities developed, literally and spiritually. Some met each other in the prison, or in other parts of the criminal legal system on the way in or out. Others found community in the bars and growing social infrastructure of lesbian life (some of which sprung up literally in the shadow of the prison), and still others would throw themselves into the burgeoning homophile movement developing in Greenwich Village.

Along the way, many of these people lost their parents, jobs, friends, husbands, homes, and children; they were arrested, abused, and vilified; they lived lives that were called lonely, stunted, and perverted—yet they lived, and loved, and fought to create space to live and love even more. The 1950s and early '60s was a cold time for outsiders. These women, rushing through the city, brushing against each other, sparked the coming blaze.

CHAPTER 8

The Gay Crowds

EMMILENE J. WAS THE FIRST OF HER GROUP OF YOUNG FRIENDS TO show up at the Women's Prison Association. She was a sweet-faced Black woman of twenty, with deeply dimpled cheeks and a whistling gap between her top front teeth. It was the summer of 1956, and Emmilene was in a terrible bind: her husband, William, had been arrested for grand larceny and was now in Sing Sing prison, leaving Emmilene behind to care for their two kids, who were both under the age of five.

Emmilene and her family lived in Edenwald, a public housing development in the Bronx. Since the 1930s, New York City had been building public housing at a quick clip, mostly at the urging of master planner Robert Moses. Never an elected official, Moses amassed power through being appointed to various positions in the city government (at one point, he held twelve different titles at the same time). He used the raw power that gave him to intimidate anyone who resisted his plans. Moses saw public housing as a convenient way to reorganize the city along class lines. He demolished areas he deemed "slums" in order to create roads and other infrastructure to make it easier for (white, wealthy) suburban dwellers to access Midtown and the

Financial District. Simultaneously, he built large public housing units out on the periphery of the city—in the outer boroughs or the as of yet "unwanted" parts of Manhattan—and moved displaced people into them. If there were people there already, well, too bad.

In the 1930s, New York's public housing was conceived as a way for working-class people to move up into middle-class life. Early units integrated casework and other services, had community spaces, and attempted to give stability and a boost up the ladder to residents. But post World War II, as the city's tax base fell apart and white families were encouraged to move to the suburbs instead, New York City's public housing was ignored and allowed to fall into disrepair, as were the old neighborhoods that had been destroyed for slum clearance. These once vibrant ethnic enclaves now had highways crisscrossing them like scars, and the new projects weren't communities at all, just large masses of strangers, crammed together with little in the way of support or easy access to things like public transportation. Many of the residents were new to the city. Few had other resources to call on. Adding insult to injury, caps on the amount that a family could earn ensured that any family that *did* succeed in finding some economic stability while living in the projects was soon kicked out of their home. It was a recipe for disaster.

Depending on the area where the New York City Housing Authority (NYCHA) was building, the existing communities were usually Black or immigrant or both, and although they tried to resist, they were generally ignored. For instance, in 1956, Black religious leaders in Harlem flooded a meeting held by the city council to discuss new projects. "Four years ago I was forced to move my church for the coming project; yet in that time, not a brick has been erected on West 140th Street," testified Catholic bishop James P. Roberts. "I say, not another project built in Harlem. In the name of God, let my people live."[1] A Protestant reverend spoke next, and told the city to commit to strengthening the existing physical neighborhood in order to preserve its community. "Help us make what we have better," he begged. "We don't want to lose, as Father Roberts said, our political strength."[2] A former city assemblyman followed the religious speakers and predicted that "the Negro businessmen in the area will be wiped out."[3]

The projects went up regardless.

Moses did fail spectacularly, once, in 1955, when he tried to extend Fifth Avenue like a highway through Washington Square Park and the heart of Greenwich Village. Part of the reason the Village has grown into the tony neighborhood it is today is its physical structure, which was largely saved due to the power of wealthy and well-connected white residents and business owners who resisted Moses. So the Village got to be a neighborhood rather than becoming an en-route to somewhere else.

Similarly, the House of D might not have been such an important landmark for working-class queer women had their home neighborhoods and communities not been constantly under siege. One guide to the city, written in 1959, acknowledged that much of the street-level counterculture in the Village "belong[ed] to the boys and girls of stodgier neighborhoods who come here to try on the make-up, costumes, and manners of what they think is indigenous evil."[4] (This remains true to this day: in the early 2000s, a big part of the impetus to "clean up" Christopher Street Pier was to drive out the queer youth of color who flocked there from other neighborhoods.) By the mid-1950s, the Village was becoming a place where misfits could visit but couldn't afford to live. As one correspondent wrote at the end of '54, "High rents as well as changing times [had] forced most of the Bohemians to move on....Greenwich Village is no longer the home of so many fabulous transients."[5]

Except, of course, for those "fabulous transients" who passed, by the thousands, through the House of D. Forced to live in the Village, yet never recognized as residents, they were the collateral damage and displaced ghosts of urban renewal.

Instead of recognizing the structural forces that were destabilizing the lives of the people in public housing, the city doubled down on an individualized answer: the tenants, and other working-class people, were the problem. As an NYCHA spokesperson told the *Daily News* in 1952, public housing was "naturally" built in "blighted areas."[6] If NYCHA had the ability to demolish and replace entire neighborhoods, he argued, everything would have worked out fine, but unfortunately, the remaining neighbors "do not exert enough influence on their children to stay them from teaming up with our 'bad tenants' in wreaking havoc in and about housing property."[7]

In 1953—shortly before Emmilene moved into the Edenwald Houses—NYCHA issued a draconian list of twenty-one "non-desirability" factors that would get you booted from the projects, or serve as a reason to deny you housing in them in the first place.[8] The list included everything from not owning enough furniture to having an out-of-wedlock child, to moving too often, to using drugs, to having an irregular work history. They might as well have listed "being poor" as a disqualifying condition for living in these projects that were theoretically built to help poor people.

NYCHA did not say anything about queer people in determining tenant desirability—at least not explicitly. But included on their list of negatives were an "other than honorable discharge" from the military, any contact with a court in the last five years, and any history of mental illness that required hospitalization—an increasingly popular treatment for homosexuality after 1952, when it was added to the *Diagnostic and Statistical Manual of Mental Disorders* as a "sociopathic personality disturbance."

But even if a queer person hadn't been discharged, arrested, or hospitalized, they would still be an easy target for government housing discrimination, as another clause allowed NYCHA to deny housing to anyone they considered "obnoxious."[9] The rules were made to be bent, broken, and used by those at the top of the system to selectively punish whomever they wanted.

Furthermore, if *any* member of the family were caught violating these rules, those on the lease could be evicted. This moved the onus of enforcement onto residents themselves. If you didn't want to be kicked out, then your queer child, or your mentally ill mother, or your freshly rejected-from-the-service aunt had to go. Just as the military had taught servicemembers to constantly be on guard for homosexuality, so too did NYCHA with its tenants. By 1956, NYCHA was the largest landlord in the world, providing homes to some 342,000 New Yorkers like Emmilene.[10] How many of these families sacrificed their queer members to keep a roof over their heads? We'll never know.

For enforcement, NYCHA was given its own police force. Previously, it had unarmed watchmen patrolling the buildings and grounds. But starting in 1953, hundreds of new officers were hired to work specifically for NYCHA. As the *Daily News* reported, "After one month's training these [armed] men will police the most troubled housing projects."[11]

Sometimes, the line between being in prison and being free is much thinner and harder to locate than you might guess—as Emmilene discovered.

One day in the summer of 1956, Emmilene went to the beach, leaving a friend of hers to babysit. Unbeknownst to Emmilene, he invited a few neighbors to join him. An NYCHA officer said he grew suspicious upon seeing two teen boys headed to the apartment with a bottle of wine and followed them. By the time Emmilene got back home, he was waiting to arrest her for "impairing the morals of minors."[12] In particular, she was accused of letting the fourteen-and-a-half-year-old daughter of a neighbor have a beer (again, while she was not home). Never mind that the girl's own mother had said "she could see no reason why her daughter should not have a half glass of beer if she wanted it" and that "she could not see any real case" against Emmilene.[13] The apartment was hers, so the crime, therefore, was hers as well.

Emmilene was already on probation due to a prostitution charge a year prior, her first encounter with the law. Shortly after her husband William had been arrested, Emmilene had been picked up for soliciting an undercover cop in Harlem. It was the week before Christmas, and she had been trying to pay her furniture bill—not having enough furniture being considered an acceptable reason to push someone out of public housing, remember.[14] She spent a week in the House of D before her case was heard at the Court for Vagrant Women, as the Women's Court had been renamed when it moved to Midtown in 1954. Luckily, a friendly neighbor had hired her a lawyer—a rarity in these cases—so even though Emmilene pleaded guilty, she managed to get probation and keep her children.

Now, thanks to her morals arrest, Emmilene was facing prison time, the loss of her apartment, and the loss of her kids. Furthermore, her husband, William, would soon be up for parole, but without an apartment for him to go home to, it was unlikely he would be granted release.

All because her babysitter had given a girl a beer while Emmilene wasn't home.

Thankfully, Emmilene's probation officer from her prostitution arrest was closely connected with the WPA, and she directed Emmilene there. The WPA quickly got involved on her behalf. The morals charge was dropped, but unfortunately, the WPA couldn't stop the harassment from NYCHA, or Emmilene's eventual eviction.

By November, Emmilene and her apartment were under constant surveillance by the NYCHA police. On a Wednesday night near midnight, they raided her home. They accused her of selling drugs to minors, woke up her children, and ransacked her apartment. The taller of the two detectives claimed to find some "marijuana sticks" and demanded Emmilene come with him to the station house.[15] As she dressed the children for the trip, "shaking like a leaf," the shorter officer whispered to her, "What are you doing, are you crazy? He has nothing on you."[16] Of course, Emmilene knew there were no drugs in her apartment. But until she realized that one of the officers was on her side, protesting had seemed more dangerous than going along. When she then refused to go to the station, the tall officer switched tactics and accused her of prostitution. However, if "she should do as they asked," he said, "they would let her go and not bother her again."[17]

Emmilene grew indignant at this unsubtle sexual blackmail and demanded they prove their case—an act of incredible bravery, considering that she was twenty-one, already on probation, and alone with two white police officers who showed little compunction about breaking the law.

It worked.

The tall officer backed down, the shorter one guided him out of the apartment, and Emmilene spent a sleepless night trying to calm her children and wondering if the cops would return. "Life is miserable," she thought, and "the Housing people are just the meanest on earth."[18] The WPA agreed; they felt that, in her case, NYCHA and the Department of Welfare were "overly authoritative and punitive," but there was little they could do.[19]

In discussing all of this with the WPA, Emmilene's underlying conflict was laid bare: she wasn't sure if she loved William anymore. They had been childhood sweethearts and married young, but that felt like a long time ago. Losing the apartment—leaving him in Sing Sing—would have put things off a little longer, given her a little more time to think. They hadn't seen each other in nearly two years, and, besides, Emmilene was now seeing someone else.

Several someone elses.

When her social worker, scandalized, inquired if William knew, Emmilene assured her that he did.

> She explained without any real apparent emotion that even while her husband was home she had frequently gone to dances with girl friends and had friends, male or female, that she had met at those dances, call her and come to see her at home and her husband has never said anything and she was sure he didn't mind.[20]

Emmilene was walking a careful line in this interview, one her social worker didn't notice, which lived in the overlap between "girl friend" and "girlfriend."

When asked how she'd feel if the situation were reversed, Emmilene said "she would be glad that [William] had someone to be with."[21] Flummoxed, her worker asked if that had ever happened, and Emmilene ascended a verbal tightrope again: William "had not had other women coming to the home while she was there," she pronounced carefully, "nor had he made as many extra friends as she had."[22]

For now, they left it at that.

A few weeks later, William returned home from Sing Sing, and the WPA described him as "a handsome young man, very personable and with a charming manner."[23] They were glad he was out, glad the pair was staying together, glad they were both working. But something was off, and undergirding those happy descriptions was a whiff of deviance: William was "weak" and "dependent," and Emmilene treated him "like another one of her children."[24] Their relationship had significant issues—William could get violent and had beaten Emmilene while under the influence of drugs more than once—but to the WPA, these real problems, while concerning, paled in comparison to William's unmanliness and Emmilene's infidelity.

In March 1957, Emmilene again waded carefully into a discussion of sexuality with her social worker. "She tells us that her husband is kind and considerate and does not make too great a demand on her sexually," her worker wrote. "In fact she modifies this by saying she does not live a normal sex life with him." Her social worker sensed that there was something Emmilene wanted to talk about, but she caught the wrong hint. "Having been given this opening," she wrote excitedly, "we discussed with her contraceptives."[25]

Two weeks later, when the WPA had a birthday party for a young Black woman named Hattie Mae, Emmilene's social worker finally caught on. She accidently found herself eavesdropping on the pair when "it suddenly dawned upon [her] that Emmilene was not averse to homo-sexual activity."[26] She didn't fully understand what she was hearing, because of their "strong symbolic language," but one of the other workers "seemed to be aware of the meaning of these terms used by homo-sexuals" and explained everything to her.[27]

Hattie Mae wasn't a troublemaker, not exactly. But as one social worker put it, "As usual when Hattie is around the atmosphere was emotionally charged."[28] Hattie Mae made things happen. People—women—paid attention to her. Her name appears in the files of at least a half dozen other women involved with the WPA, usually at the center of a group of young queer people. Even straight girls found her bewitching. One night, a nineteen-year-old young woman named Janice happened to be in a group discussion with Hattie Mae and became "quite fascinated."[29] Afterward, unprompted, she turned to her social worker and asked "how it happens some people become homo-sexuals?"[30] (Her worker's answer? There was "no one definite cause," but it was usually the mother's fault.)[31]

The night of her birthday, Hattie Mae arrived with a young white woman named Connie, who had recently moved into the WPA's shelter, the Hopper Home. Connie was the archetype of a 1950s girl in trouble: Her father wasn't around, her mother died young, and Connie bounced around a series of Catholic institutions. She was seventeen when she entered her last one, the Catholic Guardian Society, and she was eighteen and pregnant when she left it. In fact, her Catholic guardians took her to court and had her brought in front of a magistrate—again, while pregnant—for the crime of "associating with undesirable companions."[32] This was a slightly reworded version of the charge under which Big Cliff had first been incarcerated some forty years earlier. As they were considered her legal guardians, their request to have her imprisoned was granted, and Connie was sent to Westfield State Farm.

Pregnant.

Her boyfriend never even knew, and now Connie had no way to get in touch with him. Much like Connie herself, the baby entered the world of Catholic charity institutions, and for the rest of the time that Connie associated with Emmilene, Hattie Mae, and the WPA, the fate of Connie's son was constantly dangling over her head.

As was the case for so many others, Connie "became involved in homosexual activity" while in prison.[33] So, unlike Emmilene's social worker, Connie's worker was warned to keep watch on her interactions with other women. Connie told the WPA that she had a new boyfriend, but she wanted to put things on hold with him until she was settled at work. Almost immediately, the WPA realized Connie was also dating several formerly incarcerated young women, all of whom were connected through their criminal legal experiences.

It started one night in March 1957, a month before Hattie Mae's party. Connie's social worker "was made aware of an intimate friendship" developing between Connie and Hattie when she overheard some of the other women discussing the queer affairs of Connie, Hattie, and a young married woman from Puerto Rico named Irma.[34]

The next day, the WPA confronted Connie. Connie was working as a beauty technician at Slenderella, a weight-loss salon in Long Island City, so her worker met her for a cup of coffee during her lunch break. Connie didn't try to hide anything: yes, "she has become involved with Hattie Mae," and also yes, "that was the reason that she hasn't been too interested in getting in touch with her boy friend."[35] Despite this, and the fact that they had been warned about Connie's previous relationships with women, the WPA didn't really consider Connie queer, probably because she was feminine and white and had a son. Her social worker's main worry was that Connie not "become active in this way," meaning she didn't want Connie to go butch, or be the one pursuing other women.[36] The WPA offered to pay for a room so that Connie could move out of the Hopper Home and thus be less likely to run into Hattie Mae.

Connie agreed, but in a desultory way—more to shut the WPA up, it seemed, than because she actually wanted to move—and she was still living at the Hopper Home on the night of Hattie's party. Or, at least, that's what the WPA thought, until the party ended and Emmilene's social worker found herself walking with Emmilene, Hattie, and Connie to the subway station. Emmilene lived in the Bronx and Hattie lived in Brooklyn—opposite ends of the NYC universe—so when they all headed toward the same train platform, Emmilene's worker thinly suggested that Emmilene would be very lonely on the long ride back to the Bronx after she'd dropped off Hattie and Connie. Emmilene saw right through her. "You are just trying to make me go back to William," she told her, "and I'm not going to do it."[37]

Suddenly, Connie grabbed Emmilene's purse and sprinted toward a Brooklyn-bound train. Now, Emmilene told her worker, she had no choice *but* to go home with the two girls. In a twinkle, the doors of the subway opened, and in the rush of people, Emmilene, Connie, and Hattie Mae were gone.

The WPA wouldn't see Emmilene again for a month, but Hattie Mae filled them in on what happened: Connie *had* gotten a new apartment, in Brooklyn, so first the trio headed there. But the landlord spotted Emmilene and wouldn't let Connie bring a Black woman into her room (the same thing had happened when Hattie tried to visit Connie at Slenderella, and the salon chain would soon be sued for their anti-Black policies). Instead, Connie and Emmilene went back to Emmilene's place in the Bronx, while Hattie Mae attended to a few errands and joined them later. The next day, Connie ditched her new apartment (and, apparently, her relationship with Hattie Mae) and moved in with Emmilene and William.

"This has happened before in the past and [William] is certain it will not last," Emmilene's social worker wrote in a scandalized tone.[38]

Many a queer woman and transmasc person who ended up at the House of D had, or at least talked about having, sexual and romantic relationships with both men and women. Often, it is hard to tell from the existing documents if their relationships with men were made up, or coerced, or had anything to do with their own desires. For some, their sexual lives ran on two parallel tracks, and it's possible that heterosexuality was just a rut they'd gotten stuck in for a while. Not so with Emmilene, who never seemed to hide her queer desires from the WPA and her husband, or her straight desires from her wide world of queer acquaintances and lovers.

It probably helped that William, her husband, was also bisexual—although it took the WPA even longer to catch on in his case.

A few months after Emmilene and Connie started dating, Emmilene's *other* other relationship, with a man named Freddie, started to get serious. Freddie had been in the navy; now he was back, and seeing quite a bit of Emmilene. When asked how William felt about all of this, Emmilene replied coolly that "William himself invited [Freddie] to come and visit with them often."[39] Suspicions raised, the WPA quickly figured out that Duke, William's drug connection, was also his sometime lover.

The difference between the WPA's response to Emmilene's sexuality and William's is telling. Once the staff understood that William had even occasional sex with men, they began to write that William "is a homosexual."[40] His interest in women, and Emmilene in particular, was attributed to a weak personality that needed babying. The idea that he might genuinely be attracted to men and women was outside their ken.

As for Emmilene?

It is our strong belief that she is not actually a homosexual but that she is simply inducing this type of feeling in herself…out of the pervert satisfaction she gets out of it. We told her she cannot convince us otherwise and…we felt that if she will really find the man who will be the right choice for her and who will be able to stimulate her properly on a sexual level that her homosexual feelings will completely disappear.[41]

This was extremely wishful thinking.

The more the WPA workers tried to dismiss or deny her sexuality, the more Emmilene seemed to enjoy tweaking them about it. She was deeply embedded in a queer community that was white, Black, and brown; male and female; cis and trans. And she wasn't afraid to push back against homophobes, either.

Emmilene had a job in Greenwich Village and was thus frequently in the subway with staff from the WPA. One evening, while waiting in the station, Emmilene noticed her WPA worker staring at a butch-femme couple holding a baby. "We must have been looking rather intensively," the worker wrote, "to ascertain the sex of the person." Emmilene, with the exasperation of a born and bred New Yorker, tried to get her worker to chill.

"What are you staring at?" she hissed.

When the worker explained that the "woman in man's clothing… looked like a female," Emmilene could barely contain her annoyance. "Well what if she is?" she snapped.

It was confusing, the worker stammered to explain, because, well, the woman was holding a baby in her arms, and dressed like a man! But she wasn't a total idiot, the worker told Emmilene. She was "aware that there are some people who are bi-sexual."[42]

Emmilene snorted. "There certainly are," she said, making a joke that her worker heard, but didn't get.[43] To her worker, "bi-sexual" meant something along the lines of transgender or intersex, an older usage that she probably picked up in a professional or academic setting. Emmilene used bisexual as we do today, to refer to a sexual orientation. *Her* sexual orientation.

For a while, the pair stood in frosty silence, waiting for the train, watching and not-watching the couple, before Emmilene made her final assessment of the situation: "That's about the size of it."[44]

A few months later, Emmilene and her social worker had a similar interaction when her worker came to visit Emmilene and William at home (in a new apartment, now in Harlem). A neighbor stopped in for a while, and after she left the worker noticed Emmilene and William smirking at each other. When pressed, they let the worker in on the secret: their neighbor was a trans woman (although none of them used that term). Emmilene explained that she was a "woman impersonator" who had retired from the stage years ago. Thoroughly confused, the worker—using male pronouns—inquired if the neighbor "was a bi-sexual person?" Once again, they were using the same words, but with very different meanings: Emmilene answered that her neighbor "goes out with men for money but gets a real kick only out of [her] relationships with women."[45]

Overwhelmed by this information, the worker stopped asking questions. She would continue talking about this "only in so far as it reflected upon [Emmilene and William]."[46]

At the end of her visit, the worker watched as Emmilene gently washed William's hair in the sink, set it with a good wave, and then lovingly trimmed his beard. "She was quite tender with him," and "[he] appeared to love this kind of treatment," the worker wrote, before concluding, "This is not really a healthy, wholesome relationship."[47]

Perhaps not. But Emmilene and William stayed together and took care of one another, and their kids and extended families, even after the WPA gave up on them.

As William had anticipated, Emmilene's relationship with Connie quickly ran its course, and after a passionate month she moved out. According to Emmilene, Connie spent too much time in "disreputable establishments where homo-sexual orgies are going on."[48]

Be that as it may, Connie soon found the father of her child, and by April 1958 she had married him, sworn off women, and was in the process of reclaiming her son from the foster care system. Emmilene was working in Greenwich Village when she heard, and she wrote a long letter to a different worker at the WPA, with a simple request:

> I would like if you will to send Connie a congratulation card on her coming marriage. That's if she hasn't done it already. Ok please do this for me. I only ask favors of you once in a while because in this matter you're the only one who really understood. And believe me when I got the news of this I didn't feel bad, but was glad and felt good all over. I can see this is what she needed in the first place because the other way would only cause trouble. What we share[d] together wasn't complete or fulfilled our every needs, but it did bring a great joy that never can really be explain[ed] in words. Just to know we belonged to one another for a while, that's one reason why we stayed away so much, to make the break easier for the both of us without having to hurt one another. The one thing I ask of her, not to get into any more trouble, be happy and healthy always. For I will never forget what joys we shared.[49]

Shortly after, Emmilene started dating Dolores, a twenty-year-old Black nurse in training. Dolores was a stud who had many girlfriends vying for her attention in the House of D, Westfield State Farm, the Hopper Home, and all the other institutions she had passed through as a wayward minor. She had once spent sixty-five days straight in the House of D for living with her girlfriend—since they were both on parole at the time, any contact between them was technically a criminal act, much like it was for Rayleen and Tommy. Her girlfriend was sent to Westfield, but it seemed Dolores was lost in the paperwork, and after more than two months at the House of D she was released.[50]

When her social worker finally realized Dolores was gay ("a revelation," as she wrote excitedly in her notes), Dolores pulled out photos of her two girlfriends from her stint at Westfield.[51] "One was a very voluptuous blonde and the other a beautiful dark haired girl in the type of Hedy Lamar. The pictures were signed 'with love' and one was signed 'Kitty' and the other 'Virginia.'"[52]

Outside of prison, however, Dolores ran almost exclusively with other Black queer women like Emmilene and Hattie. Once, when a new Black woman named Sara showed up at the Hopper Home and a white woman got in her face, Dolores threatened to kick the crap out of the white woman. The workers were shocked. Dolores had always been fun, sweet, straightforward—never the kind of person to get into a fight. When they separated the two, they asked Dolores what had happened to set her off so badly. She explained that she wouldn't let "those trashy Whites get fresh with [my] kind."[53] But whatever that white girl had done, the WPA didn't write it down.

Just as much as these queer, formerly incarcerated women were at the roots of gay pride and liberation, they were also refusing white supremacy and anti-Blackness in their everyday lives, in the context of the ascendant civil rights movement and Black power at large. In 1954, Malcolm X had come to Harlem to lead Temple Number 7, a pillar in the Nation of Islam. In 1955, Rosa Parks, a lifelong civil rights activist and Black community organizer, initiated the Montgomery bus boycott. In 1957, Dr. Reverend Martin Luther King Jr. founded the Southern Christian Leadership Conference, a backbone in the fight against white supremacy. Black organizing was in the air.

But, sadly, when organizing for Black liberation involved everyday people, not the celebrities of the movement like X and Parks and King, it was rarely entered into the historical record. The vast majority of documents we have from the American past were created by white people, or via white-majority institutions, and have been saved and disseminated by them as well. Entrance into the historical record, therefore, largely correlates with proximity to whiteness. Even if the entire world woke up tomorrow, magically disabused of all the racist notions we carry—consciously and unconsciously—we would still be left with a white supremacist and asymmetric archive from which to write our histories.

Institutional archives are weakest when it comes to organizing done by people of color, for people of color, outside the surveillance of white eyes. At best, we get brief indications of the existence of folks like Dolores and her circle of young Black lesbian, bisexual, and gender nonconforming people; at worst, they are never referenced at all, or only through a lens of white supremacy that warps reality so fundamentally, it's impossible to know what can be trusted.

Sometimes, however, the records *do* exist—particularly in instances where the boundaries of race fall apart or are intentionally concealed. Many of the women I've researched passed as straight when necessary; some also passed as white.

So it was for Irma T., a young artist and seamstress from Puerto Rico. In 1955, Irma was arrested for shoplifting in New York City and sent to a prison upstate for an indeterminate period of up to three years. While there, she married Jose, who was the father of her two children from before she was incarcerated. But their marriage, for her, was more about child-rearing and stability than romance.

Instead, she found love with another young woman from Puerto Rico named Gloria—or "Goya," as Irma affectionately called her.[54] Irma even had Goya's name tattooed in simple stick-and-poke style on her foot. When she went in front of the parole board for the first time after six months in prison, she was denied release because of their relationship.

In her initial letter asking for support from the Women's Prison Association, Irma wrote, "I am white, 22 years of age, married and the mother of two daughters."[55] However, after she was accepted for services, she explained to a social worker that her mother was white and her father was Black. Although she was bilingual, Irma's first language was Spanish, and she saw a firm distinction between her racial and ethnic identity and that of her husband, Jose (whom she explained was also from Puerto Rico, but was really Spanish and French). But in official records, Irma was listed simply as white. According to the WPA, she was "an attractive, neat looking youngster" but "seemed rather scared and pathetic."[56]

Through Irma, WPA staff learned some surprising—yet basic—facts about life behind bars for Spanish-speaking people. They were shocked to find out that Westfield State Farm, for instance, did not have books in Spanish. Irma could read fine in English, but she missed reading in Spanish, and, besides, many of the other women from Puerto Rico couldn't read English, so she asked as much for them as for herself. The WPA's response was a master class in being what Martin Luther King named "the white moderate, who is more devoted to 'order' than to justice."[57] At first, they promised to send Irma books she could read and then donate to the prison library. But after speaking to the officials at Westfield, the WPA informed Irma that

> there are several other Spanish speaking girls at the Institution who are not as fortunate as you in their knowledge of English. To them reading these books would be greatly detrimental because it would create a further block in their learning of English and hence their adjustment into the community in which they live. So you see in a set up like yours, the need of the many sometimes has to be considered over and above the need of the individual [58]

Is it any wonder that Irma was careful in discussing her race with the white people who had power over her? She was more open with her sexuality than her racial identity; for weeks after they knew about her relationships with other women, she referred to Goya as "Joan" to hide the fact that she too was Puerto Rican.[59] But the WPA files showed that Irma was friends, almost exclusively, with other women of color. Once in a while, Irma interacted with Hattie Mae and Emmilene and their circle, but mostly it was other Latinas—Goya, of course, but also Maria, with whom she went on a few dates; Theresa, with whom she lived for a while; Irma's older sister Olga; Olga's friend Marta, etc.

But as with Emmilene, the WPA refused to believe that Irma was queer, even as they helped her leave her husband. "It is our impression that she is actually not a homosexual but was simply drawn into it by the particular situation," they wrote in her file. Once she married a real man, they told Irma, "her really feminine feelings will come to the fore."[60]

After this, Irma largely avoided the WPA, and three months later she cut contact with them forever, saying just that she "was unable to come for personal reasons."[61]

The experiences of Emmilene, Hattie Mae, Connie, Dolores, and Irma are just a few examples of the informal queer social networks that were developing all around the city in the late 1950s. These relationships were powerful, but ephemeral—they touched people deeply, but left only the lightest of traces. But the creation of formal institutions for queer women and transmasculine people was predicated on the existence of these informal groups, which showed women that their desires, concerns, needs, and identities were shared by others. Soon, more official organizing would follow.

CHAPTER 9

Queer Women Get Organized

THE BREAKUP OF HONORA AND ROCKY

Honora D. and her girlfriend, Rocky, were straight out of queer central casting, a butch-femme couple for the ages. Honora was like a black diamond—beautiful, sparkling, dark-skinned, and often the center of attention, even when she wasn't on stage. She had delicate features and a lovely voice. She enjoyed dancing, singing, reading scandalous novels like *Peyton Place*, and playing the piano; although she was trained in everything from musical theater to opera, she loved pop ballads and torch songs the most. During the 1930s, she had been one of the Peter Pan Kiddies, a large youth theater in Harlem. When she was four, she performed in their one-night revue at the Ambassador Theatre on Broadway (although the performance would grow in her mother's retelling—she informed a parole officer that Honora had a solo in the Broadway show *Peter Pan*).[1] She had a few years of conservatory training under her belt, as well as a straight-A career in high school. In the mid-1950s, Honora cut an album entitled *Please Don't Fall in Love* on the extremely short-lived Flamingo Records. The label seemed to have gone under before the album was released, but she toured nightclubs for a while, mostly in the Northeast, sometimes up in Canada.[2]

Strictly speaking, Honora didn't need the money from performing, she just loved it. She was trained as an office manager and keypunch operator on the early computers that were just starting to take over the world—if you've seen the film *Hidden Figures*, Honora was trained in similar computer programming as that done by Dorothy Vaughan, the woman played by Octavia Spencer. Honora also had a fairly wealthy (if complicated) family, who were often willing to support her.

And Honora had Rocky.

The way Honora talked about Rocky, everyone expected her to be six foot two and built like a diesel truck. Court reports listed her as older and very masculine, but when Honora finally introduced Rocky to her social worker at the WPA, the worker was surprised to find a slight, shy, young white woman with a blond crew cut. She had a good job as the foreman of a toy factory, making over $75 a week. The pair had met at a mutual friend's house party sometime in 1955 and immediately hit it off. They went on adventures (horseback riding, bowling) and soon made things official.

At the time, Honora lived at home with her mother and stepfather in what one newspaper called "a luxurious mansion in St. Albans, Long Island."[3] In reality, it was a lovely (though modest) two-story Tudor Revival row house made of stucco and brick, with a peaked gable awning over the front door. It was smack dab in the center of Addisleigh Park, a little-known Black enclave in Queens, which was said in the 1950s to be the home of "the nation's richest and most gifted Negroes."[4] Addisleigh had begun life as an all-white suburb in the 1930s, but by the time Honora moved there it was home to an incredible list of Black luminaries, including Fats Waller, Count Basie, Lena Horne, Milt Hinton, Jackie Robinson, Roy Campanella, and Ella Fitzgerald.[5] There were still leases that read "no part of the land now owned by the parties hereto shall ever be used or occupied, or sold, conveyed, leased, rented, or given to Negros."[6] But still, Addisleigh was fast becoming an upper-middle-class Black neighborhood (especially after

1948, when the Supreme Court ruled that race restrictions in property leases were illegal). Honora's mother was a real estate agent, and her stepfather a well-off tailor who owned his own shop—respectable career people, if not as rich as some of their neighbors.

At first, Rocky moved in with Honora's family, but after a little over a month, they decided to get a place of their own—Honora's mother seemed to know and not know about her daughter's romantic life, all at the same time, and she made them uncomfortable. The feeling, apparently, was mutual: According to Honora's mother, their relationship was peculiar because Rocky "wouldn't permit [Honora] to lift a finger."[7] If Honora wanted a drink, or needed her cigarette lit, Rocky was always right there, waiting. This wasn't the first time Honora had left home because of her mother's disapproval; when she was sixteen, she had run away for a year because her mother accused her of having sex with a boy. But her relationship with Rocky was much more serious.

For six months in 1956, Honora and Rocky shared a residential hotel room on the Upper West Side before getting an apartment on East Tenth Street—just three blocks from the House of D. According to Honora, their year in that apartment was "ideal" and "extremely satisfying"—particularly sexually.[8] Men, she said, just couldn't compare. At first, she worked outside the home, but Rocky "was perfectly willing to support her," and soon Honora took on "the passive role, that is, [the] female in the relationship," as her parole officer described it.[9] She performed in clubs and took care of the apartment; Rocky paid the bills.

According to Buddy Kent, one of the top drag kings in New York in the 1950s, butch-femme was *the* relationship standard for queer women at the time. "Nobody ever thought or talked about it," she said. "It was just the thing to do."[10] Kent was quick to point out that many women were neither butch nor femme, and that some switched roles over time, but even those people, she said, were still judged by their ability to live up to the form. Audre Lorde, one of the seminal Black lesbian authors and activists of the twentieth century, was first stepping foot into the gay world of Greenwich Village at this time, and she remembered that if you weren't one or the other, "the butches and femmes, Black and white, disparaged [you] with the term Ky-Ky, or AC/DC. Ky-Ky was the same name that was used for gay-girls who slept with johns for money. Prostitutes."[11] Even in the queer community, the conceptual linkage between queer women and sex workers—sexually disreputable women of different stripes—was strong, if only obliquely acknowledged.

But what would domestic life have been like for a pair like Honora and Rocky, who fit the butch-femme mold? According to Buddy Kent,

At home, the femme felt that she would emasculate her dyke if she had her doing some cooking or anything. The most that the butch could do for the girl was either carry the big bundles, or shop with her. But the butch never did the cooking. The only time a butch did cook was if she was from an old big Italian family where she was really a terrific cook, but then it was never talked about, and eventually that butch tried to teach her wife how to cook, so she would know it. But if they had a party and they were serving, it would all be prepared so that the girl could be in the kitchen and have it just heated up, so that she could still come out the woman, and not emasculate the butch.

The butch always served the drinks when you were entertaining....The butch greeted you at the door, she took your coats. The femme sat you down and offered you food, and then the butch got your drink.

Also the butch went along with if you went shopping because she carried the wallet. She paid the bills. The butch always protected the femme and always carried the suitcase. If you happened to be a butch with a heart condition, you were really in trouble because you couldn't carry the suitcase and you were ridiculed.

The girl never drove the car, even if she owned it. The butch drove, or if the girl drove and the butch didn't drive, that butch made sure she parked somewhere on the side streets so nobody saw her coming out from behind the wheel. You danced and you led, and if the girl was a better dancer, you still had your hand in the leader's position, though she was pushing you into the steps. You paid the check, she handed you the money to pay her share or you paid all of it, but you never, ever allowed the girl to pay the check. It was like a real boy-girl thing. Very heavy.[12]

For Honora and Rocky, it was domestic bliss, butch-femme '50s style.

Until it wasn't.

Starting in the spring of 1957, the pair began to have a falling-out. They were bored with each other, and it seemed like the differences between them—which had once drawn them together with the frisson of the exotic—were now pulling them apart. "Of the two girls, Honora is far superior both in intelligence and also in insight and general awareness of herself," a social worker wrote after being introduced to Rocky for the first time. "[Rocky] is obviously a very insecure and unsure person."[13]

It's worth wondering how much of that insecurity had to do with the presence of the social worker herself, who clearly looked down on Rocky for her masculinity and her working-class background. But certainly both women were unhappy, and in May 1957, Rocky picked up and left. Now single and unemployed, Honora ditched their apartment and got herself a room at the Hotel Churchill on Seventy-Sixth Street.

This was when her legal troubles began.

Later, she was matter of fact about it. When interviewed by a court officer, she told them "no-one introduced her to prostitution....Anyone with common sense could become a prostitute."[14] She was short on money and had no job. The only other option would have been to return home to her mother, and Honora "would rather serve time."[15] The work wasn't easy, but at least the hours were short and you didn't need any training. Honora estimated that she worked three nights a week, and saw three or four men a night. With that, she earned about the same that Rocky had as a factory foreman.

For several months, Honora made a good living, until the evening of September 19, 1957, when a police officer arrested her for solicitation. She *had* done it, Honora admitted, but the officer lied about the circumstances—*he* approached her first, and brought up money (eight dollars) first as well.[16] If you took the police at their word, the streets of New York City were flush with wanton women throwing themselves at cops, but entrapment seemed to be an NYPD specialty.

Honora spent three weeks in the House of D before being recommended to the WPA. From the very first, Honora wanted to talk about her love life—"her lesbian feelings and her unhappy love affair."[17] The staff hoped that this meant she wanted to get help, go straight, and date men. For a little while, there was Freddy, an older Canadian man who wanted to marry her. But he was a nuisance, and did things like show up at Honora's sales counter job to bug her at lunch. In October, when he started making overtures about marriage, Honora stopped taking his calls and moved back in with Rocky.

For a while, they made a go of it. They started hanging out in the evenings at the WPA group home, where they played board games and took part in lively discussion groups with the other young women. But by March 1958, they were on the ropes again, and Rocky stormed out—although Honora was quick to say that she was going to break up with Rocky herself, probably, "in a few short weeks."[18] The differences between them had become "grossly noticeable," she told her social worker.[19]

Honora, the WPA realized, was depressed. Bored. Lonely. This being the 1950s, the staff was pretty sure it was because she was gay, but they were very careful about saying that to Honora. She had been dating women for fourteen years, since she met her first girlfriend at the age of twelve at sleepaway camp. She was independent, educated, cultured, unashamed, and beautiful, and the WPA workers almost seemed intimidated. They soft-pedaled their criticisms of her as carefully as they could. "Worker was careful not to attack in any way H's homosexual relationship to [Rocky]," her social worker noted. Instead, "we spoke about the limitations of this kind of living and about the fact that it was indicative of some sort of retreat."[20]

On the WPA's advice, Honora began seeing her mother again and repaired their relationship. She researched psychotherapy, and tried dating men experimentally. She didn't mind them, she said, but "she was trying to convince herself that she was capable of a heterosexual relationship" while knowing absolutely that she "would leave this if she found the right person and enter into a homosexual one."[21] Adjusting to sex with men, in particular, was disappointing. Soon, the WPA began to doubt that she was dating the men she mentioned at all.

Heterosexuality might not have been the answer, but the WPA had correctly diagnosed the problem: loneliness. With Rocky, Honora found romantic and sexual satisfaction, but no long-term compatibility. The other women who hung out at the WPA for the most part didn't interest her—they were too young, or too wild, or too uneducated, or too flagrantly racist. If she went to lesbian bars, she never mentioned it to her social worker. But in the summer of 1958, Honora found a new way to meet other queer people. When she dropped in for dinner at the WPA on the evening of Tuesday, August 19, she told the staff she had to leave early to go to "a lecture on homosecuality [sic]."[22] Little could she know that that particular lecture would hold a storied spot in the history of queer organizing.

In just a week, New York City was to host the fifth annual National Mattachine Society Convention, at the Barbizon-Plaza Hotel on Central Park South. The Mattachine Society had been formed in the early 1950s by a number of gay men on the West Coast, who drew on their Communist background to develop a theory of queer people as an oppressed minority that needed to be organized to secure civil rights. By 1958, even Mattachine had gotten tangled in the Red Scare, and those early Communist roots had been disavowed; still, it was the largest, oldest, and leading homophile organization in the country. Or as Mattachine put it in its newsletter, it was "an educational research organization, non-profit and non-partisan...for the purpose of studying and seeking solution to the personal and social problems of people of homosexual or bisexual orientation."[23]

Mattachine was—and would always be—mostly white, mostly male, and mostly cis. Its work focused on fighting explicitly anti-homosexual policies (from bans on government employment to laws against sodomy); convincing straight experts to testify to the harmlessness or naturalness of homosexuality; and creating social opportunities and discussion groups for queer people (again, mostly but not entirely cis white men).

By the time of the Stonewall Uprising (in *just eleven years*), Mattachine would seem like the staid old guard, fighting for some watered-down version of tolerance. But in the '50s, its work was radical. Simply coming together as gay people could get your life ruined. Mattachine members had reasons to be cautious and afraid, and the surest sign of their profound courage was the fact that they came together despite the danger.

In 1958, Mattachine was at something of a crossroads, trying to figure out what kind of organization it was going to be—how radical, how public, how assimilationist? An upstart young student from Texas named Charlie Hayden was one of the Mattachine Society of New York's first twenty members. He had to lie about his age to join, because he was under twenty-one. When his father found out, he was accepting, but he asked that his son take a new name for his activism. According to historian Eric Cervini, "From then on, in New York's gay world, Charlie called himself Randolfe Wicker. First name Randolfe, because it seemed classy and unique. Last name Wicker, because it sounded awfully similar to 'wicked.'"[24] Wicker would become a mainstay in American LGBTQ politics: co-organizer of the first gay public protest in 1964; one of the men who helped overturn laws against serving homosexuals in bars with 1966's infamous "sip-in" action; part of the Stonewall Uprising; roommates and close friends with trans activist Marsha P. Johnson; etc.

But Wicker cut his teeth by becoming a regular in the bars in Greenwich Village, where he learned that queer people "were just as diverse" as straight ones.[25] This revelation of the wideness of the queer world is perhaps what inspired him to push Mattachine to do something it was loath to do: advertise.

"I believed Mattachine had to wage a campaign against the prevailing public misperceptions," Wicker wrote some fifty years later.[26]

If it was going to change the world, it needed more people, more publicity, and more chutzpah. Like the imprisoned people in the House of D with their riots, Wicker saw—correctly—that change only happened when you demanded attention.

In the lead-up to the fifth National Mattachine Convention in New York in 1958, Wicker decided to prove his point. Mattachine had monthly meetings, which usually included some kind of talk. That August, it invited a lawyer named Leo Strauss to give a lecture on "Homosexuality and the Law." Much like Ann C.'s lawyer Dirty Gertie, Strauss specialized in gay cases. "When you got arrested in a tea-room," Wicker recalled, "he would be the one who would come and defend you."[27] ("Tearoom" was slang for a cruisy bathroom.) Usually, twenty to thirty people showed up to these meetings—primarily white men who were already on the Mattachine mailing list. That was barely a cocktail party, let alone a political one. So, as one early gay historian put it, "On his own frolicsome initiative, [Wicker] had signs printed and displayed throughout Greenwich Village" to publicize the August talk.[28]

The signs were as simple as they were revolutionary: "Citizens, a lawyer discusses homosexuality and the law. Free admission. Public invited. Mattachine Society."[29] No one had ever done this before, and other Mattachine members were convinced it was a terrible idea.

Honora must have seen one of the posters somewhere in Greenwich Village, where Wicker placed them in "restaurants, book stores, barber shops, laundries, and any other places of business that would accept them."[30] She was far from alone. On August 19, 1958, a gobsmacking three hundred people showed up for Strauss's lecture. As Mattachine gushed in their newsletter,

> The best-attended meeting in the history of the Mattachine Society in New York took place on Tuesday, August 19th, when over 300 overflowed not only our spacious office but also the large hall at Freedom House. This was the result of an experiment in publicity.... The member who undertook this staggering task did prove that publicity of this type does work.[31]

Posters and riots were very different forms of public resistance, but they were part and parcel of the same emerging queer community consciousness, much of which was centered in Greenwich Village. Being located in the same area meant that those involved in one form of queer organizing were quite likely to see, hear, or feel the effects of the other. The House of D put queer women at the center of gay life—literally.

Also in the audience at that August lecture was Barbara Gittings, an early lesbian organizer and a titan in queer history. Dimpled, bespectacled, and somehow always smiling, Gittings looked exactly like the librarian she was—which probably helped keep her alive and employed, given her radical politics. In 1956, Gittings had traveled to LA to meet the organizers of Mattachine. They told her that a new organization for queer women called the Daughters of Bilitis (DoB) had just popped up in San Francisco. Gittings rushed to meet them. "For the first time, at that meeting, I was in someone's living room—not a bar—with twelve other lesbians," she told documentary filmmakers thirty years later.[32] This was intense and inspiring, but Gittings didn't really get involved in the movement until the New York conference in '58, when she was asked to launch the New York chapter of the DoB.

Like Mattachine, DoB was mostly middle class and white, although two of the eight founders were women of color. DoB also had early Black leaders, like Cleo Bonner, who became the national president in 1963. Playwright Lorraine Hansberry was on the DoB mailing list, and contributed occasionally to *The Ladder*, its newsletter, to discuss both sexuality and race. Yet still, racism was alive and well in the organization, and how a particular chapter dealt with race often came down to the specific women in the room, at the moment. As one West Coast leader remembered, "Racism was often very present, and very difficult to deal with—at times it threatened to tear us apart—but at least we tried."[33]

DoB was also conflicted about whether it was a purely social organization or a political one as well, and one of their early ongoing debates was about gender conformity: Did butches hurt the movement? Could they require women to wear skirts? Often they did, although

Gittings remembers thinking even at the time that "we want acceptability, we want to fit in...but this is wrong."[34]

For all of these reasons, DoB did not seem to attract many of the queer people caught up in the House of D. Prisons and police issues were on its radar somewhat, but mostly in terms of people being arrested for specifically gay crimes (like drag or obscenity), not lesbians arrested for shoplifting. Moreover, the Daughters were imagined in part as an alternative to the bars; many of the women and transmasc people who flowed through the House of D were either quite happy in the bars or so far outside the queer world they didn't know about them, or they were so Black, butch, or poor that they were rarely allowed into them.

After she attended the August 19th Mattachine lecture, Honora disappeared for a few weeks. When she returned to the WPA, she informed its staff in no uncertain terms that she was not interested in men. Moreover, she hinted to them that "there is a girl whom she has seen...who interests her."[35] Someone, perhaps, that she had met through Mattachine or DoB? The records don't say. But Honora stopped coming to social events at the WPA, stopped mentioning Rocky, got a therapist, and started "showing considerable new insight into things."[36] By late in the year, her social worker was convinced that Honora was "involved in a homosexual relationship with someone," and in January 1959, the WPA closed her case.[37]

It's impossible to say how involved Honora became with either the Mattachine Society or DoB, as their early membership records are few and rife with pseudonyms. Like the informal social networks of Hattie, Emmilene, and Irma, these connections were nurtured almost entirely in private apartments, crowded subway stations, closely monitored community centers, and other noncommercial spaces.

However, for a select few people, a growing world of lesbian or lesbian-friendly bars, restaurants, and coffeehouses was reappearing in the city, mostly in Greenwich Village. These venues were smaller, more sordid, and less tourist-friendly than the pre–World War II queer venues in the Village—but there were more, and more, and more of them. Many of them were owned or under the thumb of the mafia.

Some were extremely short-lived. Some excluded people of color, butch women, trans people, prostitutes, and others who didn't live up to their idea of respectability. The drinks were expensive yet weak; the ceilings were low; the windows were blacked over; and you might get raided at any time. But inside these pocket universes, for a brief moment, queer women could experience space made specifically for them.

According to historian of butch-femme culture Alix Genter, "If you stood in Washington Square Park in Greenwich Village in the 1950s, you could walk a few blocks in almost any direction and come upon a lesbian bar....Individual gay bars were always closing and opening or switching hands, but the bar scene itself was a more permanent institution."[38]

Genter created a map of eighteen bars in the Village that served primarily queer women for at least some time in the 1950s. Smack dab in the middle—the only non-bar marked on the map—squats the Women's House of Detention.[39] Other areas of the city like Times Square and Harlem had bars for men, or mixed bars that were queer-women-friendly. But nowhere else had the sheer number of spaces intended for queer women that Greenwich Village did, and they radiated out from the House of D like stars flung from the Big Bang. For some women, these bars were a subtle indication of the existence of a life they could not yet lead themselves. For others, they were *the* social institution they visited nightly. And for a select few, the bars were a dream job: fast, fun, and full of dykes.

MAX GOES STEALTH

Maxine D.—Max, most of the time—was a young white woman who found a home for herself in the bar scene. She'd never really known any other: given up to an orphanage at birth, she was adopted at thirteen months, only to have her new family complain she wasn't "cuddly" enough.[40] By the time she was eleven, they'd tossed her back into the cold waters of New York's charity institutions. Every once in a while, she'd wash back up on their unfriendly shore, get treated like trash, and spin out again. A state psychiatrist called her foster mother "cold, strict, and rejecting," and characterized both parents as "Puritans" who "oppos[ed] dancing, smoking, etc."[41]

But the more they said no to Max, the more Max said yes to life.

Smoking, drinking, sex, prostitution, probation, incarceration, parole: Max had passed through every step of that ringer before she turned eighteen. According to her record, she was "a troublemaker, instigator, and a leader [who] made no effort to conform."[42] She didn't do drugs—that seemed to be a hard line for her—but she was willing to try everything else. Including women: when she arrived at the WPA after being incarcerated for prostitution (for supporting her boyfriend, a New Jersey pimp, when she was just seventeen), the staff were shocked to hear her say "she dislikes and distrusts men and feels that more naturally she enjoys a homosexual relationship."[43]

For the next year, she barely mentioned women. She had nightmares "about being sent to the House of Detention" (where she'd already been, briefly, several times), and tried to get a straight job.[44] She worked on an assembly line putting rhinestones into costume jewelry, and at a greeting-card company doing clerical work. No matter where she went, however, men wouldn't leave her alone. Max quit job after job because of male bosses who couldn't keep their hands off of her. Even the straight social workers of the WPA were obsessed with Max's beauty, and her file is filled with compliments and descriptions of her outfits (e.g., "8-16-1956: She looked quite neat this morning with her hair tied back in a ponytail, wearing a clean blouse and skirt"; "8-20-1956: Maxine... [wearing] a new red and gold sheath dress and black shoes").[45]

Her file also mentioned that Max was "exceptionally bright," with an IQ of 131, but her educational history was a mess.[46] No one was even sure if she'd graduated from high school, and they didn't seem much to care. She got pregnant late in 1956 and moved in with the father ("Anything would be better than being at home," she told her WPA social worker).[47] In May 1957, right before the baby was born, she went to St. Faith's Home for Unwed Mothers in Westchester, New York, where they helped see her through the birth and put the baby up for adoption. By August of that year, she was back in New York City—and done with men for good.

Or so she thought.

When Max returned to the WPA, she explained that she'd demanded an open adoption—a rarity for the time. She'd refused to give her son up until she'd met the prospective parents, a couple out on Long Island, and she was sure it was the right decision. She had not seen him again, she said, and did not plan to—it would have been too hard. Instead, "she has arranged to stay with a girl friend, 'Jackie,' who she met in one of the Clubs in Greenwich Village. She seemed well acquainted with several of the Village Clubs."[48]

After this, Max's file takes a turn. The social workers were still obsessed with her appearance, but now it was a constant stream of criticism: "8-13-1957: Max at the Hopper Home dressed in a sloppy manner in a pair of blue jeans and a man's shirt...8-20-1957: As she was wearing slacks we wondered if she didn't want to change into a skirt."[49]

Soon after she reappeared in the city, Max moved into a room above a storefront on Bleecker Street in the Village with three other young lesbians: her friend Jackie, Jackie's friend Jean, and a woman named Maureen, whom Max was dating. They shared one bed, drank heavily, and partied all day and all night. When the WPA confronted Max, she readily admitted they were all lesbians, before cheekily adding she had "no ambition and no inhibitions. I just like things the way they are."[50] She preferred life among other queer women, she told the WPA, "as long as you are not too obvious."[51]

Max's concern about being clockable as queer didn't seem to last very long. When next she showed up at the WPA, she was wearing sunglasses to cover two black eyes, and she had scratches all over her face. She'd gotten into a "male fight" at a bar, she explained—a fight over another woman with either Jean or Jackie, causing Max and Maureen to move to Thirteenth Street.[52] Needing to make money fast, she told the WPA she was headed to a club to apply for a job. When the staff commented (again) on her slacks, she laughed at them. "Don't be silly," she told her worker, "I'd never get the job if I didn't wear pants."[53] Then, perhaps just to tweak her worker's nose, she mused about whether she should get a crew cut to really butch it up.

For the next month, the WPA and Max's adopted family did everything they could to make her go straight. The WPA ambushed her with a psychiatrist—they had a great time chatting about Max's adoption; her sexuality never came up. Her adopted mother asked about having her committed to a mental institution, but she was twenty-one now, and the WPA didn't think it would work. Her mother told Max she was an embarrassment, and that they were probably going to have to sell their house and move. Max didn't care. In exasperation, her social worker asked Max point-blank if this was the kind of disreputable life she wanted. When Max told them "she is happy for the first time in life and she is not ashamed of what she is doing," they interpreted it as a call for help.[54]

All during this, Max never told the WPA whether she got that club gig, but soon she had money, and something taking up her time. She started showing up in strange outfits—slinky dresses and "extremely high heels."[55] When the WPA inquired, she demurred and mentioned an office job. Or maybe it was with a doctor? A doctor's office, one that kept very strange hours? The story never quite came together. Eventually, Max's mother told them the truth: Max was working as a dancer at the Swing Rendezvous (aka the Swing Lounge, or just the Swing), a storied Village nightlife institution.

The Swing was almost a straight shot from the House of D—five blocks down Sixth Avenue, a quick turn on MacDougal, and there you were, standing outside a small redbrick row house from the mid-nineteenth century. When it opened in 1938, the Swing was a jazz bar—hence the name—and it featured mostly Black musicians for the enjoyment of a mostly white crowd. According to the NYC LGBT Historic Sites project, "At some point, probably in the early 1950s, it morphed into a venue that served a mostly lesbian clientele until it closed in 1965."[56]

A mostly *white* lesbian clientele. Just as in Mabel Hampton's heyday in the 1920s, the Village attracted queer women of every race—but the bars mostly admitted white women. In her memoir, *Zami: A*

New Spelling of My Name, Audre Lorde wrote about the difficulties she encountered when drinking while Black. Writing about the Bagatelle (or "the Bag"), a popular beer joint just a block and a half from the House of D, she explained:

> I didn't go to the Bag very much. It was the most popular gay-girl's bar in the Village, but I hated beer, and besides the bouncer was always asking me for my ID to prove I was twenty-one, even though I was older than the other women with me. Of course 'you can never tell with Colored people.' And we would all rather die than have to discuss the fact that it was because I was Black, since, of course, gay people weren't racists.[57]

Lorde lived and socialized in the Village while she was getting her BA at Hunter College, and the House of D assumed a large, complicated, and central place in her mental landscape. "The Women's House of Detention, right smack in the middle of the Village, always felt like one up for our side," she wrote, "a defiant pocket of female resistance, ever-present as a reminder of possibility, as well as punishment."[58] Long ago, Walter Winchell had correctly identified that the queer women in the House of D were expanding the conceptual boundaries of the Village; now, far from being on the outskirts of the neighborhood, the prison was considered central.

But outside the nimbus of the prison, Lorde rarely saw other Black queer women in the area. The title of her collection of essays, *Sister Outsider*, is an homage to those women, her "exotic sister outsiders" forging new paths for themselves and those who would come after them.[59] Bars for Black queer women would appear, particularly in Harlem, in the coming years, but for now, these women found themselves squeezing around the Village edges—getting in sometimes, particularly when they were with white women, or when the bar was pretty empty, or when there weren't any other Black people already inside, or when they came in through the kitchen door.

For Elsie A., an eighteen-year-old Black runaway who wanted to escape the factory assembly line for life as a modern dancer, the service door was the only one open to her. She excelled in dance classes at community centers around the city, and she had the kind of long, lithe, androgynous body that modern dance prized. But the only dancing job she could get was at the Bohemian, another storied Village club that was famous for its jazz scene (the original Miles Davis Quintet was a featured act in the mid-1950s). Like the Swing, the Bohemian was also known for being an on-again, off-again lesbian bar, hidden in the warren of Village streets right by the House of D. But even there, Elsie was hired to work in the kitchen, and only "dances occasionally with the band."[60]

The racism of the bar scene, past and present, cannot be overstated. However, the actions of the bars themselves have come to stand in for the feelings of the women who went to them, despite the fact that almost none of these bars were owned or operated by queer women, white or Black. The rare exception was the Page Three, which was opened by Buddy Kent and a few other drag kings, but even they were still backed by the mob and had to listen to their rules: Kent insisted that their entertainment be integrated (including such major performers as Tiny Tim, Herbie Nichols, Cecil Taylor, and Sheila Jordan), but she said they served an almost exclusively white crowd until after 1960. Lorde (who occasionally went to the Page Three) documented the racism in the bar scene, even in the white women she was closest with, but still felt that "lesbians were probably the only Black and white women in New York City in the fifties who were making any real attempt to communicate with each other; we learned lessons from each other, the values of which were not lessened by what we did not learn."[61] It is impossible to know what the mid-century lesbian bar scene would have been like, absent the pressure of the mafia.

Another problem with the bars? They didn't pay well. Max worked at the Swing for only a few weeks before she moved on. She disappeared for a month, and when she called the WPA again it was to let them know that "she has a very exciting job as a strip teaser earning $100.00 per week."[62]

You might think that being a butch lesbian would be a drawback at a strip club for men, but there were a number of women who worked both sides of the aisle, as it were. When Buddy Kent wasn't working as a drag king, she was stripping as Bubbles Kent:

> I did a strip out of top hat and tails, a Fred Astaire dance and then it would break away. With one flip of the hand the pants had snaps down the sides that just flipped out from under me, and then I went into a girl strip. When I finished people didn't know if I was a boy or a girl...and the men were enjoying it. They were asking me over to tables just like the strippers. I was getting the same amount of money they were, and tips....So the bosses said she might as well stay. I stayed one year.[63]

To Max, stripping was "the most satisfying job she has ever had and she is carried away by the amount of money which she earns."[64]

For two years, Max disappeared, and the WPA assumed she was lost to a life of dissipated lesbianism. Then, out of nowhere, letters from a woman named Susan started arriving from a strange address in suburban Illinois. The first one began, "Dear Mrs. Shapiro, Well this should come as a shock to you: Maxine D. 'arch man hater' is going to be married on Nov 1."[65]

Max (aka Susan) unspooled her story over a half dozen letters to the WPA. As was true for many of the people who escaped the city's cycle of poverty and incarceration, it all started with a lucky break (and some white privilege) when she applied for and received a Cabaret Identification Card. Without a card, you couldn't legally work in any nightlife venue in the city—not because of any law, regulation, or executive order, but because of the powerful whims of the NYPD.

In 1931, at the start of the Depression, the city amended its cabaret law, placing control over nightlife venues directly in the hands of the police department, allowing it to enforce curfews, shut down venues due to violations or complaints, etc. In the lead-up to World War II, President Franklin Roosevelt, liberal darling, issued an executive order for the FBI to "prepare a list of those whose presence might be adverse to the security of the United States."[66] The next year, the New York City police commissioner used this as the pretext for a shocking power grab when he created the "NYPD Cabaret Rules and Regulations." Neither the public nor any elected officials were involved in the creation of these rules. They extended the power of the police to regulate *performers*, not just venues, via the Cabaret Identification Card. To get a card, performers had to be of "good character," which of course excluded "anyone with a criminal record."[67] Performers who qualified for a card had to be fingerprinted—to make it easy to keep track of their "good character"—and reapply every two years. A special fingerprint drive location was set up in Greenwich Village specifically for this purpose, and this was the law of the land in New York City until 1967.

Performers were considered a priori amoral in general, but the NYPD was really concerned about one group in particular: Black jazz musicians. Jazz was associated with sex, drugs, and (most threateningly) the growing racial consciousness and solidarity among Black people, particularly in northern states. The cabaret card system allowed the NYPD to track, harass, and financially damage outspoken performers. After Billie Holiday was sent to a reformatory on a drug charge, her card was revoked; Charlie Parker's was revoked for a previous arrest; Thelonious Monk had his revoked three separate times in a decade; and Miles Davis had his revoked after being beaten by the police for having a cigarette between sets outside a club in Times Square.[68]

Given the relationship between jazz venues and lesbian venues in the Village, Max was certainly aware of the dangers the NYPD posed for performers, particularly those who had been incarcerated. When she started on the stage, she asked the WPA if she would qualify for a card, but they didn't know. So, she went to the police station, where they didn't fingerprint her and only asked if she had ever been convicted of a felony, which she hadn't (a separate regulation from the Alcoholic Beverage Commission banned felons from working in nightlife). Had the police fingerprinted her and seen her record, she certainly would have been denied a card. These soft-focus benefits of white privilege, the nebulous "lucky breaks" that always landed on *some* performers and not others, were the reason Max was able to break onto the stage while Elsie remained in the kitchens.

Armed with a card, Max quickly moved up in the club world, go-ing to bigger and bigger venues. After a few months, some men who operated a network of strip clubs—almost certainly members of the mafia—invited Max to work down in Florida for more money. For a while "it went hot and heavy."[69] Max loved the Florida weather, and she was sleeping with a partner in the club. "But give me credit for this much sense," she wrote to the WPA. "I took a look at some of the old bags that had been stripping for 'nigh onto 20 years' and thought, where will you be 20 years from now?"[70]

So, Max got herself an agent, and the agent got her an even better gig: opening a new strip club in Illinois, for $175 a week (more than $1,500 in today's money) plus tips, with a legal employment contract. The best part? "I had my agent promise that I would not have some boss trying to climb in bed with me"—a promise that was easy to keep, because the club was run by a husband-and-wife pair.[71] They didn't care what she did on her own time, Max's agent told her. The only drawback was that she had to end every act fully naked. But even with that caveat, this was an almost unheard-of opportunity for a stripper, and Max jumped on it.

Because she was up on a stage, the men couldn't touch her, and "feeling the way you know I feel about men in general," she reveled in "watching their faces as [she] danced."[72]

"Then I met Johnny," she wrote.

Johnny was a regular at the strip club, which automatically put him on Max's "'get all you can, while you can' list."[73] But he was sweet, and didn't judge her for being a stripper, and they had ac-tual conversations about their lives. What room did he have to judge anyone, after all—he was a single father raising his daughter on his own, full-time, spending all his free hours at a strip club chatting up a lesbian!

Was Max madly in love? No. Was Johnny attractive? Not really. But they were compatible, he had a good job, and, most importantly, he made Max feel safe. He took care of Max in a way no one ever had. And in his daughter, Max saw a second chance at motherhood (thank-fully without all the messiness of another pregnancy).

On stage, Max had danced as Baby Sue; now, dating Johnny, she started going by Susan. When he asked her to marry him, she had her name legally changed, to make it harder for anyone from her old life to find her. They met each other's families, and Max told the WPA that Johnny's mother "thinks John got a real gem and *my* mother thinks that John got a bad deal."[74] But their upcoming wedding went a long way toward repairing the rift between Max and her adopted parents.

After their honeymoon, Max and Johnny moved into a two-bedroom, fully air-conditioned, newly built apartment in an all-white suburb of Chicago, in a building so big and beautiful it felt to Max "like a small scale Grand Central Station!" What impressed her most, though, was "the complete built in kitchen" where "everything has a button or a knob."[75]

In one of her last letters, she grew wistful: "Sometimes I miss the glamor & fun of dancing & being admired & petted but I keep thinking [that] would be over in a while and this will stay like this for all my life." The tradeoff, she decided, was worth it.

"You have my address," she told the WPA, but "please don't forget to write Susan" on the envelope.[76]

And just like that, Max D., "arch man hater," evaporated into the suburban air.

It's easy, after hearing a single story like Max's, to rush for a simple answer—she was really heterosexual, she just had some bad experiences; she was really a lesbian, she just went into hiding; she was really bisexual all along. After reading hundreds of similar stories, however, it feels more intellectually honest to approach sexual orientation as a limited, useful, but ultimately unstable and unclear category of existence. Like political parties, our "sexual orientations"—gay, bisexual, lesbian, invert, pan, etc.—are cloud formations: indistinct at the edges and always shifting, yet discussed as though everyone sees the same vision in the mist.

Prisons, like all "single-sex" spaces, expose the limitations of sexual orientation: both the idea of it as the sole arbiter of our sexual and romantic relationships and, more fundamentally, its very existence as a permanent and unwavering aspect of our personality. It is rather more accurate to see sexual orientation as one part of our sexual identity, perhaps more fundamental for some of us than for others, which works in concert with other forces to create sexual desire, and which has the capacity to shift over time with new experiences or under different conditions.

What truly differentiates sexual orientation from all the other aspects of sexual and romantic desire is the vast (yet unacknowledged) cultural scaffolding we have built around it—scaffolding that, to a degree, falls away the moment you are arrested.

Twenty years after Max became Susan, one of America's most prominent lesbian feminist scholars and artists, the poet Adrienne Rich, would explore this idea of "compulsory heterosexuality" in an essay that questioned the existence of "innate [sexual] orientation" and "whether, in a different context, or other things being equal, women would *choose* heterosexual coupling and marriage."[77] (Her answer, largely: probably not. But Rich believed that the more important feminist questions have nothing to do with men—who are implied in all heterosexuality—and more with women's relationships to other women, sexual or non.)

Conversely, the queer experiences of imprisoned people have often been swept under the rug as "compulsory *homosexuality*"—a forced, unnatural condition in which lonely and desperate heterosexuals engage in sordid homosexual acts because they have no other option. Amazingly, sometimes this desperate loneliness took hold of women just a few minutes after they entered prison; sometimes it reappeared, on and off, for the rest of their lives. Yet in the face of stubborn evidence that a hard binary of sexual orientation does not sufficiently capture how we live our sexual lives, prison officials (and psychiatrists) would perform ever more complicated mental gymnastics to maintain heterosexuality's normality, permanence, and primacy.

Few women who lived heterosexual lives outside of their imprisonment spoke publicly and without shame about queer life on the inside. Even in the files of the WPA, it is hard to know what to make of these stories because the recording situation was so coercive: the wrong word, to the wrong social worker, could see these women cut off from their only source of support in the world. If they tried to write about their experiences—and were honest—their words would have been deemed obscene. Thanks to the motion picture code, their lives could never be shown on the big screen. No out gay characters would appear in television until 1971 (the year the House of D was closed), when the sitcom *All in the Family* had a sympathetic gay character for one episode.

But as the 1950s bled into the 1960s, cracks began to appear in this wall of silence. In 1959, one startlingly honest and insightful voice on issues of sexual orientation emerged from the House of D. Commissioner of Corrections Anna Kross would proclaim her "the most intelligent prisoner we've ever had."[78] Her arrest was broadcast with giant photos in major newspapers around the country, but her version of the story was shunted to pulp paperbacks and seamy dime-store tabloids—and even there, she had to maintain a thin veneer of heterosexuality. Infamy would force her to disappear after publishing her memoir, *Not for Love*, in 1960, but she would forever be remembered as Virginia McManus, "city school marm [and] V-Doll."[79]

NOT FOR LOVE

Virginia "Jinny" McManus's first brush with fame came at the tender age of three, when the *Chicago Tribune* described her as an "extraordinary" child prodigy, with a vocabulary better than a kid twice her age, studded with adjectives like "delightful," "luscious," and "exquisite."[80] But even then, people went out of their way to discredit her intelligence and focus on what really mattered: her looks. "These facts in black and white fail to describe Jinny," the *Tribune* wrote, before explaining that to really understand the young McManus what you needed to know was that she was "physically perfect...an elfin beauty, with golden hair and hazel eyes."[81]

At the age of eight, McManus started publishing poetry in newspapers around the country, including in the *Chicago Tribune* (which published her poem, "Carolina Garden," in 1944).[82] At twelve, she was lauded by journalists and financial institutions alike for selling $17,000 worth of war bonds during a single middle-school sales drive—approximately $250,000 in today's money.[83] She would go on to get her bachelor's in education at Western State University in Illinois and do some graduate coursework at the University of Chicago.[84] But it was her time as a sex worker in New York City that made her one of the House of D's most infamous prisoners, and gave her the platform from which to share startling truths about life on the inside.

It all began around 1955, when McManus was living in Chicago with a friend named Ann, who worked as a private pilot, above a friendly pair of "bachelors."[85] In her memoir, *Not for Love*, McManus described their landlords' apartment as "three rooms filled—no, packed—with gold, crystal, baroque; with carvings, paintings, tapestries, dark green velvet, purple velvet and undisturbed, feathery dust...teaspoons, silver teapots, hand-painted China, [and] miniature dogs."[86] In case her readers didn't catch the hint, McManus wrote that one of the movers she hired declared it 'a fairy lan'."[87]

McManus's description of her life with Ann is similarly a master class in gay vague—the art of declaring your sexuality mostly through what you *don't* say. Although McManus talked about several apartments the pair shared, she never specified their sleeping arrangements or how many bedrooms they had. Their social circle was filled with same-sex duos, like their landlords John and Don or their friends Jan and Lee, who are depicted as couples in all but name. Their apartment was in the center of Chicago's Near North neighborhood, by the famous Ambassador East Hotel. To gay readers familiar with Chicago's demimonde, McManus didn't need to mention that this put them right in a busy cruising ground in one of Chicago's gayest areas.

This incredibly queer subtext was especially invisible to mainstream readers because of the relentless heterosexuality of the text itself—*Not for Love* is, after all, "the outspoken, unashamed autobiography of the school teacher who became a call girl."[88] For decades, the queer hints that McManus left behind were a trail that led nowhere, a shadow story always nipping at the heels of the one she told publicly. However, in the self-published memoirs of a painter named

George Deem, I discovered the real name of McManus's roommate Ann. Sixty-five years after the pair went their separate ways, Ann—in reality, Nan McTeer—shared with me the true story that Virginia McManus never got to tell.

Nan and Virginia did live together in Chicago, for about a year, as a couple. Nan wasn't a pilot, though she did know how to fly a plane, thanks to her father. McManus worked at a private school for rich kids who had been kicked out of every other private school; *Nan* was the one taking classes at the University of Chicago, not McManus (although McManus had been a student there, too, a few years earlier). McTeer was just twenty when they met; McManus was older, more experienced, "a thorough lesbian," as far as McTeer ever knew.[89] She was also "brilliant," "a grandstander," a person with "a wild past," and "a very good teacher" when it came to sex.[90] After her university classes ended for the day, Nan would pick Jinny up, and the pair would cruise around Chicago with some friends in Nan's white Ford two-door, or go get a cup of tea in Chinatown, just the two of them, before retiring to their apartment—which really was as chock-a-block with antiques as McManus described.

In *Not for Love*, McManus told a straight version of her introduction to prostitution. First, she became the mistress of a man named Holt, the father of one of the teens at her school, a businessman who hired secretaries who didn't mind doubling as call girls when there were out-of-town clients to impress. Initially, McManus was *just* seeing Holt, but as he explained the ins and outs of the business to her, McManus became intrigued. Like Honora D., she was matter of fact about sex work, describing it much in the same way she did her job as a teacher: as something she did for money that was frequently annoying but had its perks. After her first time with professional clients, she reflected,

> It didn't amaze me that I had been able to go to bed with five men, all complete strangers, without guilt or horror or even as much revulsion as I had anticipated. I hadn't enjoyed it—I hadn't expected to enjoy it. I had simply used the most expedient means of getting

the money that I had to have. And when I left the bed after being with the second man, a college business representative, I had thought, When I drove stock cars to pay for my sophomore year, no one could see why I did it. It was dangerous and filthy and I still have scars from glass slivers, but I knew it wouldn't kill me and I was poor and I had to do something that was drastic enough to pay well. That got me partly through college and this will get me through my doctorate and it's nobody's business but my own.[91]

(It says something about the state of heterosexuality in 1960 that McManus could compare straight sex to "filthy" stock car racing, discuss how little she enjoyed it, and still not tip off anyone's gaydar.)

Through Holt, McManus wrote, she met a number of sex workers from New York City, mostly call girls like Bobby, "a slightly masculine girl with large dark eyes and a Southern accent," and Milly, "a *Vogue* fashion-plate type who affected elegant manners."[92] In the book, they are the closest McManus comes to giving a reason for moving to New York, writing only that she arrived home one day to find Ann packing her bags to head to Europe, so she decided she'd leave and join them.

"That's all fiction," Nan McTeer snorted over the phone.

There was no "Holt" to introduce McManus to prostitution, McTeer told me. Instead, it was Vicki, "a pimp-type lesbian—very good looking," who first turned McManus out.[93] According to McTeer, although McManus had no sexual interest in men, she enjoyed the work. "She liked being a prostitute because it drew attention to her," McTeer said. Soon, Vicki and Virginia started having an affair, though McTeer didn't know it right away. But their friends noticed that things seemed off between them. During a party at George Deem's apartment, Virginia "accused [Nan] of poisoning her drink," and the friends all knew that "Virginia was soon to go her own way and [Nan] was going hers and their beautiful apartment on Chestnut was going to be left," Deem wrote.[94]

He was right.

Through Vicki, McManus met Kay Jarrett, "Chicago's symbol of vice and bawdy good times during the late '40s, '50s, and early '60s."[95]

Jarrett ran At Your Service, Inc., and while she would later claim that it was merely for dates, and she would have fired any woman who sold sex under her name, McTeer said it was an old-fashioned "whore house" on Rush Street, elaborately decorated with deep purple walls on the first floor, where the women waited. Jarrett was a canny, manipulative operator. New hires were told they were joining a dating service, but Jarrett had a list of ringers she used as their first clients, who pressured them into having sex for money. If they refused, Jarrett fired them. If they agreed, she let them keep the money...the first time. In the future, she took a cut of all their profits.[96]

Rush Street was both disreputable and gay; in fact, it was so infamously gay that Alfred Kinsey drew much of his sample of gay men for his 1949 groundbreaker *Sexual Behavior in the Human Male* from the social scene there.[97] According to the 1950 guidebook *Chicago Confidential*,

> [Rush Street] contains hundreds of premises which violate one or more, or all, of the laws concerning: B girls soliciting at bars, clip joints, catering to homosexuals, bars and cocktail lounges operated after hours (many run around the clock and never close), gambling, assignation houses, permitting soliciting for immoral purposes in lobbies, and allowing bartenders, etc., to sell narcotics. Similar conditions exist in many sections, but nowhere are there as many infractions in so small an area.[98]

McTeer got a kick out of visiting Jarrett's place when McManus was working. When Jarrett was away, she said, "we'd just gather the girls and go to the nearest gay bar!"[99]

The real reason McManus left Chicago for New York?

Kay Jarrett wanted to go on vacation (rumor had it that she and her lover, the Italian actor Rossano Brazzi, had purchased a private island off the coast of Italy right after World War II). McManus smooth-talked Jarrett into letting her run the business while Jarrett was gone, and in return, said they'd split the profits. When Jarrett returned after more than a month away, and McManus handed her a measly thousand bucks—and then requested half of it back, as her take—Jarrett was furious. By this point, McTeer had realized that McManus was having an affair with Vicki, so she'd broken off their relationship. She soon moved out and married another member of their queer social circle, a drag queen who performed under the name Elynda McKay—"a marriage of convenience for both of us," McTeer said.[100]

The last time George Deem saw McTeer and McManus, it was around 1957. He went out dancing with Elynda, Nan, and Virginia; they took a few "up pills," and McManus announced she was moving to New York.[101] Deem didn't understand why she wanted to leave— her life seemed pretty fun to him—until Elynda clued him in: "She had been in such a violent fight with her roommate, another girl" (likely either Vicki or Kay Jarrett) that her eye was blackened and she needed to get the hell out of Chicago.[102] Without a job, girlfriend, sidepiece, or place to live, McManus headed to New York.

Once McManus left Chicago, McTeer said, they didn't keep in touch. When she saw George Deem for the last time, in the mid-1990s, he said he and some members of their old Chicago gang had ended up in New York and tried to help McManus out, but it was no use. She was on her own path.

Instead of checking in with old friends, McManus started working as a substitute teacher in Brooklyn. Soon, however, she called up a woman she had met while working with Kay Jarrett, Bea—a statuesque redhead who lived in an adamantly "modern" apartment in swank Midtown Manhattan, which was sparse and hard and covered in black and white geometric patterns.[103] When McManus came back to see Bea again a week later, the place was raided, and the NYPD picked up "two models, a dress designer, two purported actresses, an embarrassingly mercenary madam who insisted on cash before pleasure and a blonde Brooklyn high school teacher"—the last two, of course, being Bea and Virginia.[104] Virginia's arrest "caused the biggest furor of all because it isn't often a school teacher gets bagged in a vice crackdown," the *Daily News* reported.[105]

If you went just by the papers, it would seem these women were magically serving ghost patrons. Certainly, no johns were ever identified in the press, while McManus's photo, address, name, and parents' names were blasted in front-page articles across the country. According to the NYPD, Bea was running a "$50,000-a-month call girl ring," which employed over twenty girls a night and had a written roster of over two hundred customers.[106] Those arrested in the raid were rushed to the Women's Court, then paddy-wagoned down to the House of Detention.

McManus was only briefly at the House of D (this time), but it was still nightmarish. She was able to pay her bail—unlike most people who passed through the Women's Court—but she wasn't allowed to do so until she had been processed through the House of D, which ended up taking nearly thirty hours. As she waited for the enema and genital search, packed into a room with forty other newly admitted women, she watched as one, "recovering from a miscarriage the night before," hemorrhaged severely with no medical assistance.[107] Instead, the matrons "wandered back and forth with cartons of coffee and stood chatting in little groups."[108]

When she finally got to her court hearing, police testified that on the night in question they "went off to a room with Virginia and Connie. When the girls disrobed, the detectives said, the cops revealed their identities and made the arrests."[109]

A salacious story—substitute teacher turned lesbian sex worker!— if only it were true.

Virginia *had* been at Bea's that night, on a social call. But everyone was drunk, and the women were all in a bad mood because the johns were mean, so she'd left. In the hall, a plainclothes officer stopped her and asked for ID, then brought her back into Bea's apartment. For an hour, the police ransacked the apartment for drugs and shot the shit with Bea while at least a few of the officers had sex with some of the women; one officer told Bea she should move her whole operation down to the Forties, where the cops were less vigilant. When the superior officers arrived to discover that the vice cops hadn't found any drugs, and that everyone but Bea was guilty of just Section 877 (vagrancy prostitution) misdemeanors, they were more annoyed than anything else. "The other cops should have let you go before we got here," one of the superiors sighed, "now we got to at leas' take you down to the station."[110]

Bea got herself a lawyer, and when they got to the actual trial the police admitted that McManus was telling the truth—she hadn't been in the apartment until they dragged her in themselves, and she certainly hadn't gone into any private rooms with anyone. The charges against McManus were dropped and she declared her intention to go back to teaching, but she was quickly fired, and under a thin pretext her substitute teaching license was revoked. She had been living in the Barbizon, a women's hotel, which promptly kicked her out when her name hit the papers. As had so many before her, McManus discovered that once you were arrested it didn't matter if you were found innocent.

If she was going to be tainted for life, she decided she might as well run with it. Within a few weeks, McManus had a book full of clients, and, a year later, in February 1959, she was raided again at Bea's place. Again, she protested her innocence; again, the cops claimed to have caught her in the middle of a lesbian sex act with another sex worker and a john. This time, however, McManus was guilty.

At trial, McManus was convicted and sentenced to three months in the House of D. When she got out, she penned an explosive exposé on the experience entitled "Love Without Men in Women's Prison."[111] This being 1959, however, McManus could only publish it in the tabloid magazine *Confidential*, which boasted that it "tells the facts and names the names." McManus nabbed the front cover with a photo of her lighting a cigarette and looking like a Pink Lady from *Grease*. She shared it with two other, smaller headlines: one article proclaimed Frank Sinatra was a cry baby, and the other that "car exhausts cause lung cancer!"[112] (In a funny coincidence, Nan McTeer said that she had first learned the word *homosexuality* from an issue of *Confidential*, years earlier.)[113]

All too often, uncomfortable truths about sex in prison are told only in places like *Confidential*, which value these stories not for their insight into suppressed and concealed aspects of human life but for their salacious amusement. Doing so distances the magazine (and the teller) from the story being told. It allows the truth to be expressed and disavowed simultaneously. For this reason, McManus's article is accompanied by multiple shots of her in a bathing suit, applying lotion, and reading on her couch while wearing a blouse unbuttoned to her navel. Although the coercion here was different from what McManus might have experienced had her story been captured in social work notes, it's worth highlighting that this was still a narrative shaped to please the outside expectations of people in power, particularly straight white men.

At the start of the ten-page spread, in bold, McManus proclaimed, "The prison was a breeding ground of homosexuality for the uninitiated; a Utopia for lesbians."[114] A full 50 percent of the women at the House of D understood themselves to be queer, she wrote, and "40 to 45 per cent of the rest accepted homosexuality at least during their imprisonment."[115] The strictly straight remainder were considered uncool and left alone, as "there were plenty of willing ones."[116]

As another prisoner—"a bull dyke"—explained to McManus, it was easy for women to hook up with one another because "honey, [the guards] don't want to catch us. They'd be too embarrassed. Besides, what good would it do?"[117] They couldn't put the entire prison in segregated cells—there wasn't room!—and if the women weren't having sex they would find some other physical outlet, probably fighting.

The easiest time to hook up was after dinner, before lights out, when the cells on each floor were unlocked. Couples would take the cells farthest down the corridor, out of sight of the guard station at the center of the floor. Other women would sit in the corridor, acting as both speed bumps and lookouts. If a guard insisted on getting past them, they would call out, "Getting those cigarettes, Mary?" and by the time the guard made it through, Mary—and her partner—would be on their way back.[118]

Just as McManus had avoided spelling out the sleeping arrangements in her apartment with Nan in Chicago, in the article she carefully skirted the issue of which camp of women—lesbian, willing, or uncool—she fell into. But she used the opportunity to express several controversial, progressive ideas about human sexuality.

First, she emphasized that homosexuality in prison "is necessary to preserve emotional and mental stability," and told the story of an older woman who was devastated by her incarceration until an older jailhouse "daddy" turned her out.[119] Further, she elaborated, a woman like that (who lived a heterosexual life outside of prison but engaged in queer relationships on the inside) "will probably come out of jail at the end of a year a wiser woman, but virtually unchanged from the wife and mother she was before" because "the habits of a half century are not so easily revolutionized."[120] Finally, McManus emphasized that while straight women might have lesbian sex in prison, lesbians could not be turned straight (and most would not want to be, if they were left alone). The best thing psychiatrists could do, McManus believed, was to teach them "to adapt to an understanding of themselves and their relationship to the heterosexual world."[121]

The only exception, McManus thought, should be the diddy bops, the fifteen-, sixteen-, and seventeen-year-olds who were in danger of being set on a path of lesbianism for life—girls who would otherwise unthinkingly become heterosexual adults, because other opportunities had never been presented to them. McManus explored this idea in terms of compulsory homosexuality, suggesting that these young women initially engaged in lesbian relationships because they had sexual and emotional needs that could not be met any other way. But in the process, McManus accidentally demonstrated the power of compulsory *heterosexuality*, as her real fear was that outside of prison—where there would be men they could date—these teens would continue to choose other women instead.

McManus's silence around her personal sexual experiences in prison is so glaring, it feels purposeful: another attempt to say something by not saying anything. Given that she was writing in 1959, this isn't surprising. Twelve years later, in 1971, Florrie Fisher, a drug addict turned penitent antidrug campaigner (who inspired Amy Sedaris's character Jerri Blank on the cult TV show *Strangers with Candy*), was able to be much more open. As she began chapter eighteen of her memoir, *The Lonely Trip Back,*

It was in jail that I learned to be a lesbian, both sides of it. How to be a mommy, and how to be a daddy....During the very first sentence I ever served, in the House of D, I discovered I could get emotionally involved with another woman. She was the first of about ten women I had lesbian relationships with during my years in jail.

Yet outside of prison, I had no homosexual desires at all, just as I had none at all before I was locked up the first time.

For me, and I think for many other normally heterosexual in-mates, men and women both, homosexuality is something imprison-ment forces upon you. You are locked away in a cage in a completely artificial society; you are treated like some kind of subhuman, a num-ber without a face, part of an impersonal system which can operate only if the animals in the cages do exactly what they are supposed to do at the times they are supposed to....You want affection, and in prison you make do with what you've got.[122]

Fisher's extraordinary honesty was possible not just because of the feminist, gay, and sexual revolutions that were happening around her, but also because she was writing from the position of a penitent. Her book is largely a confession, a category of expression that allows (even celebrates) boldly stating your worst transgressions. In other words, par-adoxical as it might sound, her adamancy around her heterosexuality is exactly what allowed her to write about her queerness. Virginia Mc-Manus, as "a thorough lesbian," had to be much more circumspect.[123]

However, some people—*queer* people—did seem to pick up on McManus's not-so-subtle hints. One in particular was Jerry Herman, a twenty-eight-year-old composer and lyricist who would soon be fa-mous for writing some of the most enduring Broadway musicals of the twentieth century, including *Hello Dolly!* and *La Cage aux Folles*. In 1960, he wrote a comedic revue entitled *Parade!*, featuring the song "Save the Village"—originally entitled "Don't Tear Down the House of Detention."[124]

Sung from the point of view of a formerly incarcerated woman, the song declares the House of D to be the "cornerstone of Greenwich Village charm." It is "our landmark," she sings, and "a symbol of my youth," where she met the "chums" she "adored"—including "Jinny McManus," who gets namechecked in the third verse.

Why does this narrator want to save the House of D? Because of "the love" in "the laundry," "the clinic," and "the showers." As Herman wrote,

'Twas built with love
My lovely House in town

Like Jay Toole, like Audre Lorde, like Joan Nestle, Herman's pickpocket protagonist recognized that the House of D was the only visible expression of the existence of women who loved women; it was their one true landmark, their house that could never be a home.

That same year, lyricist and composer Jeanne Bargy wrote the off-Broadway show *Greenwich Village, U.S.A.*, which had its own song set in the House of D, "Ladies of the House." Not much is known about Bargy's personal life, but the year her show debuted she was living at 95 Christopher Street, just three short blocks from the prison. Although she didn't mention Jinny McManus, Bargy did make frequent references to queer life and incarceration, showing just how closely imbricated the House of D, Greenwich Village, and lesbianism had become in the popular imagination.

In Bargy's song, "three darling distaff delinquents" tell the audience how they ended up in the House of D. Each one has at least a whiff of sexual abnormality about her: the first tells us that her brother "had pierced ears"; the second, that she was arrested at a raid on a party where she ended up naked and "the host [was] wearing my dress"; and the third that, "strictly entre nous dear"

I might make my debut here...
I've found a friend in Gladys

Another phrase for making one's debut? Coming out.

In fact, the entire nation was going through a coming-out experience of a kind, as the activists of the late 1960s, the people who would become the Black Panthers, the Radicalesbians, the Gay Liberationists, the Young Lords, etc. began to come of age in every corner of the country. As the 1960s wore on, more and more of them would refuse to maintain the polite walls of silence and conformity upon which the postwar 1950s era of conservatism and peak heterosexuality were built.

At the same time that Jerry Herman and Jeanne Bargy were writing their musicals, the Living Theater (directed by Judith Malina, who had been incarcerated in the House of D) put up *The Connection*, a play about heroin addicts in the Village, which it dedicated to "Thelma Gadsden, dead of an overdose of heroin at the Salvation Army in 1957, and to all other junkies dead and alive in the Women's House of Detention."[125]

Attention was coming to the prison in a way it never had before, but its biggest theatrical moment was yet to come. In the mid-1960s, the multitalented Black auteur and actor Melvin Van Peebles found himself sleeping on a park bench outside the prison. As he recalled the scene on the sidewalk outside,

> There was this whole wonderful, wonderful world of people talking to their loved ones. I thought, "Wow, this would make a great song." So, I composed this song, "Hey, fourth floor. Hey, sugar, that your light? Make some kind of sign so I know it's you." So, the women would blink some kind of light so their people would know it was them. They would open their hearts up to their loved ones.... It was wonderful, it was poignant, but no one was capturing this. So, I started capturing these sorts of stories and I put them into an album.[126]

That album was called *Brer Soul*, and it formed the basis for Van Peebles's incredible Broadway show *Ain't Supposed to Die a Natural Death*. His song about the woman calling up to a window in the House of D—"10th and Greenwich"—was the first lesbian love song on Broadway. Now, the show is set to be revived by Van Peebles's son, Mario, in 2022.

Even the straight white public was beginning to grapple with the existence of queer women, particularly incarcerated ones. As the foreword to the prison novel *My Name Is Rusty* asked in 1958,

> In this highly developed age, with man's increasing knowledge of the universe, and of the nature of man himself, why devote all the time and effort it requires to write a novel on the allegedly deleterious subject of **Lesbianism**?
>
> …Books lead to knowledge; knowledge in turn becomes power; it is hoped that the smallest part of the immense power of knowledge will lead to a greater understanding of the female homosexual and her problems. For, despite all efforts to cloak their existence, there **are** Lesbians.…
>
> **Who** are they? **What** do they do? **How** do they function? Why do some women, **who have always before preferred men**, allow themselves to be seduced by a Lesbian?
>
> **Why? Why? Why?**[127]

As the staid 1950s gave way to the revolutionary '60s, three women who had "always before preferred men" (at least publicly) would find the answers to these questions in the House of D. One was an eighteen-year-old college freshman protesting the Vietnam War. Another was a pregnant community organizer acting as her own lawyer in an eight-month-long trial where she faced a sentence of over three hundred years in prison. The third was a fast-rising philosophy professor, on the run from the FBI for a murder she didn't commit. All three were queer, all three were leaders in the fight for social justice, and all three were held at the House of D. We know them today as Andrea Dworkin, Afeni Shakur, and Angela Davis.

CHAPTER 10

The City's Search for the Perfect Victim

"YOU CAN'T KNOW HOW IT IS FROM THE OUTSIDE"

In 1963, Kim Parker lived just off Central Park, in the fuzzy boundary between the Upper West Side and Harlem—an area sometimes referred to as Bloomingdale or Manhattan Valley, bucolic names that referenced the nineteenth century, when it was a farming village along the Hudson River. By the time Parker moved in, it was mostly small apartment buildings and row houses, but her block would soon be home to the Eugenio Maria De Hostos apartments, a public housing complex with over 220 units. There was a small but significant working-class gay area just a little bit to the south, which was more ethnically diverse than the residential parts of Greenwich Village but lacking in places for lesbians. Mostly, however, Parker's neighborhood was known for being on the skids (like much of the city at the time). As one resident described it,

> Today's Upper West Side is so gentrified and expensive that it is difficult to imagine just how dangerous and rundown it was in the

late 1960's. It was hit hard and early by postwar middle-class flight to the suburbs, as well as Robert Moses' slum clearance of the 1950's and 1960's. The superblock created by Lincoln Center destroyed the entire neighborhood of San Juan Hill. Then came city-service cuts, which meant fewer cops, more trash on the streets and less maintenance of basic amenities like playgrounds and park grass. The Upper West Side quickly became the territory of drug dealers, pimps and absentee landlords.[1]

Kim Parker was one of those disreputables: a heroin user, perhaps an occasional dealer, and a sex worker. Instead of being seen as city residents in need of care, poor Black women like Parker are usually viewed as bellwethers of its dissolution. They are signs, rather than citizens.

At thirty-five, Parker already had thirteen arrests under her belt—twelve for prostitution and one for drug possession. On the occasion of her fourteenth arrest, in August 1963, "it was figured from her record that she had spent a total of 390 days in the House of Detention, exclusive of time served there while awaiting trial."[2] If anyone could be called an expert on life in the House of D, it was Parker.

A few years earlier, Catholic anti-poverty activist Dorothy Day (the same person who compared the lesbians in the House of D to animals) had said that women like Parker were serving "a life sentence, on the installment plan."[3] In, out, junkie tank, hospital, mental ward, shelter, back inside, back outside, back in, back on the streets—that was, and is, life for far too many people caught in the revolving door of our prison system.

Since 1950, the city had seen an astounding 84 percent rise in the average daily census of incarcerated women, with no increase in space for them.[4] On Easter Monday, 1962, the House of D held a jaw-dropping 718 people.[5] State and city officials thought that around 80 percent of the sentenced women were drug users like Parker.[6] Also like Parker, 70 percent had served time previously—at least, that was the city's "best estimate."[7] For all the reams of paperwork it produced, the correctional system was (and is) remarkably opaque, poorly tracked, and misunderstood, even by those directing it. Commissioner Anna Kross, who had been in charge of the system for nearly a decade at this point, often said that if she "were given an unlimited budget [she] would not know how to spend it in rehabilitation because no basic research has been done."[8] Shortly after Parker was arrested for the fourteenth time, Kross began a research department, but their work didn't do much to help the women in the House of D.

In a weaselly burst of doublespeak, one deputy commissioner admitted in a memo in 1962 that "our failure to successfully solve the problem of crime is our failure to utilize that which we utilize in almost all areas of our national development, viz the intellect. The fact is this area of correction is traditionally a non-intellectual area."[9]

In other words, the prison system in New York City was an abject failure, organized around outdated ideas, biases, guesses, prejudices, theories, assumptions, and anything but facts.

Kim Parker didn't need a research department to tell her that.

On the occasion of her fourteenth arrest, Parker was slapped with two charges: drug possession (a misdemeanor) and possession with intent to sell (a felony). The felony charge was routine bullshit and everybody knew it—it was (and is) common for the police to stack charges, so the court could magnanimously allow the arrested person to plead down to the lesser one. After all, what defines "intent to sell"? At no point did the police say they'd seen Parker selling drugs, nor had she ever been arrested for dealing before. Parker had enough heroin on her for four shots, easily an amount she could have taken in a day or two. "Possession with intent to sell" laws are like "loitering with intent to commit prostitution" laws—a way to criminalize the existence of people already assumed to be criminals, largely Black, working-class, and gender nonconforming people. In 2016, Human Rights Watch referred to these kinds of practices as "flimsy pretext(s) to bolster charges that lack real evidence to support them."[10] Parker was a dark-skinned Black woman with short natural hair, a long arrest record, and an irregular (legal) work history. Her very existence constituted "intent to sell" in the eyes of the police.

Laws around intent are insidious attempts to create harsh sentences that would not otherwise be justifiable. Like fingerprinting, they move the conversation away from the evidence in front of the court and toward a magical calculation of a person's likelihood to commit another crime. Clearly, as 70 percent of incarcerated people in New York City were supposedly recidivists, the courts were terrible at making these kinds of calculations, but that didn't—and doesn't—stop them. According to a US Department of Justice study from 2019, today, the recidivism rate for state prisoners is 83 percent.[11] That statistic alone should be enough to confirm that our criminal legal system is a disaster.

On Wednesday, October 23, 1963, Parker finally had her day in court, after spending two more months in the House of D. Her trial was at best a formality, a set piece in which Parker wasn't supposed to have any lines. The judge read the charges; the district attorney said he recommended the court accept a guilty plea to the misdemeanor and drop the felony; and Parker's Legal Aid attorney advised her to accept the deal. Easy-peasy, everyone would be out in just a few minutes—well, except for Parker, who was looking at another year in the House of D.

Then Kim Parker interrupted the proceedings. She would plead guilty to the felony, she announced. She would take a five-year sentence outside the city rather than return to the House of Detention for one year. As she said to the court, "I won't feel any different about this in a week or a month. I'll never change my mind or statement. I want to plead guilty to the felony for my own mental stability. I can't begin to explain to you. You have to have done time and been there... you can't know how it is from the outside."[12]

The courtroom erupted into chaos. The judge was inclined to accept Parker's admission of guilt: she was, after all, the one on trial. He wanted the Probation Department to do a presentence investigation, which was normally done to determine if a person should go on probation, but in this case presumably would have discovered whether she was dealing. But in an indicator of just what a sham the whole felony case was, the district attorney—the one who *brought* the charges—objected, saying this would be a violation of Parker's rights. Parker's appointed attorney refused to back her up in court, instead asking for time to talk to her separately. The judge, at the end of his rope, yelled, "You're too rigid!" at Parker's lawyer, then snarled at the DA, "You're out of line. Don't tell me how to run my court. Simmer down."[13] For the moment, the case was adjourned, which meant Parker was sent right back to the one place she didn't want to be: the Women's House of Detention.

Parker was never given a chance to fully explain her objection to the House of D, but the basic outline of the problem was obvious and had been for years: the prison was severely overcrowded, with many people, like Parker, going through forced drug withdrawal, after which they were given nothing to do. The boredom was toxic, and most women knew that they would be back inside again soon, so even the hope of release was tainted. Lacking staff, programming, or space, the prison turned to one darkly ironic solution: they drugged their inmates to the gills.

The records of this drug program are spotty and difficult to reconstruct, but it seems to begin in earnest around 1955, when a Diagnostic Clinic was opened in the House of D. The year the clinic opened, the House had an average population of 466 incarcerated people, who made about 40,000 visits to one of the prison's medical clinics.[14] The year *after* the Diagnostic Clinic opened, the average population was slightly smaller, but the clinic recorded a shocking 104,613 visits.[15] By 1962, there were nearly 300,000 visits per year to clinics in the House of D. What was happening?

In a word: Thorazine.

In 1951, French scientists created a compound called chlorpromazine, sold under the name Thorazine. In 1952, researchers realized that Thorazine "produced disinterest without loss of consciousness" and began promoting its use for "controlling excitement and agitation."[16] It was particularly recommended for the treatment of psychotics and schizophrenics—diagnoses that were vastly overrepresented in the House of D. In 1954, Thorazine was approved for psychiatric usage in the United States—mostly on institutionalized women like Serena C.—and "quickly rose to become a staple of asylum medicine.

Cash-strapped and overcrowded state hospitals flocked to the cost-effective treatment."[17]

Prisons, it turned out, did too.

In 1954, according to Commissioner Anna Kross, the Department of Correction had a budget of $8.5 million—of which a piddly $50,000 was spent on rehabilitation and treatment personnel.[18] As a result, by 1958, prisons all around New York City (and the state) were proclaiming the wonders of Thorazine. The superintendent of Westfield State Farm wrote an article on the "Institutional Treatment of Women Offenders" for *Correction* magazine, in which she enthused about "another recent innovation…the use of thorazine and other tranquilizing drugs" in prisons.[19] That same year, the superintendent of the House of D admitted that drug users like Kim Parker (again, estimated to be 80 percent of the population) were put through a "complete withdrawal" program (aka cold turkey in the tank) upon entry to the House of D, but now, "tranquilizing drugs [are] administered during the withdrawal period."[20]

Already, however, there were whispers about much broader usage of tranquilizers in the House, beyond women actively going through withdrawal. In a 1958 article about disciplinary problems in the prison, one woman told a journalist, "I am very nervous. I can't stand to be hollered at. I go to pieces. I want to go to the diagnostic clinic."[21] Why she wanted to go to the clinic isn't stated, but the suggestion was obvious.

In 1960, the Department of Correction made a surreptitious reference to Thorazine in their annual report, writing that "special diets with high vitamin intake and tranquilizers, including those with anti-emetic properties, have been instituted for treatment purposes when needed."[22] Thorazine was also used as an anti-nausea/anti-vomiting (aka antiemetic) medication—a useful side benefit in an institution where people may have been tempted to vomit up their (unneeded) medications.

In 1963—the year Kim Parker was arrested for the fourteenth time—a young sociologist was approved to study "play family" formation among women in the House of D (aka lesbian relationships). She found that the over-drugging of "very nervous" women was endemic:

> A great deal of conscious anxiety is manifested by most inmates a great deal of the time. Fits of extreme depression or "nervousness" are reported continuously and there is a perpetual demand for solace, diagnostic help, tranquilizing medication—or all three. Almost all inmates ask for such medication at some time during their incarceration and most of them receive such "help" despite the fact that the therapists are aware of how temporary and dubious a solution this is and the physicians tend to regard these inmates as "pill lovers" or hypochondriacs.[23]

In 1965, the medical director of the Department of Correction wrote in a letter to one of his staff physicians, "On my various visits to the House of Detention for Women the chief problem has been the over-treatment of inmates. I took up this problem with the Director of Psychiatry and we plan on several conferences with the staff to distinguish more clearly between psychiatric and disciplinary problems."[24] The same superintendent who had previously mentioned the use of Thorazine in treating withdrawal told the press that year that "most of the girls are sick, either mentally or physically. Half of them are on tranquilizers for one reason or another."[25]

The casualness of that "one reason or another" betrays the true barbarity of this program. Some of these women could have benefited from psychotropic medication (properly administered, with other treatments as well), but instead of using them as a targeted, acute intervention, tranquilizers were passed out like candy. For instance, one woman reported that in 1965, her prescribed epilepsy medication was taken from her on admission to the prison, and she was instead given two unlabeled pills, three times a day, from the Diagnostic Clinic. She was given no information about what the pills were, or why they were prescribed to her, or what the effects might be. "I didn't take but one because they were very strong," she later told the New York

State Assembly, who verified with the prison that this had indeed occurred.[26]

That same year, in an internal memo, doctors at the House of D wrote that they prescribed to one woman (who had no psychiatric diagnosis on file) the following:

December 24—Tranquilizers
December 26—Sleeping medication
December 29—(twice) Receiving tranquilizer
December 30—Received a different tranquilizer...
December 31—Another tranquilizer was prescribed 3 times per day for 10 days.[27]

If that sounds insane, consider this testimony from another woman incarcerated that year:

I had a very bad cold when I went in, the kind that makes you cough all night and keeps you and everybody around you awake, and the following morning when clinic call was announced, Barbara, who was recovering from the flu, and I, who had a very bad cold, both answered the call for the clinic. We were sent in the elevator to another floor. I think there was no doctor present at all.

We stood in a line, and we were told to tell a matron what our complaint was. I told the matron that I had a very bad cold and that I would like something to ease the coughing, particularly at night. She said "Hold out your hand," and I did, and she poured fourteen pills into my hand of various sizes and colors, and I said, "what do I do with them?" And she said, "You swallow them. She'll give you some water," pointing to another matron, who did hand me a paper cup of water, and I swallowed the pills.

Well, of course, the coughing wasn't relieved at all, and when I returned to my cell block, I told one of the other inmates about the medication I received, and she laughed and she said, "Well, that's what everybody gets. That's withdrawal medication." I was very angry.

So I coughed all night that night, and the next day I reported at clinic call again, and this time I said, "I'm not suffering any withdrawal symptoms. I have a cold and would like something for a cold. I would like something to make me stop coughing all night." And this time there was a nurse present, and I made it very clear to her that I was a civil rights defendant with a cold, not a narcotics addict with withdrawal symptoms, and after insisting rather loud and clear, I was given a little paper cup of cough syrup, which by the way I was ordered to drink then, although it was quite early and wasn't going to help much that night.[28]

The most damning assessment of the Diagnostic Clinic, however, would come from the psychiatrists who worked in it themselves. In 1966, the director of psychiatry for the entire Department of Correction wrote a widely circulated memo, which blasted poorly trained guards for over-relying on drugs to control incarcerated women, resulting in ever increasing disciplinary incidents. As he wrote,

There is a significant increase in the quantity and severity of unusual occurrences from that institution....The correction force at the House of Detention for Women appear to be unknowing in how to handle the disciplinary problems....These problems have been shunted off to the Diagnostic Clinic where, for a lack of a better solution, they were medicated. This very often occurred at the request of correction officers who did not know how to handle the problem. This procedure has resulted in an enormous increase of inmates seen at the Diagnostic Clinic, together with increased amounts of medication prescribed.[29]

How much "medication" was given out, to how many women, will probably never be known. What we do know, thanks to the courage of many formerly incarcerated women, is that this drugging continued for as long as the House of D was open. In 1972, just after the prison was relocated to Rikers Island, a political prisoner and nursing student named Joan Bird (a member of the Black Panther Party) wrote about the year and a half she had spent in the hole at 10 Greenwich:

> There is the diagnostic area, which a lot of sisters are in, where a quack doctor fills you up with thorazine and chloralhydrate to keep you from shouting out how awful and horrible the place actually is, they just drug you up. Many women walk around like zombies from these drugs called medication. They just walk around all day in a daze and don't relate to anything except being high.[30]

So this was the fate Kim Parker was trying to avoid: being sent to a prison where she would have to kick cold turkey, only to be forced onto an entirely different regime of drugs, which would keep her sufficiently anesthetized and quiet until it was time to release her back onto the streets, where she would go back on heroin, which would get her sent back to the House of D, where she would have to kick cold turkey…forever, on an endless loop. Although Thorazine is considered not mentally addictive, the abrupt stoppage of high doses causes all of the physical symptoms of withdrawal, meaning formerly incarcerated women were being released to the streets poor, drugged, and on their way to a brutal comedown.

But Kim Parker was the one arrested for dealing drugs, and our legal system called that justice.

After she asked to plead guilty to the felony and her trial was adjourned, Parker was sent back, again, to the House of D, but this time, someone followed her: Commissioner of Correction Anna Kross, who used the occasion of Parker's astonishing statement—which was carried in many of the daily New York papers—to lead a public shaming tour of the House of D.

In 1963, Kross was seventy-two years old, already well past the official age of retirement for her position. She had nearly fifty years of fighting against the correctional system—often from the inside, often fruitlessly—behind her. She was a tough, tiny woman, whose family had fled anti-Semitic persecution in Nyasvizh, Russia, before landing on the Lower East Side. Kross was only sixteen when she was accepted into Columbia University, and just twenty-one when she was admitted to practice law in New York State (at a time when women still could not vote). She fought for women's suffrage and was the first woman appointed assistant corporation counsel for the city of New York. Consistently, throughout her career, Kross argued that the vast majority of people in prison (particularly women) were not criminals and, therefore, their issues could not be fixed in the criminal legal system, and they did not belong in prison. Without her unceasing activism, the correctional system in New York City would certainly have been much worse; unfortunately, even with her, it was very, very, very bad.

Kross had been feeding negative stories to the press for years, in an attempt to bring outside pressure to force change. She'd even gone so far as creating and distributing photos of some of the prison's worst aspects—a group of users, slumped in a hallway, abandoned to withdrawal; a hospital operating room that looked like an empty warehouse; cells so cramped with bodies no one could move. Internally, Kross pushed for more (and more honest) reporting and written policies, which she also made available to outside agencies. Much of the official information that appears in this book was created or preserved by Kross or at her direction. By 1963, she appeared to be reckoning with the imminent end of her career and how little she had been able to change. Knowing that she would be forced to retire soon, upon hearing the news about Kim Parker, perhaps she simply had no fucks left to give.

"If I were in her place, I would ask the same," Kross snapped at reporters. She commended Parker "on her good judgment," and announced that the House of D "is a horrible place. I can hardly bear to visit it."[31] Then she showed reporters exactly what she meant.

Six hundred twelve people were in the House of D on the day of Kross's press tour; the New York Times reporter seemed genuinely frightened as the "nervous guards accompanying Mrs. Kross jangled their big key rings warningly [and] the prisoners' voices swelled to an angry chorus."[32] Kross was unperturbed. In a tight-knit tweed fuchsia suit and little flowered hat, she zoomed through the prison, greeting prisoners and guards alike by name. The reporters were shocked as "one inmate complained that roaches get in her ears at night; another said four rats got into her cell."[33]

None of it would have surprised Commissioner Kross, who received the yearly inspection reports of the prison from the State Commission of Correction, which the state wrote and then ignored. In 1963, the "condition of many of the mattresses [was] deplorable"; they had so few pillows that people awaiting trial had to do without; there were no cups, the dishwashers were all broken, and they had run out of cleaning products for the utensils; the sewing machines were either ancient, broken, or simply not set up—and the sewing room was so cold it made it physically impossible to sew; etc.[34]

Kross showed the reporters the pitiful education services ("This is supposed to be a library. Can you imagine that?"); the seven-by-six-and-a-half-foot cells holding "two and sometimes three women"; and the two ancient elevators, which caused endless bottlenecks as they tried to move as many as a thousand people across twelve floors, day in and day out. Perhaps most tragically, she introduced them to a woman much like Kim Parker, except without whatever reserve of strength had enabled Parker to fight back in court.

The anonymous thirty-two-year-old woman was stuck in the junkie tank, the only person there not going through withdrawal. "I'm not an addict," she told a curious reporter, but she had been once, so this was where they continued to put her. They asked if she too would prefer the prison upstate to the House of D. "Oh no," she answered. "I'm 32 years old. Westfield is for rehabilitation. I'm hopeless. I got out of here Monday and was back in Wednesday. Prostitution. I went out with 25 cents with no place to stay. I had to make some money. What else could I do?"[35]

Two days after Commissioner Kross's prison tour, a Republican New York State Assembly member from Queens demanded the mayor give "immediate attention" to the House of D.[36] Parker's testimony alone would have been "bad enough," he told the newspapers, but "when Anna Kross says she doesn't blame her—this is it. I don't think we can wait any longer for improvement."[37]

Of course, they did.

Kross pushed for one immediate remedy: the relocation of all felony prisoners (who were generally serving the longest sentences) from the House of D to a more appropriate, non–maximum security facility, with more space, outside the city. This would have removed about one-third of the women currently imprisoned in the House of D, bringing it narrowly within the limit it had been built to hold. The state refused, and in a cruel twist, claimed they were doing so on be-half of the women, who would otherwise be far from home and hard to visit. As the state made literally zero other efforts to help these women receive visits from their families, this sudden concern for their loneliness seemed convenient, to say the least.

On October 28, Kim Parker returned to court, where she was al-lowed to plead guilty to the felony charge. The judge seemed annoyed at the whole affair, and after questioning her pointedly, adjourned the case for sentencing until December 16.[38] Parker was sent back yet again to do *another* two months in the House.

The next day, "the city got cracking on a cleanup probe" of the House of D.[39] Mayor Robert Wagner ordered a "speed-up in plans to replace the Women's House of Detention with a new institution on Rikers Island."[40] In 1967, he thought, they'd have an entirely new women's prison. In December, the judge grudgingly sentenced Kim Parker to two years in an upstate prison on felony drug charges, sug-gesting as he did so that the real reason she wanted to go there wasn't problems in the House of D, but some "friend" that she had in the other prison—a hint that he believed her to be queer. By that point, the uproar around Parker's case had died down again, and concerns about the House of D returned to the city's back burner.

The city had for years—decades—been discussing alternatives, ex-pansions, and new buildings, only to push them off, year after year, when the budget came due. Parker's case alone might not have made a difference, despite the public outcry. But it was followed, every few months, by another major embarrassment at the House of D, as cur-rently and formerly incarcerated women fought the wall of silence that surrounded the prison. Helena, Benita, Eloise, Ellen, Irene, Valerie,

Judith, Grace, Dorothy, Jemera, and so many more—each arrested, incarcerated, violated, and released. Arrested, incarcerated, violated, released. Arrested, incarcerated, violated, released.

In the heart of Greenwich Village, just a few years before the Stonewall Riots.

Each woman had her complaints dismissed for one reason or another: she was an addict; she was a whore; she had a record the length of my arm. The city seemed to require a perfect victim, one who could not be silenced, swept aside, or deemed to have deserved the treatment she got.

When an eighteen-year-old white college student—not yet a feminist icon—was arrested for protesting the Vietnam War in 1965, they found her.

"HOW MANY BENNINGTON GIRLS ARE VIRGINS?"

Friday, February 19, 1965, dawned cool and sunny in New York City: a perfect day for a peace protest. Eighteen-year-old Andrea Dworkin, a freshman attending Bennington College, woke up that morning in the small apartment on 110th Street that she shared with two other anti-war organizers. She was on a nine-week work program in the city, volunteering with the Student Peace Union, an intercollegiate organization that had been around since the mid-1950s. As a college freshman, Dworkin was an idealist, a bon vivant, and only a nascent feminist; a short, frizzy-haired bundle of energy committed to fighting injustice and having a good time. The familiar caricature of Dworkin as a shrill, anti-sex harpy—which would never really be true—had little to do with the teen headed to the United Nations to protest the war in Vietnam that February morning, except for this: Dworkin had, and would always have, a keen identification with marginalized people, especially women. The events of the next seventy-two hours would hone her politics like a knife, throwing her, for the first time, into the national spotlight.

America had officially been part of the Vietnam War for just under a year, since the Gulf of Tonkin incident in August 1964, when a

US ship engaged in a firefight with several North Vietnamese torpedo boats. The incident was later revealed to have been much exaggerated, but it provided the necessary pretext for the United States to publicly enter a war it had privately been part of for years.

Fast-forward six months: On February 7, the North Vietnamese attacked a US helicopter base in South Vietnam, and in response, the United States began a series of bombing campaigns. The most famous was Operation Rolling Thunder, which lasted for three years. By its end, the United States had dropped 864,000 tons of explosives on North Vietnam, killing an estimated 52,000 people and causing $500 million in damages.[41] The brutality of these bombing campaigns, which was captured in horrifying detail by journalists and photographers, helped turn much of America against the war.

But that was still years in the future. The radical 1960s were only beginning to take form. The brave souls protesting on February 19 were valiant Cassandras, fighting an injustice that most people did not yet recognize. They were a small group, mostly college students, who met weekly on the steps of UN Plaza, holding signs that read "End U.S. Support for South Vietnam Dictatorship" and "War on Poverty, Not on Vietnam."[42] Every week, a few were arrested. But that Friday it got late, and the police still hadn't shown, so some of the protestors began to leave. One, a woman in her early forties, offered to take any supplies those remaining didn't want to hold on to. Dworkin handed off a bundle of extra clothes, with a plan to get them back next week—a chance decision that would have unexpected, life-changing ramifications in just a few days.

Shortly after that woman left, the police descended en masse, and the fourteen people who were still "sitting-in" on the UN steps were offered a choice: walk to the paddy wagon and be arrested for disorderly conduct, or be dragged to the paddy wagon and be arrested for disorderly conduct and resisting arrest.

Dworkin walked, along with two other women—eighteen-year-old Lisa Goldrosen, and twenty-eight-year-old Rachel Esrick. All three were taken to a nearby police station, where they were searched, fingerprinted, and booked. The process took hours. Dworkin was allowed to send a message to a friend, letting them know that the three women were on a hunger strike to protest the outrageous, five-hundred- to thousand-dollar bonds they had been given, as well as the mistreatment of one of the men who had been arrested with them. That message was sent at 11:20 p.m., after which the three women were brought to the Night Court, where a judge remanded them to the House of D until Tuesday, when they would be tried (Monday was President's Day). Around 1:30 a.m. Saturday morning, they finally made it to the prison.

From here, accounts about what happened to Dworkin, Goldrosen, and Esrick diverge sharply. The reconstruction below is synthesized from four sources: contemporaneous newspaper reports; an internal investigation conducted by the House of D staff (some parts of which I was not allowed to quote); Dworkin's own published writings; and internal communications between city and state government officials. Regardless of the differences in these accounts, what is inarguable is that the next seventy-two hours caused explosive turmoil at the highest level of New York's government, and hastened the demise of the House of D.

After they left the Night Court, the women languished in the busy prison lobby for hours, where a nurse searched them vaginally and took Dworkin's pants (which were not allowed) and Esrick's fur coat (which she worried might have gotten stolen). Later, correction officers claimed the three women refused the opportunity to make free phone calls; all three denied that ever happened. Internally, prison officials admitted that phone calls for incarcerated people were not placed over the weekends or on holidays; however, they would never publicly admit that Dworkin and the others had told the truth. Instead, they suggested it was merely a coincidence that all three women waited until Tuesday afternoon to call their lawyers. (Although "call" wasn't quite the right word, since the prison rules actually only allowed women to write messages and phone numbers on call slips; the actual calls were made by prison staff.)

Toilet paper in the House of D was distributed in tight, per-person rations, during the guards' evening rounds. Getting to their cells at

4 a.m., Dworkin, Goldrosen, and Esrick had to do without. When Dworkin asked for some, she was told to use her hand. In the prison's internal report, much was made of the fact that this was *probably* said by another incarcerated woman, not a guard; the actual fact that the women did not have toilet paper—after being given an enema and cavity search—was downplayed. Similarly, when the three announced they were on a hunger strike the next morning, the House of D correctional staff said that they "rallied around" the young women and tried to get them to eat for their own health; in Dworkin's telling, this "rallying" consisted of correctional officers saying that if the three did not eat, they "would be taken for psychiatric examination, which would postpone the date of [their] hearing and result in longer prison stays not only for the three women demonstrators, but for the five men demonstrators who would not post bail."[43]

The judge who remanded them to the prison had, in court, specified that the two eighteen-year-olds should be kept separate from adult incarcerated women. Dworkin was housed with another adolescent, but Goldrosen was housed with a sentenced adult—although here again, prison reports would only admit that at 4 a.m. (when the women were finally finished being processed into the system) it was hard to find adequate housing, and that Goldrosen had been housed on a *floor* that held adolescents. They avoided saying anything specific about her cellmate, except that she had no known history of homosexuality—which they brought up repeatedly, because in the morning, Goldrosen woke up to find two women holding her down, while a third tried to sexually assault her.

The official responses to Goldrosen's assault were muted, and elided quickly into a conversation about homosexuality in general—not sexual violence. To prison officials and outsiders on all sides of the conversation, homosexuality among incarcerated people was viewed a priori as a violent degradation. All of the liberal crusaders who condemned the House of D in the wake of the Dworkin incident condemned lesbianism, wholesale, as a by-product of the prison's terrible conditions. No one could *want* to be a lesbian, they believed, so any sexual activity must have had a coercive, pathological aspect. When the superintendent of the House of D conducted her internal investigation, instead of discussing sexual violence in the prison, all eighteen officers interviewed claimed to have never, not once, in their entire careers, seen any kind of homosexual activity in the prison—except for one officer, who allowed that once, two years ago, she found "two inmates engaged in improper sexual activities" and stopped them immediately.[44] The lies in the prison's investigation were so blatant, they called the entire process into question.

At the time, even Dworkin herself found it impossible to separate homosexuality in the House of D from violence, telling the press that "the homosexuality was rampant and pretty hard to take. It was very well tolerated by the officers. It was orgies all the time and the sex play was constant. There were hands all over me."[45] Later, in an essay in the book *Lavender Culture*, Dworkin (herself a queer woman) wrote about her extreme regret in conflating lesbianism with sexual violence, but she had been young and scared. Moreover, she maintained that sexuality in the prison *was* frightening, and that "the dykes were 'like men'—macho, brutish, threatening."[46]

This was Dworkin's personal experience, but it was informed by—and indicative of—a shift that was happening in feminist and queer women's culture generally, away from the butch-femme paradigm of earlier years, and toward an embrace of a kind of androgyny. Joan Nestle, the founder of the Lesbian Herstory Archives, was a young femme in the bars near the House of D at this time, and she would characterize this anti–butch-femme attitude as part of "the new purity movements of the '70s."[47] These new attitudes went hand in hand with the emerging homophile, gay liberation, and feminist movements, which rejected the exploitative, mafia-controlled gay bars in the Village—and all too often ended up rejecting the butches and femmes who made sanctuaries of those spaces. In Nestle's view, the House of D "was really a butch/femme meeting place in many ways," which was partly why it was such an embarrassment to the government.[48] But this also made it an embarrassment to the newly political queer women, like Dworkin, who would define the liberatory politics of radical white people over the next few decades. Part of the reason the House of D disappeared from our cultural memory is because the white queer and feminist movements left these women behind. They were anachronisms from the bad old days.

According to Alix Genter, the historian of butch-femme culture,

> In the late 1960s and early 1970s, the women's liberation movement established a new approach to lesbianism....Harshly condemning "role-playing" as heterosexist and misogynistic, radical feminists championed lesbianism as a strictly egalitarian, supremely political stance against the patriarchy....Many lesbians involved in feminist activism learned that butch-femme had no place among liberated women....[However,] lesbians of color, poor and working-class women, rural women, and those simply not involved in feminism often maintained butch-femme identities.[49]

The world outside the prison was changing. The world inside was not.

While the attempted sexual assault of Lisa Goldrosen garnered some attention, a different kind of sexual violence was what truly inflamed the press: Dworkin's descriptions of the brutal, dehumanizing medical examination she went through. One male doctor examined her, while another (a trainee) watched; both asked questions about her sex life, her experiences with drugs, and "how many Bennington girls are virgins?" The examination was physically and mentally scarring, unsanitary, and in view of several other women, who were waiting to be run through the same mill of state-sanctioned terror. As Dworkin described it in an open letter to Mary Lindsay, the superintendent of the House of D,

> I do know that I was severely hurt, that I bled for several days after my release due to a vaginal infection, which my doctor, because of the timing, attributes to the examination or some contamination immediately thereafter....I was told that I had been "severely traumatized," i.e. bruised....No internal examination is conducted with such gross disrespect for the human body and for human dignity and

with such obvious pleasure in the embarrassment and pain of the patient/victim....The doctor's conversation with me was not "an attempt to relax" me, it was an attempt to humiliate and frighten me.[50]

These systematic violations had been part of the prison since day one, and remain the norm for many incarcerated people today. The first public protest against these examinations at the House of D took place in 1936, just four years after the prison opened, when the League of Women Shoppers assailed the mayor over the medical examination of picketers arrested during labor disputes. The mayor ordered the examinations stopped; in covering the story, the *Daily News* drolly noted that "the Mayor issued a similar order two years ago," which had been completely ignored.[51]

Despite decades—generations!—of women protesting, nothing had (or has) changed. Until a class-action lawsuit in 2005, guards at Rikers Island gave women a choice: consent to these dehumanizing exams, or spend their entire sentence in isolation.[52] Even though the city lost the suit, much like the mayor's 1934 decree, the outcome was frequently ignored. In 2010, plaintiffs won a $33 million class-action lawsuit against the city over strip searches and nonconsensual gynecological exams.[53] In 2013, a woman was forced into a brutal exam and then repeatedly raped by guards at Rikers; although it took six years, the city was eventually found at fault and forced to pay $1.2 million.[54] In 2014, a woman incarcerated at Rikers won a lawsuit against the city because she was threatened into submitting to an exam; her award was a mere $80,000.[55] Those of us not in prison have simply come to accept a consistent amount of sexual violence as part of our "justice" system.

And this isn't a New York City problem. In 1994, the National Commission on Correctional Health Care issued a paper on "Women's Health in Correctional Settings," which included the milquetoast recommendation that "evidence is insufficient to recommend routine pelvic examinations on asymptomatic, nonpregnant women."[56] The recommendation was reaffirmed in 2005, 2014, and as recently as 2020. Similarly, in 1993, 2005, and 2016, the World Medical

Association passed (or reaffirmed) resolutions stating that "a request to conduct a body cavity search puts the physician in the untenable position of potentially violating the ethical standards of his/her profession. Physician participation should be in exceptional cases only."[57] If they did anything more than issue a recommendation, it was ignored.

Every person in the House of D must have been an exceptional case, judging from their stories. Jay Toole, the activist who leads history tours of Greenwich Village to ensure that the House of D is remembered, was incarcerated for the first time around the same year as Dworkin. Toole's account of the vaginal examinations matches Dworkin's to a frightening degree:

> The worst thing was the physicals. They were horrendous, you know....He's telling me to get on the table and put my feet in the stirrups and this and that, and it felt like his whole arm went in there. They checked everywhere, every hole you have that's where they went.
>
> Then he was like, "Alright, get off the table. Hurry up, we got to bring the next one in."
>
> Hurry up? I couldn't move, the pain was so bad. I don't know what he did up in there but it was so, so bad. When I looked down I was covered in blood, you know? And they didn't do nothing.[58]

Why didn't anyone do anything? If these assaults were so routine and traumatic, why was Andrea Dworkin the only one the wider world paid attention to? Obviously, she was traditionally gendered, in college, young, white, not using drugs, and part of an organization that had some clout. She was also brilliant, brave, and outspoken: after being released, she spent days trying to tell journalists about what had happened to her. But her parents, with whom she was staying, were unsupportive and embarrassed by the entire situation. Dejected, Dworkin left their home in New Jersey and went to Greenwich Village to collect the underwear she had left with the kindly woman at the UN protest—who turned out to be none other than the writer Grace Paley. It was Paley who made Dworkin's story national news.

Paley was already a committed activist, a highly respected author, and a long-term Greenwich Village resident familiar with the horror stories about the House of D. When Dworkin showed up on her doorstep, Paley took her in. Concerned about the pain and bleeding Dworkin was experiencing, Paley sent her to a doctor, who confirmed that Dworkin had been wounded internally. Paley then used her name and connections to help Dworkin contact journalists, and "within a day or two the media started calling."[59] Together, the two women triggered an avalanche.

Within a month, the doctor responsible for Dworkin's examination was fired after refusing to testify, write up a report, or cooperate in any way.

Within two months, five separate government investigations were launched to look at conditions in the House of D.

Within three, the New York City police commissioner had resigned (although the House of D scandal was only part of that decision).

Within four, the House of D had become a major issue in local politics, leading three-time mayor Robert Wagner not to run for reelection and handing soon-to-be-elected Mayor John Lindsay a cudgel with which to batter the outgoing administration and its "tired, self-perpetuating bureaucratic ways of the past."[60]

And within a year of Dworkin's arrest, Commissioner of Correction Anna J. Kross would be forced out of her position, replaced by a man who had never worked in New York's city or state government before, who received a significant bump in salary.

With Kross gone, there would be a sudden and drastic clampdown on information coming out of the Women's House of Detention and the Department of Correction as a whole. For example, the 1962 annual report of the department was a dense treatise that ran over a hundred pages, including nearly thirty tables charting everything from the age of each person incarcerated (broken down by charge), to the amount of cash fines received at each institution in the system. The 1966 report, on the other hand, was a slick twenty-four-page pamphlet, printed in color on expensive stock, with no statistical information or tables at all.

The only thing Dworkin's imprisonment didn't have much effect on, in fact, were conditions in the Women's House of Detention—what Dworkin would one day refer to as "the common sadomasochistic structure of the prison experience no matter what the crime or country or historical era."[61] Dworkin's testimony would be instrumental in getting the prison shut down, but she could not get conditions in the prison improved—an instructive lesson for those who advocate for prison reform over abolition. The reason that overcrowding is often the only problem prison officials admit to is that it can be fixed easily (with a lot of money), and does not require any kind of fundamental questioning of the system itself. The official answer to prison problems is always more prisons.

In the immediate aftermath of the Dworkin scandal, the city engaged in some disturbing sleight of hand, shuffling imprisoned women from one institution to another in order to get the official headcount at the House of D within its limit. These moves were temporary, and without regard for the needs or experiences of the women transported. Since they involved leaving one institution and entering another, the transfers triggered additional vaginal and rectal searches on all of the people involved. According to the Medical Division of the Department of Correction, the Brooklyn House of Detention had "no special clinic facilities" available for women.[62] As a result, the Brooklyn House of Detention ripped out their library to make room for unspecified clinical facilities. Three months later the women were sent right back to the House of D.

Once the initial outcry had quieted, the official whitewash began. Mayor Wagner's administration conducted two investigations in quick succession; both found that all of the charges against the prison (other than overcrowding) "were without substance."[63] Herman T. Stichman, the New York State commissioner for special investigations, contended in the press that the government was lying, and that *his* investigation into the prison upheld nearly every charge Dworkin had made.[64] Shortly after he turned in his findings, Stichman's entire office was defunded and he and his staff were let go from the state government; I was never able to find a full copy of his report.

In November 1965, Republican John Lindsay won the New York City mayoral race, which meant that the House of D was no longer a problem he could pin on his political opponents but a situation he had to fix himself. In early December, Mayor Lindsay told the press that everyone knew the House of D was a disaster "almost since its opening day in 1932."[65] But soon he cooled his rhetoric. Later that month, the grand jury wrapped their investigation, finding that the prison had acted properly in all regards, nothing had been done to Lisa Goldrosen, and—except for overcrowding—there were no real issues at the Women's House of Detention. Once again, recommendations for moving the incarcerated women to Rikers Island were endorsed, as were recommendations for more liberal bail processes, twenty-four/seven medical coverage in the House of D, the development of a separate institution for prostitutes, alcoholics, and addicts, and the creation of a separate area inside the House of D for lesbians.[66] Very few of these recommendations were ever followed. A few weeks later, Lindsay's incoming deputy mayor visited the House of D and made a surprise announcement: "In no physical sense could the 11-story structure at the intersection of Greenwich Avenue and Avenue of the Americas be called a 'snake pit and hell hole,' terms that have been used by former inmates and staff to describe it."[67] Like many politicians, Lindsay campaigned on social justice, but governed on the status quo.

Three former inmates, along with a long-term volunteer, quickly wrote a letter of protest to all the New York City papers, saying they believed "the grand jury sought only to discredit testimony offered by critics of the House of Detention and to whitewash—and even commend—the very people responsible for its shocking conditions."[68] But after publishing a few angry letters, most newspapers seemed willing to let the state tell the story.

In 1966, an author named Sara Harris, who wrote sensational exposés on sex work, cults, and the sexual revolution, invited Dworkin to tell her side of the story as part of a book Harris was writing. After meeting several times, Dworkin was horrified by the chapter Harris wrote about her, calling it "false, malicious…purposeful fiction."[69]

Harris went forward with her project anyway, although without Dworkin's participation. The resulting book, *Hellhole*, is the only other full-length examination of the Women's House of Detention. Although sympathetic to the plight of the women incarcerated, the manuscript is so overblown, poorly sourced, homophobic, and riddled with inaccuracies that it does not seem worth quoting.

The one consistently critical voice inside the government was Brooklyn State Assemblyman Joseph Kottler, who conducted his own investigation, condemned the House of D soundly, and announced that he was "start[ing] proceedings to close the prison."[70] Those proceedings never manifested, but Kottler's continued criticism kept pressure on the city and state even after public interest faded away. The nebulous plan to open a detention center for women on Rikers Island took on new urgency, and by the end of 1966, the city announced that "final plans and specifications have been completed.... Completion is anticipated by the Summer of 1969 at an estimated cost of $20,125,258."[71] It actually took until 1971, but there were no more holds, no more surveys, no more new ideas or alternate proposals. The House of D, from here on out, was leaving the Village, headed for Rikers. It was just a matter of when.

As for Dworkin? The entire experience—her imprisonment, the subsequent public embarrassments, her family's lack of support, and the prison's ultimate vindication—was excruciating. But also eye-opening, helping her to identify and name all kinds of openly supported, public violence against women. A decade after her imprisonment, as she was starting her career as an author, Dworkin wrote a book proposal on the systemic violence and misogyny of the prison system. Unfortunately, it was rejected by every publisher she contacted. But Dworkin was unwilling to let the underlying issues go, and so she cast around for a new subject that would let her cover the same ground. She found the one that would make her infamous: pornography. Dworkin wrote in her memoir,

> I decided to write on pornography because I could make the same
> points—show the same inequities—as with prisons. Pornography and

prisons were built on cruelty and brutalization; the demeaning of the human body as a form of punishment; the worthlessness of the individual human being....Each was a social construction that could be different but was not; each incorporated and exploited isolation, dominance and submission, humiliation, and dehumanization. In each the effort was to control a human being by attacking human dignity. In each the guilt of the imprisoned provided a license to animalize persons....Arguably (but not always), those in prison had committed an offense; the offense of women in pornography was in being women.[72]

All too often, of course, the same was true of the people in the House of D: their only crime was in being women—the wrong kind of women: too masculine, too gay, too Black, too poor, too angry, too ill, too resistant, too strong, too vocal.

For years, these women had fought back, when and where they could, against the injustice of our "justice" system. Still, they were always on the margin of someone else's political agenda. But in 1966, the year after Andrea Dworkin's arrest, two college students in California launched a radical organization to empower the Black community and resist racist policing: the Black Panther Party for Self-Defense. Its focus on community organizing meant that Black women were working with other Black women to develop every aspect of the Panthers' agenda. The Panthers weren't without problems—including the endemic misogyny of the Left (and the entire world) at this time—but they were one of the first organizations to take the needs of these Black women seriously, and not demand they present as perfect victims before fighting for their rights. Black queer women quickly rose to become some of the most visible leaders in the Panther movement, although their sexuality often went unacknowledged. Three of these women—Afeni Shakur, Joan Bird, and Angela Davis—would be incarcerated in the House of D in its final years. The experience would fundamentally alter the political perspectives of these women, and for the first time, a broad coalition of radical organizations would come together to publicly fight against the House of D, and the prison industrial complex generally.

CHAPTER 11

Gay Lib and Black Power

AFENI SHAKUR, RADICAL GAY LIBERATIONIST

Afeni Shakur is today remembered for many things, including her leadership in the Black Panthers; her brilliant legal mind; the incredible life and work of her son, rapper and actor Tupac Shakur; and her autobiography, *Evolution of a Revolutionary*, which she cowrote with actor Jasmine Guy. Forgotten, though, is her history as a gay liberation radical, her presence at the Stonewall Riots, and her own bisexuality. But *all* of these parts of her history connect in one spot: the Women's House of Detention at 10 Greenwich Avenue. In fact, a close look at Shakur's time in the House of D shows the powerful ways in which Black liberation influenced gay liberation, and vice versa.

Shakur's time at the House of D began the night of April 2, 1969, when the NYPD tried to crush the Black Panther Party in New York City. There had been other skirmishes between the two groups before, but that night the police were out to decapitate the party, conducting at least thirteen simultaneous, "heavily armed" midnight raids on the homes of Panther leaders.[1] Doors were kicked in, children were held at gunpoint, and friends and acquaintances who were unlucky enough to be present were rounded up along with the intended targets—a group that would be known as the Panther 21, one of the most infamous causes célèbres of the late 1960s.

Shakur was just twenty-one years old the night of the raid—twenty-one, six months in the party, and already one of its East Coast leaders. Not all the Panthers were quite so young, but youth was a common thread that united sixties radicals across all factions—from the Young Lords to the Gay Liberation Front, to the Radicalesbians, to the Black Panther Party.

Shakur had been raised in North Carolina until she was eleven, then moved with her mother and sister to the Bronx. Like her son, she was a talented artist who qualified for the city's prestigious High School for the Performing Arts (where the movie *Fame* would soon be set). But the school was never a great fit, and after some disciplinary trouble, she transferred to Bronx Science, a public magnet school that boasts eight Nobel laureates among its alums. She didn't last long there either. It was the mid-sixties, a time of dropping out and tuning in, so Shakur left high school and soaked up Black New York. She went to be-ins and political rallies, studied Yoruba culture, dropped acid to Jimi Hendrix, and was given the name Afeni—"dear one" or "lover of the people."[2] But it wasn't until she heard Bobby Seale, cofounder of the Panthers, give a sidewalk speech in Harlem, that she found herself. She remembered that day, thirty years later:

So there I was wrapped in my Africanness. For the first time, loving myself and loving, now that there was something I could do with my life. There was now something I could do with all this aggression, and all this fear....Before I joined the party, I was fucked up. I would slap a motherfucker in a minute....So, the Panther Party for me, at that time, clarified my situation....They took my rage and channeled it against them [she points outside], instead of us [she holds her heart]. They educated my mind and gave me direction. With that direction came hope, and I loved them for giving me that. Because I never had hope in my life....They took me and looked at me and said: "Afeni, you are so strong, so use your strength to help the weak. You are smart, so use your mind to teach the ignorant."[3]

She soon met Lumumba Shakur, who led the Black Panther section in Harlem and was steeped in the Black radical tradition—his father had been a follower of Marcus Garvey, who espoused a powerful theory of pan-Africanism. She converted to Islam, they got married, she joined the party, and she quickly rose to be a leader, giving passionate speeches to raise money and helping establish a breakfast program for schoolkids in Harlem. To the rest of the Panthers, Afeni and Lumumba were a power couple, like Eldridge and Kathleen Cleaver, although Afeni was uncomfortable with that kind of celebrity and didn't feel like she deserved a place in that pantheon.[4] But three months after they got married, when Lumumba was arrested, she found herself one of the leaders of the party in New York. Three months after that, in April 1969, the police kicked in her door on 117th Street and arrested her and Lumumba while they were sleeping. The charges? "Conspiracy to murder, arson, reckless endangerment, and possession of weapons and explosives."[5]

Specifically, the Panther 21 were accused of planning to bomb a startling array of targets simultaneously, from the police station on 106th Street to the Brooklyn Botanical Gardens, to the Easter shopping crowds at Macy's and Bloomingdale's.[6] Additionally, several other existing cases involving members of the party were rolled into this trial. All told, they were charged with thirty counts of conspiracy, and faced a total of 356 years in prison—*each*.

Joan Bird was the only other woman among the Panther 21. A nursing student at Bronx Community College, she had just turned twenty a month before the raids. She was asleep in her parents' apartment in Harlem when the cops broke in "at 5am…with shotguns, you see, armed. Armed pigs, breaking down doors."[7] She knew exactly how much danger she (and her mother and father) were in, as this was her second Panther-related arrest that year. In January, she'd been picked up on charges of trying to bomb a police station in New Jersey. She had been beaten badly by the police at the time, who lamely claimed that she had received a black eye, a bruised forehead, a split lip, and contusions all over her body when trying to duck the bullets they fired at her.[8] The truth, according to Bird?

> One of the police told me "to crawl out of the car, bitch."...[They] dragged me by my arms, while on the ground on my back....With a short black club [one] beat me across my face and head....I became dizzy....My mouth was bleeding....They put handcuffs on me and turned me over face down....They began to kick me and walk on my back and legs.[9]

After this, she was held for a while and then bailed out. This initial case against Bird and her codefendants was one of the cases rolled into the Panther 21 trial.

Given the vastness of the conspiracy alleged, the number of homes raided, and the months of advance surveillance that had already been conducted by the government, one would imagine the police captured a grand haul of weapons and explosives during their raids. But in truth, they found only "one carbine, one rifle, six revolvers, one shotgun, one saw-off [sic] shotgun, two switchblade knives and one dagger."[10] All the dynamite the Panthers were going to plant in department stores—allegedly on the *very* day they were arrested—was never found.

In court, Bird and Shakur were each given a $100,000 bail and sent to the House of D. Joan Bird spent the next year and a half in a dark, dirty, seven-by-six-foot cell. Except to go to court, she wouldn't see the outside world again until July 1970. Afeni Shakur was an exceptional speaker, so the Panthers and their allies bailed her out a little faster, so she could help raise money for the rest of the 21. She only spent nine months in the House of D (this first time), but they were some of the most turbulent in Greenwich Village history—and they would have a profound effect on Shakur's political thinking.

Just two months after Shakur and Bird were incarcerated, the cops conducted an ill-planned raid on the Stonewall Inn, kicking off days and nights of queer resistance. On the very first night, as a rowdy crowd de-arrested one of their own and forced the police to take refuge in the bar, a few people—women—looked to the House of Detention. About five hundred feet separated the prison and the bar, the incarcerated and the liberated, the forgotten and the immortalized. Five hundred feet between those who "birthed" the modern gay rights movement and those the movement has ignored. Some of those incarcerated had windows that looked down Christopher Street. They would have heard the sirens and the screams, smelled the burning trash, and flocked to see what was happening.

Arcus Flynn was driving home late that night from her job as a nurse, wending through the streets around Washington Square when she noticed something strange: small points of light, flying through the sky. When she pulled over, she realized they were fires—little burning things being thrown from the windows of the House of D. As she got out of her car, she could hear them inside: dozens, maybe hundreds, of voices screaming, "Gay rights, gay rights, gay rights!"[11] That, she would later tell interviewers, was how she first realized Stonewall was happening.

Author Rita Mae Brown was on the street, in the crowd, closer to the bar. Years later, she wrote about her frustration with the way the people in the House of D had been left out of history: "At the women's house of detention, the women heard the noises and started rioting inside the prison.... [They] burned mattresses and shoved them through the bars. This never got written up because all the accounts of that period were given by men."[12]

Jay Toole was also in the crowd that night, one of the many homeless youth who are often generically recognized as a vital part of the Stonewall Uprising, yet rarely singled out for recognition by name, or even as part of the queer community. According to Toole, Stonewall was a turning point *because* of the diversity of the crowd: "It was every form of human being, every shade of human being, every sexuality of human being, all coming together as one. It was just like, enough is e-*fucking*-nough."[13]

And yet that diversity has been underplayed—in consistent ways—since the very next day. In one of the first articles written about

Stonewall, *Village Voice* journalist Lucian Truscott IV mentioned the "rough street people," who were not genuinely interested in gay rights or fighting police repression, but instead "saw a chance for a little action."[14] That narrative has held ever since, furthering an imagined divide between "rough street" and "gay." But many of the street kids in the Village, like Jay Toole, were there *because* they were gay—a situation that remains true today, when poor queer youth still flock to the neighborhood because of its reputation. David Carter, author of the first book-length history of the Uprising, *Stonewall*, was one of the rare few who recognized this truth, telling journalist Richard Burnett that "the people who resisted most were gay street youth, non-gender-conforming butch lesbians and effeminate young men."[15]

Some of those gender nonconforming butch lesbians weren't on the street because they were gay, they were in the House of D because they were gay. Who were those women setting fires and chanting for their rights? Like the rough street kids, they're rarely recognized as part of the Uprising, let alone named and honored like other Stonewall veterans. None of the extant records of the prison talk about that night, but a week later, the *New York Amsterdam News*—the same historically Black paper that had covered the arrest of Serena C. back in the 1930s—ran an article entitled "Women Held in Assault on Guard," which detailed how eight incarcerated women attempted to escape the prison on the night of Stonewall.[16] Verna, Beverly, Nancy, Marie, Mildred, Sylvia, Veronica, and Jean: forgotten queer women Stonewall veterans? "Rough street people" who "saw a chance for a little action"? For far too long, our frame of reference for Stonewall has been too small, cropping the story down to a narrow sliver of its true self and then enlarging that image until it blots out everything else. The memory of these eight women has fallen into the crack between what happened and what we remember; research as I might, I cannot bridge this divide.

But there were definitely two queer women in the House of D during the Stonewall Uprising: Afeni Shakur and Joan Bird. And they were there one month later, when the newly formed Gay Liberation

Front protested the House of D—in fact, protesting the prison was one of the reasons GLF formed.

In the wake of Stonewall, a few young people, already active on the Left, "posted notices for a demonstration in support of the Black Panther Party members currently jailed in the Women's House of Detention."[17] When older leaders from the homophile movement shot the idea down (worried that it would "prove offensive to the authorities"), the young radicals spontaneously announced they were forming a new group called the Gay Liberation Front to sponsor their protests.[18] They put together a flyer calling for a rally outside the House of D on August 2—one month earlier than their oft recognized "first protest" at the offices of the *Village Voice*.[19]

According to historians of gay liberation, this protest, and their support for the Black Panthers generally, caused a nearly instantaneous fracturing of the GLF. A year later, a group of (mostly white, mostly male, mostly cis) members split off to form the Gay Activists Alliance, which didn't consider prisons or the House of D gay issues:

> When GLF agreed to march with the Panthers to the New York City Women's House of Detention, Marty Reynolds broke away from the movement. [Jim] Owles and [Arthur] Evans followed. They would focus on building a single-issue, homosexual rights movement, rather than at maintaining a broad coalitional politics with other Left groups. And rather than emphasizing the destruction of capitalism and existing political structures, their efforts...were directed at using the existing "system" to the advantage of gay and lesbian Americans.[20]

The radicals continued to focus on the prison, however. Afeni Shakur and Joan Bird were *still* incarcerated there when the GLF made protesting the House of D a regular activity. Much of this was initiated by the lesbian and bisexual women in the group. Karla Jay, a leading lesbian activist, remembered that "after the start of women's liberation, the House of D became a rallying point. From Christmas

Eve 1969 through New Year's Day, men and women, including my-self, kept a vigil in front of it night and day."[21] Other groups there that week included the Black Panthers, the Red Stockings, Youth Against War and Fascism, and many other organizations that were part of the New Left.

The Gay Liberation Front returned to the House of D again on In-ternational Women's Day 1970, to support feminist groups in an anti-prison protest that turned violent, pitting angry cops against women determined to "free our sisters."[22] And the GLF came back in August 1970, when a march for gay and feminist rights ran into another po-lice raid, on another gay bar, turning the streets of Greenwich Village into a bloody battlefield between "700 demonstrators and 100 police men"—the forgotten Haven Riot.[23] In describing *that* riot, GLF mem-ber Kenneth Pitchford highlighted the political consciousness—and daring—of the homeless people who are so often dismissed. "It was the street people fighting at our side who were in the vanguard that night (and the next), risking more, staying longer, getting it all to-gether," he wrote.[24] (Still though, they were seen as fighting *alongside* gay liberation, not as part of gay liberation.) A month after that, GLF banners could be spotted in the crowd of a Panther organized protest, which was captured on NYPD surveillance footage.[25] Again and again and again, the Women's House of Detention was the place where Black liberation, women's liberation, and gay liberation came together to battle the carceral state.

This support was not one way. When Huey P. Newton, cofounder of the Black Panthers, was freed from jail in the spring of 1970, he announced that one of his goals for the party was to make common cause with feminist and gay liberation. When he came to New York, he held a famous press conference in the apartment of Jane Fonda. Afeni Shakur was there that day, and she arranged for him to meet with three members of the Gay Liberation Front: John Knoebel, Angela Lynn Douglas, and Nikos Diamon. Newton was looking to create a new world with a new "revolutionary value system."[26] To achieve this, the Panthers were organizing a Revolutionary People's Constitutional

Convention in Philadelphia, in September 1970, and he invited the GLF to participate.

At the convention, the women's meeting (which Joan Bird was part of) was riven by homophobia. Afeni Shakur attended the gay men's workshop instead, and talked about the significance of the queer protests outside the House of D. According to a report written by a Chicago-based group of queer people of color,

> [Shakur] told us about how she had looked out of her prison cell window during a demonstration to free the N.Y. 21. Seeing a Gay Liberation banner in the crowd made her think for the first time about gay people and Gay Liberation. She then began relating to the gay sisters in jail beginning to understand their oppression, their anger and the strength in them and in all gay people. She talked about how Huey Newton's statement would be used in the Panther Party, not as a party line, but as a basis for criticism and self-criticism to overcome anti-homosexual hang-ups among party members, and in the black community. She also helped us to formulate what we wanted to say in our list of demands.
>
> When the Panther sister left, some of us went over to thank her for helping us. She said, "I didn't help you, but I want to thank you. You really helped me to understand things."[27]

But what Shakur saw out her window was only part of her journey in the House of D.

As protestors filled the streets of the Village day in and day out, Shakur sat in a tiny punishment cell, because she refused to allow the prison doctors to perform the same barbaric genital examinations on her that they did on Joan Bird, Andrea Dworkin, and hundreds of thousands of other women over the last forty years. According to Bird,

> These "punishment" and "psychiatric" cells are without beds, mattresses, or toilets. They have wash basins and water. There is no hot water in the punishment cells, but there is hot water in the

psychiatric cells. Women live in these cells for months. They have to ask officers when they need to go to the bathroom.[28]

In fact, it was worse than Bird even knew. People in these cells could only be brought to a bathroom when there were two guards on the floor who had time to take them—which meant rarely. In just a few months, Angela Davis would be tossed into one of these, and she wrote that "absolutely nothing was allowed inside the cells—not only were cigarettes and matches banned, but also books, writing materials, toothbrushes, soap, washcloths, clothes, and shoes."[29]

In prison, it is almost impossible to tell a punishment cell from one designed for someone in acute psychiatric distress. And this isn't some archaic practice. In Mariame Kaba's phenomenal *We Do This 'Til We Free Us*, she described the experiences of Tiffany Rusher, a woman serving a five-year sentence on sex work charges in Illinois in 2013. After being placed in solitary due to a fight with her cellmate, her mental health began to slip, she attempted suicide, and she was placed in a psychiatric cell on crisis watch, which meant

being stripped of all clothing and belongings, and placed in a bare cell with only a "suicide smock" (a single piece of thick woven nylon, too stiff to fold, with holes for one's head and arms). During this time, Rusher was monitored through a plexiglass wall, with the lights on, twenty-four hours a day. Rather than receiving mental health care, Rusher was kept naked, except for her rigid smock, in an empty cell. She was given strict, dehumanizing instructions about how to wipe herself and manage her menstrual hygiene, which included a requirement that her hands be visible to the guard watching her at all times. In order to read, Rusher had to persuade a prison guard to hold an open book against the glass of her cell…as time wore on, Rusher asked her attorney: "Who in her situation wouldn't want to kill themselves?"[30]

Today, solitary confinement is widely recognized as physical and psychological torture; while I was writing this chapter in June 2021, courageous, committed activists won a years-long campaign to have it banned in New York City.

But in the late 1960s and early 1970s, many Black leaders were held in solitary as a way of breaking them, and preventing them from speaking with other imprisoned people. Huey P. Newton was held in solitary for spans of up to twenty-two months at a go, and recent historians have suggested this torture played a large part in his later difficulties outside of prison.[31]

Shakur was at least given a cot; still, her months in solitary confinement were brutal. Shakur says she survived it by sheer exhaustion. "I slept through the rats, the isolation, the Spam, the fake white bread, and all of that," she wrote.[32]

Aside from being imprisoned on false charges, part of the reason Shakur was so exhausted was that she acted as her own attorney during the Panther 21 trial—despite having left high school long before graduating. None of the other Panthers—including Shakur's husband, Lumumba—thought this was a good idea. But as Shakur put it in her autobiography, "I was young. I was arrogant. And I was brilliant in court…because I thought this was the *last* time I could speak. The last time before they locked me up forever.…I was writing my own obituary."[33] Today, it is largely believed that it was Shakur's statements, and her perceptive questioning of government infiltrators on the witness stand, that exposed FBI corruption and saved the Panther 21.

But it was the other incarcerated people in the House of D who enabled Shakur to survive those daily court battles. The older women, the ones serving life on an installment plan, the disregarded and downtrodden like Kim Parker. They taught Shakur to put Vaseline on her stretch marks when her pregnancy with Tupac began to show; they took her one court outfit and rubbed their precious reserves of toothpaste on it, so it would look fresh pressed and starched in the mornings; and every day, they told Shakur "to go in there tomorrow and shame" the men who had put her in prison.[34]

And she did.

"Women have to find strength from other women, because that is what gets us through," Shakur wrote in her autobiography. But more than just strength, Shakur found love among the women in the House of D, as did Joan Bird.

Even though it was more than fifty years ago, Carol Crooks—Crooksie—remembers clearly the first time she saw Shakur in the House of D.

> I had come from court, and she was talking to a group of girls in the back of the hallway....She was telling us whatever we asked about....
> She explained to us what [the Panthers] were fighting for....She had a smile, she was very, very soft in her manner, and everybody did everything for her.[35]

Crooks was only eighteen when they met, in the House of D briefly on a drug setup. The police claimed to have watched her do a direct sale, but Crooks had people underneath her to do that work. "I didn't let people know who I was, and nobody was allowed to talk to me," she said of that time.[36] Crooks grew up in Brooklyn when the borough was considered uncool, unsafe, and decidedly ungentrified. From the age of nine, she was in the streets, "playing cards and shooting dice with men and stealing food to help support her mother and sister."[37] She was also an accomplished athlete, running with the Police Athletic League program and training for the Junior Olympics, but all that was derailed by the need to make money to survive.

The House of D, in its last few years of existence, was "very tightly controlled," according to Crooks.[38] It wasn't like Bedford Hills (where she would eventually spend more than thirteen years). The elevators were slow and old, which meant that you saw virtually no one who wasn't on your floor, unless you worked delivering the laundry—a useful gig for passing notes and contraband along with uniforms and sheets. Nothing happened between the two women while they were in the prison, Crooks remembered, but she managed to give Shakur her mother's number and the names of a few places where she hung out. When the trial was finally over in 1971, Shakur came looking for Crooksie, and soon the pair was a couple.

"She was very nervous," Crooks remembered. "The feds were shooting them, killing them left and right."[39] Shakur was looking for a safe house, a place where no one would think to find her. She located it less than a half mile from the House of D, in an apartment on West Fourth Street, which was owned by a wealthy white woman who allowed Panthers, Gay Liberation Front members, and other radicals to crash there for months at a time.

"Sometimes there were as many as four or five people living there," remembered Giles Kotcher, a Gay Liberation Front member who ended up sharing the apartment with Shakur, Joan Bird, and Bird's girlfriend, Bern, who had also just been released from the House of D.[40] "Bern was the butch to Joan's femme," said Kotcher.[41] Kotcher slept on a couch in the living room, while Bird and Shakur took the two bedrooms at the back of the apartment.

Kotcher said the few months they shared were the best time he ever had in New York. Shakur had a sharp sense of humor and could be incredibly sarcastic; Bird was shy but sweet; and Bern was a born performer, who kept the whole group in hysterics. Kotcher was closer to Bird and Bern than to Shakur, who was often in Brooklyn with Crooksie, or out working for the Panthers, or visiting her husband Lumumba. It was a wild time. One night, Bern showed up at West Fourth Street wearing a perfectly fitted, robin's egg-blue leather suit, packing a gun and some cocaine. Bird put on a giant wig, and the two of them and Kotcher got high and went to Times Square to watch people.

The three were living together when Afeni Shakur gave birth to her son, Lesane Parish Crooks. "He had my last name," Crooks told me, wistfully. "When the nurse brought the baby in, 'Feni said don't pass him to me, pass him to Crooksie."[42] A year later, his name would be changed to Tupac Amaru Shakur, but he stayed close with Crooks throughout his life.

Charlotte Marchant was a young white activist just beginning to question her own sexuality when she met Shakur at this time, during a long weekend at a socialist commune in Vermont. According to Marchant, Shakur told us that the male co-defendants in the Panther 21 were unhappy with her jail relationship. One of the struggles was over the naming of her son. She and her girlfriend in jail wanted to name him Parish, after a soap opera star they admired. The other Panthers said the name was bourgeois and not revolutionary. She was really conflicted about her sexual feelings and her identity as a Black Panther, and wasn't sure how to reconcile them.[43]

One thing the two questioning women agreed on: sex was better with other women.

Denise Oliver-Velez, a leader in the Young Lords and a friend of Shakur's, said despite the difficulties, Shakur had no interest in hiding her relationship with Crooks, and that many in the party assumed Crooks was a man (at least at first). "The Party was not happy with Afeni announcing she was pregnant—and Crooksie was the father!" Oliver-Velez laughed, remembering.[44] They would go out dancing at the Hilltop, a lesbian bar in Harlem, or Trude Heller's, a queer and wild dance club just one block from the House of D, or to the Bon Soir on lesbian nights, when Owen Watson, a Black Panther martial arts expert, would act as the bouncer "to stop girls from getting hassled going to lesbian nights in the Village."[45]

However, Shakur was more than capable of dealing with homophobia on her own. Giles Kotcher remembered that while they lived together, he would sometimes help out with young Tupac, babysitting and changing diapers. One afternoon, Lumumba Shakur—Afeni's husband—"made a fuss about [me] handling 'the family jewels,'" and "Afeni was all over him."[46]

"Shut the fuck up," she told Lumumba. "This guy is helping me! You can go back the fuck where you came from."[47]

After that, Kotcher remembered, he, Afeni, and Lumumba had a revealing conversation about sexuality and incarceration. For both Lumumba and Afeni, incarceration had put them in close contact with out queer people, but in vastly different ways. In the House of D, as in most women's prisons, there was little effort to consistently segregate queer people, creating the possibility for real connections. Moreover, its location in Greenwich Village meant Afeni was also exposed to the revolutionary-minded queer folks protesting outside. For radical women, prisons made a spectrum of sexuality visible, encouraged anti-prison solidarity across identities, and propelled women to explore their own emotions away from men and heteronormative society.

In contrast, on Rikers Island, where Lumumba was incarcerated, he told Kotcher, "gay people were segregated in their own section"— the island's infamous "fairy wing," which closed in 2006.[48] Not all queer men were placed in segregation. It was really used to segregate transgender women, feminine men, and people arrested for specifically gay crimes—thus in 2015, when a modified version was reinstated, it was called the Trans Housing Unit. When Lumumba was there, masculine men who were attracted to other men were not housed in segregation, or acknowledged as gay by the prison, and were considered "asshole bandits," who would rape you.[49] And because Rikers was an island, there was no way for gay revolutionaries to protest the prison within hearing distance of those incarcerated. Thus, the prison taught Lumumba there were two kinds of homosexuals: feminine men who were weak, needed to be segregated, and rarely had contact with other imprisoned people; and lying rapists. Because of these experiences, Lumumba told Kotcher, "there was no possibility" of solidarity between gay and straight male prisoners.[50]

As Lumumba wrote in *Look for Me in the Whirlwind: The Collective Autobiography of the New York 21*,

Homosexuality is out in the open in prisons. In prison you're only a faggot or a homosexual if you play the role of the woman. Some faggots actually thought they were women, and walked, talked, and acted just like women. Most faggots in prisons have women's names. After five years in prison, I came to the conclusion that faggots became faggots out of psychological reasons rather than physical reasons. Most men who came to prison and became faggots did so because they would not fight for their manhood. The manly response in prison if somebody says he wants to fuck you—you must fight the person who said he wanted to fuck you immediately. If you fight and lose and the person who wanted to fuck you asks you again, you better get a pipe and beat that person in the head. The institutional official will tell you that you were right for fighting for your manhood, and discipline the person who tried to fuck you (that is, if you don't kill him). Sometimes the person who was fighting for his manhood got knocked out fighting. Then while he was knocked out, the other person would fuck him. When he woke up and dug that he got fucked, if he went and piped the person in the head who fucked him, in this way he could restore his manhood and win the respect of the other inmates. Here's the other situation: if a person went over to another inmate and told him he wanted to fuck him and the other person said no and didn't want to fight for his manhood and said something like, "If you ask me again I'll tell the officers," the person who asked the other inmate to fuck, or as we call these persons, asshole bandits, the asshole bandit would put some mass psychological pressure on the punk who refused to fight for his manhood. The asshole bandit would tell about four hundred inmates constantly to ask the punk to fuck. Word was already out that the punk would not fight for his manhood. Within three months, he would be a faggot because he could not stand the psychological pressures. Most faggots became faggots like that. Some punks became faggots for protection. In Comstock the faggots got married in the yard, with a wedding, rice-throwing, a big picnic in the yard, and a so-called honeymoon. In the prisons I've been in, many correctional officers were faggots.[51]

For men, prisons created a narrow, negative binary of what it meant to be gay, and discouraged any kind of solidarity, or even honesty, between straight and non-straight people. Institutional officials encouraged them to kill one another to maintain a veneer of heterosexuality, even while acknowledging that men were having sex with each other. This may go a long way toward explaining the seeming divide between women and men in the Black Panther Party when it came to their attitudes toward queer sexuality—yet another way in which experiences *inside* prison have had a tremendous impact on the history of sexuality *outside* of prison. Rather than repeating tired, racist tropes of Black men as inherently homophobic, we must reckon with the complexities of sex and violence in men's prisons, and how the state reinforces terror against queer and trans people in these cages—most of whom are people of color.

According to Carol Crooks, even while Afeni was connecting the Panthers and gay liberation, she was pushing Crooks to go further. "'Feni wanted me to be involved with the gay people....She wanted me to come out and do speeches for it, and get support for it. I still wanted to make money."[52] Crooks gave a lot of that money to the causes Shakur supported, but she didn't want to be the face of anything. Plus, if she were publicly connected to one of those causes (or even to Shakur), her history as a dealer could have been used to discredit the entire movement—a fear she took so seriously that when a journalist took photos of her outside the court on the day the Panther 21 were found innocent on all charges, Crooks made the photographer destroy the film.

But it was jealousy, not politics, that eventually tore the two apart. Shakur had told Crooks that among the Panthers she was close with, many people had multiple partners, well-known to their wives or husbands. Crooks became convinced that Shakur was going to cheat on her, or perhaps already had, and threatened Shakur (with the very gun Shakur had bought her). After that, they stopped being together. But Shakur came to Crooks's aid a few years down the line in 1974, when Crooks was repeatedly assaulted by guards at Bedford Hills. Crooks led a resistance movement that culminated in another now forgotten prison riot, and she needed a lawyer. Shakur got Crooks's story publicized in *DYKE: A Quarterly* and connected her with Stephen Latimer, an attorney Shakur worked with at Bronx Legal Services. According to law professor Amber Baylor, the resulting case

> marked a pivotal moment in women's collective work challenging prison conditions. The women at Bedford Hills advanced the struggle for recognition of their rights in federal courts, forging a path for modern prisoners' rights claims. Their litigation, and similar work of women at other institutions, was a critical contribution to modern constructions of prisoners' rights in the United States.[53]

Crooks and Tupac remained close for his entire life; after he died, Crooks spent ten days with the Shakur family down at the house in Georgia he had purchased for them.

None of this is in Shakur's book, *Afeni Shakur: Evolution of a Revolutionary*, except for one tiny mention at the end. In a list of "men who had raised Tupac," Carol Crooks appears in one tender sentence: "It was Crooksie who painted Afeni and Tupac's first bedroom when Afeni moved in with [her sister] Glo."[54]

Shakur passed in 2016, without ever publicly discussing her relationship with Crooks, her incredible work connecting Black and gay liberation movements, or queer sexuality in prison in general. As for Joan Bird, after leaving the House of D, she disappeared and hasn't been seen or heard from since the early seventies.

Shortly after Shakur was declared innocent in the Panther 21 case, another queer Black revolutionary leader was chased across the country by the FBI, before finally being caught in a Howard Johnson Motor Lodge in Times Square and brought to the House of D for two and a half months: Angela Davis. Davis didn't publicly discuss her own sexuality until the late 1990s, but her autobiography delved deeply into queer life in the House of D.

Davis saw the prison in its final moments before its closure in 1971, when the people incarcerated inside were transferred to Rikers Island, and the neighborhood (and world) began the process of forgetting that they had ever been in Greenwich Village in the first place.

THE HUNT FOR ANGELA DAVIS

In the early evening of August 9, 1970, assistant UCLA philosophy professor Angela Yvonne Davis donned a bad fake wig, left her friend Helen's apartment in the Echo Park neighborhood of Los Angeles, and stepped into the wind, a fugitive from injustice. For the next two months, she crisscrossed the country, living a life of safe houses, disguises, and constant fear, on the FBI's "Ten Most Wanted List" for kidnapping and murder.

Forty-eight hours earlier, a seventeen-year-old boy named Jonathan Jackson had walked into the Marin County Courthouse on a mission. His older brother George had been in prison for most of Jonathan's life. In 1960, George had been involved in the robbery of a gas station—he was driving the car when his friend went inside and stole $70. George maintained he hadn't known the robbery was going to happen, or that his friend had a gun. His friend said the robbery was George's idea, and that he had a toy cap gun, not a real one.[55] They both pled guilty to armed robbery, so there was never a trial or any evidence collected. No one was shot—no one, in fact, was hurt at all. George's sentence? One year to life.

He was eighteen years old. He never left prison again.

Jonathan was just seven when all that went down, and he grew up smart but introverted, always worried about his brother. They became close through prison visits and censored letters, but more than anything, Jonathan wanted his brother to be free. Ten years for seventy bucks—was that justice? So, Jonathan got involved in the mass movement to free his brother and two other prisoners, who were collectively called the Soledad Brothers. But perhaps the movement was moving too slowly for an impatient teenager, or he'd lost hope that the system would ever give his brother (or any Black man) justice. Somewhere along the line, Jonathan started developing his own plan to secure his brother's freedom—at any cost. George Jackson was kept in a series of maximum-security facilities in California; a jailbreak was impossible. Instead, Jonathan Jackson decided to take hostages and exchange them for the Soledad Brothers.

Jackson got several guns, duct tape, and baling wire and went to the Marin County Courthouse, where a different man was on trial for an assault on a guard in San Quentin State Prison. Two other imprisoned men from San Quentin were there to act as witnesses. As the trial began, Jackson brandished a gun and took the judge and several jurors hostage. The three imprisoned men joined him. They demanded that the Soledad Brothers be freed or they would kill the judge. After a tense standoff, they taped a sawed-off shotgun to the judge's head and proceeded to walk their terrified hostages to a nearby van that Jackson had rented a few days before. They didn't know that a roadblock had already been set up to stop them, or that most of the San Quentin guards there that day were nervous rookies, or that the prison had a policy that "escapees are to be stopped without regard for the lives of hostages."[56]

Who fired the first shot was never determined—even one of the prosecution's own witnesses thought it was the San Quentin guards.[57] But by the time all was said and done, four people—Jonathan Jackson, two of the incarcerated witnesses he'd tried to free, and the judge they had taken hostage—were dead, and three others were seriously wounded.

What's missing from this tragic story? Angela Davis.

The evidence of her involvement in the events at the Marin County Courthouse was circumstantial, revolving primarily around three things: her close relationship to the Jackson brothers, several witnesses who thought they had seen her with Jonathan in the rented escape van in the days before the shootout, and the fact that Davis had purchased the guns used in the kidnapping. But the guns had been purchased over a two-year period, for self-defense, and stored in a place where Jackson could access them; other (friendly) witnesses put Davis far from the scene in the lead-up; and while Davis did love the Jackson brothers, it was the love of comrades in struggle, not the blind, girlish passion the prosecution tried to suggest. Moreover, much of this information was not available to the police and government at the time they began their manhunt, suggesting that they had decided Davis was guilty before they had any evidence at all.

But why did Davis disappear that August evening if she was innocent? Seeing footage of the events on the news that night, she said she recognized the guns as her own and knew the police would be coming. She was a Communist and Black liberationist in a country that hated both. Black liberationists were dying at police hands regularly; most recently, Fred Hampton and Mark Clark had been murdered in a predawn police raid in Chicago just nine months earlier (in a case with tragic echoes of the murder of Breonna Taylor in 2020). Although at the time they couldn't prove it, Davis, the Black Panthers, the Gay

Liberation Front, the Young Lords, and many other radical organizations were being targeted by COINTELPRO, an FBI program that spread disinformation, incited and directly committed violence, and in many other ways tried to destroy radicals. Guilty or innocent, Davis had good reason to be afraid of what might happen to her now that a manhunt had been announced. How many rookie cops were after her, how many weekend warriors owned a gun and knew her face, how many undercover agents were planted God knows where in her life?

From Los Angeles, Davis fled to Chicago, where her friend David Poindexter lived. (In her memoir, Davis seemed to hint that Poindexter was gay. She described how Poindexter introduced her to his "'very close friend'" [quotation marks hers] Robert, who lived in the same building, and with whom he had a "jointly owned automobile."[58] However, some contemporary newspaper articles also reported he was married.) Together, Davis and Poindexter drove to New York, then took a train to Miami, then returned to New York. After being on the run for more than two months, they were broke, and everyone they knew was under constant surveillance, so they couldn't reach out for help. One afternoon, they went to a movie in Times Square. As they returned to the Howard Johnson Motor Lodge, Davis began to notice a higher than usual number of conspicuous white men. She thought for a second about running but convinced herself she was being paranoid. Besides, she "remembered how [the police] had murdered li'l Bobby Hutton, how they shot him in the back after telling him to run," and wasn't sure she'd be any safer if she did.[59] Better to walk forward like normal, hold her head up high, and try to ignore the pounding in her chest. As they opened the door to their room, the hallway seemed to explode with police. The two were separated, searched, questioned, and brought to FBI headquarters. Several hours later, Davis found herself cuffed in the back of a squad car, approaching a "red brick wall surrounding this tall archaic structure"—the House of D.[60]

Davis recognized the building right away. Although she was born and raised in Birmingham, Alabama, she attended high school at Elisabeth Erwin High, just a few blocks from the House of D. As a teenager, she had been disturbed by the sight of people calling up to the imprisoned women inside; now, she wondered, "Would I scream out at the passing people in the street, only to have them pretend not to hear me as I once pretended not to hear those women?"[61]

After her time in the House of D, Davis never ignored incarcerated women again—in fact, prison abolition has been a major focus of her life ever since. As she told the radio program *Democracy Now!*, despite being incarcerated for a much longer time in California, the House of D "was the only time I was ever in general population," meaning the only time she had regular, direct contact with other imprisoned women.[62] That contact, along with urging from George Jackson, who was a brilliant revolutionary and philosophical thinker himself, changed the way Davis looked at prisons. Before, she had seen the political aspect of prisons as primarily being the repression of political dissidents like herself. But after hearing the stories of the hundreds of women imprisoned with her—often on trumped-up charges, or because they couldn't pay a $50 bail, or because they were homeless and mentally ill—she realized prisons played a larger, more insidious role, "deeply connected to the maintenance of racism" in general in America.[63] Moreover, as Davis told an interviewer in 2014, being in the House of D made her think specifically about how "we were missing so much by focusing only or primarily...on male political prisoners."[64] She estimated that 95 percent of the people incarcerated in the House of D were women of color. This was vastly at odds with official Department of Correction statistics, but records suggest Davis was more accurate than the government.

The last year that the Department of Correction included race as a category of analysis in its "Annual Statistical Report" while the House of D was open was 1965 (probably not coincidentally, this was also the last year Anna Kross was commissioner of the department).[65] They put the population at 45 percent white and 55 percent Black, which was shocking considering that the Census Bureau estimated Black people were only 18 percent of New York City's total population that year.[66] However, two years earlier, the House of D had allowed a young sociologist named Halle Wise into the prison to conduct a study of the women. She (and other sociologists who were working in the prison around the same time) found that the population was 68 percent Black, 16 percent Puerto Rican, and only 16 percent white.[67] In fact, every year the prison was open, the population was less white than the year before. Although it is impossible to extrapolate to an exact number, by the time Angela Davis was imprisoned there in late 1970, white women were vastly in the minority. (In March 2021, the New York City Department of Correction noted that only 5.9 percent of incarcerated people were white, though they didn't break that number down by gender, at a time when approximately 33 percent of the city was white, non-Hispanic.)[68]

Like Afeni Shakur, Angela Davis was at first kept in the psych and punishment corridor on the fourth floor, which "was far worse than [her] worst fantasies of solitary confinement."[69] It was excruciating to hear (and occasionally see) so many women in desperate pain being warehoused like animals. Davis's new understanding of the depth of prison depravity began here, in the worst part of the House of D, surrounded by drug users trying to kick cold turkey, psych patients doped to hell and back on Thorazine, and women too mentally ill to understand where they were, let alone the laws they had supposedly broken. As Davis later wrote, she became

> increasingly persuaded that something had to be done about this maximum security arrangement camouflaged as a therapeutic cell-block. Regardless of why the women in 4b had been placed there, they were all being horribly damaged. Whatever problems they had had initially were not solved, but rather systematically aggravated.[70]

Prison officials told Davis and her lawyers that she was being kept in solitary for her own protection, as the other prisoners hated Communists. But every time she interacted with them—walking through the halls to the elevator to see her attorneys, or when someone came with fresh laundry—they were cordial at worst, curious always, and often downright excited to see her. Finally, after a week, she was transferred to the tenth-floor dormitory, the former surgical room in the hospital that had been cannibalized to deal with overcrowding. Davis estimated there were about a hundred other women in there with her. On her first day, some of the women asked her if it was true, that she was a Communist, and Davis "snatched the opportunity to tell them that most of what they had heard about Communism was a carefully woven network of lies."[71]

First thing the next morning, the guards put her back in solitary.

This time, it was worse: Instead of being on 4b, they put her in special isolation on the sixth floor, far from anyone else. A guard was on her door at all times, and any time she had to leave—say to shower—the other women on the floor were all moved out to avoid contact. Some of the guards were sympathetic, and a few even expressed their support for Black liberation, but most were indifferent or hostile. Her presence was disruptive, the prison insisted. Her isolation was warranted.

Davis knew immediately that she couldn't let this stand, or it would set a precedent for all future political prisoners. So, she went on hunger strike until she was reintegrated into the general population. Her strike succeeded where Andrea Dworkin's failed, for several reasons. One, she was in the prison longer, so the stakes were higher. Davis's strike ended up lasting ten days, during which she had only juice and water. Two, she had supporters on the outside who could publicize her strike and put pressure on the administration. Three, she had an actionable goal in mind: whereas Dworkin and her friends had been protesting the treatment of prisoners *in general*, Davis articulated a specific demand the prison needed to meet. And finally, perhaps most importantly, Davis had support from the other incarcerated women. Dworkin was an eighteen-year-old white college student, from an almost all-white school, who cared about the other imprisoned women but also seemed scared of them, and removed from them. Davis, on the other hand, came to the prison with deep roots in the Black community, and her vast organizing experience meant she knew how to meet people where they were and talk frankly about difficult issues and personal matters. The other incarcerated women saw her as a symbol of resistance. When rumors of her hunger strike spread through the prison grapevine, other women joined in. When they walked on her floor, they chanted, "Free Angela! Free our sister!" A huge rally was organized outside the prison, and Davis got to hear her sister Fania's voice on a megaphone. Finally, on the tenth day of her hunger strike, a federal court ruled that she could no longer be kept in isolation, and Davis was finally permitted to join the general population. (As an unexpected side effect of the ruling, the prison actually ended up reshuffling many people, because the added attention to Davis's housing made apparent the fact that juveniles were *again* not being kept separately from adults.)

Like every other person held in the House of D, Davis found prison life stultifying: there were almost no activities, the food was disgusting, and the library was terrible (although she was glad to find a few old Communist books, which she hoped had passed through the hands of Claudia Jones in the 1950s). In fact, Davis became a vegetarian while in the House of D, a practice she has continued ever since.[72] But these were all aspects of the official and prescribed experience of the prison; little by little, Davis found herself drawn into the private world of prison culture, which exists in all detention facilities "in order to shield [imprisoned people] from the open or covert terror designed to break their spirits....This culture is one of resistance, but a resistance of desperation."[73] In particular, she wrote, "Homosexuality emerged as one of the centers around which life in the House of Detention revolved."[74]

The most obvious manifestation of queer culture in the House of D was "the family system," in which women got married and/or adopted each other as sister, or brother, son, daughter, cousin, aunt, ad infinitum.[75] The system was "not closed to straight women," but it revolved around lesbian relationships.[76] Being in a family gave these women sexual and emotional support, a way to resist "being no more than a number," and an extended network of caregivers who would teach you the ropes, share their knowledge and possessions with you, and—should you be transferred elsewhere—provide people who could vouch for you in an unfamiliar institution.[77]

Davis didn't join an existing family, but one of the diddy bops told her "plainly and simply one day that she was going to consider me her mother."[78] Davis took the sixteen-year-old under her wing, answered her questions about Black liberation, and shared her commissary with her. For the most part, however, Davis heard about the families from other women more than she observed them directly. Halle Wise, the sociologist who had been invited into the House of D in 1963, spent a month documenting what she called "the play family" in the House of Detention, which she wrote was "endemic to women's and girls' penal institutions" but almost completely absent in institutions for men.[79] Her observations about its prevalence and functions match what Davis learned to a T.

Wise documented the clever ways that those incarcerated found to express their love. One of her first observations was that there were a surprising number of Black Jewish women in the prison—at least, that was what she thought until she started talking to the Black women who were wearing Stars of David. They called themselves the Sammy Davis Club, after the popular Black Jewish entertainer, but explained that the stars were given to them by their Jewish girlfriends.[80] There was no jewelry allowed inside the prison except for crucifixes and Stars of David (both of which were distributed by a religious volunteer organization), so to non-Jewish femmes, the stars were the height of chic. As well, Wise noted that women of Puerto Rican descent (especially those who primarily spoke Spanish) developed mostly separate communities and families, disconnected from those of Black and white women who were not Puerto Rican (as was true for Irma T. and her circle of queer Puerto Rican women in the 1950s). Wise also documented that certain "known lesbians"—most likely butches, though she didn't make that clear—were segregated by the administration, always kept in single cells, and had to wear a "D" (for "degenerate") on their uniforms.[81] Of this, she wrote, "I understand their resentment."[82] Overall, she estimated that about 75 percent of the women in the House of D were involved with a family—almost the exact same percentage of people that Virginia McManus estimated were involved in queer relationships in the prison in 1959.[83]

Carol Crooks said that in her experience in the House of D, the families weren't as big a thing as they were in institutions like Bedford

Hills, where people were incarcerated for years at a time.[84] Wise's research bears out this assertion: although she found husbands, wives, mothers, fathers, daughters, and sons, the more extended relationships she heard about were either legacy (brought over from previous institutions) or otherwise beyond the walls of the House of D.

Crooks, Wise, and Davis all noted that many of the women who were sexually involved with other women—butch and femme—did not consider themselves queer. But removed from the broader culture of compulsory heterosexuality, they found they could have sexually, emotionally, and romantically nurturing relationships with other women and trans men.

Perhaps the lack of such families in men's institutions is related to the same prison segregation of "gay" inmates that Lumumba Shakur said precluded the chance for solidarity between incarcerated gay and straight men. However, alternative family formations did arise among the queer men and trans women in men's institutions—most famously, many early members of the ballroom scene (like Willi Ninja) trace the evolution of voguing back to the fairy wing of Rikers Island. Although the first ballroom house was established in Harlem by Crystal and Lottie LaBeija in 1972, the connections between these institutions and other alternative family formations among queer people (who are often forced out of their birth families) and incarcerated people (who are separated from their birth families by the state—and sometimes abandoned by them as well) require further study. For instance, Denise Oliver-Velez, the Young Lords cofounder who was friends with Afeni Shakur, noted in her later work that most prisons in Puerto Rico were controlled by one of two gangs, the Netas or the Latin Kings, and that one of the main areas of opposition between the two groups was homosexuality. The Kings were completely opposed; the Netas "were allowed to have gay members, but they had to get married in jail."[85] Our refusal to see prisons as sites of queer culture goes hand in hand with our refusal to see these queer/chosen families as legitimate and our obsession with a limited idea of "sexual orientation" as the sole, permanent, inborn determinator of our attractions.

Wise and Davis were both empathetic to the people in these families but ultimately found the families limited and limiting. Wise saw
them as a chance for these women to work out the psychodramas of
previous traumas and experiment with families they never had on the
outside. She believed the families were reflective of these women's
"minimal" inner resources and poor value systems, but hoped they
would allow the women to survive incarceration and develop better
habits for heterosexual family life on the outside—sort of like the way
people often describe girls kissing each other at sleepovers for quote-
unquote practice.[86]

Like Andrea Dworkin and Elizabeth Gurley Flynn, Davis was uncomfortable with butch incarcerated people, saying that she could not
bring herself to use masculine pronouns for any of the people who
wanted them. Davis's ultimate analysis of the family system was in
line with many Communists' at the time, who saw homosexuality as
a distracting by-product of rapacious capitalism. As she wrote,

> Certainly, [homosexuality] was a way to counteract some of the pain
> of jail life; but objectively, it served to perpetuate all the bad things
> about the House of Detention. "The Gay Life" was all-consuming;
> it prevented many of the women from developing their personal
> dissatisfaction with the conditions around them into a political dis-
> satisfaction, because the homosexual fantasy life provided an easy
> and attractive channel for escape.[87]

Davis's PhD graduate work was done under two of the leading neo-
Marxist thinkers of the mid-twentieth century, Theodor Adorno and
Herbert Marcuse. Perhaps the common leftist view of homosexuality as
bourgeois or escapist was part of the reason she did not come out publicly until 1998, when she told an interviewer for *Out* magazine that
her "lesbianism…is 'something I'm fine with as a political statement.
But I still want a private space for carrying out my relationships.'"[88]

. Whatever their qualms, Wise and Davis were infinitely less homophobic than most mainstream commenters on queer sexuality in
prisons. The year after Davis was incarcerated, the *New York Times*

wrote a sensational article entitled "The Terrifying Homosexual World of the Jail System," which opined that

> many former inmates and criminologists find this indirect effect of the distorted sexuality of prison life even more disturbing than the immediate brutality of rape in shadowed corners of stairways and shower rooms. Quite simply, the distorted sexuality serves to widen the distance between prison society and the world outside. Some prisoners, particularly those young people who spend their pre-adolescent and adolescent years in such a society, may have their sexual definition affected for life.[89]

Yes, that's right, the *New York Times* argued that it was better to be raped than end up gay. Despite the heterosexual world's fixation on sexual assaults in prisons, Wise found them to be rare to nonexistent in the House of D. Although prison officials warned her that many of the women would lie to her about their backgrounds and crimes, she found them to be fundamentally honest. She also felt it critical to note something she did not expect: "the cheerfulness and gaiety which abound in the House of Detention so much of the time."[90] This should in no way distract from our understanding of the prison as a brutal place; rather, it reflects the strength and hope of those incarcerated. As activist Jay Toole said, "A lot of us called it the playground. A lot of us called it a prison. I called it both."[91]

Whatever cheerfulness existed in the House of D, it was created by the incarcerated people themselves, *despite* the prison and its administration. When she was there, Angela Davis grew close to many of the other imprisoned women, sharing books with them, answering their questions about Communism, imperialism, and Black liberation, and even starting a karate exercise class that convinced the administration that she was planning an insurrection. As she learned more about their situations, Davis began to develop ideas for concrete, community organizing projects that would center *their* needs, and not focus on well-known activists like herself. Quickly, she realized "the biggest problem jail prisoners face is how to get out on bail," and that the broader implications of this issue could have profound effects on all people in the House of D.[92]

Remember, the House of D held two main populations: people on/ awaiting trial who were technically "in jail" but presumed to be innocent, and those who were serving sentences who were technically "in prison." A shocking number of people incarcerated in the House of D were there for months because they could not afford even minuscule bail amounts of fifty dollars, meaning that they were considered innocent but held in a maximum-security prison because they were poor.

The concept of bail goes back to English common law of the seventeenth century. It's not enshrined in the Constitution, but the Eighth Amendment prohibits "excessive bail." Legally, bail is intended—and can only be used—to ensure that an arrested person shows up at trial. It cannot be used to punish them, or give them "a taste" of jail to scare them straight, or be applied willy-nilly—though of course, that's how bail often gets used. If a person is able to afford their bail, they are released until trial, and when they show up for trial, they get their money back. If they can't afford bail, they can turn to bondsmen, who furnish their bail for a certain percentage up front. Although in New York State this percentage has been enshrined in law, in practice, many bondsmen take advantage of families desperate to bail out their loved ones, and set painful terms. This was simply an evolution of the "evils of the station house" that the Women's Night Court had been created to preempt in 1910.

In fact, as early as 1927, legal studies recognized that pretrial "detainment was based on wealth and not facts."[93] A 1963 study of all New York City penal institutions found that nearly sixty thousand people were in jail because they could not afford bail.[94] The average length of their detention was twenty-eight days for adults—and thirty-two days for juveniles.[95]

What happens to that person who can't afford bail? According to a 1964 New York City legislative committee, pretrial detention has three layers of debilitating effects.

First, it ruins the accused person's financial health and ability to receive a fair trial:

His detention prevents his working, and thereby sentences his dependents to poverty and the relief rolls. Unable to produce funds, he cannot hire the counsel of his choice....Lacking income, he cannot accumulate funds to purchase his freedom. Without freedom he cannot seek out witnesses or other evidence for his defense...and if the defendant loses his job before trial, he loses with it perhaps his best argument, if convicted, for a suspended sentence.[96]

Second, it destroys their spirit and hope:

Detention—particularly in the oppressive and depressing maximum security facilities which we found in use in New York—may have an unhealthy or even debilitating psychological effect....The enforced inactivity, compounded by the uncertainty as to his fate and that of his dependents, can be destructive of the defendant's moral resolve and mental stamina.[97]

And finally, it debilitates the communities they come from and puts strain on the entire city:

Relief funds must be expended for support of the dependents. Employers must perforce seek new employees, and train them. The community, through the Department of Correction, must pay for food, housing, custodial service and transportation. Otherwise productive real estate must be devoted to prison use, and the tax rolls suffer.[98]

In 1961, a wealthy chemical engineer named Louis Schweitzer decided to fund a project in New York City, which aimed to prove, in essence, that bail was a bad idea—that community ties, *not* financial burdens, were a better (and more equitable) indicator of a person's flight risk before trial. Law students were hired to interview arrested individuals before arraignment, and if they had strong community ties, those students recommended that they be released on their own recognizance ("RoR"), meaning they would be allowed to live free until their trial and verdict. Critically, the program also included several layers of linguistically appropriate follow-up (mostly phone calls and mailings) to ensure that the person understood RoR and showed up for their hearing.[99]

This "Manhattan Bail Project" ran for three years, from 1961 to 1964. The House of Detention, as a central site for arrested women, was one of its primary locations. The project was an incredible success at every level of the criminal legal process—so much so that the organization founded to oversee it, the Vera Institute of Justice, is still a leading legal nonprofit. The Bail Project was far from perfect: it relied on metrics that were racist and classist, and (like the Vera Institute still to this day) it placed an unreasonable amount of faith in our carceral system. Yet still it proved a vast improvement over the bail system as it had been run before.

First, the Bail Project found that the initial idea that community ties were a better indicator of later court attendance was correct: over three years, the project conducted ten thousand interviews and recommended four thousand people for RoR. Fewer than 1 percent missed their court date.[100]

To take the study further, it also created a control group—people for whom the project *would* have recommended RoR were they not in the control group. Only 16 percent of these people received RoR when they came in front of a judge, compared to a whopping 59 percent of those who were given a positive recommendation by students in advance.[101] This showed that judges, on their own, were not good at evaluating risk.

Once they made it to trial, 60 percent of those who had been given a recommendation for RoR were acquitted or had their cases dismissed. In the control group—again, people who qualified for an RoR recommendation but did not get one—a measly 23 percent were found innocent.[102] The facts of their cases were broadly the same, but the experience of pretrial detention seemed to ensure posttrial detention. As the saying goes, "the rich get bail, the poor get jail."

Finally, when it came to those people who were ultimately convicted, the statistics were the starkest. Just 16 percent of people who were found guilty and received an RoR recommendation were given prison sentences, as compared to 96 percent of the control group.[103] Simply having someone advocate for them, even if the judge disagreed that they deserved RoR, kept many people out of prison.

In essence, the Manhattan Bail Project proved that bail was destructive to the individual, and bloating to the system.

The project was *so* successful that over the course of it, they went from recommending release in 28 percent of cases, to 65 percent of cases.[104] Faced with these glaring facts, in 1963, New York City judges and administrators pushed for the city to take on these services and make them permanent. They requested $175,000 to establish a program within the Office of Probation, but the mayor stonewalled them until the case of one woman, held in the House of Detention, became an embarrassing public scandal. That woman was Kim Parker, and thanks to her public protests, the city adopted the Manhattan Bail Project as an official part of their work.[105]

Then, the city promptly ruined it.

The Office of Probation cut the interview time to determine whether someone should be granted RoR down to almost nothing, and defunded all of the notifications and reminders originally intended to ensure that people who received RoR would attend their trials. By 1967, the percentage of people who were not showing up had skyrocketed, from fewer than 1 percent to 15.4 percent.[106] That same year, only 4.4 percent of those who paid a bond or bail missed their trial. Thus, judges began to ignore the Probation Office's recommendations and simply granted RoR to whomever they felt like (as a scattershot method to reduce overcrowding in city jails), which further reduced the efficacy of the program as a whole. Suddenly, RoR began to look like a bad risk. In 1976, a public policy analyst summed up the shift from the pilot program thusly: "The Office of Probation ... drift[ed] from an effective operation to an ineffective one without being aware of their role in the deterioration."[107]

None of these studies factored in race or gender, but Essie O. Murph—the second Black superintendent of the House of D, who oversaw its final year in Greenwich Village—reported to a researcher that in her experience white women, having the advantage of families or resources in the nearby community to assist them at the time of arrest, received bail, [or] were released on their own recognizance, or [were] diverted to a pre-trial intervention program. Lacking those advantages, Afro-American women were held in detention and at the time of sentencing rarely received probation.[108]

Between 1955 and 1969 (the last year for which there are available statistics), the number of women detained (aka awaiting trial) in the House of D increased by over 70 percent.[109] Most of these women were Black, poor, and without anyone to advocate for them. At the close of 1969, the House of D held 576 people, 61 percent of whom were awaiting trial. Over the course of the entire year, 8,179 people were detained in the House of D for some period of time. And from these women and trans men, the city made bank. The Department of Correction collected nearly $500,000 in bails and bonds from people in the House of D that year. To put this in perspective, the Manhattan House of Detention for Men had 105,916 people admitted for detention, and collected slightly less than $700,000.[110] Average that out, and women were paying *ten times* the amount men were in bails and bonds. Incarcerated women and their families were exorbitantly gouged to fund a terrible system that never gave them justice.

This was the state of bail when Angela Davis was incarcerated in the House of D. Around the time Davis was forced to go on the run, a small group of white, middle-class women had begun to organize in Manhattan to find a way to "effectively help women and also begin to talk to white women about the concepts of class and race and how the women's movement, if it is going to get anywhere, is going to have to deal with these issues."[111] It took six months before they hit on the issue of bail, and a little longer before they were finally able to communicate with incarcerated women in the House of D to find out who needed what. To guide them, they turned to four radical Black women: Afeni Shakur, Joan Bird, Angela Davis, and Denise Oliver-Velez.

Upon first being contacted by them, Shakur recommended they start a bail fund for those women who only needed $50 or $100 to be free. "This was my first contact with a lot of white women," Shakur said in her autobiography, "and these women tried to help." Some asked racist, exoticizing questions about Black men; others acted superior to the women they were assisting. But many were old-school leftists and new-school feminists, and they were serious about the work. Together, they developed what came to be known as the Women's Bail Fund. Shakur and Bird advised them to be methodical: bail out one woman, see how the process went for her, and evaluate. Angela Davis worked on the inside of the prison to let them know who needed bail and how much. She also worked out a system to ensure that the program was equitable, and that it developed into a mass movement, not a social service organization. Each corridor of detained people in the jail met as a committee and elected the person who should be bailed out next. Once free, that person "would have to work with the fund, helping to raise money, making whatever political contributions she could to the development of the organization."[112]

Denise Oliver-Velez designed a poster for the fund and helped organize a massive December 20th kick-off rally outside the House of D. For her, a large part of the issue was the misogyny that kept communities from bailing out women.

> If families had a son who went to jail it was not a smear in the community, and people would go and bail their son out. But the stigma for women being arrested was such that literally, women could be busted and their bail would be $25 and no one would come....Dudes could get out and swagger around, whatever, but to have a daughter who got picked up for selling drugs, or prostitution? Forget about it! We took on that support. Because it was sexist!...Not bailing your daughter out? How are you going to let a woman sit in jail for months?[113]

Other radical women quickly signed on to support. After lesbian activist Karla Jay and other feminists staged a sit-in at the offices of the *Ladies Home Journal*, they were paid $10,000 to write an eight-page supplement that would be distributed with the next issue.[114] Much of that money was donated to the bail fund. Later, when another group of feminists took over the offices of Grove Press, they similarly demanded that the press provide money to immediately free one hundred political prisoners, "most of whom are prostitutes," from the House of D (though they ultimately did not get the money).[115] These (mostly white) feminists helped raise cash and spread the word about the other demands of the incarcerated people—which included "no restrictions on women's relationships."[116]

Paul was one of the first people bailed out by the Women's Bail Fund. Just twenty-two years old, she was "a poor, Black, gay woman" who'd been inside for six months because she couldn't afford a $100 bond.[117] Her crime? A family friend had accused her of stealing $10 worth of groceries.

"I did everything a person would do when they're shooting drugs," Paul admitted. "But you know, I never robbed a bank or stole from a store. I didn't do anything so wrong I should go to jail for it."[118]

Paul was one of six children; by the time she was fourteen, she'd been sent to "a shelter for girls whose mothers don't want them."[119] They kicked her out at seventeen, and she ended up at the Salvation Army, where she met a group of girls who'd all done time "upstate"— probably Bedford Hills, maybe the Hudson Training School.[120] They taught her about heroin. When the Salvation Army caught them using and kicked them all out, Paul's life started to get really wild.

Even before she ended up in the House of D, she'd heard so much about it, she said, "I just felt I had been there all my life."[121] Her first stint wasn't so bad, but something happened the second time. Her case was dropped from the court calendar, and for months she had no idea what was happening, no lawyer, and no one on the outside to support her—which meant no money for the commissary and no letters from home.

Without an advocate, it's easy to disappear into the system, but Paul made friends in the jail. "Everyone liked Angela [Davis]," she said, and when there were protests for her freedom outside, everyone inside would yell, "Right on!" and, "Power to the people!" That kept her going.[122] "It means a whole lot. If someone comes to see [you,] it makes [you] feel like somebody cares....If you know somebody on the outside cares about you on the inside, well you're all right. Other than that you feel nothing, you're sad, gone."[123]

Carol Crooks used to come back, after she got out, to say hi to those still inside. She'd walk her two big Doberman pinscher dogs around the base of the prison and yell up to her friends, much like the character that Melvin Van Peebles had written into his show, *Ain't Supposed to Die a Natural Death* (which opened in 1971, right as the prison was closing).

But the guards were a whole different story. At times, Paul worried she'd end up back in for homicide, the way they kept at her. She never fought back, so the guards wouldn't have "an opportunity to get [her] all drugged up," but they tried to provoke her.[124] If she told them she felt sick in the afternoon, they would get angry she hadn't told them in the morning. They refused to let her have aspirin because she'd been a drug user—to which Paul said, "Yeah, you want to get high, but no aspirin is going to get you high!"[125] Overall, she said, the House of D was "a concentration camp" that "shouldn't be standing."[126]

Paul was bailed out on December 20, 1970, the same day the Women's Bail Fund announced their existence at a protest rally outside the House of D.

The next night, around 2 a.m., Angela Davis was awoken by a guard shining a flashlight in her face, who told her that her lawyers were there for a special meeting. When she got down to the first floor, she realized she had been lied to and they were preparing her for a predawn extradition flight to California. When she refused to go along, she was thrown to the ground by four correctional officers and taken bodily to a waiting van. Even some of the House of D staff tried to physically prevent her from being taken, but it was no use. Her trial in California lasted eighteen months, until finally, on June 4, 1972, she was acquitted on all charges.

One year earlier, on June 13, 1971, the Women's House of Detention was closed for good. It was replaced by a larger institution on Rikers Island, called the New York City Correctional Institute for Women, which cost $22 million to build and had room for 679 people.[127] When it opened, the *Daily News* called it a "plush country rest-and-recreation spa."[128] By the time it closed in 1988, it was over-crowded, understaffed, and violent, stuffed to the gills with 1,500 incarcerated people—500 of whom were male adolescents.[129]

The institute was replaced by the Rose M. Singer Center in 1988, which cost $106 million to build—but could only hold 800 people.[130] Newspapers and reformers championed its nursery and other services for incarcerated pregnant women, but by the time it opened, those had been sacrificed to make room for more human cages, just like the elaborate hospital that had originally been planned for the House of D.[131] The *Daily News* called the Singer Center "woefully inadequate" already on the day it opened.[132]

Yet "Rosies" is still in operation, and will be until 2026. The eponymous Singer's own granddaughter, a New York City rabbi, said in 2020, "It has devolved into a torture chamber, where women are routinely abused, housed in unsanitary conditions, and denied medical and mental health services. They are treated as less than human."[133]

But in truth, that is what prisons have always been. They have neither evolved nor devolved. They have simply grown, and grown, and grown. Moments of liberal reform effect small changes, at great cost, usually involving the creation of bigger prisons. When public attention fades away, they return to business as usual. We live in the age of mass incarceration. Right now, as I write these words, nearly 250,000 people are incarcerated in women's detention facilities in America—a small sliver of our massive, 2.3-million-person sprawling system of captivity and punishment.[134]

In 2020, at the start of the COVID-19 pandemic, 70 percent of those incarcerated in Rosies were there because they could not make bail.[135] Two-thirds were mentally ill.[136] Without space, proper medical intervention, privacy, or protective equipment, the pandemic has torn through America's mass detention facilities. As of July 2020, incarcerated people in the United States were five times more likely to contract the disease than those who were not incarcerated, and the mortality rate was higher as well.[137] Officially, at least 2,700 incarcerated people have died, as of April 2021.[138] Prison activists are convinced the real number is much higher.

As for Greenwich Village? "Since the city began tracking COVID-19 rates by ZIP code, Greenwich Village has consistently registered near the very lowest seven-day positive rates in the five boroughs."[139]

The rich get vaccinated, the poor get decimated.

When the House of Detention was removed from the Village, almost no one was happy. Those incarcerated were now further separated from their loved ones. There were no more street visits. Most of the existing volunteers quit, because of the onerous commute.[140] On Rikers, incarcerated people were escorted by guards at all times when they were out of their cells.[141] According to a journalist who was allowed to tour the new facility shortly after it opened,

> Nothing works…the health system is a horror…the prison itself is run on strict military regimentation. And it is badly located, so it takes two hours and two fares to get there from Bed-Stuy….No visitor under 16 is allowed, meaning that inmates can't see their own children, the cruelest possible punishment.[142]

Overall, he reported, "Many of the inmates say they actually preferred the old, ugly, rat-filled women's jail in Greenwich Village."[143] How miserable the new prison must have been, to make them miss the House of D.

Even the staff was unhappy. "There was more friendliness and warmth at Greenwich Avenue," the prison superintendent told journalists, once the move was done.[144] Three months in, the guards began having sick-outs and wildcat strikes. They petitioned the mayor, saying they had "waited in vain for your concern and promised alleviation of our poor work conditions….We have moved and our situation is 10-fold more cumbersome."[145] The Correction Benevolent Association led a protest march to the Manhattan Criminal Court.[146] Nothing was done.

With the incarcerated people gone, Greenwich Village began the busy work of destroying their very memory.

First, they went after the building itself. Many different uses for the structure were proposed, from a home for the elderly to an extension of the nearby library, to a social center for gay and feminist groups.

Immediately after the House of D closed, "more than 1000 chanting, shouting, militant Gays…converged on the abandoned Charles Street (Sixth Precinct) Police Station and the old Women's House of Detention to reinforce demands that the city turn over abandoned Village buildings to Gays and other community groups."[147]

This was not to be, as Village landowners strenuously opposed any use for the building. Why? Because "if allowed to stand, the building could at any time be re-used as a correctional institution."[148] They recognized that public housing and facilities for the elderly were noble causes, but "[they] must be sought in other ways and places."[149] In other words, not in my backyard.

They preferred that the building be replaced by a small garden. To ensure that it was, the powerful Association of Village Homeowners flexed their financial muscle in government meetings and letters sent to city officials. "Of all the several thousand buildings in Greenwich Village, only about 400 are occupied as residences by their owners," they wrote. "This small but committed group of Manhattan families…[holds] about fifteen acres of Manhattan land among us."[150]

Because they owned the most land, they seemingly believed they had the right to dictate what happened to the land they did not own. Because they owned the most land, they believed they were the only ones whose concerns mattered. Because they owned the most land, they believed they *were* Greenwich Village.

As the plans for the garden came together, a high priority was making sure it was "not open to [the] public generally."[151] A variety of strategies to do so were discussed, including requesting extra police, hiring private security, making the park itself private (like Gramercy), or having people enter only through the nearby library. In the end, they went with a tall fence and locked gate. The explicit goal was to prevent disreputable elements, who did not own property in the Village, from enjoying this new green space. As one homeowner wrote to city officials,

If the space is simply paved and equipped with benches and swings, it will become the same kind of trouble spot we know all too well three blocks south at the corner of 6th Avenue and 3rd Street where police have recently had to intervene in force when brawls broke out between groups of people who do not live in Greenwich Village and have no roots in our community.[152]

But roots are a tricky thing to measure. Queer and incarcerated people had been coming to the Village for over a century, giving it the very "bohemian air" that now made it so desirable to the middle-class and wealthy. Most of these newly arrived gentrifiers did not know or care that much of the vibrant culture in the Village "belong[ed] to the boys and girls of stodgier neighborhoods who come here to try on the make-up, costumes, and manners of what they think is indigenous evil."[153] And if they did know it, they regretted it, lamenting the Village's "traditional permissiveness," which caused "many people to come down here who want to 'do their own thing.'"[154]

In order to erase the prison, they rewrote the history of Greenwich Village.

"The site was such a civic center through all the changes of the centuries," opined the head of the Association of Village Homeowners, "*until* the present detention building was erected."[155]

Never mind that prisons preceded most other uses of the Village, or that incarcerated people and their loved ones were a huge part of the population that made 10 Greenwich a "civic center." According to Caroline Ware, the sociologist who studied the Village for the entirety of the 1920s (its supposed heyday), "It was the general opinion of the neighborhood that…landing in jail was a matter of accident, and…no serious blot on a person's reputation."[156] Previously, incarcerated and formerly incarcerated people had been seen as *part* of the community. Now, they were a cancer on it, which needed to be excised from both the present and the past.

Not all Village residents concurred with the NIMBY majority. "It would seem the 'haves' of Greenwich Village continuously dictate to the 'have-nots' what they should not have!" thundered one resident at a contentious Landmarks Commission meeting.[157]

But they were overruled; the prison was destroyed; and—as one fifth-generation Village resident told me tearily—"the heart was torn out of Greenwich Village."[158]

Soon, those same homeowners would lead a crackdown on Washington Square Park, and a thankfully unsuccessful attempt to have it entirely fenced in. Then they went after the trucks in the Meatpacking District where men met for sex, then the Christopher Street Pier— long a destination for queer people (especially queer people of color) and artists. Then they tore down the remains of the Westside Highway, where many queer street people lived (including trans activist Sylvia Rivera). Every spot in the Village that provided free space for queer existence was targeted, surveilled, destroyed, and recreated as a gentler, safer place…for whom? Certainly not the queer people who had once gathered there, or the ones who still do today.

All that remains now is a plaque, which preserves the memory of these women and transmasculine people as a plague on the rightful owners of Greenwich Village:

> In the late 1960s, GVA and Community Board 2 held town meetings to discuss the removal of the Women's House of Detention and the creation of a "passive recreation area" on the site. At the time, friends and families of inmates lingered outside the House at all hours of the day or night, yelling their news and greetings. Nearby residents were disturbed by the noise. Gawkers came to watch the scene. The facility was overcrowded and had become obsolete. The Women's House of Detention was demolished in 1973, after 42 years of use.

But that building was just a cage, a collection of sticks and stones and broken bones. It was never the queer people it held, or the queer communities they created, or the queer communities they are *still* creating.

Desire is like a river. Build a dam, try to stop it—maybe you buy yourself a few decades. But the water is waiting, and one day, it will rise.

Epilogue

THE FIRST WORDS NAN MCTEER EVER SAID TO ME WERE, "I'M CURRENTLY in hospice care. I have lung cancer, it has metastasized to my brain, but my mind is still okay! You've got awhile to pump me for information."

Nan had been Virginia McManus's girlfriend, back in Chicago, in the fifties. That's why I'd called her originally. I'd suspected Virginia was a lesbian the moment I read her book, but it was a thing I thought I'd never be able to pin down, a message sent in code words and pseudonyms, received sixty years too late. But the self-published memoir of a painter who'd known Virginia gave me Nan's real name, which led me to a 1957 wedding announcement—which gave me Nan's married name—which led me to a Facebook account with a photo of a steel-haired woman rowing a kayak. After a few messages, she agreed to talk about Virginia.

But the longer we talked, the more I wanted to know *Nan's* story: the high school girl who could solo land a single-engine plane on the Calumet River; the college student who was hounded out of her all-women's school by a closeted, homophobic dean; the woman who married a gay man in 1957, and a gay woman in 2013.

For every story told in this book, there are fifty I didn't tell—and a hundred I never found.

I started with the simplest idea: that the Women's House of Detention *mattered*. And it wasn't even my idea. I was just listening to Joan Nestle, to Audre Lorde, to Jay Toole—to the queer elders who came before me, pointed to the prison, and said, "There, there! We were there."

Ever done one of those Magic Eye puzzles, where you can't see anything and you can't see anything and you can't see anything— then, suddenly, your eyes or your brain snaps into focus, and a century's worth of queer women and transmasculine people are staring back at you? That's what it was like, writing this book.

Greenwich Village is perhaps the most studied place in all of queer history. It should be a dry well for untold stories. But sometimes, the things we know—or think we know—can obscure the things we don't. When we refract all of queer American history through a single bar, which mostly catered to white cis men, it's not surprising that the stories of queer women, trans men, and people of color get lost, glossed over, and ignored.

For my entire life, I have been trying to see clearer, to listen closer, to let go of what I know so I can learn what I don't. Twenty years ago, I got two tattoos on my wrists: "see" on my left, "speak" on my right—a commitment to trying to tell the truth, or close as I can get. It's a daily practice, like hope or abolition. Every day, something slips into history that we will never recover: a memory, a document, the sound of a dead woman's voice.

Save what you can.

* * *

Nan McTeer died on Sunday, February 13, 2021, at the age of eighty-four. In 2011, she conducted an oral history with Arden Eversmeyer, just one of more than two hundred that Eversmeyer has collected for the Old Lesbian Oral Herstory Archive. Should you want to know the rest of Nan's story, it is kept at Smith College.

Acknowledgments

This book would not have been possible without the incredible archives that have collected, preserved, and made available the documents from which we craft our stories. In particular, I must thank the Lesbian Herstory Archives, the New York Public Library, the American Jewish Archives, the ONE Archives, the San Francisco GLBT Historical Society, the Municipal Archives of New York City, the New York State Archives, the Schomburg Center for Research in Black Culture, Smith College Libraries, the Human Sexuality Collection at Cornell University, the Beinecke Library at Yale University, the LGBT Community Center National History Archive, the Kinsey Institute, the Library of Congress, the Prison Public Memory Project, the Interference Archives, the Stonewall National Museum and Archives, the Schlesinger Library at Radcliffe, the June L. Mazer Lesbian Archives, and the New York City Trans Oral History Project. Without my position as a research associate at Smith College, many of the databases and other academic resources I used would not have been available to me. Most importantly, I am indebted to the Women's

Prison Association for access to their archive, which provided unique and invaluable insight into the lives of queer people caught up in our carceral system.

I received generous support for researching and writing this book from the New York Foundation for the Arts, and spent perhaps the best month of my writing career finishing a first draft at the Corporation of Yaddo.

Brian Ferree provided critical research and thought throughout the development of this book. I also received vital assistance from two wonderful research interns, Michael Waters and Mathilde Denegre, and from Professor Hans Vermy. I'm deeply indebted to my early readers Alejandro Varela, Naomi Gordon-Loebl, Senja Spackman, Nicole Pasulka, Nick Seeley, Phil Andrews, and Eileen Maher.

An incredible number of people shared their memories and insights with me, including Carol Crooks, Nan McTeer, Jay Toole, Eve Rosahn, Sarah Schulman, Giles Kotcher, Charlotte Marchant, Barbara Police, Jonathan Ned Katz, Joan Nestle, Bettina Aptheker, Ericka Huggins, Denise Oliver-Velez, Leslie Cagan, Jim Fouratt, David De Porte, Marcia Gallo, Martha Shelley, Diamond Durant, Carole Elizabeth Boyce Davies, Martin Boyce, Kevin Powell, Michela Griffo, Bob Lederer, Ellen Broidy, Gwen Shockey, Jen Jack Gieseking, Andrea Weiss, Ken Lustbader, Sydney Baloue, Lee Lynch, Ron Punit Auerbacher, Ilan Meyer, Martin Duberman, Elena Rossi-Snook, Ariel Federow, Lisa Davis, Stephen Kent Jusick, Emily K. Hobson, KJ Rawson, Saskia Scheffer, Rachel Corbman, Nicholas Martin, Allen Young, Karla Jay, Reed Ide, Anja Milde, Scott W. Stern, C. John Knoebel, Sharon Raphael, Alix Dobkin, Sheryl Kaplan, Susan Wiseheart, Arden Eversmeyer, Amber Baylor, Judy Greenspan, Laura Whitehorn, Rich Wandell, Laura Vogel, Anna Wahrman, George Chauncey, Michelle O'Brien, Flavia Rando, Eileen Maher, Sarita Daftary, and Zakiya Collier.

Without the support of my supporters on Patreon, I would not have had the time or mental energy to finish this book. In particular, I want to thank Mohammed Fakhro, Patricia Ryan, and David Zinn.

Thank you to my parents, my partners, my brothers, my cousins, my aunts, and my fellow denizens of Cat House for making sure I occasionally slept, ate, and took a break from writing.

Finally, my great thanks to my agent, Robert Guinsler, and the entire editorial team at Bold Type Books—Claire Zuo, Remy Cawley, Hillary Brenhouse, Ben Platt, Kelly Lenkevich, Jennifer Top, and Cecillia Nowell—who saw the potential in this book, and helped me reach it.

Notes

Introduction: Jay Toole Marks the Land

1. Author interview with Jay Toole, September 11, 2017.

2. "Jay London Toole Interview Transcript," New York City Trans Oral History Project, https://s3.amazonaws.com/oral-history/transcripts/NYC+TOHP +Transcript+003+Jay+London+Toole.pdf, accessed June 18, 2020.

3. Author interview with Jay Toole, September 11, 2017.

4. Ilan H. Meyer, Andrew R. Flores, Lara Stemple, Adam P. Romero, Bianca D. M. Wilson, and Jody L. Herman, "Incarceration Rates and Traits of Sexual Minorities in the United States: National Inmate Survey, 2011–2012," *American Journal of Public Health* 107, no. 2 (2017): 267–273.

•5. "Incarceration Rate of LGB People Three Times the General Population," Williams Institute, UCLA School of Law, https://williamsinstitute.law .ucla.edu/williams-in-the-news/incarceration-rate-of-lesbian-gay-bisexual -people-three-times-the-general-population, accessed May 17, 2019.

6. Aleks Kajstura, "Women's Mass Incarceration: The Whole Pie," Prison Policy Initiative, October 29, 2019, www.prisonpolicy.org/reports/pie2019 women.html.

7. Cheryl Hicks, *Talk with You Like a Woman: African American Women, Justice, and Reform in New York, 1890–1935* (Chapel Hill: University of North Carolina Press, 2010).

8. "Arcus Flynn, Tape 1. of 1, November 1, 1987," *Herstories: Audio/Visual Collections of the LHA*, http://herstories.prattinfoschool.nyc/omeka/document /Flynn_Arcus_tape1of1_1987nov1, accessed September 5, 2019.

9. Michael D. Shear, "Obama May Create Monument to Gay Rights Movement," *New York Times*, May 3, 2016.

10. "Historical Musings: Women's House of Detention, 1931–1974," Out History, http://outhistory.org/exhibits/show/historical-musings/womens-house -of-detention, accessed May 17, 2019.

11. Nicole Hahn Rafter, *Partial Justice: Women, Prisons, and Social Control* (London: Routledge, 1990).

12. Jen Manion, *Liberty's Prisoners* (Philadelphia: University of Pennsylvania Press, 2015).

13. Sara Harris, *Hellhole* (New York: Dutton, 1967).

14. Matt Clarke, "Long-Term Recidivism Studies Show High Arrest Rates," *Prison Legal News*, May 3, 2019.

15. Allen J. Beck, Marcus Berzofsky, Rachel Caspar, and Christopher Krebs, *Sexual Victimization in Prisons and Jails Reported by Inmates, 2011–12* (Washington, DC: Bureau of Justice Statistics, May 2013), www.bjs.gov/content/pub /pdf/svpjri1112.pdf.

16. Mariame Kaba, *We Do This 'Til We Free Us* (Chicago: Haymarket Books, 2021).

17. "Jay London Toole Interview Transcript," New York City Trans Oral History Project.

18. "Jay London Toole Interview Transcript," New York City Trans Oral History Project.

19. Áine Duggan, "'Nobody Should Ever Feel the Way That I Felt': A Portrait of Jay Toole and Queer Homelessness," *The Scholar & Feminist Online*, no. 10.1–10.2. (Fall 2011/Spring 2012), http://sfonline.barnard.edu/a-new-queer -agenda/nobody-should-ever-feel-the-way-that-i-felt-a-portrait-of-jay-toole -and-queer-homelessness/0.

20. "Huey P. Newton Interview," Pacifica Foundation, August 11, 1970.

Chapter 1: The Prehistory of the Women's House of Detention (1796–1928)

1. "The Weather," *New York Daily News*, July 5, 1924.

2. Mabel Hampton Case File, Westfield State Farm inmate case files, New York State Archives.

3. Mabel Hampton Oral History, Lesbian Herstory Archives, http://herstories.prattinfoschool.nyc/omeka/collections/show/29.

4. Mabel Hampton Oral History, Lesbian Herstory Archives.

5. Mabel Hampton Oral History, Lesbian Herstory Archives.

6. John Strausbaugh, *The Village* (New York: HarperCollins, 2013).

7. Hugh Barbour et al., eds., *Quaker Crosscurrents: Three Hundred Years of Friends in the New York Yearly Meetings* (Syracuse, NY: Syracuse University Press, 1995).

8. Hugh Entwistle McAtamney, *Cradle Days of New York (1609–1825)* (New York: Drew and Lewis, 1909).

9. Mary K. Stohr and Anthony Walsh, *Corrections: The Essentials*, 3rd ed. (Thousand Oaks, CA: SAGE, 2017).

10. Nicole Hahn Rafter, "Prisons for Women, 1790–1980," *Crime and Justice* 5 (1983): 129–181.

11. Michelle Alexander, *The New Jim Crow* (New York: The New Press, 2010).

12. Strausbaugh, *The Village.*

13. Strausbaugh, *The Village.*

14. Strausbaugh, *The Village.*

15. "By-laws and Ordinances of the Mayor, Alderman, and Commonalty of the City of New York, 1845," https://books.google.com/books/about/By_laws_and_Ordinances_of_the_Mayor_Alde.html?id=6WQtAAAAYAAJ, accessed September 22, 2021.

16. "The Public Institutions," *New York Times*, December 22, 1871.

17. Nicole Hahn Rafter, *Partial Justice: Women, Prisons and Social Control* (London: Routledge, 1990).

18. "Newkirk's Death," *Indianapolis News*, December 8, 1871.

19. "The Weather of the Week," *New York Times*, December 3, 1871.

20. "Newkirk's Death," *Indianapolis News.*

21. "Gleanings from the Department of Public Works," *New York Times*, January 1, 1872.

22. "Newkirk's Death," *Indianapolis News.*

23. "A Sad Death," *Sunbury Gazette*, December 23, 1871.

24. "A Sad Death," *Sunbury Gazette.*

25. "The Grand Jury and the Prison System," *New York Times*, December 10, 1871.

26. "The Grand Jury and the Prison System," *New York Times.*

27. "The Grand Jury and the Prison System," *New York Times.*

28. "Current Events," *Brooklyn Daily Eagle*, April 4, 1878.

29. "Tragedy in a Cell," *New York Daily Herald*, October 29, 1878.

30. Frederick H. Whitin, "The Women's Night Court in New York City," *Annals of the American Academy of Political and Social Science* 52 (March 1, 1914).

31. "Magistrates Elect House," *New York Times*, July 23, 1907.

32. "The Social Evil in New York City," Committee of Fourteen, New York, 1910.

33. "The Social Evil in New York City," Committee of Fourteen.

34. "The Social Evil in New York City," Committee of Fourteen.

35. "Item #1523, Committee of Fourteen Bulletin Book #14, April 1922 to December 1, 1922," Committee of Fourteen Collection, Box 88, New York Public Library.

36. Anna M. Kross, "Report on Prostitution and the Women's Court," 1934, Box 37, Folder 14, Anna Cross Collection, American Jewish Archives.

37. *People ex rel. Miller v. Brockman et al.* (1916) 35 N.Y. Crim. Reps. 337, 341.

38. Bruce W. Cobb, *Inferior Criminal Courts Act of the City of New York* (New York: Macmillan, 1925).

39. Cobb, *Inferior Criminal Courts Act.*

40. People v. Anonymous, 161 Misc. 379 (1936).

41. Kross, "Report on Prostitution and the Women's Court."

42. "Item #1522, Committee of Fourteen Bulletin Book #14, April 1922 to December 1, 1922," Committee of Fourteen Collection, Box 88, New York Public Library.

43. "Item #1522, Committee of Fourteen Bulletin Book #14."

44. Kross, "Report on Prostitution and the Women's Court."

45. Kross, "Report on Prostitution and the Women's Court."

46. Lewis A. Erenberg, *Steppin' Out: New York Nightlife and the Transformation of American Culture, 1890–1930* (Chicago: University of Chicago Press, 1981).

47. Bertha Rembaugh, "Problems of the New York Night Court for Women," *Women's Law Journal* 45 (1912).

48. Maude E. Miner, *Slavery of Prostitution: A Plea for Emancipation* (New York, 1916).

49. Eve Rosahn interview with author, October 12, 2018.

50. Eve Rosahn interview with author, October 12, 2018.

51. Mae Quinn, "Revisiting Anna Moscowitz's Critique of New York City's Women's Court," *Fordham Urban Law Journal* 33, no. 2 (2006).

52. O. O. M'Intyre, "The Talk of N' Yawk," *St. Joseph Gazette*, May 8, 1919.

53. M'Intyre, "The Talk of N' Yawk."

54. "Gritty Attraction: New York City's Night Court Now a Tourist Stop," Associated Press, March 18, 2014, www.nbcnews.com/business/travel/gritty -attraction-new-york-citys-night-court-now-tourist-stop-n55886.

55. "Sightseers End Women's Night Court," *New-York Tribune*, August 11, 1918.

56. Andrea Barnet, *All-Night Party: The Women of Bohemian Greenwich Village and Harlem, 1913–1930* (Chapel Hill, NC: Algonquin Books of Chapel Hill, 2004).

57. Caroline Ware, *Greenwich Village, 1920–1930* (London: Octagon, 1977).

58. Annual Report of the City of New York Department of Correction for the Year 1929, New York City Municipal Archives.

59. Simon A. Cole, *Suspect Identities: A History of Fingerprinting and Criminal Identification* (Cambridge, MA: Harvard University Press, 2001).

60. Cole, *Suspect Identities*.

61. Cole, *Suspect Identities*.

62. Annual Report of the City of New York Department of Correction, 1929.

63. Annual Report of the City of New York Department of Correction, 1929.

64. Gabrielle S. Mulliner, "A Court for Women," *Brooklyn Daily Eagle*, May 2, 1909.

65. Mulliner, "A Court for Women."

66. Mabel Hampton Oral History, Lesbian Herstory Archives.

67. Mabel Hampton Oral History, Lesbian Herstory Archives.

68. Malcolm Crowley, "The Vice Squad Carries On," *New Republic*, June 25, 1930.

69. Mabel Hampton Case File, Westfield State Farm inmate case files, New York State Archives.

70. "Notorious Stool Pigeon for Police Engaged in Trapping Decent, Hard-Working Girls," *New York Age*, July 5, 1924.

71. "Woman Is Removed as NY Magistrate," *New York Times*, June 26, 1931.

72. Cheryl Hicks, *Talk with You Like a Woman: African American Women, Justice, and Reform in New York, 1890–1935* (Chapel Hill: University of North Carolina Press, 2010).

73. Rafter, *Partial Justice*.

74. "Denies Brutality at Reformatory," *New York Times*, November 23, 1919.

75. Elizabeth Trondle File, Box 106, Women's Prison Association Collection, New York Public Library.

76. Nancy D. Campbell and Elizabeth Ettorre, *Gendering Addiction: The Politics of Drug Treatment in a Neurochemical World* (Basingstoke, UK: Palgrave Macmillan, 2011).

77. Ware, *Greenwich Village, 1920–1930*.

78. Ware, *Greenwich Village, 1920–1930*.

79. Ware, *Greenwich Village, 1920–1930*.

80. Ware, *Greenwich Village, 1920–1930*.

81. Ware, *Greenwich Village, 1920–1930*.

82. Ware, *Greenwich Village, 1920–1930*.

83. Letter from Richard C. Patterson Jr., Commissioner of the Department of Correction, to Mayor James J. Walker, January 16, 1928, Municipal Archives of the City of New York, Collection of Correspondence Received by Mayor James Walker from the Department of Correction, Box 25.

Chapter 2: Psychiatrists, Psychologists, and Social Workers—the Prison's Eyes, Ears, and Record Keepers

1. Virginia Commonwealth University, "Stock Market Crash of October 1929," https://socialwelfare.library.vcu.edu/eras/great-depression/beginning-of-great-depression-stock-market-crash-of-october-1929, accessed March 27, 2020.

2. "Walker Enters Queens for Big Rally Tonight," *Brooklyn Standard Union*, October 30, 1929.

3. Linda Poon, "Charting the Booms and Busts of NYC's Skyscraper History," *Bloomberg CityLab*, October 27, 2015.

4. "The New House of Detention," *On Guard*, April, 1932.

5. "New 'Jail' for Naughty Girls a Ritzy Place," *Democrat and Chronicle*, March 11, 1931.

6. "New 'Jail' for Naughty Girls a Ritzy Place," *Democrat and Chronicle*.

7. Clarice Feinman, "Imprisoned Women: A History of the Treatment of Incarcerated Women in New York City, 1932–1975" (PhD diss., New York University, 1976).

8. "Will Revise Plans for Women's Prison," *New York Times*, September 10, 1927.

9. Feinman, "Imprisoned Women."

10. "State Commissioner of Correction's Report on Conditions at the House of Detention for Women," 1935, Box 22, Folder 15, Anna Cross Collection, American Jewish Archives.

11. "State Commissioner of Correction's Report on Conditions at the House of Detention for Women," 1938, Box 22, Folder 15, Anna Cross Collection, American Jewish Archives.

12. "State Commissioner of Correction's Report on Conditions at the House of Detention for Women," 1943, Box 22, Folder 15, Anna Cross Collection, American Jewish Archives.

13. "State Commissioner of Correction's Report on Conditions at the House of Detention for Women," 1934, Box 22, Folder 15, Anna Cross Collection, American Jewish Archives.

14. "State Commissioner of Correction's Report on Conditions at the House of Detention for Women," 1934.

15. "Seventh Annual Report of the State Commission of Correction, for the Year 1933," Ossining, February 15, 1934.

16. "Jail Welfare Stores Do $300,000 Business Yearly," *Daily News*, January 18, 1934.

17. "State Commissioner of Correction's Report on Conditions at the House of Detention for Women," 1933, Box 22, Folder 15, Anna Cross Collection, American Jewish Archives.

18. "Seventh Annual Report of the State Commission of Correction, for the Year 1933."

19. "Seventh Annual Report of the State Commission of Correction, for the Year 1933."

20. Nicole Hahn Rafter, *Partial Justice: Women, Prisons and Social Control* (London: Routledge, 1990).

21. Women's Prison Association Collection, New York Public Library, Box 67.

22. Women's Prison Association, Box 67.

23. Women's Prison Association, Box 67.

24. Movement Advancement Project and Center for American Progress, "Unjust: How the Broken Juvenile and Criminal Justice Systems Fail LGBTQ Youth," August 2016, https://www.lgbtmap.org/policy-and-issue-analysis/criminal-justice-youth.

25. Author interview with Ilan Meyer, April 14, 2020.

26. Cheryl Hicks, *Talk with You Like a Woman: African American Women, Justice, and Reform in New York, 1890–1935* (Chapel Hill: University of North Carolina Press, 2010).

27. Hicks, *Talk with You Like a Woman.*

28. Merril Sobie, "The Family Court: An Historical Survey," Elisabeth Haub School of Law Faculty Publications no. 615 (July 1988), http://digitalcommons.pace.edu/lawfaculty/615.

29. "Juvenile Reentry," Office of Juvenile Justice and Delinquency Prevention, August 2017, https://ojjdp.ojp.gov/sites/g/files/xyckuh176/files/media/document/aftercare.pdf.

30. Women's Prison Association, Box 67.

31. Gillian Rodger, *Champagne Charlie and Pretty Jemima* (Champaign: University of Illinois Press, 2010).

32. Jen Manion, "Female Husbands," *Aeon*, May 7, 2020.

33. Women's Prison Association, Box 67.

34. Women's Prison Association, Box 67.

35. Women's Prison Association, Box 67.

36. Women's Prison Association, Box 67.

37. Women's Prison Association, Box 67.

38. Women's Prison Association, Box 67.

39. Women's Prison Association, Box 67.

40. Women's Prison Association, Box 67.

41. Virginia Maynard, "I Was a New York Gun-Girl! Pt 1," *Sunday Mirror*, July 24, 1938.

42. Maynard, "I Was a New York Gun-Girl! Pt 1."

43. Virginia Maynard, "I Was a New York Gun-Girl! Pt 3," *Sunday Mirror*, August 7, 1938.

44. Maynard, "I Was a New York Gun-Girl! Pt 3."

45. Women's Prison Association, Box 88, 91.

46. Women's Prison Association, Box 91.

47. Women's Prison Association, Box 91.

48. Women's Prison Association, Box 67.

49. Women's Prison Association, Box 67.

50. Women's Prison Association, Box 91.

51. Women's Prison Association, Box 91.

52. Women's Prison Association, Box 91.

53. Women's Prison Association, Box 91.

54. Women's Prison Association, Box 91.

55. Women's Prison Association, Box 67.

56. Women's Prison Association, Box 67.

57. Women's Prison Association, Box 67.

58. "Girl Wins Honor at Swarthmore," *Philadelphia Evening Public Ledger*, June 12, 1922.

59. Marianne Kelsey, "Don't Call Them Do-Gooders," *Florida Today*, March 25, 1971.

60. Kelsey, "Don't Call Them Do-Gooders."

61. Letter from Barbara Philips to E. Mebane Hunt, June 5, 1939, Women's Prison Association, Box 19, Folder "House of Detention 1937–1947," New York Public Library (NYPL).

62. Letter from Barbara Philips to E. Mebane Hunt, December 20, 1939, Women's Prison Association, Box 19, Folder "House of Detention 1937–1947," NYPL.

63. State Commissioners of Correction Report on the Women's House of Detention, 1936.

64. Brad H. v. City of New York, 716 N.Y.S.2d 852 (App. Div. 2000).

65. "Coming Home Checklist," New York State Department of Corrections and Community Supervision, https://doccs.ny.gov/coming-home-checklist.

66. Letter from Barbara Philips to E. Mebane Hunt, December 20, 1939, Women's Prison Association, Box 19, Folder "House of Detention 1937–1947," NYPL.

67. Annual Report of the City of New York Department of Correction for the Years 1940–41, New York City Municipal Archives.

68. Lorna Collier, "Incarceration Nation," *American Psychological Association Newsletter* 45, no. 9 (October 2014).

69. Women's Prison Association, Box 67.

70. Women's Prison Association, Box 67.

71. Women's Prison Association, Box 67.

72. Women's Prison Association, Box 67.

73. Women's Prison Association, Box 67.

74. Women's Prison Association, Box 67.

75. Women's Prison Association, Box 67.

76. Women's Prison Association, Box 91.

77. Women's Prison Association, Box 67.

78. Women's Prison Association, Box 91.

79. "Ex-Girl Bandit, Out on Parole, Ends Her Life," *New York Daily News*, November 16, 1948.

80. "Star Grill Cook, City Bred, to Do Bit as Farmerette," *New York World-Telegram*, May 14, 1942.

81. "Star Grill Cook, City Bred, to Do Bit as Farmerette," *New York World-Telegram*.

82. "Star Grill Cook, City Bred, to Do Bit as Farmerette," *New York World-Telegram*.

83. "Star Grill Cook, City Bred, to Do Bit as Farmerette," *New York World-Telegram*.

84. "Boarding Kennel," *Poughkeepsie Journal*, August 28, 1960.

85. "Charlotte Alice B—," *Poughkeepsie Journal*, November 21, 1984.

Chapter 3: Where the Girls Are: Greenwich Village and Lesbian Life

1. Sacramento High School Year Book, 1931.

2. Women's Prison Association Collection, New York Public Library, Box 67.

3. Women's Prison Association, Box 67.

4. Women's Prison Association, Box 67.

5. Women's Prison Association, Box 67.

6. Women's Prison Association, Box 67.

7. Women's Prison Association, Box 67.

8. Women's Prison Association, Box 67.

9. Richard Freiherr von Krafft-Ebing, *Psychopathia Sexualis* [1886].

10. Women's Prison Association, Box 67.

11. Women's Prison Association, Box 67.

12. Women's Prison Association, Box 67.

13. Women's Prison Association, Box 67.

14. Women's Prison Association, Box 67.

15. Women's Prison Association, Box 67.

16. Women's Prison Association, Box 67.

17. Women's Prison Association, Box 67.

18. Women's Prison Association, Box 67.

19. Women's Prison Association, Box 67.

20. Women's Prison Association, Box 67.

21. Women's Prison Association, Box 67.

22. Women's Prison Association, Box 67.

23. "Statistical Report, Year 1937, Parole Commission, City of New York," New York Correction History Society, www.correctionhistory.org/html/chronicl/nycparole/parolerpt37.html.

24. *Seventy-First Annual Report of Prison Association of New York* (Albany: J. B. Lyon Company Printers, 1916).

25. Elizabeth Hinton, *From the War on Poverty to the War on Crime* (Cambridge, MA: Harvard University Press, 2016).

26. Scott W. Stern, *The Trials of Nina McCall* (Boston: Beacon Press, 2018).

27. Stern, *The Trials of Nina McCall*.

28. Stern, *The Trials of Nina McCall*.

29. "An Act to Amend the Public Health Law, in Relation to Certain Contagious Diseases," Laws of New York, 1919.

30. Annual Report of the Department of Corrections, 1940–1941, New York City Municipal Archives.

31. Annual Report of the Department of Corrections, 1940–1941, New York City Municipal Archives.

32. "State Commissioner of Correction's Report on Conditions at the House of Detention for Women," 1938, Box 22, Folder 15, Anna Cross Collection, American Jewish Archives.

33. Women's Prison Association, Box 67.

34. "Bars Medical Exam of Women Pickets," *New York Daily News*, August 15, 1936.

35. Author interview with Jay Toole, September 11, 2017.

36. State Commissioners of Correction Report on the Women's House of Detention, 1935.

37. Women's Prison Association, Box 67.

38. Women's Prison Association, Box 67.

39. Women's Prison Association, Box 67.

40. Women's Prison Association, Box 67.

41. Women's Prison Association, Box 67.

42. "Stewart's Cafeteria," NYC LGBT Historic Sites Project, www.nyclgbt sites.org/site/stewarts-cafeteria, accessed May 19, 2020.

43. "Sheridan Square Dramalet," *Broadway Brevities*, November 2, 1933.

44. Women's Prison Association, Box 67.

45. Women's Prison Association, Box 67.

46. Women's Prison Association, Box 67.

47. Women's Prison Association, Box 67.

48. Albert C. Lammert and Roger B. Scott, "Hazard in the Intravaginal Use of Potassium Permanganate," *American Journal of Obstetrics and Gynecology* 68, no. 3 (September 1954).

49. Annual Report of the Department of Corrections, 1940–1941, New York City Municipal Archives.

50. Women's Prison Association, Box 67.

51. Women's Prison Association, Box 67.

52. Women's Prison Association, Box 67.

53. "Deaths," *Sacramento Bee*, August 26, 1944.

54. "Deaths," *Sacramento Bee*, January 5, 1953.

55. "Remembrances," *Sacramento Bee*, September 18, 2011.

56. Women's Prison Association, Box 69.

57. Women's Prison Association, Box 69.

58. Women's Prison Association, Box 69.

59. Women's Prison Association, Box 69.

60. Women's Prison Association, Box 69.

61. Regina Kunzel, *Criminal Intimacy* (Chicago: University of Chicago Press, 2008).

62. 1935 Women's House of Detention Inspection Report, State Commission of Correction, Box 22, Folder 15, Anna Kross Papers, American Jewish Archives.

63. Clarice Feinman, "Imprisoned Women: A History of the Treatment of Incarcerated Women in New York City, 1932–1975" (PhD diss., New York University, 1976).

64. "Incarceration Rate of LGB People Three Times the General Population," Williams Institute, UCLA School of Law, https://williamsinstitute.law

.ucla.edu/williams-in-the-news/incarceration-rate-of-lesbian-gay-bisexual
-people-three-times-the-general-population, accessed May 17, 2019.

65. Women's Prison Association, Box 69.

66. Women's Prison Association, Box 69.

67. Women's Prison Association, Box 69.

68. Women's Prison Association, Box 69.

69. Women's Prison Association, Box 69.

70. Women's Prison Association, Box 69.

71. Women's Prison Association, Box 69.

72. Women's Prison Association, Box 69.

73. Women's Prison Association, Box 69.

74. Women's Prison Association, Box 69.

75. Women's Prison Association, Box 69.

76. Annual Report of the Department of Correction, 1940–1941, New York City Municipal Archives.

77. Christian Salazar, Deepti Hajela, and Randy Herschaft, "Black Undercount Found in 1940 Census Records," *San Diego Union-Tribune*, May 20, 2012.

78. Annual Report of the Department of Correction, 1940–1941, New York City Municipal Archives.

79. Andrea Ritchie, *Invisible No More: Police Violence Against Black Women and Women of Color* (Boston: Beacon Press, 2017).

80. Annual Report of the Department of Correction, 1940–1941, New York City Municipal Archives.

81. "Fred M. Bryan, Pianist and Composer, Dies After Four Weeks of Illness," *New York Age*, August 24, 1929.

82. Women's Prison Association, Box 68.

83. Women's Prison Association, Box 68.

84. Women's Prison Association, Box 68.

85. Women's Prison Association, Box 68.

86. Women's Prison Association, Box 68.

87. Nicole Hahn Rafter, *Partial Justice: Women, Prisons and Social Control* (London: Routledge, 1990).

88. Rafter, *Partial Justice.*

89. *General Laws of the State of New York* (St. Paul: West Publishing Co., 1921).

90. Annual Report of the Prison Association of New York, vols. 73–76, https://books.google.com/books?id=TugTAAAAIAAJ&pg=RA3-PA27&lpg=RA3-PA27, accessed September 22, 2021.

91. Hinton, *From the War on Poverty to the War on Crime.*

92. Anna Lvovsky, *Vice Patrol* (Chicago: University of Chicago Press, 2021).

93. Women's Prison Association, Box 68.

94. Women's Prison Association, Box 68.

95. Women's Prison Association, Box 68.

96. Andrea Barnet, *All-Night Party: The Women of Bohemian Greenwich Village and Harlem, 1913–1930* (Chapel Hill, NC: Algonquin Books of Chapel Hill, 2004).

97. Barnet, *All-Night Party*.

98. Barnet, *All-Night Party*.

99. Mabel Hampton Oral History, Lesbian Herstory Archives.

100. Yolanda Retter, "Eva La Gallienne," *GLBTQ Encyclopedia*, 2015, www.glbtqarchive.com/arts/legallienne_e_A.pdf.

101. Jason Clevett, "Interview—Bernie Koppel," *Gay Calgary Magazine*, October 2008, www.gaycalgary.com/magazine.aspx?id=60&article=561.

102. Women's Prison Association, Box 68.

103. Women's Prison Association, Box 68.

104. Walter Winchell, "Walter Winchell on Broadway," *Daily Mirror*, April 18, 1939.

105. Women's Prison Association, Box 68.

106. Women's Prison Association, Box 68.

107. Women's Prison Association, Box 68.

108. Women's Prison Association, Box 68.

109. Women's Prison Association, Box 68.

110. Women's Prison Association, Box 68.

111. Women's Prison Association, Box 68.

112. Women's Prison Association, Box 68.

113. "Held in Rare Book Theft," *Brooklyn Citizen*, December 24, 1941.

114. Women's Prison Association, Box 68.

115. Women's Prison Association, Box 68.

116. Women's Prison Association, Box 69.

117. Women's Prison Association, Box 68.

118. "Jim Crow in Prisons Disavowed," *New York Amsterdam News*, April 6, 1932.

119. "State Commissioner of Correction's Report on Conditions at the House of Detention for Women," 1936, Box 22, Folder 15, Anna Cross Collection, American Jewish Archives.

120. Women's Prison Association, Box 69.

121. Martin Duberman, *Stonewall* (New York: Plume, 2019).

122. Duberman, *Stonewall*.

123. Women's Prison Association, Box 69.

124. Women's Prison Association, Box 69.

125. Women's Prison Association, Box 68.

126. Women's Prison Association, Box 68.

127. James Baldwin, *Notes of a Native Son* (Boston: Beacon Press, 2012).

128. "1943 Harlem Riot Killed 5, Hurt 500; It Began When a Policeman Shot a Negro Soldier," *New York Times*, July 19, 1964.

129. Women's Prison Association, Box 68.

130. Women's Prison Association, Box 68.

Chapter 4: Rosie the Riveter Gets Fired

1. Mariano-Florentino Cuéllar, "Administrative War," *George Washington Law Review* 82, no. 5 (October 2014).

2. Christina D. Romer, "The Hope That Flows from History," *New York Times*, August 13, 2011.

3. Mary M. Schweitzer, "World War II and Female Labor Participation Rates," *Journal of Economic History* 40, no. 1 (March 1980).

4. Schweitzer, "World War II and Female Labor Participation Rates."

5. "State Commissioner of Correction's Report on Conditions at the House of Detention for Women," 1943, Box 22, Folder 15, Anna Cross Collection, American Jewish Archives.

6. Letter from Ruth Collins to Peter Amoroso, June 22, 1943, Box 22, Folder 15, Anna Kross Collection, American Jewish Archives.

7. Annual Report of the Department of Corrections, 1940–1941, New York City Municipal Archives.

8. Clarice Feinman, "Imprisoned Women: A History of the Treatment of Incarcerated Women in New York City, 1932–1975" (PhD diss., New York University, 1976).

9. Annual Report of the Department of Corrections, 1947, New York City Municipal Archives.

10. Annual Report of the Department of Corrections, 1940–1941, New York City Municipal Archives.

11. "State Commissioner of Correction's Report on Conditions at the House of Detention for Women," 1943.

12. "State Commissioner of Correction's Report on Conditions at the House of Detention for Women," 1944.

13. "State Commissioner of Correction's Report on Conditions at the House of Detention for Women," 1944.

14. "State Commissioner of Correction's Report on Conditions at the House of Detention for Women," 1944.

15. "State Commissioner of Correction's Report on Conditions at the House of Detention for Women," 1944.

16. "Minutes: 1940–1944," Women's Prison Association Collection, Box 3, New York Public Library.

17. "Federal Jurors Fete," *Brooklyn Daily Eagle*, May 31, 1942.

18. Annual Report of the Department of Corrections, 1960, New York City Municipal Archives.

19. Women's Prison Association, Box 96.

20. Women's Prison Association, Box 96.

21. Women's Prison Association, Box 96.

22. Women's Prison Association, Box 96.

23. Women's Prison Association, Box 96.

24. Women's Prison Association, Box 96.

25. Allan Bérubé, *Coming Out Under Fire: The History of Gay Men and Women in World War II* (Chapel Hill: University of North Carolina Press, 2010).

26. Women's Prison Association, Box 68.

27. Women's Prison Association, Box 68.

28. Women's Prison Association, Box 68.

29. Women's Prison Association, Box 68.

30. "Queer Doings Net Suspension for Vill. Clubs," *The Billboard*, December 2, 1944.

31. "Queer Doings Net Suspension for Vill. Clubs," *The Billboard*.

32. "Tony Pastor's Downtown/Gay Community Center," NYC LGBT Historic Sites Project, www.nyclgbtsites.org/site/tony-pastors-downtown-gay-community-center, accessed June 12, 2020.

33. J. Stanley Lemons, *The Woman Citizen* (Champaign: University of Illinois Press, 1973).

34. Judith Schwarz, *Radical Feminists of Heterodoxy* (Norwich: New Victoria Publishers, 1986).

35. "Village History," Greenwich Village Society for Historic Preservation, www.gvshp.org/_gvshp/resources/history.htm#beat, accessed June 16, 2020.

36. Women's Prison Association, Box 69.

37. Women's Prison Association, Box 69.

38. Women's Prison Association, Box 69.

39. Women's Prison Association, Box 69.

40. Women's Prison Association, Box 69.

41. "Assail Discrimination of WPA Authorities in Case of Negro Workers," *New York Age*, June 25, 1938.

42. "Discover Family of Five in Starving Conditions," *New York Amsterdam News*, June 25, 1938.

43. "Floor Scrubbing, No Clerical Jobs for Negro Girls," *Daily Worker*, June 20, 1938.

44. Women's Prison Association, Box 71.

45. Women's Prison Association, Box 71.

46. Women's Prison Association, Box 71.

47. Women's Prison Association, Box 71.

48. Women's Prison Association, Box 71.

49. Women's Prison Association, Box 71.

50. Women's Prison Association, Box 71.

51. Women's Prison Association, Box 71.

52. Raymond L. Hayes, "Report of the Committee on Scholarships, Prizes, and Awards," *The Dentoscope* 21, no. 2 (July 1941).

53. Women's Prison Association, Box 71.

54. Women's Prison Association, Box 71.

55. Women's Prison Association, Box 71.

56. Women's Prison Association, Box 71.

57. Women's Prison Association, Box 71.

58. Women's Prison Association, Box 71.

59. Women's Prison Association, Box 71.

60. Women's Prison Association, Box 71.

61. Women's Prison Association, Box 71.

62. Women's Prison Association, Box 71.

63. Women's Prison Association, Box 71.

64. Richard D. Schwartz and Jerome H. Skolnick, "Two Studies of Legal Stigma," *Social Problems* 10, no. 2 (Autumn 1962).

65. Elizabeth Hinton, *From the War on Poverty to the War on Crime* (Cambridge, MA: Harvard University Press, 2016).

66. "Summary Report, R-Two," Box 29, Folder 4, Anna Kross Collection, American Jewish Archives.

67. "Summary Report, R-Two," Box 29, Folder 4, Anna Kross Collection.

68. Women's Prison Association, Box 69.

69. Women's Prison Association, Box 69.

70. Women's Prison Association, Box 69.

71. Women's Prison Association, Box 69.

72. Women's Prison Association, Box 69.

73. Author interview with Christopher Mitchell, June 6, 2019.

74. Author interview with Christopher Mitchell, June 6, 2019.

75. R. B. Sullivan, "Should We All Be Fingerprinted?," *New York Daily News*, January 28, 1940.

76. Sullivan, "Should We All Be Fingerprinted?"

77. Sullivan, "Should We All Be Fingerprinted?"

78. Sullivan, "Should We All Be Fingerprinted?"

79. Cuéllar, "Administrative War."

80. Theo Wilson, "Depravity and Fear Scar Life of an Addict," *New York Daily News*, February 29, 1968.

Chapter 5: The Long Tail of the Drug War

1. Magistrate Court's Annual Report, 1932, Municipal Archives of NYC.

2. "State Commission of Correction Report of August 14 and 15, 1952," Anna Kross Collection, American Jewish Archives.

3. Department of Correction Annual Statistical Report, 1965, Box 26, Folder 9, Anna Kross Collection, American Jewish Archives.

4. "Minutes of the Regular Meeting of the Women's Prison Association," June 9, 1964, Women's Prison Association Collection, Box 4, New York Public Library.

5. National Institute on Drug Abuse, "Criminal Justice DrugFacts," June 1, 2020, www.drugabuse.gov/publications/drugfacts/criminal-justice on 2021.

6. "Still Clings to Her Male Attire," *Daily Standard Union: Brooklyn*, August 30, 1913.

7. "Girl Masquerader Is Miss Trondle," *Brooklyn Daily Eagle*, August 29, 1913.

8. "Still Clings to Her Male Attire," *Daily Standard Union: Brooklyn*.

9. "Trondle Girl in Dresses," *Brooklyn Daily Eagle*, September 3, 1913.

10. Elizabeth Trondle File, Box 106, Women's Prison Association Collection, New York Public Library.

11. Kathleen J. Frydl, *The Drug Wars in America: 1940–1973* (New York: Cambridge University Press, 2013).

12. Dale Gieringer, "The Opium Exclusion Act of 1909," *CounterPunch*, February 6, 2009.

13. "'Dope' Coined by Chinamen," *Elmira Star-Gazette*, December 8, 1910.

14. Edward M. Brecher, "The Consumers Union Report on Licit and Illicit Drugs," 1972, www.druglibrary.org/schaffer/library/studies/cu/cu8.html, accessed April 9, 2021.

15. Marie Nyswander, "Drug Addicts in the General Hospital," *Hospital Administration*, ed. Louis Linn, Box 27, Folder 14, Medical Advisory Board, Anna Kross Collection, American Jewish Archives.

16. "Character of the Mexican Proper and Improper," *Buffalo Sunday Morning News*, May 17, 1914.

17. Richard J. Bonnie and Charles H. Whitebread, "The Forbidden Fruit and the Tree of Knowledge: An Inquiry into the Legal History of American Marijuana Prohibition," *Virginia Law Review* 56, no. 6 (October 1970).

18. "New Anti-Drug Law Is in Effect Today," *New York Times*, July 1, 1914.

19. "New Anti-Drug Law Is In Effect Today," *New York Times*.

20. "Muzzles the Dogs All the Year 'Round," *New York Times*, July 29, 1914.

21. "New Anti-Drug Law Is In Effect Today," *New York Times*.

22. Florrie Fisher, *The Lonely Trip Back* (New York: Doubleday, 1971).

23. Polly Adler, *A House Is Not a Home* (New York: Rinehart, 1953).

24. Elizabeth Trondle File, Box 106, Women's Prison Association Collection.

25. Elizabeth Trondle File, Box 106, Women's Prison Association.

26. Elizabeth Trondle File, Box 106, Women's Prison Association.

27. Elizabeth Trondle File, Box 106, Women's Prison Association.

28. Elizabeth Trondle File, Box 106, Women's Prison Association.

29. Elizabeth Trondle File, Box 106, Women's Prison Association.

30. Donald J. Cantor, "The Criminal Law and the Narcotics Problem," *Journal of Criminal Law and Criminology* 51, no. 5 (Winter 1961).

31. "13 Seized in Dope Raids Here and Over 500 Held After Nationwide Roundup," *Brooklyn Times Union*, December 9, 1934.

32. "1,909 Jailed in Treasury Crime Drive," *Rochester Democrat and Chronicle*, March 16, 1935.

33. "Four Narcotic Violators Get Long Terms," *Wilkes-Barre Evening News*, July 9, 1937.

34. Elizabeth Trondle File, Box 106, Women's Prison Association.

35. Elizabeth Trondle File, Box 106, Women's Prison Association.

36. Elizabeth Trondle File, Box 106, Women's Prison Association.

37. Elizabeth Trondle File, Box 106, Women's Prison Association.

38. "Police Hunt Man in Hotel Murder," *Brooklyn Daily Eagle*, June 26, 1942.

39. Frydl, *The Drug Wars in America: 1940–1973*.

40. Frydl, *The Drug Wars in America: 1940–1973*.

41. Lily Rothman, "How World War II Still Determines Your Tax Bill," *Time Magazine*, April 14, 2016, https://time.com/4289687/1942-tax-day-history.

42. Women's Prison Association, Box 66.

43. Women's Prison Association, Box 66.

44. Women's Prison Association, Box 66.

45. Women's Prison Association, Box 66.

46. Women's Prison Association, Box 66.

47. Women's Prison Association, Box 66.

48. Frydl, *The Drug Wars in America: 1940–1973*.

49. Frydl, *The Drug Wars in America: 1940–1973*.

50. "Blues Singer Sentenced as Drug Addict," *Binghamton Press and Sun Bulletin*, May 28, 1947.

51. Hector R. Cordero-Guzman, "The Latino Population in New York City," *Footnotes: A Publication of the American Sociological Association* 47, no. 3 (June–August 2019).

52. Sam Roberts, "New York, 1945," *New York Times*, July 30, 1995.

53. Frydl, *The Drug Wars in America: 1940–1973*.

54. Martha Biondi, *To Stand and Fight* (Cambridge, MA: Harvard University Press, 2003).

55. "Brownsville Plan Should Hasten City Action for More Police," *Brooklyn Daily Eagle*, November 22, 1954.

56. "Brownsville Plan Should Hasten City Action for More Police," *Brooklyn Daily Eagle*.

57. Michelle Alexander, *The New Jim Crow* (New York: The New Press, 2010).

58. William J. Horvath, "The 1950s 'War on Narcotics': Harry Anslinger, the Federal Bureau of Narcotics, and Senator Price Daniel's Probe," *Harvey M. Applebaum '59 Award* (2020), https://clischolar.library.yale.edu /applebaum_award/21/.

59. Memo on August 14, 1949, Box 40, Frederic Wertham Collection, Library of Congress.

60. Women's Prison Association, Box 66.

61. Women's Prison Association, Box 66.

62. Women's Prison Association, Box 66.

63. Women's Prison Association, Box 66.

64. Women's Prison Association, Box 66.

65. Women's Prison Association, Box 66.

66. Women's Prison Association, Box 66.

67. Women's Prison Association, Box 66.

68. Women's Prison Association, Box 66.

69. Women's Prison Association, Box 66.

70. Women's Prison Association, Box 66.

71. Women's Prison Association, Box 66.

72. Women's Prison Association, Box 66.

73. Women's Prison Association, Box 66.

74. Women's Prison Association, Box 66.

75. Women's Prison Association, Box 66.

76. Women's Prison Association, Box 66.

77. Fisher, *The Lonely Trip Back*.

78. Fisher, *The Lonely Trip Back*.

Chapter 6: Flickers of Pride

1. Women's Prison Association Collection, Box 100, New York Public Library.

2. Women's Prison Association, Box 100.

3. Women's Prison Association, Box 100.

4. Women's Prison Association, Box 100.

5. Women's Prison Association, Box 100.

6. Women's Prison Association, Box 100.

7. Women's Prison Association, Box 100.

8. Women's Prison Association, Box 100.

9. Women's Prison Association, Box 100.

10. Women's Prison Association, Box 100.

11. Women's Prison Association, Box 100.

12. Women's Prison Association, Box 73.

13. Women's Prison Association, Box 73.

14. "Burr and Burton Notes—Enrollment Reaches 180," *Bennington Evening Banner*, October 10, 1940.

15. "Death Notice," *Windsor Vermont Journal*, January 18, 1924.

16. Women's Prison Association, Box 73.

17. Women's Prison Association, Box 73.

18. Women's Prison Association, Box 73.

19. Women's Prison Association, Box 73.

20. Women's Prison Association, Box 73.

21. Women's Prison Association, Box 73.

22. Women's Prison Association, Box 73.

23. Women's Prison Association, Box 73.

24. Women's Prison Association, Box 100.

25. Women's Prison Association, Box 100.

26. Women's Prison Association, Box 100.

27. Women's Prison Association, Box 100.

28. Women's Prison Association, Box 73.

29. Women's Prison Association, Box 73.

30. Women's Prison Association, Box 100.

31. Women's Prison Association, Box 100.

32. Women's Prison Association, Box 100.

33. Women's Prison Association, Box 100.

34. Women's Prison Association, Box 100.

35. Women's Prison Association, Box 73.

36. Women's Prison Association, Box 73.

37. Tourmaline, "Filmmaker and Activist Tourmaline on How to Freedom Dream," *Vogue*, July 2, 2020, www.vogue.com/article/filmmaker-and-activist -tourmaline-on-how-to-freedom-dream.

38. Allan Bérubé, *Coming Out Under Fire* (Chapel Hill: University of North Carolina Press, 2010).

39. David K. Johnson, *The Lavender Scare* (Chicago: University of Chicago Press, 2004).

40. Johnson, *The Lavender Scare*.

41. Johnson, *The Lavender Scare*.

42. Johnson, *The Lavender Scare*.

43. Johnson, *The Lavender Scare*.

44. Rusty Brown interviewed by Len Evans, July 7, 1983.

45. Rusty Brown interviewed by Len Evans, July 7, 1983.

46. Rusty Brown interviewed by Len Evans, July 7, 1983.

47. Rusty Brown interviewed by Len Evans, July 7, 1983.

48. Rusty Brown interviewed by Len Evans, July 7, 1983.

49. Rusty Brown interviewed by Len Evans, July 7, 1983.

50. "Julius and Ethel Rosenberg Executed for Espionage," History.com, November 24, 2009, www.history.com/this-day-in-history/rosenbergs-executed.

51. Elizabeth Gurley Flynn, *My Life as a Political Prisoner* (New York: International Publishers, 1963).

52. Wendy McElroy, "Smith Act Tyranny Against Communists," Future of Freedom Foundation, December 1, 2017, fff.org/explore-freedom/article /smith-act-tyranny-communists.

53. McElroy, "Smith Act Tyranny Against Communists."

54. McElroy, "Smith Act Tyranny Against Communists."

55. Flynn, *My Life as a Political Prisoner.*

56. Flynn, *My Life as a Political Prisoner.*

57. Flynn, *My Life as a Political Prisoner.*

58. Flynn, *My Life as a Political Prisoner.*

59. Flynn, *My Life as a Political Prisoner.*

60. Flynn, *My Life as a Political Prisoner.*

61. Bettina Aptheker, "Keeping the Communist Party Straight, 1940s–1980s," *New Politics* 12, no. 1 (Summer 2008).

62. Aptheker, "Keeping the Communist Party Straight, 1940s–1980s."

63. Aptheker, "Keeping the Communist Party Straight, 1940s–1980s."

64. Aptheker, "Keeping the Communist Party Straight, 1940s–1980s."

65. Flynn, *My Life as a Political Prisoner.*

66. Rosa Collazo, *Memorias de Rosa Collazo* (San Juan: Los Libros de la Iguana, 2017).

67. Collazo, *Memorias de Rosa Collazo.*

68. William Laas, "The Suburbs Are Strangling the City," *New York Times Magazine*, June 18, 1950.

69. "Total and Foreign-Born Population New York City, 1790–2000," New York City Department of City Planning Population Division, www1.nyc.gov /assets/planning/download/pdf/data-maps/nyc-population/historical-population /1790-2000_nyc_total_foreign_birth.pdf.

70. Annual Report of the New York City Department of Correction, 1954, NYC Municipal Archives.

Chapter 7: Conformity and Resistance

1. Women's Prison Association Collection, Box 69, New York Public Library.

2. Women's Prison Association, Box 69.

3. Women's Prison Association, Box 69.

4. Women's Prison Association, Box 69.

5. Women's Prison Association, Box 69.

6. Women's Prison Association, Box 69.

7. Women's Prison Association, Box 69.

8. Women's Prison Association, Box 69.

9. "The Supreme Court Ruling That Led to 70,000 Forced Sterilizations," *Fresh Air*, NPR, March 7, 2016, www.npr.org/sections/health-shots/2016/03/07 /469478098/the-supreme-court-ruling-that-led-to-70-000-forced-sterilizations, accessed April 13, 2021.

10. Women's Prison Association, Box 71.

11. Women's Prison Association, Box 71.

12. Women's Prison Association, Box 71.

13. Women's Prison Association, Box 71.

14. "Women Get Unruly in Detention Home," *Fort Myers News-Press*, September 26, 1954.

15. "Women Prisoners Here in 2-Hour Uproar; Protest Disciplining of One for a Remark," *New York Times*, September 25, 1954.

16. "Prison Riots of 1952," Michigan State University Lab for Education and Advancement in Digital Research, http://projects.leadr.msu.edu/statesofin carcerationmi/exhibits/show/resistance/riot, accessed April 13, 2021.

17. Women's Prison Association, Box 73.

18. "Four Years Progress Report: Administrator, 1954–1957," Box 33, Folder 7, Anna J. Kross Collection, American Jewish Archives.

19. Clarice Feinman, "Imprisoned Women: A History of the Treatment of Incarcerated Women in New York City, 1932–1975" (PhD diss., New York University, 1976).

20. Department of Corrections Annual Report, 1954, NYC Municipal Archives.

21. Department of Corrections Annual Report, 1954, NYC Municipal Archives.

22. Department of Corrections Annual Report, 1954, NYC Municipal Archives.

23. Feinman, "Imprisoned Women."

24. Department of Corrections Annual Report, 1954, NYC Municipal Archives.

25. Feinman, "Imprisoned Women."

26. Department of Corrections Annual Report, 1960, New York City Municipal Archives.

27. Feinman, "Imprisoned Women."

28. Department of Corrections Annual Report, 1955, NYC Municipal Archives.

29. Department of Corrections Annual Report, 1960, New York City Municipal Archives.

30. Department of Corrections Annual Report, 1960, New York City Municipal Archives.

31. Feinman, "Imprisoned Women."

32. Feinman, "Imprisoned Women."

33. "Comments of City Administrators, Grand Jury, and Investigators Regarding Department of Corrections," Box 30, Folder 1, Anna J. Kross Collection, American Jewish Archives.

34. Halle Wise, "The House of Detention for Women—a Field Study," 1963, Anna Kross Archive, Smith College.

35. Jay Toole, interview with author, September 11, 2017.

36. Department of Corrections Annual Report, 1955, NYC Municipal Archives.

37. Letter to Honorable Anna Kross, May 12, 1958, Anna Kross Collection, Box 33, Folder 11, American Jewish Archives.

38. "Accuse Blonde of 2d Try at 5 & 10 Con Gag," *New York Daily News*, August 28, 1954.

39. Women's Prison Association, Box 75.

40. Women's Prison Association, Box 75.

41. Women's Prison Association, Box 75.

42. Women's Prison Association, Box 75.

43. Women's Prison Association, Box 75.

44. Women's Prison Association, Box 75.

45. Women's Prison Association, Box 75.

46. Women's Prison Association, Box 75.

47. Women's Prison Association, Box 75.

48. Women's Prison Association, Box 75.

49. Women's Prison Association, Box 75.

50. Women's Prison Association, Box 75.

51. Women's Prison Association, Box 75.

52. "Minutes of the Advisory Committee, Meeting of March 19, 1957," Box 27, Folder 14, Anna Kross Collection, American Jewish Archives.

53. "Department of Correction Press Release June 27, 1958," Box 33, Folder 3, Anna Kross Collection, American Jewish Archives.

54. "City Studying Riot of Women in Jail," *New York Times*, April 28, 1958.

55. "Police Commissioner Requests Further Information RE: Disturbance at Woman's House of Detention," May 3, 1958, Departmental Files 1954–1965, Department of Correction, Roll 13, Mayor Robert Wagner's Papers, Municipal Archives of NYC.

56. "Riot by Women Prisoners Blamed on Overcrowding," *Rochester Democrat and Chronicle*, April 28, 1958.

57. "Unusual Occurrences," Memo from Superintendent, House of Detention for Women to Commissioner of Correction, April 28, 1958, Departmental Files 1954–1965, Department of Correction, Roll 13, Mayor Robert Wagner's Papers, Municipal Archives of NYC.

58. Wise, "The House of Detention for Women—a Field Study."

59. "Transcription of Ken Banghart WCRA Report on the Women's House of Detention, July 30, 1958," Box 23, Folder 1, Anna Kross Collection, American Jewish Archives.

60. "Unusual Occurrences," Memo from Superintendent, House of Detention for Women to Commissioner of Correction, April 28, 1958.

61. "Unusual Occurrences," Memo from Superintendent, House of Detention for Women to Commissioner of Correction, April 28, 1958.

62. "Incidents Involving Correction Officers vs. Inmates," Memo to Commissioner of Correction, from Superintendent, House of Detention for Women, May 22, 1958.

63. "Incidents Involving Correction Officers vs. Inmates," Memo to Commissioner of Correction, from Superintendent, House of Detention for Women, May 22, 1958.

64. Women's Prison Association, Box 73.

65. Women's Prison Association, Box 102.

66. Women's Prison Association, Box 73.

67. Women's Prison Association, Box 73.

68. Women's Prison Association, Box 73.

69. Women's Prison Association, Box 102.

70. Women's Prison Association, Box 102.

71. Women's Prison Association, Box 102.

72. Women's Prison Association, Box 102.

73. Women's Prison Association, Box 102.

74. Judith Resnik, Hirsa Amin, Sophie Angelis, Megan Hauptman, Laura Kokotailo, Aseem Mehta, Madeline Silva, Tor Tarantola, and Meredith Wheeler, "Punishment in Prison: Constituting the 'Normal' and the 'Atypical' in Solitary and Other Forms of Confinement," *Northwestern University Law Review* 115, no. 1 (2020), https://scholarlycommons.law.northwestern.edu/nulr/vol115/iss1/3.

75. "Riot Scare Sends Sing Sing Guards to Women's Prison," *Elmira Star-Gazette*, June 9, 1958.

76. Robert McCarthy and Jack Smee, "Sing Sing Guards Quell Bedford Hills Women," *New York Daily News*, June 9, 1958.

77. Women's Prison Association, Box 66.

78. Robert McCarthy and Jack Smee, "Call Sing Sing Guards in Women's Pen Riot," *New York Daily News*, June 9, 1958.

79. Women's Prison Association, Box 66.

80. McCarthy and Smee, "Call Sing Sing Guards in Women's Pen Riot."

81. Hannah Walker, "From a Whisper to a Rebellion: Examining Space, Race, Sexuality, and Resistance Within the Confines of the Bedford Hills Correctional Facility," *Women's History Theses and Capstones* 33 (2017), https://digitalcommons.slc.edu/womenshistory_etd/33/.

82. Women's Prison Association, Box 73.

Chapter 8: The Gay Crowds

1. "Councilmen Hear Angry Tenants," *New York Age*, April 21, 1956.

2. "Councilmen Hear Angry Tenants," *New York Age*.

3. "Councilmen Hear Angry Tenants," *New York Age*.

4. Kate Simon, *New York: Places and Pleasures* (New York: Harper and Row, 1971).

5. Hal Boyle, "Greenwich Village, Intelligentsia's Tarnished Arcady, Crumbling Away," *Daily Independent Journal*, December 14, 1954.

6. Michael O'Brien, "Of Kings and Queens," *New York Daily News*, December 15, 1952.

7. O'Brien, "Of Kings and Queens."

8. Nicholas Dagen Bloom, *Public Housing That Worked* (Philadelphia: University of Pennsylvania Press, 2008).

9. Bloom, *Public Housing That Worked*.

10. "You Can Smell a Slum," *New York Daily News*, November 28, 1956.

11. O'Brien, "Of Kings and Queens."

12. Women's Prison Association Collection, Box 86, New York Public Library.

13. Women's Prison Association, Box 86.

14. Women's Prison Association, Box 86.

15. Women's Prison Association, Box 86.

16. Women's Prison Association, Box 86.

17. Women's Prison Association, Box 86.

18. Women's Prison Association, Box 86.

19. Women's Prison Association, Box 86.

20. Women's Prison Association, Box 86.

21. Women's Prison Association, Box 86.

22. Women's Prison Association, Box 86.

23. Women's Prison Association, Box 86.

24. Women's Prison Association, Box 86.

25. Women's Prison Association, Box 86.

26. Women's Prison Association, Box 86.

27. Women's Prison Association, Box 86.

28. Women's Prison Association, Box 86.

29. Women's Prison Association, Box 71.

30. Women's Prison Association, Box 71.

31. Women's Prison Association, Box 71.

32. Women's Prison Association, Box 67.

33. Women's Prison Association, Box 67.

34. Women's Prison Association, Box 67.

35. Women's Prison Association, Box 67.

36. Women's Prison Association, Box 67.

37. Women's Prison Association, Box 86.

38. Women's Prison Association, Box 86.

39. Women's Prison Association, Box 86.

40. Women's Prison Association, Box 86.

41. Women's Prison Association, Box 86.

42. Women's Prison Association, Box 86.

43. Women's Prison Association, Box 86.

44. Women's Prison Association, Box 86.

45. Women's Prison Association, Box 86.

46. Women's Prison Association, Box 86.

47. Women's Prison Association, Box 86.

48. Women's Prison Association, Box 86.

49. Women's Prison Association, Box 86.
50. Women's Prison Association, Box 63.
51. Women's Prison Association, Box 63.
52. Women's Prison Association, Box 63.
53. Women's Prison Association, Box 63.
54. Women's Prison Association, Box 106.
55. Women's Prison Association, Box 106.
56. Women's Prison Association, Box 106.
57. Martin Luther King Jr., "Letter from a Birmingham Jail" [1963].
58. Women's Prison Association, Box 106.
59. Women's Prison Association, Box 106.
60. Women's Prison Association, Box 106.
61. Women's Prison Association, Box 106.

Chapter 9: Queer Women Get Organized

1. Women's Prison Association Collection, Box 75, New York Public Library.
2. Women's Prison Association, Box 75
3. "Two Mrs. Frank Grahams Set St. Albans on Ears," *New York Age*, February 28, 1953.
4. Suzanne Spellen, "Queenswalk: Addisleigh Park, Part Two," *Brownstoner*, February 11, 2015, www.brownstoner.com/history/queenswalk-addisleigh-park-part-two/.
5. Theresa C. Noonan, "Addisleigh Park Historic District Designation Report," NYC Landmarks Preservation Committee, February 1, 2011.
6. Spellen, "Queenswalk."
7. Women's Prison Association, Box 75.
8. Women's Prison Association, Box 75.
9. Women's Prison Association, Box 75.
10. Interview between Buddy Kent, Deb Edel, and Joan Nestle, Lesbian Herstory Archives.
11. Audre Lorde, *Zami Sister Outsider Undersong* (New York: Quality Paperback Book Club, 1993).
12. Interview between Buddy Kent, Deb Edel, and Joan Nestle, Lesbian Herstory Archives.
13. Women's Prison Association, Box 75.
14. Women's Prison Association, Box 75.
15. Women's Prison Association, Box 75.
16. Women's Prison Association, Box 75.
17. Women's Prison Association, Box 75.

18. Women's Prison Association, Box 75.

19. Women's Prison Association, Box 75.

20. Women's Prison Association, Box 75.

21. Women's Prison Association, Box 75.

22. Women's Prison Association, Box 75.

23. *New York Mattachine Newsletter: Convention Issue* 3, no. 4 (September 1958).

24. Eric Cervini, *The Deviant's War* (New York: Picador, 2020).

25. Cervini, *The Deviant's War.*

26. Randy Wicker, "A Life Lived on the Front Line of the Gay Rights Battle," *Dallas Voice*, January 25, 2007, https://dallasvoice.com/a-life-lived-on-the -front-line-of-the-gay-rights-battle.

27. Benjamin Shepard, "Dancing in the Streets: Contested Public Spaces and the History of Queer Life," *Dissent Magazine*, June 24, 2011.

28. John Loughery, *The Other Side of Silence: Men's Lives and Gay Identities: A Twentieth-Century History* (New York: Henry Holt, 1998).

29. Shepard, "Dancing in the Streets."

30. *New York Mattachine Newsletter: Convention Issue.*

31. *New York Mattachine Newsletter: Convention Issue.*

32. Manuela Soares, "Barbara Gittings and Kay Tobin, Tape 1 of 3, February 20, 1988," *Lesbian Herstory Archives Audio Visual Collections*, http://herstories .prattinfoschool.nyc/omeka/document/MV-36, accessed December 7, 2020.

33. Marcia Gallo, *Different Daughters* (Emeryville, CA: Seal Press, 2007).

34. Manuela Soares, "Barbara Gittings and Kay Tobin, Tape 1 of 3, February 20, 1988."

35. Women's Prison Association, Box 75.

36. Women's Prison Association, Box 75.

37. Women's Prison Association, Box 75.

38. Alix Buchsbaum Genter, "Risking Everything for That Touch: Butch-Femme Lesbian Culture in New York City from World War II to Women's Liberation" (PhD diss., Rutgers University, May 2014).

39. Genter, "Risking Everything for That Touch."

40. Women's Prison Association, Box 74.

41. Women's Prison Association, Box 74.

42. Women's Prison Association, Box 74.

43. Women's Prison Association, Box 74.

44. Women's Prison Association, Box 74.

45. Women's Prison Association, Box 74.

46. Women's Prison Association, Box 74.

47. Women's Prison Association, Box 74.

48. Women's Prison Association, Box 74.

49. Women's Prison Association, Box 74.

50. Women's Prison Association, Box 74.

51. Women's Prison Association, Box 74.

52. Women's Prison Association, Box 74.

53. Women's Prison Association, Box 74.

54. Women's Prison Association, Box 74.

55. Women's Prison Association, Box 74.

56. "Swing Rendezvous," NYC LGBT Historic Sites Project, 2017, www .nyclgbtsites.org/site/swing-rendezvous, accessed December 22, 2020.

57. Lorde, *Zami*.

58. Lorde, *Zami*.

59. Lorde, *Zami*.

60. Women's Prison Association, Box 64.

61. Lorde, *Zami*.

62. Women's Prison Association, Box 74.

63. Interview between Buddy Kent, Deb Edel, and Joan Nestle, Lesbian Herstory Archives.

64. Women's Prison Association, Box 74.

65. Women's Prison Association, Box 74.

66. Sarah Lynne Ramshaw, "Sign of the Times: Celebrity, Truth, and Legal Storytelling" (master's thesis, Allard School of Law at the University of British Columbia, 2009).

67. Ramshaw, "Sign of the Times."

68. Nate Chinen, "The Cabaret Card and Jazz," *Jazz Times*, April 26, 2019, https://jazztimes.com/features/columns/the-cabaret-card-and-jazz.

69. Women's Prison Association, Box 74.

70. Women's Prison Association, Box 74.

71. Women's Prison Association, Box 74.

72. Women's Prison Association, Box 74.

73. Women's Prison Association, Box 74.

74. Women's Prison Association, Box 74.

75. Women's Prison Association, Box 74.

76. Women's Prison Association, Box 74.

77. Adrienne Rich, "Compulsory Heterosexuality and Lesbian Existence," *Signs* 5, no. 4 (1980): 631–660, www.jstor.org/stable/3173834.

78. Virginia McManus, "Love Without Men in Women's Prison," *Confidential*, September 1959.

79. Virginia McManus, *Not for Love* (New York: Dell Publishing Co., 1960).

80. "Jinny McManus Is Little Girl of Great Many Words," *Chicago Tribune*, December 8, 1935.

81. "Jinny McManus Is Little Girl of Great Many Words," *Chicago Tribune*.

82. Virginia McManus, "Carolina Garden," *Chicago Tribune*, April 2, 1944.

83. "Doorbells Ring $17,000 Tune for Bond Seller, 12," *Chicago Tribune*, July 1, 1945.

84. McManus, *Not for Love*.

85. McManus, *Not for Love*.

86. McManus, *Not for Love*.

87. McManus, *Not for Love*.

88. McManus, *Not for Love*.

89. Author interview with Nan McTeer, January 13, 2021.

90. Author interview with Nan McTeer, January 13, 2021.

91. McManus, *Not for Love*.

92. McManus, *Not for Love*.

93. Author interview with Nan McTeer, January 13, 2021.

94. George Deem, "There's a Cow in Manhattan, Part 05," https://georgedeem.org/search/view/Theres-a-Cow-in-Manhattan-Part-05-1965-01-01, accessed January 8, 2020.

95. Bob Greene, "'Queen of Sex and Sin,'" *Green Bay Press-Gazette*, September 11, 1978.

96. Author interview with Nan McTeer, January 13, 2021.

97. "Gays and Lesbians," *Encyclopedia of Chicago*, www.encyclopedia.chicagohistory.org/pages/509.html, accessed January 15, 2021.

98. Jack Lait and Lee Mortimer, *Chicago Confidential* [1950].

99. Lait and Mortimer, *Chicago Confidential*.

100. Author interview with Nan McTeer, January 13, 2021.

101. George Deem, "There's a Cow in Manhattan, Part 06," https://georgedeem.org/search/view/Theres-a-Cow-in-Manhattan-Part-05-1965-01-01, accessed January 8, 2020.

102. Deem, "There's a Cow in Manhattan, Part 06."

103. McManus, *Not for Love*.

104. "Plush V-Gal Rendezvous Hit in East Side Raids," *New York Daily News*, October 26, 1958.

105. "Plush V-Gal Rendezvous Hit in East Side Raids," *New York Daily News*.

106. "Former Child Prodigy—New York School Teacher Freed on Call Girl Charge," *Tampa Tribune*, October 10, 1958.

107. McManus, *Not for Love*.

108. McManus, *Not for Love*.

109. "Say Teacher Won Her 'V' as a Call Girl," *New York Daily News*, October 4, 1958.

110. McManus, *Not for Love*.

111. McManus, "Love Without Men in Women's Prison."

112. McManus, "Love Without Men in Women's Prison."

113. "Nan McTeer Oral History," Old Lesbian Oral History Project, 2011, Smith College.

114. McManus, "Love Without Men in Women's Prison."

115. McManus, "Love Without Men in Women's Prison."

116. McManus, "Love Without Men in Women's Prison."

117. McManus, "Love Without Men in Women's Prison."

118. McManus, "Love Without Men in Women's Prison."

119. McManus, "Love Without Men in Women's Prison."

120. McManus, "Love Without Men in Women's Prison."

121. McManus, "Love Without Men in Women's Prison."

122. Florrie Fisher, *The Lonely Trip Back* (New York: Doubleday, 1971).

123. Author interview with Nan McTeer, January 13, 2021.

124. "House of D Vets to Get Their Song," *New York Daily News*, January 29, 1960.

125. "Review: The Connection," *Variety*, July 22, 1959.

126. "Melvin Van Peebles Red Bull Music Academy Interview," 2008, www.redbullmusicacademy.com/lectures/melvin-van-peebles-dont-write-a-check-your-ass-cant-cash, accessed April 4, 2021.

127. Kay Johnson, *My Name Is Rusty* (New York: Castle Books, 1958).

Chapter 10: The City's Search for the Perfect Victim

1. Roberta Brandes Gratz, "O Urban Pioneers!," *New York Times*, September 1, 2010.

2. Jack Roth, "A Woman Prefers 5 Years in Prison to One in City Jail," *New York Times*, October 24, 1963.

3. Dorothy Day, "Vocation to Prison," *The Catholic Worker*, September 6, 1957.

4. Department of Corrections Annual Report, 1962, New York City Municipal Archives.

5. Department of Corrections Annual Report, 1962, New York City Municipal Archives.

6. New York State Commission of Correction Report, 1962, Box 23, Folder 1, Anna Kross Collection, American Jewish Archives.

7. "Institute of Correctional Research and Operation," Memo from David D. Jones to Anna M. Kross, August 21, 1962, Box 27, Folder 5, Anna Kross Collection, American Jewish Archives.

8. "Institute of Correctional Research and Operation," Memo from David D. Jones to Anna M. Kross, August 21, 1962.

9. "Institute of Correctional Research and Operation," Memo from David D. Jones to Anna M. Kross, August 21, 1962.

10. Human Rights Watch, "Every 25 Seconds: The Human Toll of Criminalizing Drug Use in the United States," October 12, 2016, https://www .hrw.org/report/2016/10/12/every-25-seconds/human-toll-criminalizing -drug-use-united-states#.

11. Matthew Clarke, "Long-Term Recidivism Studies Show High Arrest Rates," *Prison Legal News*, May 2019.

12. Roth, "A Woman Prefers 5 Years in Prison to One in City Jail."

13. Roth, "A Woman Prefers 5 Years in Prison to One in City Jail."

14. Annual Report of the Department of Correction, 1955, New York Municipal Archives.

15. Annual Report of the Department of Correction, 1956, New York Municipal Archives.

16. Thomas A. Ban, "Fifty Years Chlorpromazine: A Historical Perspective," *Neuropsychiatric Disease and Treatment* 3, no. 4 (August 2007): 495–500, www.ncbi.nlm.nih.gov/pmc/articles/PMC2655089.

17. Wes Lindamood, "Thorazine: Purpose Antipsychotic," *Chemical and Engineering News* 83, no. 25 (June 25, 2005).

18. Annual Report of the New York City Department of Correction, 1954, NYC Municipal Archives.

19. Henrietta Additon, "Institutional Treatment of Women Offenders," *Correction* 22, no 4, Box 13, Folder 16, Anna Kross Collection, American Jewish Archives.

20. Annual Report of the Department of Correction, 1958, New York Municipal Archives.

21. "Women's Prison: Crowded, Tense," *New York Herald Tribune*, June 2, 1958.

22. Annual Report of the Department of Correction, 1960, New York Municipal Archives.

23. Halle Wise, "The House of Detention for Women: A Field Study," July 1963, Anna J. Kross Collection, Smith College.

24. "Complaints from Inmates Regarding Medical Treatment," from Dr. Hans Abeles to Dr. George James, March 18, 1965, Box 28, Folder 1, Anna Kross Collection, American Jewish Archives.

25. Marlene Nadle, "Superintendent Says Women's Jail: Prisons Reflect What Public Wants," *Village Voice*, April 15, 1965.

26. "NY State Assembly Committee on Penal Institutions Testimony," April 19, 1965, Box 14, Folder 2, Anna Kross Collection, American Jewish Archives.

27. "Letter to Anna Kross from an Inmate, January 14, 1958," Correction Department: 1956–1959, Box 13, Folder 8, Anna Kross Collection, American Jewish Archives.

28. "NYS Assembly Committee on Penal Institutions," Box 19, Folder 2, Anna Kross Collection, American Jewish Archives.

29. "Unusual Occurrences at the House of Detention for Women," Memo from Director of Psychiatry (Correction) to Commissioner of Correction, February 25, 1966, Box 28, Folder 12: Psychiatry: Stanley L. Portnow, 1965, Anna Kross Collection, American Jewish Archives.

30. Joan Bird, "Joan Bird," *Ain't I a Woman* 2, no. 8 (May 1972).

31. Edith Evans Asbury, "Mrs. Kross Bares Crowding in Jail," *New York Times*, October 25, 1963.

32. Asbury, "Mrs. Kross Bares Crowding in Jail."

33. "Mrs. Kross: Kim Is Right," *New York Daily News*, October 25, 1963.

34. Women's House of Detention Inspection Report, 1965, State Commission of Correction, Box 23, Folder 1, Anna Kross Papers, American Jewish Archives.

35. Asbury, "Mrs. Kross Bares Crowding in Jail."

36. Edith Evans Asbury, "Legislator Hints Jail Inquiry Here," *New York Times*, October 26, 1963.

37. Asbury, "Legislator Hints Jail Inquiry Here."

38. Jack Roth, "New Women's Jail Ordered Speeded," *New York Times*, October 29, 1963.

39. "Prisoner's Plea Stirs Probe of Women's Jail," *New York Daily News*, October 29, 1963.

40. Roth, "New Women's Jail Ordered Speeded."

41. Andrew Glass, "LBJ Approves 'Operation Rolling Thunder,' Feb. 13, 1965," *Politico*, February 13, 2019, www.politico.com/story/2019/02/13/lbj-operation-rolling-thunder-feb-13-1965-1162618.

42. "Pickets Arrested," *Ithaca Journal*, February 20, 1965.

43. Andrea Dworkin, "Answering Mrs. Lindsay," *Village Voice*, April 22, 1965.

44. "Inquiry into Conditions in Receiving and Housing Areas . . . ," April 22, 1965, Box 33, Folder 9, Anna Kross Papers, American Jewish Archives.

45. William E. Farrell, "Inquiry Ordered at Women's Jail," *New York Times*, March 6, 1965.

46. Andrea Dworkin, "A Letter to M," in *Lavender Culture*, ed. Karla Jay and Allen Young (New York: NYU Press, 1994).

47. Author interview with Joan Nestle, December 19, 2015.

48. Author interview with Joan Nestle, December 19, 2015.

49. Alix Buchsbaum Genter, "Risking Everything for That Touch: Butch-Femme Lesbian Culture in New York City from World War II to Women's Liberation" (PhD diss., Rutgers University, May 2014).

50. Dworkin, "Answering Mrs. Lindsay."

51. "Bars Medical Exam of Women Pickets," *New York Daily News*, August 15, 1936.

52. "NYC Jails to Stop Forced Gynecological Tests," Associated Press, July 14, 2005.

53. Matt Clarke, "$33 Million Settlement in New York City Jails Strip Search Class-Action," *Prison Legal News*, February 15, 2011, www.prisonlegal news.org/news/2011/feb/15/33-million-settlement-in-new-york-city-jails -strip-search-class-action.

54. Andrew Denney, "Ex-Rikers Inmate Who Says She Was Raped by Guards Gets $1.2M," *New York Post*, July 1, 2019.

55. John Marzulli, "Woman Who Claims She Was Forced into Gynecological Exam at Rikers Island Will Collect $80k from Lawsuit Against City," *New York Daily News*, December 31, 2014.

56. National Commission on Correctional Health Care, "Women's Health Care in Correctional Settings," https://www.ncchc.org/womens-health-care.

57. World Medical Association, "World Medical Association Statement on Body Searches of Prisoners," www.wma.net/policies-post/wma-statement -on-body-searches-of-prisoners.

58. Author interview with Jay Toole, September 11, 2017.

59. Martin Duberman, *Andrea Dworkin: The Feminist as Revolutionary* (New York: The New Press, 2020).

60. Frank A. Schneiger, "Liberal Social Change in a Conservative Bureaucratic Setting: A Case Study" (PhD diss., Columbia University, 1977).

61. Andrea Dworkin, *Heartbreak: The Political Memoir of a Feminist Militant* (New York: Basic Books, 2002).

62. "Monthly Report March, 1965," Memo from Dr. Hans Abeles to Commissioner Kross, May 7, 1965, Box 28, Folder 1, Anna Kross Papers, American Jewish Archives.

63. William E. Farrell, "Cavanagh Denies Jail Is 'Snake Pit,'" *New York Times*, April 28, 1965.

64. "Stichman Attacks Cavanagh's Report as Jail 'Whitewash,'" *New York Times*, April 29, 1965.

65. Clarice Feinman, "Imprisoned Women: A History of the Treatment of Incarcerated Women in New York City, 1932–1975" (PhD diss., New York University, 1976).

66. Feinman, "Imprisoned Women."

67. "Costello Suggests Penal Study by City," *New York Times*, December 23, 1965.

68. "Conditions in Women's Prison," Letters to the Editor, *New York Times*, January 1, 1966.

69. "Letter from Andrea Dworkin to Sara Harris," December 6, 1966, Box 42, Folder 14, Andrea Dworkin Collection, Schlesinger Library, Harvard University.

70. Richard Madden, "Rockefeller Proposes Legislation to Ease Overcrowding in the City's Jails," *New York Times*, March 30, 1966.

71. Annual Report of the Department of Correction, 1966, New York City Municipal Archives.

72. Dworkin, *Heartbreak*.

Chapter 11: Gay Lib and Black Power

1. Morris Kaplan, "Bomb Plot Is Laid to 21 Panthers," *New York Times* News Service, April 3, 1969.

2. Afeni Shakur and Jasmine Guy, *Afeni Shakur: Evolution of a Revolutionary* (New York: Atria Books, 2004).

3. Shakur and Guy, *Afeni Shakur*.

4. Shakur and Guy, *Afeni Shakur*.

5. Kaplan, "Bomb Plot Is Laid to 21 Panthers."

6. Morris Kaplan, "Panther Backers Hiss at the Judge," *New York Times*, April 4, 1969.

7. dequi kioni-sadiki and Matt Meyer, eds., *Look for Me in the Whirlwind* (Oakland, CA: PM Press, 2017).

8. Rudy Johnson, "Joan Bird and Afeni Shakur, Self-Styled Soldiers in the Panther 'Class Struggle,'" *New York Times*, July 19, 1970.

9. "Student Nurse Tortured," *Black Panther Paper*, February 17, 1969.

10. "N.Y. Police Nip Panther Plot to Attack Department Stores," *Hackensack Record*, April 3, 1969.

11. "Arcus Flynn, Tape 1 of 1, November 1, 1987," *Herstories: Audio/Visual Collections of the LHA*, http://herstories.prattinfoschool.nyc/omeka/document/Flynn_Arcus_tape1of1_1987nov1, accessed September 5, 2019.

12. "Rubyfruit Jumble," *Dignity Houston Newsletter* 11, no. 7 (July 7, 1984).

13. Naomi Gordon-Loebl, "How Stonewall Veteran Jay Toole's Life Has Changed Since the Riots—and How It Hasn't," *The Nation*, July 2, 2019.

14. Lucian Truscott IV, "Gay Power Comes to Sheridan Square," *Village Voice*, July 2, 1969.

15. Interview between David Carter and Richard Burnett, 2009, http://bugsburnett.blogspot.com/2011/04/sordid-real-story-behind-stonewall.html, accessed March 29, 2021.

16. "Women Held in Assault on Guard," *New York Amsterdam News*, July 5, 1969.

17. Martin Duberman, *Stonewall* (New York: Plume, 2019).

18. Duberman, *Stonewall*.

19. "Gay Liberation Front Newsletter," August 1969, p. 5, FBI Gay Liberation Front—New York 100-167120 Section 1.

20. Chet Meeks, "Eros, the Lifeworld, and Difference: Case Studies in Sexual Politics (1969–1999)" (PhD diss., University of Albany, 2003).

21. Karla Jay, *Tales of the Lavender Menace* (New York: Basic Books, 2000).

22. Nina Sabaroff, "It's Dark but It's Gonna Get Light," Liberation News Service, March 11, 1970.

23. "'Gay Power' Marches Have Clash with Police," *Louisville Courier-Journal*, August 31, 1970.

24. Kenneth Pitchford, "We're Not Gay We're Angry," *Rat*, September 9, 1970.

25. "Rally to Free the Black Panther 21," September 8, 1970, NYPD Surveillance Films Collection, NYC Municipal Archives, https://nycma.lunaimaging.com/luna/servlet/detail/NYCMA~3~3~1105~1233787:nypd_f_0760, accessed April 14, 2021.

26. Huey P. Newton, "An Open Letter About Women's—and Gay—Liberation," *Berkeley Barb* 11, no. 8263 (September 2, 1970).

27. "Gays Discover Revolutionary Love," Chicago Gay Liberation Subject Files, ONE Archive.

28. kioni-sadiki and Meyer, *Look for Me in the Whirlwind*.

29. Angela Davis, *Angela Davis: An Autobiography* (New York: International Publishers, 1988).

30. Mariame Kaba, *We Do This 'Til We Free Us* (Chicago: Haymarket Books, 2021).

31. Joe Street, "The Shadow of the Soul Breaker: Solitary Confinement, Cocaine, and the Decline of Huey P. Newton," *Pacific Historical Review* 84, no. 3 (August 2015).

32. Shakur and Guy, *Afeni Shakur.*

33. Shakur and Guy, *Afeni Shakur.*

34. Shakur and Guy, *Afeni Shakur.*

35. Author interview with Carol Crooks, December 29, 2020.

36. Author interview with Carol Crooks, December 29, 2020.

37. J. B. Nicholas, "August Rebellion: New York's Forgotten Female Prison Riot," *Village Voice*, August 30, 2016.

38. Author interview with Carol Crooks, December 29, 2020.

39. Author interview with Carol Crooks, December 29, 2020.

40. Author interview with Giles Kotcher, July 30, 2019.

41. Author interview with Giles Kotcher, July 30, 2019.

42. Author interview with Carol Crooks, December 29, 2020.

43. Charlotte Marchant, "Unpublished Autobiography," email to author, March 14, 2021.

44. Author interview with Denise Oliver-Velez, March 6, 2021.

45. Author interview with Denise Oliver-Velez, March 6, 2021.

46. Author interview with Giles Kotcher, July 30, 2019.

47. Author interview with Giles Kotcher, July 30, 2019.

48. Paul von Zielbauer, "New York Set to Close Jail Unit for Gays," *New York Times*, December 31, 2005.

49. Von Zielbauer, "New York Set to Close Jail Unit for Gays."

50. Von Zielbauer, "New York Set to Close Jail Unit for Gays."

51. kioni-sadiki and Meyer, *Look for Me in the Whirlwind.*

52. Author interview with Carol Crooks, December 29, 2020.

53. Amber Baylor, "Centering Women in Prisoners' Rights Litigation," *Michigan Journal of Gender and Law* 109 (2018).

54. Shakur and Guy, *Afeni Shakur.*

55. Earl Caldwell, "Jackson an Enigma in Life and Death," *New York Times*, September 20, 1971.

56. Lawrence V. Cott, "San Rafael Shootout: The Facts Behind the Angela Davis Case," *Human Events*, June 17, 1972.

57. Cott, "San Rafael Shootout."

58. Davis, *Angela Davis.*

59. Davis, *Angela Davis.*

60. Davis, *Angela Davis.*

61. Davis, *Angela Davis.*

62. "Angela Davis on Running from the FBI, Lessons from Prison and How Aretha Franklin Got Her Free," *Democracy Now!*, December 30, 2018.

63. Angela Y. Davis, *Abolition Democracy: Beyond Empire, Prisons, and Torture* (New York: Seven Stories Press, 2005).

64. Tony Platt, "Interview with Angela Davis," *Social Justice* 40, no. 1 (2014).

65. "Annual Statistical Report, 1965," Department of Correction, City of New York.

66. "Social and Economic Conditions of Negroes in the United States," US Department of Commerce, Bureau of the Census, October 1967.

67. Halle Wise, "The House of Detention for Women: A Field Study," Department of Correction, Division of Research and Planning, July 1963.

68. "NYC Department of Corrections at a Glance: Information for 1st 6 months 2021," City of New York Department of Correction, https://www1.nyc.gov/assets/doc/downloads/press-release/DOC_At_Glance_first6_months_FY2021-030921.pdf.

69. Davis, *Angela Davis*.

70. Davis, *Angela Davis*.

71. Davis, *Angela Davis*.

72. "Angela Davis on Running from the FBI, Lessons from Prison and How Aretha Franklin Got Her Free," *Democracy Now!*

73. Davis, *Angela Davis*.

74. Davis, *Angela Davis*.

75. Davis, *Angela Davis*.

76. Davis, *Angela Davis*.

77. Davis, *Angela Davis*.

78. Davis, *Angela Davis*.

79. Wise, "The House of Detention for Women."

80. Wise, "The House of Detention for Women."

81. Wise, "The House of Detention for Women."

82. Wise, "The House of Detention for Women."

83. Wise, "The House of Detention for Women."

84. Author interview with Carol Crooks, December 29, 2020.

85. Author interview with Denise Oliver-Velez, March 6, 2021.

86. Wise, "The House of Detention for Women."

87. Davis, *Angela Davis*.

88. Sara Miles, "Angela at Our Table," *Out*, February 1998.

89. Linda Charlton, "The Terrifying Homosexual World of the Jail System," April 25, 1971.

90. Wise, "The House of Detention for Women."

91. "Jay London Toole Interview Transcript," New York City Trans Oral History Project, https://s3.amazonaws.com/oral-history/transcripts/NYC+TOHP+Transcript+003+Jay+London+Toole.pdf, accessed June 18, 2020.

92. Davis, *Angela Davis*.

93. Lee S. Friedman, "The Evolution of Bail Reform," *Policy Sciences* 7, no. 3 (September 1976).

94. Bernard Botein, "The Manhattan Bail Project: Its Impact on Criminology and the Criminal Law Processes," *Texas Law Review* (February 1965).

95. Botein, "The Manhattan Bail Project."

96. Botein, "The Manhattan Bail Project."

97. Botein, "The Manhattan Bail Project."

98. Botein, "The Manhattan Bail Project."

99. Botein, "The Manhattan Bail Project."

100. Botein, "The Manhattan Bail Project."

101. Botein, "The Manhattan Bail Project."

102. Botein, "The Manhattan Bail Project."

103. Botein, "The Manhattan Bail Project."

104. Botein, "The Manhattan Bail Project."

105. Friedman, "The Evolution of Bail Reform."

106. Friedman, "The Evolution of Bail Reform."

107. Friedman, "The Evolution of Bail Reform."

108. Clarice Feinman, "An Afro-American Experience: The Women in New York City's Jail," *Afro-Americans in New York Life and History* 1, no. 2 (July 1977): 201.

109. NYC Department of Correction Annual Report, 1969.

110. NYC Department of Correction Annual Report, 1969.

111. "Bail Fund," *Rat*, no. 17 (1970).

112. Davis, *Angela Davis*.

113. Author interview with Denise Oliver-Velez, March 6, 2021.

114. Jay, *Tales of the Lavender Menace*.

115. Ann-Marie Russo, "The Feminist Pornography Debates: Civil Rights vs. Civil Liberties" (PhD diss., University of Illinois at Urbana Champaign, 1990).

116. "Letters," *Up from Under* 1, no. 3 (January–February 1971).

117. Ruth McCormick, "Woman's Liberation Cinema," *Cinéaste* 5, no. 2 (Spring 1972).

118. Veronica Golos, "Get Me Out!," *Battle Acts*, March 1, 1973.

119. Golos, "Get Me Out!"

120. Golos, "Get Me Out!"

121. Golos, "Get Me Out!"

122. Golos, "Get Me Out!"

123. Golos, "Get Me Out!"

124. Golos, "Get Me Out!"

125. Golos, "Get Me Out!"

126. Golos, "Get Me Out!"

127. Department of Corrections Annual Report, 1968, New York Municipal Archives.

128. Phil Santora, "They're Only Birds in a Gilded Cage," *New York Daily News*, September 12, 1971.

129. Susan Milligan, "Coed Rikers Jail Draws Criticism," *New York Daily News*, August 6, 1987.

130. Richard G. Carter, "A Peek Behind the Walls of Rikers Island," *Daily News*, June 28, 1988.

131. Paul La Rosa, "The Cage Is 'Gilded'—and Bursting," *Daily News*, September 24, 1988.

132. La Rosa, "The Cage Is 'Gilded'—and Bursting."

133. Suzanne Singer, "The Women's Jail at Rikers Island Is Named for My Grandmother. She Would Not Be Proud," *New York Times*, May 12, 2020.

134. Aleks Kajstura, "Women's Mass Incarceration: The Whole Pie," Prison Policy Initiative, October 29, 2019.

135. Singer, "The Women's Jail at Rikers Island Is Named for My Grandmother."

136. Singer, "The Women's Jail at Rikers Island Is Named for My Grandmother."

137. "Covid-19's Impact on People in Prison," Equal Justice Initiative, April 16, 2021, https://eji.org/news/covid-19s-impact-on-people-in-prison.

138. "Covid Prison Outbreak," *New York Times*, April 10, 2021, www.nytimes.com/interactive/2021/04/10/us/covid-prison-outbreak.html.

139. Gus Saltonstall, "Greenwich Village ZIP Codes All Under 3 Percent COVID Rate: Data," Patch.com, February 24, 2021, https://patch.com/new-york/west-village/greenwich-village-zip-codes-all-under-3-percent-covid-rate-data.

140. "Minutes of the Meeting of the Board of Correction, October 18, 1971," https://www1.nyc.gov/assets/boc/downloads/pdf/1971-oct-18.pdf, accessed September 22, 2021.

141. Angela Taylor, "Rikers Island May Be Posh, but They Miss the House of Detention," *New York Times*, July 9, 1971.

142. Jack Newfield, "New Women's Prison: Parody of Progress," *Village Voice*, December 2, 1971.

143. Newfield, "New Women's Prison: Parody of Progress."

144. Taylor, "Rikers Island May Be Posh, but They Miss the House of Detention."

145. "Guards Petition Mayor," *Village Voice*, December 2, 1971.

146. "Correction Officers in Protest," *New York Amsterdam News*, December 18, 1971.

147. "Ired Village Gays Demand City Donate Social Centers," *The Advocate*, August 18–31, 1971.

148. "West Ninth Street Block Association: The Women's House of Detention: Facts of the Issue," Village Committee for the Jefferson Market Area Collection, New York Public Library, Box 1.

149. "Community Board #2 Ad Hoc Committee Women's House of Detention, in Support of Board of Estimate," April 20, 1972, Village Committee for the Jefferson Market Area Collection, New York Public Library, Box 1.

150. "Memo from Verna Small, Landmarks Chairman, Association of Village Homeowners," July 19, 1973, Village Committee for the Jefferson Market Area Collection, New York Public Library, Box 1.

151. "Agenda for the Village Committee for the Jefferson Market Area.," June 5, 1974, Village Committee for the Jefferson Market Area Collection, New York Public Library, Box 3.

152. "Letter from George C. Stoney to Mrs. Phillip Wittenberg, Chairman, Village South Committee of the Community Board," December 17, 1973, Village Committee for the Jefferson Market Area Collection, New York Public Library, Box 1.

153. Kate Simon, *New York: Places and Pleasures* (New York: Harper and Row, 1971).

154. Lawrie Mifflin, "Village Prison Is Now Free to Be a Garden," *New York Daily News*, June 9, 1975.

155. "Memo from Verna Small, Landmarks Chairman, Association of Village Homeowners," July 19, 1973.

156. Caroline Ware, *Greenwich Village, 1920–1930* (London: Octagon, 1977).

157. Reed Ide, "Inside the Infamous House of D: Where Today a Lush Garden Blooms, a Sad Women's Prison Once Loomed," *The Villager*, October 17, 2013.

158. Author interview with Barbara Police, July 5, 2018.

HUGH RYAN is a writer and curator. His first book, *When Brooklyn Was Queer*, won a 2020 New York City Book Award, was a *New York Times* Editors' Choice in 2019, and was a finalist for the Randy Shilts and Lambda Literary Awards. He was honored with the 2020 Allan Bérubé Prize from the American Historical Association. In 2019–2021, he worked on the Hidden Voices: LGBTQ+ Stories in United States History curricular materials for the NYC Department of Education.